Debt Defaults and Lessons from a Decade of Crises

Debt Defaults and Lessons from a Decade of Crises

Federico Sturzenegger and Jeromin Zettelmeyer

The MIT Press
Cambridge, Massachusetts
London, England

MIT Press books may be purchased at special quantity discounts for business or sales promotional use. For information, please email special_sales@mitpress.mit.edu or write to Special Sales Department, The MIT Press, 55 Hayward Street, Cambridge, MA 02142.

This book was set in Palatino on 3B2 by Asco Typesetters, Hong Kong.
Printed and bound in the United States of America.

Library of Congress Cataloging-in-Publication Data

Sturzenegger, Federico.
Debt defaults and lessons from a decade of crises / Federico Sturzenegger, Jeromin Zettelmeyer.
    p.   cm.
Includes bibliographical references and index.
ISBN-13: 978-0-262-19553-9 (hardcover : alk. paper)
ISBN-10: 0-262-19553-4 (hardcover : alk. paper)
1. Debts, External—Developing countries. 2. Debt relief—Developing countries. 3. Developing countries—Economic policy. I. Zettelmeyer, Jeromin. II. Title.
HJ8899.S83   2007
336.3′435091724—dc22   2006027582

10 9 8 7 6 5 4 3 2 1

To the memory of Rudi Dornbusch
Our teacher and friend

Contents

Preface

The 1980s were supposed to be the time of "the" debt crisis. But since the tequila crisis in 1995, and particularly after the 1998 Russian default, questions related to sovereign debt have once again been at the forefront of policy discussions about emerging market economies. For the first time since the 1930s, a series of crises and restructurings have taken place that focused on sovereign bonds. Each crisis has given rise to new debates about crisis prevention and resolution, moral hazard, globalization hazard, and the international financial architecture. They have also given impetus to a large new literature on economic and legal aspects of sovereign debt.

The purpose of this monograph is to give an account of the past decade of sovereign debt and debt crises in emerging market countries, at three levels. First, the facts. How did the crises develop? What was restructured, and on what terms? How did investors fare, and how did countries emerge from the crisis? Second, the new thinking on sovereign debt and debt crises. How do risky debt structures arise? What are the fundamental causes of costly debt crises? Why are crises costly and what are the costs, for both debtor countries and investors? Finally, the policy debate, with particular attention on the perspective of the emerging market policymaker. What are appropriate prevention measures? How should a restructuring be implemented? How can an economic collapse following a debt crisis be avoided? And at the international level, how can the financial architecture provide a safety net that protects debtor countries and investors and, at the same time, imparts good incentives to countries and capital markets alike?

This book stands on the shoulders of a tradition in economics and law, going back to the nineteenth century that has periodically reflected on the causes and consequences of sovereign debt crises. Bill Cline's fine account of the debt crisis of the 1980s, *International Debt*

Reconsidered, is a recent work in this tradition. We have also benefited from several other recent monographs on international capital flows, financial crises, and "architecture" reforms by Barry Eichengreen (1999, 2002), Peter Kenen (2001), Jean Tirole (2002), Lex Rieffel (2003), Nouriel Roubini and Brad Setser (2004), and Peter Isard (2005). What distinguishes this book from these monographs is its focus on privately held sovereign debt and its primary objective of providing an overview of both facts and ideas, rather than putting forward new proposals. This said, we certainly have views on these topics, some of which are reflected in chapters 11 and 12.

The monograph is anchored in a series of case studies of emerging market countries that undertook post-Brady debt restructurings in distressed circumstances. From a social science perspective, this is not ideal: focusing on crises that have happened, while excluding crises that were avoided (perhaps narrowly) may create a bias. In part for this reason, we complement the case studies with three broad survey chapters in which we review the history, economics, and law of sovereign debt and debt crises. The policy chapters at the end of the book—one written from the perspective of the domestic policymaker and one from an international perspective—draw both on the case studies and this broader experience.

We hope this volume will provide a useful starting point for policymakers, financial market participants, and academics who are new to the subject of sovereign debt. Our aim is to provide these readers with a comprehensive, nontechnical review of the theory and facts needed to understand the current policy debates and analyze a future debt restructuring scenario. While the bust cycle that began in 1998 is over, debt crises and restructurings are likely to be a recurrent issue in international financial markets. Thus, this volume may be useful for quite some time. We would have preferred to say otherwise.

Acknowledgments and Disclaimer

This book grew out of a project initiated in 2002, with the encouragement of Sara Calvo and Brian Pinto, to describe recent debt defaults and restructurings and draw some general lessons from the experience. Its scope has since increased far beyond what we imagined at the beginning. In the process, we have become indebted to more friends and colleagues than we can name for providing us with data, answering our questions, and providing comments and suggestions. However, we would like to express our special gratitude to the following: Fernando Alvarez, Roberto Benelli, Charlie Blitzer, Mike Bordo, Eduardo Borensztein, Luis Cubeddu, Tina Daseking, Matthew Fisher, Anna Gelpern, Paul Gleason, Olivier Jeanne, Thomas Laryea, Eduardo Levy-Yeyati, Cheng-Hoon Lim, Atsushi Masuda, Paolo Mauro, Guillermo Nielsen, Jonathan Ostry, Andy Powell, Roberto Rigobon, Nouriel Roubini, Axel Schimmelpfennig, Mercedes Vera, Michael Waibel and Mark Wright, as well as participants in seminars at the Bank of England and the Swiss National Bank. We also thank our editor, Elizabeth Murry, for her encouragement and patience throughout the process. None of these individuals, however, bear responsibility for any remaining errors. All views expressed in the book are those of the authors and not of any institutions that they are affiliated with. In particular, the views expressed in this book do not necessarily reflect those of the International Monetary Fund.

Several research assistants helped us gather and process the information contained in this book. We are particularly grateful to Francisco Ceballos, Federico Dorso, Luciana Esquerro, Pryanka Malhotra, Carolina Molas, Luciana Monteverde, Maria Fernandez Vidal, Victoria Vanasco, and Sofia Zerbarini.

Federico Sturzenegger gratefully acknowledges financial support by the Centro de Investigacion de Finanzas of Universidad Torcuato Di

Tella, as well as the Japanese Bank of International Cooperation. Jeromin Zettelmeyer is grateful to the IMF Research Department for allowing him to spend far more time on this project than was initially envisaged. Most important, we are both grateful to our families for bearing with us over the last two and a half years.

I History, Economics, and Law

1 Sovereign Defaults and Debt Restructurings: Historical Overview

Debt crises and defaults by sovereigns—city-states, kingdoms, and empires—are as old as sovereign borrowing itself. The first recorded default goes back at least to the fourth century B.C., when ten out of thirteen Greek municipalities in the Attic Maritime Association defaulted on loans from the Delos Temple (Winkler 1933). Most fiscal crises of European antiquity, however, seem to have been resolved through "currency debasement"—namely, inflations or devaluations—rather than debt restructurings. Defaults cum debt restructurings picked up in the modern era, beginning with defaults in France, Spain, and Portugal in the mid-sixteenth centuries. Other European states followed in the seventeenth century, including Prussia in 1683, though France and Spain remained the leading defaulters, with a total of eight defaults and six defaults, respectively, between the sixteenth and the end of the eighteenth centuries (Reinhart, Rogoff, and Savastano 2003).

Only in the nineteenth century, however, did debt crises, defaults, and debt restructurings—defined as changes in the originally envisaged debt service payments, either after a default or under the threat of default—explode in terms of both numbers and geographical incidence. This was the by-product of increasing cross-border debt flows, newly independent governments, and the development of modern financial markets. In what follows, we begin with an overview of the main default and debt restructuring episodes of the last two hundred years.[1] We next turn to the history of how debt crises were resolved. We end with a brief review of the creditor experience with sovereign debt since the 1850s.

Boom-Bust Cycles, Defaults, and Reschedulings, 1820–2003

There have been hundreds of defaults and debt restructurings involving privately held sovereign debt since the early nineteenth century.[2]

In some cases, these were a reflection of the tumultuous political history of the period: the by-product of wars, revolutions, or civil conflicts that made debtor governments unwilling or unable to pay. For example, Turkey, Bulgaria, and Austria-Hungary suspended debt payments to enemy country creditors at the beginning of World War I; Italy, Turkey, and Japan did the same at the beginning of World War II. Mexico (1914), Russia (1917), China (1949), Czechoslovakia (1952), and Cuba (1960) repudiated their debts after revolutions or communist takeovers.[3] Some countries, such as Austria (1802, 1868) and Russia (1839), defaulted after losing wars; others, such as Spain (1831) and China (1921), defaulted after enduring major civil wars. In some of these cases—particularly revolutions and civil wars—economic causes may well have played an important role in triggering the political events that in turn led to a default. However, the defaults or repudiations were sideshows compared with the political and social upheavals with which they were associated, and any economic causes were largely domestic in origin.

As it turns out, the majority of defaults and debt restructurings involving private debtors that have occurred since the early nineteenth century—including almost all that were experienced since the late 1970s—do *not*, in fact, belong to this category, but reflect more subtle interactions between domestic economic policies and shocks to the economy, including changes in the external environment and sometimes, though not always, political shocks. In the remainder of the chapter, we concentrate on this class.

The striking fact about these defaults is that they are bunched in temporal and sometimes regional clusters, which correspond to boom-bust cycles in international capital flows. Based on Lindert and Morton (1989), Marichal (1989), and Suter (1989, 1992), one can distinguish eight lending booms since the early nineteenth century: (1) in the early 1820s, to the newly independent Latin American countries and some European countries; (2) in the 1830s, to the United States, Spain, and Portugal; (3) from the 1860s to the mid-1870s, to Latin America, the United States, European countries, the Ottoman Empire, and Egypt; (4) in the mid- to late 1880s, to the United States, Australia, and Latin America; (5) in the decade prior to World War I, to Canada, Australia, South Africa, Russia, the Ottoman Empire, the Balkan countries, and some Latin American countries; (6) in the 1920s, to Germany, Japan, Australia, Canada, Argentina, Brazil, and Cuba; (7) in the 1970s, to Latin America, Spain, Yugoslavia, Romania, Poland, Turkey, Egypt, and Indonesia, as well as some African countries; (8) in the 1990s, to Latin America, emerging Asia, and former Communist countries in eastern Europe.[4] The main sources of these capital flows were the United Kingdom and France in the nineteenth century; the United Kingdom, France, Germany, the Netherlands, and the United States in the early twentieth century; the United States and the United Kingdom in the interwar period; the United States and some western European countries in the 1970s; and the United States, western Europe, and Japan in the 1990s.

The origins of these lending booms varied. Several were initiated by political change that created a demand for capital or opened new investment opportunities. For example, the 1820s boom was triggered by the end of the Napoleonic wars in Europe and the emergence of the newly independent countries of Latin America; the 1920s boom was triggered by the end of World War I and the financing of German reparations; flows to Africa in the 1960s and 1970s were triggered by African decolonization and independence; and a portion of the 1990s boom was triggered by the collapse of Communism. On other occasions, new lending booms were driven by economic changes in the debtor countries—sometimes resulting from technical progress, sometimes from reform or stabilization policies, and sometimes from improvements in the terms of trade. For example, the lending booms of the nineteenth century were largely directed to infrastructure investments, particularly railway construction, and they often accompanied booms in commodity exports. The boom of the 1990s was in some part a reaction to economic reforms in debtor countries that appeared to usher in a new era of growth. In such cases, new booms set in soon after the defaults that had accompanied the preceding bust had been cleared up.

Cycles in economic growth and private savings, and changes in the financial systems and lender liquidity in *creditor* countries also played an important role. For example, the 1970s boom in bank lending to developing countries originated in the 1960s, when U.S. banks lost a portion of their domestic business to corporate debt markets and began to look for lending alternatives abroad. This incipient boom received a boost after the oil price shocks of 1973–1974 led to high oil earnings in search of investments (Beim and Calomiris 2001). Easy monetary conditions in the United States and Europe contributed to the latest boom in emerging market lending that began in the second half of 2003 (IMF 2005d).

All lending booms so far have ended in busts in which some of the beneficiaries of the preceding debt inflows defaulted or rescheduled their debts. Busts were usually triggered by at least one of the following factors: (1) a deterioration of the terms of trade of debtor countries; (2) a recession in the core countries that were the providers of capital; (3) a rise in international borrowing costs driven by events in creditor countries, such as tighter monetary policy; and (4) a crisis in a major debtor country, transmitted internationally through financial and trade linkages. For example, the 1830s boom ended after a collapse in cotton prices that decimated the export earnings of southern U.S. states and tighter credit in England, which led to an outflow of gold, a fall in the price level, and higher real debt levels (English 1996). Terms of trade deteriorations also played an important role on several other occasions in the nineteenth century (e.g., the collapse of guano prices due to the rise of artificial fertilizers in the 1870s) as well as the 1930s, when commodity prices fell across the board, and the 1990s, when sharply lower oil prices contributed to debt servicing difficulties in Russia. The 1890s bust was triggered when mounting doubts about Argentina's macroeconomic sustainability led to the collapse of Baring Brothers, a London bank that had underwritten an Argentine bond that the market was unwilling to absorb; this was followed by a sudden stop in lending to Latin America (Fishlow 1985, 1989). The main cause of the 1930s bust was the collapse of commodity prices in the late 1920s and the Great Depression in the United States (Kindleberger 1973). Following a period of overlending to developing countries in the 1970s, the 1980s debt crisis was triggered by sharply higher interest rates in the United States and the ensuing 1980–1984 U.S. recession (Sachs 1989; Cline 1995; Easterly 2001). Finally, the 1990s bust was a result of contagion from the 1998 Russian default, which led to a sharp increase in emerging markets borrowing costs.

As table 1.1 shows, each bust was associated with a cluster of default cases: in the late 1820s, the 1870s, the 1890s, just before and during World War I, the 1930s, the 1980s, and 1998–2004. (The only boom phase whose default counterpart is not recorded in the table is the 1830s boom, which led to defaults only at the U.S. state level. See English 1996.) Of the default clusters shown, the 1980s default wave affected bank loans, while all others involved mainly sovereign bonds. Obviously, only a subset of the countries that had borrowed during a preceding lending boom defaulted during each bust, depending on their overall indebtedness, the uses of the debt during the preceding

Table 1.1
Selected government defaults and restructurings of privately held bonds and loans, 1820–2004

	Default or restructuring clusters						
	1824–1834	1867–1882	1890–1900	1911–1921	1931–1940	1976–1989	1998–2004
Europe							
Austria		1868		1914	1932		
Bulgaria				1915	1932		
Greece	1824		1893				
Germany					1932		
Hungary					1931		
Italy					1940		
Moldova							2002
Poland					1936	1981	
Portugal	1834		1892				
Romania				1915	1933	1981	
Russia[a]				1917			1998
Serbia/ Yugoslavia			1895		1933	1983	
Spain[a]	1831	1867, 1882					
Turkey		1876		1915	1940	1978	
Ukraine							1998, 2000
Latin America and Caribbean							
Argentina	1830		1890	1915[b]	1930s[b]	1982	2001
Bolivia		1874			1931	1980	
Brazil	1826		1898	1914	1931	1983	
Chile	1826	1880			1931	1983	
Colombia	1826	1879	1900		1932		
Costa Rica	1827	1874	1895		1937	1983	
Cuba					1933	1982	
Dominica							2003
Dominican Republic		1869	1899		1931	1982	
Ecuador	1832	1868		1911, 1914	1931	1982	1999
El Salvador	1827			1921	1931		
Grenada							2004
Guatemala	1828	1876	1894		1933		

Table 1.1
(continued)

	Default or restructuring clusters						
	1824–1834	1867–1882	1890–1900	1911–1921	1931–1940	1976–1989	1998–2004
Honduras	1827	1873		1914		1981	
Mexico[a]	1827	1867		1914		1982	
Nicaragua	1828		1894	1911	1932	1980	
Panama					1932	1982	
Paraguay	1827	1874	1892	1920	1932	1986	2003
Peru	1826	1876			1931	1978, 1983	
Uruguay		1876	1891	1915	1933	1983	2003
Venezuela[a]	1832	1878	1892, 1898			1982	
Africa							
Angola						1988	
Cameroon						1989	
Congo						1986	
Côte d'Ivoire						1984	2001
Egypt		1876				1984	
Gabon						1986	1999, 2002
Gambia						1986	
Liberia		1874		1912		1980	
Madagascar						1981	
Malawi						1982	
Morocco						1983	
Mozambique						1984	
Niger						1983	
Nigeria						1983	
Senegal						1981	
Seychelles							2002
Sierra Leone						1977	
South Africa						1985	
Sudan						1979	
Tanzania						1984	
Togo						1979	
Uganda						1981	
Zaire						1976	
Zambia						1983	

Table 1.1
(continued)

	Default or restructuring clusters						
	1824–1834	1867–1882	1890–1900	1911–1921	1931–1940	1976–1989	1998–2004
Asia and Middle East							
Indonesia							1999
Jordan						1989	
Philippines						1983	
Pakistan						1981	1999
Vietnam						1985	

Sources: Lindert and Morton (1989), Beim and Calomiris (2001), and Standard & Poor; news reports.
Notes: Cases shown are defaults and/or debt restructurings (including reschedulings) in distressed circumstances, involving external creditors. Defaults triggered by wars, revolutions, occupations, and state disintegrations are generally excluded, except when they coincide with a default cluster. Payment delays and other technical defaults that eventually resulted in full repayment are also generally excluded. Unless otherwise noted, all restructurings and defaults refer to federal or central government obligations; in particular, defaults of U.S. states in the 1840s are not shown. In the event of a sequence of debt reschedulings, the year listed refers to the initial rescheduling.
[a] Russia also defaulted in 1839, Spain in 1820 and 1851, Venezuela in 1847 and 1864, and Mexico in 1859.
[b] Default at provincial/state level only.

boom period, political and fiscal institutions, the magnitude of the shocks suffered, and so on. The defaults in the nineteenth century were concentrated mainly in Latin America as well as a handful of countries in the European periphery, those in the 1930s in Europe and Latin America, and those in the 1980s in Latin America and Africa.

Several interesting facts emerge from the table. First, many countries and regions—even some that received substantial debt inflows—never defaulted. This includes the United States at the federal level, Canada, Australia, South Africa (except for an episode related to sanctions in 1985), most Asian countries, and most Arab countries. Second, most Latin American countries defaulted repeatedly, and Latin America as a region is represented in all default waves since the 1820s. Third, some countries appear to "graduate" from repeated defaults. No western European country has defaulted since the interwar period. Among the Latin American countries, Argentina, Ecuador, and Uruguay defaulted in the most recent wave as well as most previous waves (though Argentina is notable for not defaulting in the 1930s, at least at the federal level). Most Latin American countries, however, defaulted for the last time in the 1980s, and some, notably Colombia, have not defaulted since the 1930s. Fourth, among the seven default clusters shown in the table, two—the 1930–1940s, and particularly the 1980s—are outliers in the sense that many more countries defaulted than in the other clusters. The 1930s prove to be a testimony to the depth and reach of the Great Depression, the worst global financial crisis in history. The debt crisis of the 1980s, in turn, affected many more countries than previous crises because debt had been flowing to so many new countries in the preceding boom period, including to dozens of newly independent countries in Africa.

In contrast, the latest default cycle (1998–2004) appears to have been about in line with the default clusters of the nineteenth century in terms of the number of sovereign defaults and restructurings. Following the spectacular debt crisis of the 1980s, many developing countries—particularly in Africa, and some Latin American countries, such as Bolivia—lost access to international capital markets altogether. Hence, far fewer developing countries were exposed to significant levels of privately held debt than at the beginning of the 1980s. In addition, compared with the 1970s, a much higher share of lending to emerging markets, particularly in the Asian countries, was absorbed directly by the private sector, namely, it did not directly give rise to sovereign debt. When the lending boom to these countries ended in 1997, the result was a *private* debt crisis that led to thousands of corporate defaults and debt restructurings in the Asian crisis countries but not to sovereign debt restructuring (except for a comparatively marginal commercial bank debt rescheduling episode involving Indonesia). Since these private sector defaults—which are without counterpart in most previous periods—are not reflected in table 1.1, the table understates the comparative gravity of the last bust phase. Finally, international official creditors, led by the International Monetary Fund (IMF), played a more aggressive role in preventing debt restructurings in the 1990s than in the 1980s, through large lending packages to countries such as Mexico, Brazil, and Turkey. Without these lending packages and the fiscal adjustment programs that they supported, these countries probably would have had to restructure their public debts in the late 1990s.

Resolving Debt Crises

The great majority of defaults in the nineteenth and twentieth centuries eventually led to some form of settlement between creditors and the debtor country. In the following, we summarize how the resolution of debt crises evolved in history, along three dimensions: (1) the negotiation process—in particular, the way creditor coordination was achieved; (2) the content of the settlement; and (3) the involvement, if any, of an official third party—either creditor country governments or international institutions—in the negotiation process.

Creditor Coordination

Between the 1820s and 1870, negotiations between debtors and creditors proceeded through ad hoc creditor committees. Negotiations under this model appear to have been inefficient, at least from a creditor perspective, for several reasons: lack of specialization and experience; weak coordination across creditors; and sometimes competing creditor committees (Suter 1992; Eichengreen and Portes 1986, 1989). According to Suter, one indication of the inefficiency of the process was the long average duration (fourteen years) of settlements prior to 1870.

This changed after 1868 when the British Corporation of Foreign Bondholders (CFB), the most institutionalized, powerful, and celebrated creditor association in history was established (Wright 2002a; Mauro and Yafeh 2003; Mauro, Sussman, and Yafeh 2006, chap. 7). After its reconstitution in 1898 through an act of parliament, the council (board) of the CFB consisted of twenty-one members, six of them appointed by the British Bankers' Association, six appointed by the London Chamber of Commerce, and nine miscellaneous members of which at least six were to be substantial bondholders; thus, it represented the entire British financial sector as well as the bondholders.[5] The corporation had two functions: (1) information provision on debtor countries, and (2) creditor coordination and negotiation of settlements. The latter was achieved through committees specific to particular debtor countries, which negotiated an agreement that was presented to a general meeting of bondholders for approval or rejection. Although the agreement was not legally binding on individual bondholders, "holdouts" generally did not pose a problem, in part, because the chances of successful legal action against sovereigns were much lower than they are today.[6] As a result, the corporation effectively had control over the sovereign debtor's access to the London market. Following a practice adopted in 1827, the London stock exchange would refuse to list new bonds by creditors that were in default, but it relied on the CFB to determine who should be considered in default and who should not.

Based on this power—and rare interventions by the British government—the CFB was able to negotiate settlements with all major problem debtors, including Spain, Portugal, Greece, Turkey, Peru, Mexico, Brazil, and Argentina. By 1906, the volume of loans in default had declined from about 300 million pound sterling in the late 1870s to less than 25 million (Mauro, Sussman, and Yafeh 2006). The corporation was unsuccessful only with regard to a few Central American countries and a small group of U.S. states, to which the London capital market and trade relations with Britain were less important (Kelly 1998). Coordination with U.S. creditors would have been critical here, but was lacking, in part, because U.S. creditors had an incentive to exploit their regional power to obtain better terms (Mauro, Sussman, and Yafeh 2006). The average duration of defaults between 1870 and the default wave of the 1930s fell to about six years, though other factors, including more assertiveness on the side of creditor country governments, also may have contributed to this outcome. CFB-type organizations were eventually set up in France and Belgium (1898), Switzerland (1912), Germany (1927), and the United States (1933) (Esteves 2004). The CFB and its counterpart organizations in other countries remained active until the 1950s, when the last defaults of the 1930s (except those of some Soviet bloc countries that had repudiated their prewar debts) were settled.

Creditor representation and debt renegotiation did not return as an issue until the 1970s. By then, the structure of international private capital flows had changed radically, from bonds dispersed among thousands of holders in a handful of creditor countries to loans by a few hundred commercial banks. By the mid-1970s, most bank lending was channeled through syndicates involving groups of typically ten to twenty banks. In the late 1970s, when several developing country debtors—Zaïre, Peru, Turkey, Sudan, and Poland—began to experience debt servicing difficulties, a coordinated negotiating procedure for the restructuring of commercial bank debt began to emerge: the "Bank Advisory Committee" (BAC) process, also referred to as the "London Club."[7]

BACs consisted of a group of banks, rarely more than fifteen, which represented bank creditors—usually several hundred—in debt restructuring negotiations (see Rieffel 2003 for a detailed account). Like the CFB, a BAC did not have the legal authority to agree to a debt restructuring that would bind all creditors. Rather, it would negotiate a deal, initially in the form of a "term sheet," followed by a documentation package that became legally binding for each individual creditor only after that creditor's signature. Institutionally, however, BACs differed significantly from the bondholder organizations of the nineteenth and early twentieth centuries. First, BACs were international and universal, representing all commercial bank creditors rather than just creditors residing in a particular country. Also, unlike bondholder corporations, the BACs had no charter, no secretariat, and no physical infrastructure. Moreover, they had no information provision function outside a specific debt restructuring. (In 1983, the banks created a parallel institution, the Washington-based Institute of International Finance, specifically to provide regular information about borrowing countries to its members.) BACs were formed ad hoc, usually chaired by a senior official of the creditor bank with the largest exposure, and with subcommittees drawn from the staff of the major banks on the BAC.

The debt restructuring agreements that began to be negotiated by BACs in the early 1980s required unanimity for changes to the payment terms negotiated under the agreement. This created problems in subsequent debt restructurings, as initial acceptance typically fell short of unanimity. As the debt crisis progressed, the share of dissenters increased, and the period between the date on which the agreement was opened for signature and the date on which "the last straggler signed up" widened (Buchheit 1991, 1998c). Ultimately, however, holdouts were dealt with through a mix of pressure from officials in creditor countries, debt buy backs, buyouts or, in rare cases when the amounts involved were very small, full repayment. Cases of holdout litigation against the debtors were very rare (see chapter 3).

As in the case of the CFB, the power of the London Club vis-à-vis debtors derived from the fact that it blocked new lending from its members prior to agreement on a debt restructuring deal. Unlike the CFB, however, this effect was not achieved through a formal mechanism but merely through informal adherence to the "cartel." Compared with earlier debt restructurings involving bonds, the BAC process tended to be very efficient; debt rescheduling deals in the early 1980s were often concluded in months, while the more comprehensive Brady deals of the late 1980s and early 1990s, in which creditors accepted large losses, generally took one or two years. This said, the final resolution of the 1980s debt crises, from the initial declaration of debt servicing difficulties to the final Brady deals, took longer than the average CFB restructuring; for example, it took about eight years for Mexico and eleven years for Argentina. However, these long time periods had

less to do with the negotiation process per se than with overly optimistic assumptions about the solvency of the debtors, regulatory incentives faced by banks, and perhaps the presence of the official sector as
an implicit "third party" in the negotiations.

The London Club continues to play a role today. Two of the debt
crises covered in detail in this book, Russia and Pakistan, involved
agreements with BACs. However, most debt crises and restructurings
between 1998 and 2005 focused on sovereign bonds held by a heterogeneous group of creditors which were mostly nonbanks. As far as the
negotiation process is concerned, the striking difference between this
most recent set of crises and earlier default waves between the 1860s
and the 1930s is the lack of representation of bondholders by a formal
committee such as the CFB. Bondholder representation in the 1998–
2005 restructurings was, at best, ad hoc, resembling the practice from
1820 to the 1860s more than any other period. An Emerging Markets Creditors Association (EMCA), based in New York, was founded
in 2000, but did not serve as a negotiating body. The Argentine debt
crisis led to the creation of a Global Committee of Argentina Bondholders in January 2004, which claimed to represent investors holding
about 45 percent of Argentina's total defaulted bonds (about two-
thirds of the bonds held outside Argentina). However, the Argentine
government avoided formal negotiations with this committee, and
Argentina's 2005 exchange offer achieved an acceptance rate of 76 percent in spite of the fact that the committee urged bondholders to reject
the offer (see chapter 8).

Given the lack of formal creditor coordination, it is perhaps surprising that the 1998–2005 debt restructurings were undertaken relatively
quickly. Most of them were undertaken in a matter of months (only
Argentina's most recent debt restructuring, which lasted for about
four-and-a-half years from default until settlement, took more than
two years). This was achieved through a novel approach, namely,
take-it-or-leave-it offers to exchange the existing bonds for new ones
with payment streams of lower present value. The offers were preceded by informal discussions with creditors, but rarely formal
negotiations. This worked well as long as the terms of the exchange
offer—usually designed with the help of an investment bank as
financial advisor—were sufficiently attractive enough to invite wide
participation, given the alternatives faced by creditors (i.e., uncertain
litigation or sale at depressed prices).

A powerful device to minimize the coordination problem was to make these offers contingent on their acceptance by a supermajority of creditors (80–90 percent). Only Argentina's most recent restructuring lacked such a threshold. While not removing the temptation of hold-outs to free ride at the expense of a majority of creditors (see chapter 3), this removed the risk of being stuck with a debt deal that had been rejected by most other creditors, and hence might not result in a sustainable debt burden. Participation thresholds therefore allowed creditors to evaluate the quality of an offer on the assumption that the country's debt burden would indeed be reduced by a large amount, with a corresponding improvement in debt service capacity. Other devices that helped achieve high participation rates included the use of majority amendment clauses in Ukraine's debt exchange, and changes in the *nonpayment* terms of the old bond contracts in Ecuador and Uruguay (see chapter 3).

The Content of Debt Restructuring Agreements

During the first long era of bond finance, from the 1820s until the postwar settlements of defaults in the 1930s, settlements generally took the form of an agreement on (1) the capitalization of interest arrears (which could be extensive, given average default periods of ten years or more); (2) a payments moratorium or maturity extension; and (3) in some cases, a reduction of interest payment and/or principal. The latter (face value reductions) was rare in the first half of the nineteenth century, but became more prevalent in the second half, particularly as transfers of property or revenue streams to the creditors became more common as components of a settlement. Eichengreen and Portes (1989) report that as a matter of principle, bondholder committees tried to avoid forgiving interest arrears and writing down principal on the grounds that "these obligations had been incurred prior to any renegotiation of the bond covenants." However, they cite several examples from settlement negotiations of the 1930s defaults where the CFB ultimately agreed to principal write downs and even to reductions in interest arrears.

In some cases, banks participating in the negotiations (usually the issuing banks) extended new loans to provide liquidity for continuing interest payments. For example, the March 1891 settlement with Argentina initially involved a £15 million loan to enable the government to continue servicing its debt and appreciate the currency; in view of continuing payments difficulties, this was replaced in 1893 by a new restructuring arrangement envisaging a reduction in interest payments by 30 percent over five years and a suspension of amortization payments until 1901. After Brazil experienced payment difficulties in 1898, a settlement was negotiated that envisaged a "funding loan" of £8 million to cover continue interest expenses, and a suspension of amortization payments for thirteen years (Fishlow 1989). While settlements were mostly negotiated only after the country had defaulted in the sense that debt service payments had been missed, there were also a few occasions, including the Brazilian funding loan in 1898, when a debt restructuring agreement was concluded ahead of a default.

A substantial subset of settlements between the midnineteenth century and World War I—seventeen out of a total of about fifty-seven settlements, according to Suter (1992)—included the transfer of property or income streams, such as tax or customs revenues to the creditors. This included the transfer of land or railway concessions, in return for a cancellation of principal and/or interest arrears. For example, in the Peruvian debt settlement of 1889, $30 million in outstanding debt and $23 million in interest arrears were canceled in return for the right to operate the state railways for sixty-six years, two million tons of guano, and the concession for the operation of steamboats on Lake Titicaca (Suter 1992). Similar settlements involving either railways or land took place in Colombia (1861 and 1873), Costa Rica (1885), the Dominican Republic (1893), Ecuador (1895), El Salvador (1899), and Paraguay (1855).

Control over specific revenue streams accompanied settlements with Tunisia (1869–1870), Egypt (1876), Turkey (1881), Serbia (1895), Greece (1898), Morocco (1903), the Dominican Republic (1904 and 1931), and Liberia (1912). The assigned revenues were typically collected by a "debt administration council" composed of creditor and debtor government representatives. In some cases, such as Turkey, the power of these councils and of creditor representatives within the councils was very strong (Flandreau 2003; Mauro, Sussman, and Yafeh 2006). In a few instances, including Egypt and Liberia, creditors essentially took over the management of the public finances of the country. Creditor attempts to gain direct revenue control in debtor countries disappeared after World War II; however, the idea of exchanging debt for nondebt claims had a comeback in the form of the "debt-equity swaps" of the 1980s.

Unlike the classical bond finance period, most major debtors that began to experience debt servicing difficulties in the late 1970s and early 1980s avoided "outright" default by renegotiating their debts with creditor banks before missing debt service payments. The content of settlements in this period evolved in several phases. During the first negotiations in the late 1970s, banks tried to rely entirely on refinancing: providing new loans to the debtors that enabled them to continue servicing the old loans, without formal debt restructuring. There were two reasons for this strategy. First, there was a belief that the debt crisis that began in the late 1970s was fundamentally one of liquidity rather than solvency. With an improvement in the external environment and some internal adjustment, developing countries were expected to be in a position to repay (Cline 1995). Second, regulatory incentives played a role. By maintaining debt service financed by new lending, banks could avoid classifying loans as impaired, which would have forced them to allocate income to provision against expected losses (Rieffel 2003).

After large debtors, such as Poland (1981) and Mexico (1982), began to renegotiate their debts, settlements typically involved a mix of new financing to enable countries to stay current on interest payments and rescheduling of principal. As it became clear that the debt crisis was not as transitory as had been initially expected, these annual rescheduling deals were replaced by "multiyear rescheduling agreements" (MYRAs). For example, Mexico's September 1984 MYRA rescheduled principal payments over a six-year period, extending from 1984 to 1989. Some MYRAs also contained new features such as debt-to-equity conversion options, and some lowered the interest rate spread over the London Interbank offer rate (LIBOR) in which coupon payments where expressed (Chuhan and Sturzenegger 2005; Rieffel 2003).

With continuing stagnant growth, it became clear that the net present value (NPV) debt reduction embodied in MYRAs was far too small to put an end to the continuing debt servicing difficulties of developing countries. A final initiative to avoid major write downs, the 1985 "Baker Plan" to stimulate growth in the debtor countries by combining structural reforms with new financing, failed by about 1987, when unilateral debt service moratoria were imposed by Peru and Brazil. Bank creditors began to view debt forgiveness as inevitable and began to provision for future losses. Provisioning was also a response to the development of a secondary market for defaulted debt that began in 1986. The existence of market prices for the unpaid loans entailed the risk that regulators might force banks to mark these loans to market, with a large potential negative impact on the balance sheet. One way to cover this risk was by provisioning the loans or by accepting a workable debt deal.

As a result, during 1987–1988, Mexico, Argentina, Brazil, and Chile negotiated debt restructuring agreements which included exchanging bank debt for "exit bonds" with lower face value, and debt buy backs at lower market prices. But with the exception of the Chilean buy back, even these deals proved insufficient to achieve a sustainable debt burden. Beginning in 1989, they were superseded by the United States and IFI-sponsored "Brady Plan," which combined IMF-monitored adjustment programs, significant NPV debt reduction, and official "enhancements" which were supposed to protect creditors from a new default round. The basic idea was to make debt relief acceptable to commercial bank creditors by offering a smaller but much safer payment stream in exchange for the original claim that clearly could not be serviced in full. "Enhancements" took the form of full collateralization of principal using U.S. Treasury zero-coupon bonds, which countries bought using reserves and financing by international financial institutions (IFIs); in addition, reserves were placed in escrow to cover an interruption in interest payments of up to one year.

In the next eight years—from Mexico in 1989–1990 to Côte d'Ivoire and Vietnam in 1997—BACs negotiated Brady deals with seventeen debtor countries. In all cases, creditor banks were presented with a "menu"—a choice of new claims—which typically included "par bonds" of same face value as the outstanding loan but a low fixed interest, "discount bonds" with a market interest expressed as a markup over LIBOR but a reduction in face value; a debt-equity option yielding a local currency claim that could be exchanged for shares of government enterprises being privatized, and a cash buyback option where banks could sell the loans back to the debtor country at a substantial discount. Par and discount bonds were thirty year bonds which included the enhancements described above, but the menus typically also contained shorter-dated bonds, such as "PDI (part due interest) bonds" issued in exchange for past due interest, without these enhancements.

The bond restructurings of 1998–2005 have generally followed the example of the Brady deals in offering investors a "menu" (though this was often limited to two options) and reducing the debt burden through a mixture of interest reduction, principal reduction, and maturity extension. Debt-equity conversions did not feature in these restructurings. In four out of the six bond exchanges affecting externally issued bonds—namely, Pakistan (1999), Ukraine (2000), Argentina (2001), and Uruguay (2003)—the existing debt was serviced up to the time of the exchange offer. In the cases of Russia (1998–2000), Ecuador (1999–2000), and Argentina (2002–2005), governments defaulted first and announced a debt exchange offer later.

The Role of the Official Sector

Creditor country government intervention in disputes between sovereign debtors and private creditors has been the exception rather than the rule. Lipson (1989) and Mauro, Sussman, and Yafeh (2006) report for the 1870–1914 period that the British government was usually reluctant to intervene on behalf of investors who had sought higher returns abroad and generally regarded defaults as the consequence of imprudent investment. Eichengreen and Portes (1989) characterize the interwar period in a similar way. However, British diplomats did provide the CFB with some degree of practical and administrative support, by receiving payments on behalf of the CFB or collecting securities for the CFB. In addition, creditor countries intervened more actively in support of private bondholders on a number of occasions and through several means, ranging from diplomatic suasion, to withholding of official credits to countries in default, to threat of trade sanctions and, in rare cases, armed intervention.

According to Mauro, Sussman, and Yafeh, diplomatic pressure was applied on several Central American countries in the 1870s. In 1875, Honduras was the subject of a parliamentary examination. In 1903, the CFB asked the British government not to recognize the new Republic of Panama. In 1913, the continued default of Guatemala was finally resolved as a result of diplomatic pressure. In a handful of famous cases, official intervention went beyond diplomatic pressure or threat of sanctions (Lipson 1985, 1989; Suter 1992; Suter and Stamm 1992; Mitchener and Weidenmier 2005). In 1863, France, initially supported by Spain and Britain, invaded Mexico after the republican regime of Benito Juarez refused to honor Mexico's debt service obligations, briefly installing the Austrian archduke Maximilian as emperor. (Maximilian was dethroned and executed in 1867, after which Mexico repudiated for good.) In 1882, Britain invaded Egypt, which had defaulted in 1876 and whose public finances were already under the control of a

Franco-British debt administration council. Venezuela suffered a maritime blockade by Germany, Britain, and Italy in 1902–1903 after Venezuela did not resume debt service payments after the end of its civil war. Finally, U.S. Marines were sent to the Dominican Republic (1905) and Nicaragua (1911) to take over customs revenues following attempted defaults.

While these episodes provide illustrations of official intervention benefiting private bondholders, enforcing debt repayments was often not the main motive for many of these interventions (Tomz 2006). Colonial or imperial ambitions played an obvious role in the French and British invasions of Mexico and Egypt, respectively, and the blockade of Venezuelan ports was partly the result of a border dispute between Venezuela and British Guyana as well as tort claims associated with the Venezuelan civil war (Kelly 1998; Tomz 2006). Hence, the defaults that preceded these interventions may only have been a pretext for legitimizing these interventions, rather than their main cause. Nevertheless, armed intervention may still have deterred defaulters to the extent that providing the major powers with such a pretext made an intervention more likely. Whether this was the case as an empirical matter is controversial (see Mitchener and Weidenmier 2005, for arguments in favor of, and Tomz 2006, for arguments against this view).

During the 1930s, the British and U.S. governments supported creditors through a combination of "diplomatic representations," the principle that the British Treasury would generally not lend to countries that had defaulted on British creditors, and threats of trade-related sanctions, including through the suspension of trade credits granted by government controlled institutions and the creation of "clearing arrangements" that would sequester a portion of payments of creditor country importers to debtor country exporters for the purpose of repaying creditor country bondholders (Eichengreen and Portes 1989, 19–23). Under the threat of such an arrangement, backed by a 1934 Act of Parliament creating a clearing office to regulate British trade with Germany, Germany agreed to continue servicing Dawes and Young Plan bonds held by British citizens, while U.S. bondholders, which lacked a corresponding threat, received only partial interest from June 1934 forward. However, just like military intervention prior to World War II, the threat of trade-related sanctions in the 1930s was the exception rather than the rule. Moreover, government pressure could go both ways. In some cases when government interests conflicted with bondholder interests, bondholder committees were pressured to accept a settlement, as occurred on the eve of World War II with respect to some debtor countries, such as Egypt and Greece, with which Britain was trying to conclude treaties.

After World War II, the role of the official sector in debt disputes changed in two respects. First, with very few exceptions such as U.S. sanctions against Cuba, which were imposed for much broader reasons than just Cuba's 1960 default, there have been no direct sanctions and certainly no military interventions against defaulting governments. Second, creditor governments have influenced debt restructuring agreements through several channels that did not exist or were less common prior to the war, including regulatory pressure or forbearance with respect to creditor banks, legal channels, which became viable after the narrowing of the concept of sovereign immunity, and multilateral organizations (see Buchheit 1990 for an overview of the roles of the U.S. government played in sovereign debt negotiations in the 1980s). An example for the legal channel is the "Allied Bank" case, in which a legal opinion issued by the U.S. Department of Justice was pivotal in the 1984 reversal of a lower court ruling that had sided with a defaulting debtor (Costa Rica) against a U.S. creditor bank (see chapter 3). Government agencies in creditor countries have also played the role of mediators or hosts during debtor-creditor negotiations, such as the U.S. Treasury and Federal Reserve during Mexico's 1989 Brady plan negotiations and the Bank of England during the 1976 negotiations between creditor banks and Zaïre (Rieffel 2003). Finally, international financial institutions, particularly the IMF, have had an important influence on settlements between creditors and debtors. However, the IMF's role has been more nuanced than simply helping creditors get their money back, and it has evolved over time.

The stated objective of the IMF has been to make the international financial system more efficient by preventing disruptive debt crises and accelerating debt settlements. To do so, it has used two main instruments. First, the IMF provided crisis lending to countries that required temporary financing, which allowed them to adjust in order to be able to repay their debts. This role is not new, though the actors, motives, and terms of crisis lending have evolved over time (see Bordo and Schwartz 1999 for a survey). During the nineteenth century and the interwar period crisis lending was undertaken by private investment banks on commercial terms, and on some occasions by the central banks of England and France; in the 1930s, by the Bank for International Settlements (Fishlow 1985; Eichengreen and Portes 1986, 1989;

Flandreau 2003). During the 1980s renegotiations of commercial bank loans, this role was shared by the IMF and bank syndicates providing "new money" loans. The main difference between the IMF and private crisis lenders is that IMF lending has always been conditional on policy adjustments, and has generally taken place at lower interest rates (Haldane 1999; Higginbotham and Schuler 2002; Zettelmeyer and Joshi 2005).

Second, IMF-supported programs with countries with debt servicing difficulties have served as commitment devices for debtors to undertake steps to restore solvency, lowering the uncertainty associated with debt settlement negotiations, and implicitly helping to define the resource envelope available for a settlement. Rieffel (2003) reports that IMF staff was regularly present during BAC negotiations with creditors in the 1980s, presenting their medium term projections of a debtor country's balance of payments as a starting point from which creditors could form their own views on the country's capacity to repay.

Armed with these instruments, the IMF was a critical presence during the early stages of the 1980s debt crisis, when it helped define and execute the initial crisis resolution strategy by which countries would seek to regain their debt service capacity through a mix of IMF-supported adjustment and fresh financing. "As a referee for the extension of new credit," the IMF was "especially important for creating a cooperative environment for avoiding outright default" (Jorgensen and Sachs 1989, 48). The IMF was also part of the Brady Plan that ultimately ended the crisis, both by negotiating adjustment programs with debtor countries that accompanied their agreements with the banks and by financing some of the Brady bond "enhancements" (Boughton 2001; Rieffel 2003).

However, the IMF's role during the debt crisis has also been criticized. First, the IMF and, more generally, the official sector have been accused of contributing to the long delay in the resolution of the crisis, both by "producing short-run cosmetic agreements with little clear resolution of the underlying disagreement over resource transfer" in the early and mid 1980s, and by implicitly holding out the prospect of a public sector bailout (Lindert and Morton 1989, 78; Bulow and Rogoff 1988). Partly in reaction to this criticism, the IMF has generally become more reluctant to rescue countries with debt servicing difficulties, in some cases refusing to lend to countries unless they sought a debt restructuring with their creditors at the same time. While the fundamental rule under which the IMF lends—namely, only to countries which are solvent, or at least conditionally solvent after appropriate policy adjustments—remained unchanged, judgments on what should be regarded as solvent became more conservative in the 1990s, after several crisis countries of the 1980s had accumulated arrears to the IMF.

Second, the IMF was accused of playing the role of a "bill collector for the banks" in the 1980s, that is, of a bias in favor of the creditor side. The basis for this criticism was the IMF's longstanding policy of not lending to countries that were in arrears with the creditors, hence strengthening the creditors' capacity to exclude recalcitrant debtors from access to credit, and thus their bargaining power during debt settlement negotiations. In response to this criticism, the IMF changed its policy in 1989, to one that allows it to lend to debtors in arrears so long as they are engaged in "good faith negotiations" with their creditors. However, what constitutes "good faith" is debatable. In recent years, the IMF has been accused of overshooting in the direction of harming creditor interests—and by extension, those of the sovereign bond market—by encouraging unilateral debt exchange offers, and lending even to countries with a defiant stance vis-à-vis their creditors (Cline 2001; Rieffel 2003, EMCA 2004). In response, the IMF has argued that its support of debtor countries benefits both sides by improving the debtors' debt servicing ability, and that it always encourages countries to service their debts in line with this ability.

How Investors Fared

A central question—perhaps *the* question—in the study of sovereign defaults is how defaults and the subsequent settlement affect the parties involved. The economic literature on sovereign debt generally assumes that defaults have benefits and costs for the debtor, and that the decision to default is based on a comparison of these. In contrast, a default always harms the creditor, but for sovereign debt to exist, this harm must be made up by positive returns in normal times. In the following we briefly summarize the evidence on the losses that defaults have inflicted on creditors, as well as the overall average returns earned by investors holding risky sovereign debt. The question of how defaults impacted debtor countries is taken up in the next chapter.

To summarize the losses suffered by creditors as a result of specific debt restructurings, one would ideally like to compare the (remaining) payment stream that was originally promised to investors with the payment stream associated with the restructured instruments, both discounted at a common interest rate (see Sturzenegger and Zettelmeyer 2005 and pages 88–90, this volume). Unfortunately, there is no study that compares all debt settlements since the 1820s using such a summary measure. Instead, several authors have compared debt restructurings in various aspects, such as the face value reductions suffered, the average reduction in interest payments, and so forth, that contribute to the overall reduction in the investors' claim.

In an extensive historical study of debt and defaults since the 1820s, Suter (1992) compares debt restructurings during 1820–1870, 1871–1925, and 1926–1975, in terms of (1) the extent to which interest arrears were repaid; (2) reduction in interest rates; and (3) reduction in face value. He finds that, by these measures, debt settlements seem to have become tougher for investors over time. In the first period, there were hardly any face value reductions, interest rates were typically reduced by about 15 percent, and 81 percent of the outstanding arrears were capitalized into new bonds (this ignores compound interest on arrears). In the second period, the rate of capitalization of arrears was only 72 percent, interest rates were reduced by about 16 percent, and face value by 23 percent. However, the latter is, in part, a reflection of the increasing use of land and railway concessions to "repay" investors in this period. Finally, the interwar defaults led to much larger investor losses: only 35 percent of interest arrears were recognized on average; interest payments suffered an average haircut of 34 percent; and face value was reduced by 23 percent, without any offsetting assignment of nondebt assets.

Jorgenson and Sachs (1989) compute investor losses for four major Latin American default cases in the 1930s—Bolivia, Chile, Colombia, and Peru—by comparing the present value of the principal outstanding at default to the present value of actual repayment after default, both discounted back to the default year using a risk-free international interest rate. Using this methodology, Jorgenson and Sachs show that the 1930s defaults and restructurings resulted in very large present value losses: 37 percent for Colombia, 61 percent for Peru, 69 percent for Chile, and a staggering 92 percent for Bolivia.

Rieffel (2003, 171, based on World Bank data) summarizes the terms of the Brady deals by averaging the face value reduction suffered by investors choosing discount bonds (namely, bonds with the same coupon as outstanding bank loans, but smaller face value) and the discounts reflected in the buyback component (the difference between the face value and the market price at which bonds were bought back). The average discounts range from about 35 percent for Mexico (1990) to 76 percent for Côte d'Ivoire. Importantly, these discounts significantly understate the present value discount suffered by investors, because they do not take into account the much longer maturity (thirty years) of the new Brady bonds relative to the previous bank loans, which for the most part had already come due and were being rolled over.[8]

Finally, Sturzenegger and Zettelmeyer (2005) calculate the present value losses attributable to the bond exchanges and restructurings of 1998–2005. To do so, they compare the present value of the originally promised payment stream, including both remaining interest payments and principal outstanding, to the *expected* present value of payments promised at the time of a debt restructuring; as this is unobservable, the post-restructuring interest rate (which prices in any expected future losses) is used to discount both streams. Out of the six major debt restructurings of externally issued debt in this period, investors suffered face value reductions in four cases (Russia 2000 Prins and IANs exchange, Ukraine 2000, Ecuador 2000, and Argentina 2005), while the remainder (Pakistan 1999 and Uruguay 2003) involved mainly extensions in maturity and to a lesser extent interest rate reductions.[9] Present value "haircuts," ranged from just 5–20 percent for Uruguay (2003) to over 50 percent for Russia (2000) and over 70 percent for Argentina (2005), with the remaining exchanges falling mostly in the 20–40 percent range.

One interesting implication of these results is that with the exception of Argentina (2005), investors suffered smaller losses as a consequence of the supposedly creditor-unfriendly unilateral exchange offers than the negotiated settlement with Russia, which was conducted by a BAC. Based on Rieffel's computations, it also seems that most Brady deal restructurings negotiated between banks and debtor countries involved significantly larger present value losses. Of course, it is possible that these different outcomes reflect different initial conditions, including a bigger debt overhang in the 1980s. In the absence of a systematic study that controls for initial conditions, what can be said at this point is only that unilateral debt exchanges, perhaps surprisingly, do not appear to have been associated with larger investor losses than negotiated debt restructurings.

The main limitation of "haircut" calculations of this kind is that they say nothing about how investors fared in the longer run, namely, whether defaults, as well as capital losses in crisis times in countries that did not end up defaulting, were ultimately offset by high returns in good times. To answer this question, one needs to compute investor returns over longer horizons. Several papers tackle this issue: Eichengreen and Portes (1986, 1989) track a large sample of bonds issued on behalf of overseas borrowers in the United States and the United Kingdom in the 1920s; Lindert and Morton (1989) track over 1,500 bonds issued by ten borrowing countries between 1850 and 1983 (including bonds outstanding in 1850); and Klingen, Weder, and Zettelmeyer (2004) compute returns on public and publicly guaranteed bank loans and bond flows to about two dozen emerging markets in the 1970–2000 period, using aggregate data at the debtor country level compiled by the World Bank.

The results are remarkably consistent across time periods and methodologies. The upshot of the three studies is that while investors both incurred significant losses and made large profits in specific episodes and for specific countries, the long-run average premium of emerging market debt relative to sovereign debt in the traditional creditor countries, such as the United Kingdom and the United States, has generally been positive, but small (150 basis points or less). According to Lindert and Morton (1989), the portfolio of 1,522 bonds issued by overseas borrowers over the course of one hundred and fifty years would have narrowly "beaten" a portfolio of *creditor* country sovereign bonds absorbing the same flows, by 42 basis points on average per annum. For bonds issued prior to 1914, they find a virtual tie of −14 basis points, while bonds issued between 1914 and 1945, the "generation" that suffered from the defaults of the 1930s, did slightly better with 113 basis points. Eichengreen and Portes (1986) find that foreign government bonds issued in the United States in the 1920s did slightly worse than their U.S. government counterparts, while Sterling bonds did slightly better (on the order of 100 basis points). For the 1970–2000 period and a sample of both bank and bond lending to twenty-two emerging markets countries, Klingen, Weder, and Zettelmeyer (2004) find a long-run premium of −17 to 46 basis points, depending on the methodology applied. This reflects the combined effect of negative ex post (realized) spreads during the boom-bust cycle from 1970 to the late 1980s (reflecting the debt crisis of the 1980s) and sharply positive ex post spreads, on average, since then.

Table 1.2 shows some results for specific countries, based on Lindert and Morton (1989), and Klingen, Weder, and Zettelmeyer (2004). For

Table 1.2
Emerging markets: Realized excess returns on sovereign debt, 1850–2000 (in percentage points)

	Bonds[a]				Bonds and long-term bank loans[b]		
	1850–1914	1915–1945	1946–1983	1850–1983	1970–1992	1992–2001	1970–2001
Argentina	1.71	1.95	4.70	1.96	−2.09	−17.01	−6.82
Brazil	0.89	0.70	. . .	0.83	−3.42	16.23	−0.51
Chile	1.48	−1.90	. . .	−0.22	−0.17	3.51	0.06
Mexico	−2.72	. . .	2.31	−1.92	−0.51	5.96	0.64
Australia	1.01	1.21	0.72	1.03	. . .	. . .	. . .
Canada	1.27	0.65	2.25	1.56	. . .	. . .	. . .
Egypt	2.92	−0.73	. . .	2.53	. . .	. . .	. . .
Japan	1.25	2.26	2.25	1.58	. . .	. . .	. . .
Russia	−1.63	. . .	. . .	−1.63	. . .	. . .	. . .
Turkey	−1.56	−0.88	−0.34	−1.29	0.89	0.44	0.58

Note: Difference between the realized return on sovereign debt of the respective periphery country and the return on sovereign debt of the investor's home country (for bond returns 1850–1983) or the United States (for all private external lending, 1970–2001).
[a] From Lindert and Morton (1989). Dates refer to issue dates.
[b] Adapted from Klingen, Weder, and Zettelmeyer (2004); uses their "indirect approach."

the long pre–World War I period, one important result is that investors earned positive average spreads in most debtor countries, including Argentina, Brazil, and Chile, which all defaulted at least once in this period. Thus, the defaults of these countries were more than offset by debt service in normal times. This was not the case for Russia, Turkey, and particularly Mexico. In all three of these cases, what made the difference was political upheaval, war, or revolution. Mexico repudiated completely on two occasions: after deposing the Emperor Maximilian in 1867, who had been installed by France three years earlier, and after the 1911 revolution. Russia did the same after the 1917 revolution, and Turkey did so after World War I, when the new nationalist government refused to repay prewar Ottoman debts. At the other extreme, Egypt's creditors earned exceptionally high returns because of the combination of a high ex ante spread with full repayment after the attempted default of 1876 led to the 1882 British invasion and loss of sovereignty. In short, both the negative spreads for Mexico, Russia, and Turkey, and the high positive spread for Egypt reflect forecast errors, while the moderate positive spreads for the remainder reflect repayment performance that was about in line with expectations. In the case of Argentina, Brazil, and Chile, ex ante spreads were comparatively high (Lindert and Morton 1989, Table 2.2), which was validated by a default some time in the late nineteenth century. In the cases of Australia, Canada, and Japan, ex ante spreads were lower, validated by full repayment.

It is also interesting to interpret Lindert and Morton's post–World War I returns. First, note the missing values for Mexico (1915–1945) and Russia (1915–1983). This reflects extended absences of these countries following their revolutions and repudiations in the early twentieth century. The worst return in the interwar period was that of Chile, consistent with the exceptionally large write-down associated with its interwar default (69 percent, according to Jorgenson and Sachs's methodology). High returns, both for bonds issued in the interwar period, and after World War II prior to the 1980s debt crisis, were earned by Argentina's creditors, as Argentina was the only major Latin American borrower to avoid default in the interwar period. The same was true for Japan, which repaid faithfully until the attack on Pearl Harbor and again after the war.

The right columns of the table, which are based on data and calculations by Klingen, Weder, and Zettelmeyer (2004), consider the postwar experience for the Latin American countries and Turkey. In contrast with its good repayment performance during the first half of the century, the main defaulter is now Argentina. It was the only major borrower to undergo large debt write-offs both after the 1980s debt crisis and after the boom-bust cycle of the 1990s, hence its large negative spread. Like Argentina, Brazil, Mexico, and Chile went through two major boom-bust cycles, but, unlike Argentina, only the first of these cycles ended in a default. As a result, the overall realized spread from 1970–2001 is about zero, reflecting the offsetting effects of poor returns until the resolution of the 1980s debt crisis and high returns since then.

Finally, Turkey's postwar experience was unusual. It is the only country in the group that does not exhibit negative spreads for the period 1970–1992. This reflects the absence of a large debt write-off during or after the 1980s debt crisis. After devaluing in 1979, Turkey restructured "convertible Turkish lira deposits," foreign commercial bank deposits in Turkish banks with an exchange rate guarantee from the central bank, but left medium term sovereign loans untouched (Rieffel 2003, 307–311), and managed to avoid further debt restructuring during the 1980s or 1990s. But neither does Turkey exhibit large realized spreads between the early 1990s and 2001, unlike Brazil, Chile, or Mexico. This is a result of the 2000–2001 financial crisis, which led to a limited commercial bank debt restructuring in early 2001 and depressed sovereign bond prices, which enter in the calculations underlying the returns for the period ending at end-2001. Thus, while Turkey's average result for the entire 1970–2001 period is very similar to that of Mexico, its composition is very different.

The unusually high returns during the 1990s provide clues for evaluating the behavior of international financial markets during the last decade. They signal both unusually high ex ante creditor demands, possibly due to the negative returns obtained during the 1980s, and better-than-expected outcomes.

2 The Economics of Sovereign Debt and Debt Crises: A Primer

The purpose of this chapter is to provide the economics background that is critical to understanding the major crises of the 1990s. As such, we make no attempt to systematically survey the large literature on sovereign debt.[1] Instead, we briefly review some basic ideas on sovereign debt, and then turn to recent research on the causes and consequences of debt crises.

Basics

Explaining Why Sovereign Debt Can Exist

In the corporate world, debt contracts are enforced by the courts. A corporation cannot simply repudiate, that is, decide not to repay. If it tried, it would be sued and courts would force it to hand over assets to the creditor, restructure, or (in the limit) shut it down and liquidate its remaining assets. This enforcement mechanism is lacking in sovereign debt. As we will see in the next chapter, the reason for this is not so much "sovereign immunity"—a legal doctrine that limits the extent to which sovereign assets located in foreign jurisdictions can be attached by creditors—but the fact that few sovereign assets (including future income streams) are located in foreign jurisdictions, and that a sovereign cannot credibly commit to hand over assets within its borders in the event of a default. This leads to the question of why private creditors are willing to lend to sovereigns in the first place. Much of the literature on sovereign debt, starting with a seminal contribution by Eaton and Gersovitz (1981), has focused on this question.

The simplest way to pose the question is to ask whether there would be a sovereign debt market if creditors had *no* direct control over debtors whatsoever, and their only means of retaliating in the event of default would be through the denial of future credit. Eaton and Gersovitz showed that under some assumptions, the answer is "yes".[2] If debtors have no way of insuring against output shocks other than through borrowing, and default triggers permanent exclusion from credit markets, then the threat of losing access to credit markets is a sufficient reason for repaying, up to a certain maximum level. This level is higher, the bigger the variance of output, and the more the borrowing country values the insurance function of international capital markets for given fluctuations in output.[3]

Though highly influential, Eaton and Gersovitzs' result was quickly criticized from two angles. The first, anticipated by the authors themselves in the introduction to their paper, focused on the assumption that a default could be punished through *permanent* exclusion from future credit. The problem is that in such a situation both parties— creditors and debtors—are generally worse off than in a situation in which lending resumes.[4] In technical parlance, a lending equilibrium sustained by the threat of a permanent embargo on future lending is not "renegotiation-proof," in the sense that after a default both parties potentially benefit from reaching a new agreement involving positive lending. But if such an agreement is anticipated, then this undermines the expected punishment that was sustaining positive lending in the first place (see Kletzer 1994 for details).

The second line of criticism, due to Bulow and Rogoff (1989a), focused on the implicit assumption that borrowing from international lenders is the *only* way countries can smooth consumption in response to shocks to output. What if there are other ways, including storing output, purchasing insurance, or investing a portion of one's wealth abroad so that it can be tapped in times of need? Clearly, this would diminish the dependence on international credit for insurance purposes, and thus the effectiveness of exclusion from credit markets in preventing defaults. In the extreme, if a country could purchase an insurance contract that delivers payments in low output states exactly like borrowing would, then the threat of exclusion from credit would lose its bite entirely. To see this, suppose sovereign debt could exist in these circumstances, and take the highest level of debt that can supposedly be sustained. Rather than repaying this debt to creditors, the country could use the repayment to collateralize an insurance contract delivering the same maximum transfer in bad states as the country could have borrowed under the previous debt contract, in exchange for country payments ("premia") in good states. Thus, a "cash-in-advance" insurance contract can be designed so that it exactly replicates the flows associated with international borrowing. But in addition, the country would receive interest on its collateral. Since this argument can be made for any level of debt, any borrowing is impossible.

Together, these objections posed a powerful challenge to the notion that the threat of exclusion from credit markets, by itself, makes sovereign borrowing possible. Broadly speaking, the literature has since evolved in three directions.[5]

A first group of papers, including Sachs and Cohen (1982), Bulow and Rogoff (1989b), and Fernandez and Rosenthal (1990) focused on direct punishments as the reason for repayment. Direct punishments are generally interpreted as interference with a country's current transactions, that is, trade and payments, either through seizure outside the country's borders or through the denial of *trade* credit. Renegotiations are explicitly modeled in these papers. In Bulow and Rogoff (1989b), contracts can be renegotiated at any time. The amount that a country can borrow is determined by the proportion of the debtor's output that creditors can expect to extract in this renegotiation. The fact that they can extract anything at all hinges critically on the assumption that inflicting a sanction not only harms the debtor, but also benefits the creditor directly (e.g., the creditor receives a share of the debtor country's trade payments). Thus, the threat that in the event of nonpayment the creditor will actually impose the sanction is credible. This would not be the case if imposing the sanction hurts both debtors and the creditors.

A second line of research attempts to rescue the idea that governments repay because they are worried about the repercussions of a default in the credit market. Most of these papers no longer rely on enforcement through the (implausible) threat of permanent exclusion from credit markets, and some explicitly address the renegotiation problem. One group of papers, including Cole and Kehoe (1995), Eaton (1996), and Kletzer and Wright (2000), sidestep the Bulow and Rogoff (1989a) critique by dropping the assumption that the government can safely invest abroad regardless of its past behavior. Just like the debtor countries themselves, financial institutions may not be able to commit to future payments, at least not to countries that have defaulted (e.g., because past lenders could attempt to interfere with such payments as a way of enforcing their claims). In the jargon of this literature, the "one-sided commitment problem" assumed by the sovereign debt literature of the 1980s is replaced by a "two-sided commitment problem." This said, with multiple lenders, an equilibrium sustained by credit market sanctions could still unravel if a new lender refuses to participate in the sanctions. In Kletzer and Wright's model, this is deterred by the original lender's offer to "pardon" the debtor (i.e., to let the debtor return to the original lending relationship) in exchange for defaulting on any new lender. As a result, potential new lenders "will respect the punishment of the borrower in equilibrium," that is, a defaulter will not be able to find new positive surplus lending relationships.

Most recently, several papers have demonstrated that sovereign lending could exist in a setting that *both* considers only credit market punishments *and* assumes that deposit or insurance contracts à la Bulow-Rogoff are feasible. Wright (2002b) shows that sovereign debt can be sustained in these circumstances if countries can have lending relationships with more than one bank at a time—syndicated lending, which offers banks a profit relative to competitive lending—because this creates an incentive for lenders to collude in punishing default. Banks that defect by engaging in financial relationships with a defaulting country are punished by exclusion from future syndicated lending.[6] Amador (2003) has a model in which governments undersave because they know that they may lose power, but at the same time wish to retain access to capital markets since they count on being returned to power eventually. This fits a situation in which several established parties alternate in power. This combination—a desire for insurance, combined with a chronic lack of cash that could be used to make a deposit or finance a cash-in-advance insurance contract—means that the threat of exclusion from future borrowing is sufficient to sustain sovereign lending.[7]

As far as the enforcement of repayment is concerned, Kletzer and Wright (2000) and Wright (2002b) work with infinite horizon models in which default does not trigger permanent exclusion from credit markets, but rather a new financial relationship *at terms that make the defaulting debtor no better off than permanent exclusion*. Thus, the equilibrium in the subgame following a default is just as unpleasant for the debtor as a permanent lending embargo, but it is also efficient. The creditor appropriates all gains from trade, and would thus not want to renegotiate. For example, Wright's (2002b) paper includes a model in which a country borrows from a single bank that can commit to honoring deposit and insurance contracts. The threat that enforces repayment is the replacement of the lending relationship with an insurance contract, in which the insurance "premium" after a default is so large as to leave the country without any surplus relative to permanent exclusion from capital markets.

Eaton (1996) presents a finite horizon model in which there is incomplete information about the borrower's type: "bad" types will strategically default if this is optimal, while "good" types will always try to repay. Borrowers cannot save or buy insurance. Lenders try to distinguish between the two types by observing the borrower's default history. If there is no uncertainty about the borrower's *ability* to pay, then observing a default identifies the borrower as a "bad" type. This leads to exclusion from credit markets.[8] If there is extraneous uncertainty, default does not imply that a borrower is necessarily bad, but it increases the probability that he is. This leads to higher interest rates. Either way, "bad" borrowers have an incentive to build a good credit history, at least at low levels of debt.

Finally, a third line of research is based on the idea that a default could have much broader adverse effects on a lender's reputation than just through his standing in credit markets. This was first raised as a possibility by Bulow and Rogoff (1989a), and is developed by Cole and Kehoe (1998). Like Eaton (1996), Cole and Kehoe assume that there are two types of debtor country governments: "honest" governments that always repay, and "normal" governments. If the government can save or purchase insurance and is in just one repeated relationship (with lenders), then the Bulow-Rogoff result applies, that is, no borrowing can be sustained if the lending relationship is sufficiently long so that lenders find out about the bad government's true type.[9]

Suppose, however, that there is another relationship in which the government's partners (say, workers) also have incomplete information about the government's true type. Both workers and lenders make inferences about the government's true type from the way the government behaves in the other relationship as well as in their own. Default, vis-à-vis lenders, tarnishes the government's reputation with its workers. This provides a powerful new incentive to repay. The intuition is that while the possibility of saving the defaulted debt or using it to back an insurance contract removes the need to preserve a good reputation vis-à-vis the creditors, it is no substitute for preserving a good reputation in the other relationship. In that relationship, there is no mechanism analogous to the presence of insurance contracts that would undo the damage caused by the government's loss of reputation. Think of a miser riding in a cab. If he is alone, he will not tip the driver. He does not care if this exposes him as a miser, since he does not depend on this particular cab driver for future rides. But if he is with his girlfriend, he will tip the driver in order to maintain a reputation of generosity vis-à-vis *her*.

In summary, the classic theory of sovereign debt suggests that incentives to repay sovereign debt might include credit market incentives, worries about reductions in trade and legal harassment, and broader reputational concerns. Pure credit market incentives may not be as critical as had been initially assumed. While the Bulow-Rogoff critique may not hold literally—both for the reasons raised by Wright (2002b) and Amador (2003), and because it requires highly state contingent deposit contracts, which are not observed in practice—it could hold approximately, in the sense that the importance of access to external borrowing is diminished if governments have other ways of transferring income across time. However, sovereign debt theories based on exclusion from credit markets remain influential, and have recently made a comeback.

Explaining Sovereign Debt Structures in Emerging Markets

Sovereign debt structure in emerging markets is quite different from that in advanced countries. The basic stylized fact is that emerging market governments issue some long-term debt in foreign currency as well as short-term debt in both domestic and local currency, but, until recently, very little long-term debt in domestic currency. In contrast, in advanced countries, *most* debt is domestic currency long-term debt. Moreover, average maturities tend to be longer in industrial countries than in emerging economies (Borensztein et al. 2005).

As we argue in the next section, the particular debt structure of emerging market countries is a contributing cause to debt crises. It affects both the vulnerability of a country to a debt crisis and the depth of a crisis when it happens. Because it is the source of so many other problems, some authors (Eichengreen and Hausmann 1999; Eichengreen, Hausmann, and Panizza 2005a, b) have called this debt structure the "original sin" of emerging economies. It is thus important to understand the incentives that determine the peculiar public debt structures characteristic for emerging market countries. Only then can one tell whether particular policy prescriptions for moving toward "safer" debt structures in emerging markets are likely to be successful, irrelevant, or worse.

There are two classes of explanations for the bias in emerging market debt in the direction of short-term and foreign currency debt. The first has to do with risk aversion on the side of the lender (Broner, Lorenzoni, and Schmukler 2004). In general, long-term debt is riskier than short-term debt, as witnessed by its higher price volatility. Hence, investors will require a premium to hold it. This makes long-term debt relatively expensive, which may be a reason for countries to issue short-term debt, in spite of the fact that the latter exposes them to roll-over crises. Assuming that investors like to consume or hold their asset portfolio in dollars, a similar argument could be made to explain foreign currency denomination. The appeal of this theory is its simplicity; however, it is predicated on the assumption that investors are more risk averse than countries.

A second set of explanations emphasizes commitment problems on the side of the borrower. In this story, short-term and/or foreign currency debt is common because it makes it harder for the debtor to undertake actions that hurt the creditor after the debt has been issued. If the debtor could commit ex ante not to undertake these actions, or if contracts could specify sanctions in the event that such actions are taken, then there would be no problem, and all debt would be long-term and in domestic currency. But this form of ex ante commitment may be impossible for deep institutional or legal reasons (e.g., weak institutions in the debtor countries, or weak contract enforcement at the international level).

A simple example is the moral hazard problem associated with domestic currency debt. A country that cannot commit to low inflation can avoid repayment by inflating away its debt, or by generating a depreciation (Bohn 1990; Calvo and Guidotti 1990). Hence, domestic currency debt cannot be issued, or only on terms that are prohibitive for the borrower. By issuing debt in foreign currency, a country removes the temptation to expropriate the borrower; this makes debt affordable. In the jargon of information economics, foreign currency debt prevails because it involves lower "agency costs." Note that these are "agency costs" that arise over and above the standard problem of enforcing the debt contract.

A similar argument applies to long-term debt. The chance that long-term debt is repaid could depend on certain policy actions (e.g., fiscal adjustment). If the debtor cannot commit to undertaking these actions, investors may prefer to hold short-term debt, which allows them to "get out" after observing the country's policy effort (Rodrik and Velasco 2000; Jeanne 2004). Because governments know that investors may not roll over if they observe bad policies, short-term debt acts as a disciplining device. In equilibrium, the government may exercise the high policy effort, but at the expense of a short-term debt structure that makes the country vulnerable to self-fulfilling runs or rollover crises in the event of a bad shock.

A further variant of this argument that has recently received attention is debt dilution. Here, the "bad action" from the (original) creditor perspective is not low policy effort but the issuing of additional debt, which reduces the original creditors' share of the debt recovery value in the event of a default (except to the extent that original creditors are senior or secured). Short-term debt can serve as a protection against dilution, as the original creditors can refuse to roll over their short-term loans—or roll them over at higher interest rates—when they perceive an attempt to dilute (Sachs and Cohen 1982; Kletzer 1984; Chamon 2002; Bolton and Jeanne 2005).

The Causes of Debt Crises

As we have seen, the classic literature on sovereign debt focuses on the "willingness to pay problem": Why are countries willing to repay their debts? In this perspective, defaults or debt renegotiations are most naturally interpreted as situations where the willingness to pay breaks down, as the trade-off between repaying and defaulting is somehow altered by unforeseen events. In contrast, most literature written specifically to "explain" debt crises focuses on *ability* to pay: How do countries get into situations where they can no longer repay? However, these two ways of looking at debt crises are to some extent equivalent. Countries may not be "willing" to pay because this would require unacceptable sacrifices in light of a reduction in their "ability" to do so (their resources). Conversely, they may not be "able" to pay in the sense that repaying would not be an equilibrium given the resources and political economy constraints that shape their willingness to take measures that would enable them to repay. Consequently, we focus on only one of these perspectives, and frame the discussion of debt crises by asking what economic problems might diminish a country's ability to pay. The "willingness to pay" perspective is distinguished whenever it leads to different conclusions.

Debt Runs

One tradition in the literature, going back to Sachs (1984), focuses on liquidity crises triggered by self-fulfilling runs on debt. The assumption here is that debt is short-term, and that there is a fixed pool of resources for repayment (or equivalently, in a willingness-to-pay framework, that repayment becomes increasingly painful as resources are depleted). Hence, governments will default if too many of the current creditors refuse to roll over. The interesting question is whether creditors might find it in their interest to do so even in a situation when debtors are "solvent" in the sense that the net present value of future fiscal surpluses exceeds their debt. The answer is: possibly, if one assumes that defaults are costly in the sense that they reduce future output. Because of the reduction in future output as a result of default, the government may not be able to repay investors who roll over. Therefore, if an individual creditor expects a default, it is best for him or her not to roll over. It all creditors think this way, this triggers a default, hence validating the initial expectation. The same fundamentals thus give rise to two equilibria in this type of model: a normal state where all creditors roll over and there are no defaults, and self-fulfilling debt runs where no creditors roll over and there is a default. Several authors (notably Alesina, Prati, and Tabellini 1990; Cole and Kehoe 1996, 2000) have explored this setup, and extended it to allow for complications such as the presence of new potential lenders.

The debt run story is valuable in providing the simplest possible argument for why short-term debt could be dangerous. It also meets the minimal test that any theory of debt crises should be required to pass, namely to explain why industrial countries do not appear to suffer such crises. The answer could be that—for the reasons described previously, and unlike most developing countries—industrial countries can issue long-term debt in their own currency. If this debt comes due beyond the horizon at which a default depresses the future capacity to repay, this breaks one of the links that generates the self-fulfilling debt run. Creditors that purchase long-term debt today can expect to be repaid in the future even if the government is illiquid today; hence, governments can always deal with a rollover crisis by issuing long-term debt, and the rollover problem disappears.

However, there are several reasons not to be fully satisfied with the simple debt run story. Most important, pure debt runs on just one borrower seem to be a silly reason to have a crisis. Surely there must be ways for this borrower, particularly if it is a government, to coordinate its creditors on rolling over their debt. For example, Chamon (2004) shows that debt runs can be prevented by issuing state-contingent debt contracts that require the creditor to disburse only if enough similar debt contracts have been signed by other creditors. This assures creditors that they will be required to pay only if there is no rollover crisis. Hence, all creditors should be willing to sign up for the new contingent loans, and the crisis disappears. Informal coordination mechanisms could have the same effect.

Moreover, debt crises do not seem to come out of the blue. There seem to be shocks or fragilities beyond high short-term debt in relation to liquidity that precede them, and they are often associated with currency crises (Reinhart 2002) and sometimes with banking crises. Although these other crises could in principle be interpreted as the *consequences* of a public sector debt run, this does suggest that the basic phenomenon of a debt crisis might be more complicated than in the simple debt run story.

Balance Sheet Crises and Credit Constraints

As was just mentioned, most debt crises go along with currency crises, and the debt that is defaulted on is often denominated in foreign currency. The simplest story that can explain default in these circumstances is that a currency crisis makes the government insolvent: since the government must repay its debt using mostly taxes that are denominated in local currency, its debt in dollars may exceed its capacity to repay after a devaluation (see the appendix for a more detailed discussion of this point). Put differently, in the presence of foreign currency debt, a currency crisis leads to a jump in the debt-to-GDP ratio, possibly to a level at which the debt is no longer sustainable.

Furthermore, if there is an economic link from the default back to a depreciated exchange rate, then currency and debt crises could become self-fulfilling. One simple story could be that government debt is partly in local currency and partly in dollars. Depreciation leads to a default on the foreign debt and an inflation to help repay the domestic debt; this inflation, in turn, validates the depreciation. Alternatively, either the default or the exchange rate depreciation could depress output, which in turn leads to a more depreciated exchange rate. For example, the depreciation and/or the government default could lead to a banking crisis that depresses real credit and hence output, or it could depress investment directly, as the depreciation lowers the net worth of firms which themselves may have currency mismatches in their balance sheets. A large recent literature, including Aghion, Bacchetta, and Banerjee (2001, 2004), Krugman (1999), Schneider and Tornell (2004), and Burnside, Eichenbaum, and Rebelo (2004), shows that currency mismatch problems in the banking or corporate sectors can be a source of self-fulfilling financial crises. This can be extended to include solvency problems of the government (Jeanne and Zettelmeyer 2005a). To withstand a crisis of this type, a government must not only be solvent but "supersolvent": not only must it be able to service its debt at "normal" exchange rate levels, but also at the levels of the exchange rate that might arise in a currency crisis, taking into account the weakening of the fiscal position that might result in such a crisis as a result of balance sheet crises in other sectors of the economy.

Like all economic theories of self-fulfilling crises, the literature summarized in the previous paragraph does not explain what *triggers* the crisis. However, there is a parallel literature that invokes essentially the same features typical of emerging market economies—dollar debt owed by corporations, banks, and governments, and borrowing constraints related to the net worth or current income of firms and households—while using a somewhat different class of economic models. The main substantive difference is that in this literature crises are generally not self-fulfilling but are triggered by shocks such as policy uncertainty, a fall in domestic productivity, or a sharp rise in foreign interest rates (see Arellano and Mendoza 2002 for a survey). For example, in Mendoza (2002), economies operate normally as long as borrowing constraints are not binding, but when they become binding, output collapses. Liability dollarization magnifies the effect of an adverse interest rate or productivity shock: lower production in the nontradables sector results in a real depreciation, which makes it more difficult to borrow because debt is denominated in tradables while income or net worth are partly in nontradables. While these models are not about sovereign debt per se, it is easy to see how the economy–wide financial crises they describe can affect the public sector in addition to other sectors.

Overborrowing

All theories of debt crises that have been surveyed so far have in common that debt could in fact be repaid in "normal times." What generates the debt crisis is a collapse in confidence, or a domestic or external shock whose effects are magnified by fragile debt structures, namely, currency and maturity mismatches. However, there also seem to be situations when debt crises arise because the debt burden seems so high that it would be very difficult to repay even in "normal times," that is, under optimistic growth and exchange rate assumptions. Crises like these are sometimes referred to as "solvency crises," as opposed to the liquidity crises or "conditional solvency crises" discussed previously.

By definition, a country is insolvent if its debt exceeds the net present value of income it can generate for debt repayment purposes, given constraints on fiscal adjustment (a country cannot generate arbitrarily large primary fiscal surpluses). Hence, a solvency crisis could be the result of a large adverse shock to economic fundamentals. Alternatively, a solvency crisis could be triggered by a shift in the parameters that govern the country's willingness to make sacrifices in order to repay, due to political developments (a revolution, a coup, an election, etc.). In both these cases, the level of debt could have been socially optimal before the crisis so that the solvency crisis may be a reflection of bad luck. However, in real life crises there is frequently a sense that this is not the whole story, in the sense that the crisis was caused not just by bad luck but by excessive borrowing—borrowing that was suboptimally high even from an ex ante perspective, given what was known about the risk of solvency shocks at the time of borrowing. This leads to the question why countries would ever want to borrow at "suboptimally high" levels.[10]

Three answers have been suggested in the literature. All three revolve around moral hazard problems, though these are quite different from the standard debtor moral hazard at the expense of the creditor. In a nutshell, debt accumulation can be excessive because those that decide to accumulate the debt do not bear the full costs of a debt crisis. That burden is shared with someone else. Thus, moral hazard prevails at the expense of a "third party" that cannot fully observe or control the actions of the parties that contract debt. What distinguishes the three stories is the identity of that third party.

First, the third party could be the average citizen of the debtor country, who ultimately bears the burden of an erupting crisis but may not receive the full ex ante benefits from accumulating debt. Thus, this argument revolves around a domestic political economy problem. Decisions on how much sovereign debt is accumulated and whether it is invested or consumed are taken by the government. If the government does not fully internalize the welfare of the population at large—say, it favors an elite or vested interests, or has an agenda of its own—then the country may end up with more debt than a representative citizen would have wanted to borrow, given the way it was used. There are many examples for this: excessive debt-financed spending ahead of an election, debt that finances "white elephants," debt that reflects tax breaks to specific business groups, high wage or pension payments to public employees, or simply a government that steals the money (Kremer and Jayachandran 2003).

Perotti (1996) provides a good example for this type of overborrowing. In his framework, the rich and the poor collude to support a program of public spending and redistribution financed by foreign debt. The poor do not pay taxes, and the rich avoid paying taxes by moving their assets abroad. (Perotti assumes that any agent can do this by paying a fixed cost; moving assets abroad hence makes sense for the rich but not for the middle class.) When repayment time comes, the middle class pays the entire bill. Foreign borrowing becomes a mechanism by which the political system transfers resources between different groups in society.

The second story is moral hazard at the expense of *international* (rather than *domestic*) taxpayers. The international financial community —through bilateral lending by governments and institutions such as the IMF and World Bank—operates as a "safety net" that helps countries deal with financial crises. The presence of this safety net could be a source of moral hazard, as countries may borrow too much from private sources because they expect to be "bailed out" by the official community in the event of a crisis. Note that for this argument to make sense, official loans must contain a subsidy, either by carrying an interest rate below the international risk-free rate, or because the debtor country expects part of the loan to be forgiven. If official lending is always repaid and carries at least the international interest rate, the safety net would be operated at no one's expense and hence could not be a source of moral hazard by definition (Jeanne and Zettelmeyer 2001, 2005b).

Finally, and perhaps surprisingly, a "third party" that could lose as a result of new borrowing are *existing* creditors who have been lending to the country in the past. They could lose because in the event of a default, they will have to share the recovery value of the debt with the new creditors. In a sense, the existing creditors "subsidize" the interest rate at which a country can borrow new debt, because the new (marginal) creditors know that in the event of a default, they will be able to obtain a slice of the debt recovery pie, a slice that previously "belonged" to the existing creditors. This is referred to as the debt dilution problem (see Borensztein et al. 2005 for an overview). Because the marginal interest rate is subsidized by the existing creditors, countries may have an incentive to overborrow (Detragiache 1994; Eaton and Fernandez 1995; Eaton 2004).

Empirical Evidence on the Causes of Debt Crises

There is a large empirical literature on the "causes" of debt crises—or more accurately, on the "risk factors" that are useful in predicting such crises. This literature evolved in two waves. The first, starting with seminal papers by Cline (1984) and McFadden et al. (1985), was motivated by the debt crises of the 1980s. A more recent one has taken hold in the last five years, motivated by the debt crises and restructurings that are covered in this book and to a lesser extent by debt rescheduling and debt relief in low income countries.

Most papers in this area are based on regression analyses that treat a crisis measure as the dependent variable and a number of economic and sometimes political and institutional variables as independent variables. There is considerable variation in the literature on what to call a "debt crisis." Most papers include defaults in the sense that contractual payments were missed beyond some grace period specified in the sovereign debt contract, as well as "technical defaults" labeled as such by rating agencies. These typically include both breaches in the debt contract and debt exchange offers or commercial bank reschedulings in "distressed" circumstances, that is, where the creditors suffer some loss, even if these reschedulings of debt exchanges preempt missed debt service payments. Hence, including technical defaults gives rise to a large number of debt crises. However, many papers take the view that this definition still misses some important debt crises, namely, all those that did not result in a debt restructuring or rescheduling (e.g., as a result of official crisis lending). Some of the alternative definitions of debt distress include the accumulation of arrears to any creditor (Detragiache and Spilimbergo 2001); nonconcessional IMF lending, possibly in excess of some threshold (Manasse, Roubini, and Schimmelpfennig 2003; Kraay and Nehru 2004) or secondary market sovereign bond spreads in excess of a critical threshold such as one thousand basis points, which can be assumed or determined using statistical techniques (Pescatori and Sy 2004).

The "independent" variables examined in these papers typically include solvency indicators such as the ratio of debt to GDP or debt to exports, GDP growth, the real exchange rate, export growth, and openness as well as liquidity indicators such as debt service coming due, the ratio of short-term debt in total debt, and the level or international reserves relative to (foreign currency) short-term debt. Beyond these simple indicators, relatively little attention has been paid to balance sheet variables and fragility indicators of the type discussed in the previous section (particularly as regards the private sector). This may reflect the fact that the theoretical literature in this area is fairly new and that this data is hard to come by.[11] Several recent papers, such as Catão and Sutton (2002); Reinhart, Rogoff, and Savastano (2003); Kraay and Nehru (2004); Van Rijckeghem and Weder (2004); and Kohlscheen (2005a, b) have extended the focus to other variables, including institutional and political variables, variables summarizing debt history, and variables reflecting macroeconomic volatility.

The results from these regressions are more or less in line with expectations based on theories of what might influence countries' "ability to pay" as well as "willingness to pay," and reasonably robust across sample periods and crisis definitions. Debt crises tend to be more likely the higher the debt to GDP or debt to exports ratio, the lower growth, the higher the proportion of short-term debt, and the lower reserves. "Financing needs" indicators that combine some of the liquidity-related variables also work rather well (Kruger and Messmacher 2004), and most recent studies of emerging market debt crises have emphasized the importance of these variables. Overvaluation is a significant predictor in some studies but not all. Debt history, institutions, and political factors also seem to play a role, according to several recent studies. Institutions particularly seem to matter in a larger sample that includes all developing countries and includes defaults on official creditors rather than only on private creditors (Kraay and Nehru 2004).

Though these results are intuitive, it is important to bear in mind that their interpretation is more ambiguous than might seem at first, for two reasons:

• *Endogeneity*. Many of the variables on the right hand side of debt crisis regressions are endogenous in the sense that they could depend on crises, or the anticipation of crises, or that they could be influenced by factors that also affect the crisis outcome but are not controlled for in the regression, such as economic or political shocks. This applies particularly to liquidity variables such as the ratio of short-term debt or the level of reserves. The fact that short-term debt increases and reserves decreases ahead of debt crises might be a symptom as much as a cause of these crises. For example, when sovereigns begin to experience distress, they will generally no longer be able to borrow except very short-term (Detragiache and Spilimbergo 2001).

• *Competing theories and interpretations*. Even if endogeneity is not an issue, there could be several reasons for why a particular variable might matter. Sometimes they go in different directions; in that case, an empirical coefficient can be interpreted as the net effect of the two.[12] Sometimes, however, there are competing explanations of the same phenomenon. For example, a standard notion is that short-term debt is dangerous because it exposes a country to liquidity shocks. But short-term debt will also increase the likelihood of default through a willingness-to-pay argument: if most of a country's debt is short-term (in terms of remaining maturity), this increases the temptation to default now rather than later (Detragiache and Spilimbergo 2004). Another example concerns the level of debt as a predictor of crises. The standard interpretation is that "solvency matters" as a cause of debt crises in addition to liquidity. But total debt may be high because of illiquidity, namely, lack of access to capital markets except at very high interest rates (Cohen and Portes 2004). And even if debt accumulation reflected large primary deficits rather than high interest rates, there is a need to understand how this related to deeper factors such as institutions, income distribution, and other political economy variables (Berg and Sachs 1988).

Some of the papers surveyed previously emphasize not so much what causes or predicts debt crises but what levels of debt appear reasonably safe (or "sustainable") in terms of *avoiding* debt crises. A recent paper by Manasse and Roubini (2005) explores "safe zones" systematically using binary recursive tree analysis. Furthermore, any multivariate analysis of debt crises will of course imply that relatively "safe" debt levels depend on the level of the other significant variables in the regression; for example, if countries have more liquidity or longer debt maturities, they can "afford" to have higher levels of debt. Kraay and Nehru (2004) and Van Rijckeghem and Weder (2004) also emphasize this kind of trade-off, though not between debt level and debt structure but rather between debt level and the quality of institutions, which turn out to be an important predictor of debt crises, or, conversely, of safe zones.[13] Reinhart, Rogoff, and Savastano (2003) make a similar point with respect to countries' histories of default rather than institutional quality, based on regressions that show that default history is an important determinant of the creditworthiness of sovereign borrowers, as expressed by *Institutional Investor* ratings. To be regarded as creditworthy and thus maintain access to capital markets, countries with histories of default are hence forced to keep their debt-to-GDP ratios at much lower levels than countries that have never defaulted. This result, however, appears not to be robust to the inclusion of additional economic variables in the regression (Catão and Kapur 2004).

Finally, what does the empirical literature have to say on whether countries "overborrow" in the sense described in the previous section, and if so, why they "overborrow"? We are not aware of empirical tests that would indicate whether debt is suboptimally high from a social welfare perspective, but according to the IMF (2003a), most emerging market countries have indeed overborrowed in the sense that their current debt stocks exceeds the debt stock that could be repaid if average primary balances in the future are equal to the average primary balance in the 1985–2002 period ("benchmark debt stock"). The average "overborrowing ratio" (actual debt over benchmark debt stock) in emerging markets is 2.5 to 1 (3.5 to 1 in countries with default histories) whereas it is smaller than one in industrial countries. This is just another way of saying that in order to repay their debts, emerging markets will have to run sharply higher fiscal surpluses in the future than they did, on average, between 1985 and 2002. To justify this as socially optimal, one would need to argue that the fiscal deficits of the past were the price that needed to be paid for higher incomes in the future, an argument that is doubtful in light of the fact that, as the IMF study shows, countries that overborrowed tended to be those with relatively slow growth (Asian countries have overborrowing ratios below one). The IMF study also cites some evidence suggesting that overborrowing is more likely in countries with low revenues, closed economies, and weak property rights.

The Costs of Debt Crises

Theory

What are the costs of debt crises when they do occur? In the classic economics literature on sovereign debt, the costs of debt crises are simply the counterpart of the enforcement problem discussed at the beginning of this section. Absent an international legal or political framework that forces countries to repay, costs of default are the reason why countries choose to pay their debts. This line of reasoning does not imply that costly defaults are necessarily *observed* ("in equilibrium," as economists would say). After all, it is precisely the costs of default that makes countries want to avoid debt crises. Indeed, in some models of sovereign debt, the optimal course of action is to borrow *up to* the threshold where debt becomes risky. In this setting, costly defaults would never be observed. But in general, it may be optimal to borrow more, up to a point where debt is in fact risky, so that in the event that a large economic shock hits, defaults are observed and default costs are incurred. (The classic Eaton and Gersovitz (1981) article included a model that can generate both types of behavior.) The nature of the default cost predicted in such a situation will depend on the particular type of model, as previously explained. It could be loss of access to international capital markets, reputational spillover effects, or direct sanctions of some form. Only empirical evidence can help us narrow this set of potential default costs, or tell us which effects seem to be more important than others.

A common feature of most traditional sovereign debt models is that the sovereign always suffers the same default cost regardless of whether it repudiates its debt or defaults as a result of a bad shock. In other words, in these models, crisis risk is not shared between borrowers and lenders. On the face of it, this just seems to be an implication of using debt contracts, which do not make the amount to be repaid conditional on the circumstances facing a country. (If this is the case, it begs the question why contracts are written this way, a point we address later.) However, a celebrated paper by Grossman and Van Huyck (1988) points to an intriguing possibility: perhaps lenders do in fact tailor the extent of the punishment for defaults to the degree to which defaults are "excusable" or not. In that case, there would be risk sharing between borrowers and lenders even with debt contracts. As Grossman and Van Huyck show, if lenders can observe the shocks that borrowers are exposed to, and have control over default costs, we would generally expect to observe (1) partial defaults, in the sense that the country repays as much as it can, given its fundamentals; and (2) no sanctions, since sanctions make sense only in the event of repudiations, and it is never optimal to repudiate (sovereigns will never repudiate in these models, because lenders will never allow them to accumulate debt to the point where repudiation—that is, default without an exogenous solvency shock—would make sense).

Hence, in this interpretation, rescheduling arrangements between borrowers and lenders introduce an equity-like feature into the world of sovereign debt. The implication is that it may be incorrect to view costly debt *crises* as the inevitable by-product of sovereign debt, even in a world with uncertainty and shocks to the borrower's payment capacity.

Empirical Evidence on the Costs of Default

Based on the theoretical literature, we should be looking for answers to three sets of empirical questions. First, are defaults and debt restructurings costly at all? In Grossman and Van Huyck's world, they would reflect "excusable defaults" and hence not trigger any sanction. Second, to the extent that they are costly, what exactly is the cost? Does the data favor any specific theory as to why sovereign debt exists? Third, even if it turns out that defaults are sometimes costly and not all defaults are viewed as "excusable" by lenders, is it true that the degree to which defaults seem "excusable" matters for the size of the sanction?

The answer to the first question is yes. Even though it is often difficult to disentangle the costs of defaults from the costs of the shocks or economic crisis that trigger a default, there is no serious disagreement in the empirical literature that defaults and debt restructuring result in a cost to the debtor over and above that of the underlying shock. Moreover, defaults seem to involve "deadweight losses"—that is, costs to the debtor that do not translate into an equal gain to the creditor, and vice versa. The fact that countries often desperately attempt to avoid debt restructurings even in situations where full repayment seems hopeless further suggests that there are costs of default, regardless of their origin.

Regarding the nature of default costs, the evidence is mixed. All three mechanisms that have been proposed in the literature—direct sanctions, loss of capital market access, and reputational spillovers—

have some empirical support, but there is no consensus on their relative importance. Moreover, the way in which these effects play out seem to be more nuanced and complicated than the models suggest. Furthermore, there seems to be at least one channel, through which defaults create costs—namely, the direct costs of default for the *domestic* economy, particularly the financial system—that does not seem adequately captured by any of the basic theories, perhaps because these theories are all focused on *external* sovereign debt.

• Defaults appear to have large adverse effects on *international trade* (Rose 2005; Rose and Spiegel 2004). Rose (2005) finds that defaults trigger a decline in bilateral trade between the debtor and its creditor countries of approximately 8 percent a year which persists for around fifteen years. This seems to be driven by a reduction in trade credit, and thus constitutes evidence for credit market sanctions of a particular kind, although legal sanctions could also play a role. Lane (2004) finds that countries with large trade volumes tend to have higher debt stocks. This could be interpreted as evidence in favor of the relevance of trade sanctions in making sovereign debt possible: countries exposed to such sanctions can borrow more.

• With few exceptions, defaults have indeed triggered a *loss in market access* by sovereigns, as the standard capital market exclusion story would predict. In most cases, this is a temporary effect that generally lasts only until the conclusion of a debt restructuring agreement, although getting to such an agreement has sometimes taken very long, as described in chapter 1. While it may also take emerging market countries a while to return to capital markets *after* a restructuring, this seems to be driven either by economic or political conditions in the countries that defaulted, or by a generalized "bust" in capital flows for emerging markets following a cluster of defaults, not by discrimination against former defaulters (Lindert and Morton 1989; Jorgenson and Sachs 1989; English 1996). For example, after World War II, there was a general breakdown in international debt flows until the 1960s, which affected virtually all major prewar borrowers regardless of whether they had defaulted in the 1930s or not; and in the 1990s, many emerging market countries enjoyed large debt inflows, regardless of whether they had defaulted in the 1980s or not. Several of the countries that defaulted in the late 1990s, including Russia, Ukraine, and Pakistan, reaccessed markets within a few years of their restructurings. Gelos, Sahay, and Sandleris (2004) find that the average time from default to resumption of access was four years in the 1980s, with very short exclusion periods in the 1990s.

• In contrast, defaults seem to have a longer-lasting impact on *borrowing costs*. However, the size of the effect does not appear to be very large. Controlling for a set of fundamental determinants of borrowing costs, Flandreau and Zumer (2004) find for the 1880–1913 period that having defaulted increased spreads by about 90 basis points in the first year after a debt restructuring agreement, with the effect declining to 45 basis points ten years later.[14] Özler (1993) finds that nineteenth century default history had no significant impact on average loan spreads in the 1970s, but the defaults in the 1930s did, raising the average spread by about 12–60 basis points in her sample. Using a panel regression, Dell'Ariccia, Schnabel, and Zettelmeyer (2006) find that participation in the Brady restructurings significantly raised borrowing costs in the 1990s, and that the effect increased after the Russian crisis of 1998, from about 15–50 basis points to 50–100 basis points. In contrast, Ades et al. (2000) do not find a statistically significant effect of previous default on sovereign spreads in the second half of the 1990s, though they do find that restructured debt (Brady bonds) traded at a significantly higher spread than nonrestructured debt.

• While capital outflows are a feature of all international financial crises, these seem to be exceptionally large in default cases as shown by the current account surpluses in the aftermath of defaults (IMF 2002a). This may constitute evidence for the *reputational spillover* story. A default undermines confidence that the government will respect property rights. What other assets will be confiscated? Will the rights of investors holding equity or owning businesses be curtailed? The consequence is capital flight and a large reversal of inflows.[15]

• Finally, several of the recent defaults have led to the collapse or severe impairment of the *domestic financial system* (IMF 2002a), with severe contractionary effects on credit, financial intermediation, and ultimately output. This direct domestic effect of a public debt default through the insolvency of economically important entities whose net worth and/ or cash flow depend on the debt being defaulted on has only very recently begun to attract attention in the literature (Kumhof 2004; Kumhof and Tanner 2004; Sandleris 2005; Broner and Ventura 2005).[16]

Many of these effects should combine to generate a loss in output. Sturzenegger (2004) provides an estimate from cross section and pooled growth regressions with annual data for a large sample of developing economies over the last two decades.[17] The results show a significant and sizable independent effect of default on growth, which falls by about 0.6 percentage points per year after the default. If compounded by a banking crisis, the output loss increases by about 1.6 points. Thus, a defaulter that also suffers a banking crisis would typically experience output of about 4.5 percent below trend five years after the event.

What remains largely unknown is the relative importance, from an empirical perspective, of these various default cost channels. Arellano and Heathcote (2003) suggest that if exclusion from future borrowing was the only channel through with defaulters could be sanctioned, countries could sustain debt levels on the order of only 1–3 percent of their GDP. Taken literally, this suggests that exclusion from future capital markets cannot be the main reason why sovereign borrowing is feasible. However, it is not clear to what extent this result is sensitive to the parameters used to simulate the model, or to the model specification.[18] And, obviously, it says nothing about the relative importance of channels other than exclusion from capital markets.

Finally, there is some evidence supporting the idea that economic and legal sanctions may be higher in pure repudiation cases than in defaults that seem "justified" by economic circumstances. While pure repudiations are extremely rare, default cases may vary in terms of the degree of repudiation that they embody in the eyes of creditors. Much like Grossman and Van Huyck (1988), Tomz (1999) distinguishes between "expected defaults" which are in some sense justified by economic distress, and "surprising defaults" which occur in circumstances that do not seem to warrant a default, and are thus close to pure repudiations. His main finding is that the latter have much larger reputational consequences than the former. For example, "surprising defaults" during World War II—defaults by countries that were not involved in the war—triggered an exclusion from international capital markets of twenty-eight years, on average, while "expected defaulters" took only fourteen years to regain access to borrowing. The distinction between default to "prevent a national financial disaster" and "wanton" defaults also seems to have played a role in court (Kaletsky 1985, 24).

Can the Cost of Debt Crises Be Reduced?

As we have seen, there is some evidence that (1) the costs of debt crises involve deadweight losses, and (2) the costs can be interpreted, at least in part, as sanctions for nonrepayment. These observations seem to corroborate the unsettling idea, mentioned at the beginning of this chapter, that costly debt crises are indeed an unavoidable by-product of the existence of sovereign debt, or rather, that sovereign debt might exist only because debt crises are costly. Try to reduce the costs of debt crises, and sovereign debt will vanish, because the enforcement mechanism breaks down. Ex post—in other words, while a country is experiencing a crisis—crises might appear painful and inefficient, but ex ante they might be efficient, to the extent that they enable international capital to flow to places where it is needed (Dooley 2000).

If this argument were literally true, our quest for a crisis-free world with international capital flows would stop here. But fortunately, the literature surveyed so far also implies that the argument, while posing a challenge, may not be the last word, for two reasons.

First, assuming one has some verifiable information about a borrower's ability to pay, it is of course possible to think of financial contracts that deter repudiation while allowing for better risk sharing. GDP-indexed bonds provide one example. These work like regular bonds except that they envisage higher debt service in good times and lower debt service in bad times. Thus, they function explicitly in the way that Grossman and Van Huyck were hoping that sovereign debt was functioning implicitly, by "rescheduling" debt automatically when debt service capacity is low, at no deadweight cost. In contrast, contract *violation* triggers the same costs as a default on standard debt. From an efficiency perspective, these instruments are hence clearly superior.

Why, then, are they not used more widely? One answer might be that they are hard to introduce because of thin markets, or because of a novelty premium—in other words, due to a coordination failure. If so, introducing state-contingent instruments in sufficient volume, such as, in the context of a debt restructuring, might change history and create a new market (Borensztein and Mauro 2004). The argument is more general: to the extent that today's financial instruments are the result of historical accident coupled with inertia that arises from the fact that change requires coordination among many "users" of a particular instrument or category of contract, reforms that attempt to provide that coordination can, in principle, be successful (Borensztein et al. 2005).

Alternatively, suppose that simple debt contracts are in fact optimal given current information and enforcement constraints and the moral hazard problems they breed. In that case, there might still be ways public policy can relax these information and enforcement constraints, in particular, by improving institutions (Rajan 2004a). For example, we argued that "dangerous debt structures," such as short-term of foreign currency debt or short-term debt, could be interpreted as optimal ways of dealing with debtor moral hazard. If so, creating institutions or rules that enable debtors to be able to commit not to engage in behavior that damages creditor interests may remove the underlying distortion, and hence its reflection, the "dangerous" debt structure.

There are many examples. An inflation targeting framework that precludes high inflation may create the monetary policy credibility necessary to issue debt in local currency. A commitment not to accumulate debt beyond a certain threshold—for example, by giving existing creditors the contractual right to ask for early repayment if the sovereign does exceed the threshold—may remove or mitigate the dilution problem, and hence discourage overborrowing and make long-term debt cheaper relative to short-term debt (Borensztein et al. 2005). An international bankruptcy regime that coordinates reschedulings—namely, shortens defaults and lowers their costs—if, and only if, the sovereign pursued good pre-crisis policies could similarly remove the incentive to borrow short-term. We return to these ideas in chapter 12.

3   Legal Issues in Sovereign Debt Restructuring

Sovereign lending has many characteristics and legal provisos that distinguish it from corporate debt. Most of its distinctive features have to do with the way a default situation for sovereign debt is resolved. Sovereign immunity, for example, limits the ability to sue defaulting countries or to attach their assets. The jurisdiction in which the debt instrument has been issued has implications for debt restructuring procedures. Also of relevance are bond clauses that specify remedies in case of default and define procedures for modifying the bond contract.

In what follows, we briefly review these concepts, before turning to the experience with creditor attempts to enforce sovereign bond contracts through litigation. In this context, we examine whether the possibility of uncoordinated litigation against sovereigns has impeded or delayed sovereign debt restructuring agreements, as has sometimes been argued. Finally, we ask whether some or all of the desirable characteristics of domestic bankruptcy organization could be mimicked through provisions in sovereign bond contracts, a question that has received much attention in recent years.

Legal Characteristics of Sovereign Debt

Principles Protecting Sovereign Debtors

A fundamental characteristic of sovereign debt is the lack of contractual enforcement mechanisms analogous to those that exist at the level of corporate debt. To a large extent, the reasons for this are political and practical rather than legal: it is hard to force a government to pay against its will, since most of the assets or income streams that could be used for repayment purposes (including tax revenue streams) are located inside the country. However, legal doctrine traditionally played an important role in magnifying the enforcement problem, particularly through the principle of (absolute) *sovereign immunity*, which states that sovereigns cannot be sued in foreign courts without their consent. Sovereign immunity can be derived from the equality of sovereign nations under international law: legal persons of equal standing cannot have their disputes settled in the courts of one of them (Brownlie 2003). Importantly, immunity can be waived: a sovereign can enter in a contractual relationship in which it voluntarily submits to the authority of a foreign court in the event of a dispute.

Under absolute immunity, which was the prevailing doctrine in the nineteenth century and in the first half of the twentieth century, sovereign immunity applied even to commercial transactions between foreign states and private individuals from another state. From the perspective of governments, this had the advantage that private commercial interests did not get in the way of diplomatic and political relations. As a result, unless an aggrieved creditor could persuade his own government to apply pressure, he was deprived of legal remedies to enforce repayments (except to the extent that he could successfully make a case in the *defaulting* country's courts).

In the United States, the interpretation of sovereign immunity began to change in the 1950s, in part as a consequence of the Cold War. The United States felt uneasy with granting sovereign immunity to Soviet Union state-owned companies operating in the United States. The U.S. government encouraged a more restrictive theory of sovereign immunity, under which foreign sovereigns were denied immunity for commercial activities carried on inside, or with direct effect inside, the United States. This restrictive view was embodied in the Foreign Sovereign Immunities Act (FSIA) of 1976, which allows private parties to sue a foreign government in U.S. courts if the complaint relates to commercial activity. The United Kingdom adopted similar legislation in 1978, and many other jurisdictions have followed suit (Buchheit 1986, 1995; Brownlie 2003).

As a result, sovereigns can now often be held legally accountable for breach of commercial contracts with foreign parties in the same manner as private parties. This leaves open the question of what is really a commercial transaction, and who really is a sovereign, within the terms of a foreign sovereign immunity law. With regard to the question of who is a sovereign, the U.S. FSIA, for example, defines a sovereign broadly to include agencies and instrumentalities of a sovereign.

Several court decisions have confirmed that the issuance of sovereign bonds is a commercial activity. Furthermore, a 1992 U.S. Supreme Court decision (*Republic of Argentina v. Weltover*) (Power 1996) established that suspending payments on debt contracts that call for payment in the United States entails direct effects within the United States sufficient to satisfy the U.S. nexus requirement under the FSIA. Accordingly, under U.S. law, international bond issues by a sovereign, and a subsequent default, are almost always considered commercial activities, regardless of the purpose of the issue, or the reason behind the payments interruption. Moreover, whatever protections of the sovereign remain under U.S. law can be contractually waived, and such waivers are in fact routinely included in bond covenants. As a result, under U.S. law (and that of several other major jurisdictions), sovereign immunity no longer plays an important role in shielding sovereign debtors from creditor suits.

Sovereign immunity laws may be a more effective shield against attachment proceedings, namely, creditor attempts to collect once a favorable court judgment has been obtained. Most physical assets of a sovereign located outside its borders, such as diplomatic or military property, are protected because they do not fall within the specific exceptions to sovereign immunity. Moreover, under FSIA and comparable laws, central bank assets, including international reserves, are typically immune from attachment.[1] For sovereign debt not issued by the central bank itself, this follows from the fact that although it benefits from sovereign immunity as an agency of the debtor state, it is also generally viewed as a separate legal entity that cannot be held liable for the acts of its principal. But even when the central bank itself is the debtor, most of its assets—in particular, international reserves and other assets necessary for the exercise of key central banking functions—generally enjoy immunity, unless this is explicitly waved (Lee 2003; Gramlich 1981). Moreover, as already mentioned, a sovereign or central bank can of course always attempt to limit attachable assets by locating them outside the reach of foreign courts. For example, government and central bank assets have been placed with the Bank for International Settlements (BIS) in Switzerland to take cover under the legal protections afforded to the BIS against attachment proceedings.

In addition to the principle of sovereign immunity, a number of other legal principles or conventions have been invoked by sovereign debtors in resisting creditor lawsuits during the 1980s and 1990s. Two such defenses are the "act of state" doctrine and international comity (Power 1996; Brownlie 2003). The *act of state doctrine* states that courts should not judge the validity of a foreign sovereign's acts committed on its territory: "In contrast to sovereign immunity, which acts as a jurisdictional bar to suits against a sovereign, the act of state doctrine is a judicially created rule of abstention concerning the justiciability of the acts of foreign governments. In further contrast to sovereign immunity, the act of state doctrine defense cannot be waived" (Power 1996). However, the act of state doctrine has proved to be of little use to sovereigns for a similar reason as sovereign immunity, namely, that defaulting on debtors payable in international jurisdictions is not considered to be a sovereign act worthy of judicial deference (see *Allied Bank International v. Banco Credito Agricola de Cartago*, discussed later in the chapter).

Finally, *international comity*, according to an 1895 U.S. Supreme Court decision, is defined as "the recognition which one nation allows within its territory to the legislative, executive, or judicial acts of another nation." Comity is a "softer" principle than sovereign immunity or act of state, which Power (1996) describes as "not the rule of law, but rather one of practice, convenience, and expediency." Brownlie (2003) speaks of "neighborliness and mutual respect." Comity considerations have motivated several court decisions both against and in favor of the sovereign debtor, and continue to play a role today. In practice, comity considerations in the United States seem to have boiled down to a court assessment on whether a debtor's actions could be viewed as broadly justified in light of U.S. policies on how international debt crises ought to be resolved. As such, they have given the U.S. executive branch a lever for influencing debt-related disputes before U.S. courts. Thus, comity is an unreliable principle, as "the defense's likelihood of success is subject to reassessment with each shift in U.S. policy on sovereign debt restructuring" (Power 1996).

Governing Law

Sovereign bonds can be classified as either *international bonds* issued by a government in an international financial center (e.g., New York, London, or Tokyo) under foreign law, or *domestic bonds*, issued in the debtor country under domestic legislation. International bonds are typically not denominated in the currency of the issuer, though very recently there have been some exceptions (see chapter 12). Domestic bonds are denominated either in foreign or in local currency. *Eurobonds* refer to a specific category of international bonds, namely bonds that are issued in countries other than the one in whose currency the bond is denominated. Eurobonds are often U.S. dollar-denominated bonds issued in a European jurisdiction (e.g., England, Germany, or Luxembourg), hence the name.[2]

New York law and English law are by far the most popular governing laws for the issue of international bonds, though Luxembourg law (for Brady bonds), German law and, more recently, Japanese law and Italian law (for Argentine debt) have also played a role. Traditionally, sovereign bond contracts issued under New York and English law have differed in important respects, though this was mostly a matter of "drafting momentum" rather than statutes governing sovereign borrowing, and these differences have recently narrowed.

Bond Contracts

Sovereign bonds come with an array of contractual features, or "clauses," that have important implications for debt restructurings. These include bond *covenants*, which commit the debtor to certain actions over the lifetime of the bond and prohibit others; *remedies* in the event that contractual obligations are breached; and *procedures for modifying the contract*. A brief survey follows.

Covenants are essentially formal promises by the debtor to the creditors. They define what is expected of the debtor during the lifetime of the contract. *Positive* covenants outline things that the debtor is supposed to do: most obviously, to repay the principal, and to pay an interest coupon and related payment promises (e.g., a put option that gives the creditor the right to ask for early repayment at specified points in time). Beyond this promise to pay, positive covenants typically commit the debtor to undertaking certain actions that support the base promise, for example, sharing information with the creditors and listing the bond on a specific stock market to ensure its liquidity. Another example is a "gross-up" covenant, by which the government commits to reimbursing cash flow losses from tax measures that may affect the interest or principal.

Negative covenants refer to actions the debtor promises to refrain from, because they would undermine the base promise, and hence reduce the value of the claim. The best known negative covenants in sovereign bonds are the pari passu clause and the negative pledge clause. Both are intended to ensure that an individual creditor is not discriminated against. The *pari passu clause* prohibits the debtor from subordinating the borrower, that is, from reducing his right to repayment relative to that of other creditors (Buchheit and Pam 2003).[3] The *negative pledge clause* prohibits issuing collateralized debt unless the incumbent debt holder is given equivalent collateral. This is meant to ensure that assets that a creditor could potentially attach in the event of default, or that could help to strengthen the repayment capacity of the creditor, are not assigned to other creditors.

Bond contracts also define remedies, which are legal consequences in the event that any of these covenants is breached. These remedies are typically calibrated to the seriousness of the breach. The most serious breach, obviously, is a failure to make good on any aspect of the promise to pay. To the extent that the bond is collateralized, this could trigger seizure of collateral. It could also trigger *acceleration*, which means that all principal and any accrued interest become immediately due and payable. Acceleration clauses govern the conditions under which acceleration can occur. The typical case is that 25 percent of the bondholders can accelerate unmatured principal following a default on payment terms, while a majority (50 percent) can veto or rescind a prior acceleration, if the default event has either been "cured" or waived by the bondholders.[4] For example, following Ecuador's default in September 1999, one bond was accelerated by its holders. In August 2000, Ecuador made an exchange offer to holders of this bond which was conditional on "exiting" holders voting to rescind the original acceleration, so that holders of the bond that chose not to accept the exchange offer were left with a bond that did not constitute an immediate claim on the principal.

The contract can also trigger remedies in the event of a default of the debtor on a third party (another creditor). This is called a *cross-default*. For example, a cross-default clause could define a default on a third party as an event that triggers acceleration. In order to strengthen the creditor's legal position in the event of default, bond contracts typically contain a clause in which the debtor waives sovereign immunity in the event of future disputes, that is, he promises to submit to the courts of a specified jurisdiction (the jurisdiction whose laws govern the bond, such as New York, England, or Luxembourg). In some cases, bond clauses might restrict the assets of the sovereign that may be attached in the event of default, augmenting sovereign immunity protections or limiting the extent of a sovereign immunity waiver. For example, during the 1990s, Argentina included a clause affirming that central bank reserves backing the monetary base under its currency board arrangement were unattachable.

Finally, *amendment clauses* may govern the conditions under which the terms of the bond contract can be changed. Bonds issued under U.S. law have traditionally contained a clause permitting amendments or modifications to the contract with the consent of a simple majority of bondholders, *except* for changes in the payment terms of the bond, which required the consent of each bondholder. Hence, under such provisions, important features of the bond including the applicable law, the formal definition of default, majority thresholds needed for acceleration, the negative pledge clause, listing requirements, and so forth, could be changed against the wishes of dissenting bondholders, while changes to the bond's maturity, scheduled interest payments, or principal repayment amount required unanimity. In contrast, bonds issued under English law have traditionally included a "majority amendment clause" which permits changes in the payment terms of the bond with some supermajority (usually 75 percent). These changes bind all bondholders, including those that voted against the change.

As argued by Buchheit and Gulati (2002), these traditions are rooted in differences in domestic bankruptcy law in the two countries. Until the 1930s, majority action clauses could be found in corporate debt contracts both in the United States and in the United Kingdom, but after a 1934 amendment to the U.S. Bankruptcy Act introduced a new procedure of coordinating creditors (a precursor of the modern "Chapter 11"), majority action clauses fell out of favor in the United States and were made illegal for corporate bonds (though not for sovereign bonds) by the Trust Indenture Act of 1939.[5] Sovereign bond contracts in the United States by and large followed the template of corporate debt in not containing majority action provisions until 2003, when majority amendment clauses began to be included in New York law bonds in response to pressures from creditor countries and the IMF.

As explained in chapter 1, the recent debt restructurings in Russia, Pakistan, Ukraine, Ecuador, Uruguay, and Argentina have not primarily relied on changes in the payment terms of the existing bond contracts but rather on exchanging the old instruments for new instruments with different payments terms. Nonetheless, majority amendment clauses played a role on three occasions. Majority amendment clauses were used directly to restructure an English law Eurobond issued by Moldova (June 2002) as well as one of Uruguay's nineteen externally issued bonds in May 2003 (a "Samurai bond" issued under Japanese law). Majority amendment clauses were also used to back up Ukraine's debt exchange offer in March 2000. By agreeing to the offer, holders of Ukraine's English law bonds delivered an "irrevocable proxy vote" in favor of an amendment that would bring the payment terms of the old bonds in line with the payment terms of the new bonds offered at the exchange. Hence, "holdouts faced the prospect of being left with an amended illiquid old bond that paid out no earlier than the very liquid new bond being offered at the exchange" (Buchheit and Gulati 2002).

In addition, the possibility of amending *nonpayment* terms to bonds has been used in three recent sovereign debt restructurings—Ecuador in 2000, Uruguay in 2003, and the Dominican Republic in 2005— to render the old instruments less attractive, hence creating an incentive for bondholders to accept the exchange offer (*exit consents/ amendments*) (see Buchheit 2000; Buchheit and Gulati 2000; and IMF 2003b). In the case of Ecuador, exit amendments removed a prohibition on the further restructuring of the Brady bonds tendered in the exchange, cross-default clauses, negative pledge clauses, and the requirement to list the bonds on the Luxembourg stock exchange. In the cases of Uruguay and the Dominican Republic, the sovereign immunity waiver in the old bonds was amended to protect payments on the new bonds from attachment by holders of the old bonds; cross-default and cross-acceleration clauses were removed; and the listing requirement was also dropped (IMF 2003c).

Experience with Legal Enforcement of Sovereign Debt Contracts

As we have seen, legal protections of sovereigns from court action by creditors were significantly reduced by the 1980s. From the perspective of the sovereign debt literature in economics, this should be a good thing: if the fundamental distortion in sovereign debt—the reason why sovereign borrowing is expensive, and debt financing may be suboptimally low—is lack of contract enforcement, then improvements in creditor rights should be in the interests of both debtors and creditors. However, as the literature in both law and economics recognized early on, this is not necessarily true if individual creditors use their rights to seek an advantage relative to *other creditors*, that is, if they cease to behave cooperatively. In that case, "collective action problems" among creditors could be an obstacle to the orderly resolution of debt crises. This does not necessarily imply that creditors will be worse off relative to a situation in which they had fewer rights, but it opens the door for institutional mechanisms—from contracts that force creditors to act collectively, to formal bankruptcy-like regimes at the international level—that could improve over the status quo (see chapter 12).

In what follows, we briefly survey the experience with creditor attempts to enforce repayment through the courts following a default. We organize the discussion according to whether creditor legal action was initiated before or after a debt restructuring with a majority of the creditors was completed. Each of these litigation strategies have been linked to a particular collective action problem: pre-restructuring litigation to a possible "rush to the courthouse," in which creditors attempt to obtain a favorable settlement ahead of a possible debt restructuring, and post-restructuring litigation to the "holdout problem," in which a creditor refuses to participate in a restructuring with the hope of obtaining a better settlement later on. From an economic perspective, these collective action problems are much the same: they boil down to an attempt of individual creditors to free ride at the expense of the majority of creditors, which may scuttle a cooperative outcome. From a legal perspective, however, they involve somewhat different issues, particularly with regard to the attachment strategies that creditors might pursue.

We address two questions. First, how successful has either brand of litigation been in extracting repayment, or a favorable settlement, from the sovereign debtor? Second, has creditor litigation before or after a debt restructuring proved to be an obstacle to swift and successful debt restructurings?

Post-restructuring Litigation and the "Holdout Problem"

At the corporate debt level, creditor rights can be effectively enforced through the domestic courts, by giving creditors the right to seize collateral, liquidate, or otherwise sanction a defaulting firm. In a one-creditor world, this would generally be efficient. In a world of many creditors, however, it may give too much power to an individual creditor from the perspective of creditors collectively. In particular, liquidation is often inefficient in the sense that the liquidation value of the firm is lower than the value of the firm when it is reorganized and continues operating. Hence, creditors may have a collective interest in a debt restructuring agreement that avoids liquidation. Such an agreement could be undermined by creditors who insist on full repayment in exchange for not exercising their right to liquidate (or in exchange for not inflicting a sanction that would do the debtor more damage than full repayment to an individual creditor). If creditors know that a "holdout" can obtain full repayment conditional on a previous debt restructuring, everyone will want to be that holdout, and no one will want to restructure. This could prolong the default state, leaving a debtor without access to new capital—and creditors without any re-covery of payments—for a long time. Bankruptcy legislation that imposes a court-supervised reorganization of the firm that maximizes its value as a "going concern" is often interpreted as the domestic level solution to this holdout problem.

The question is whether there is a similar holdout problem at the level of sovereign debt. Prior to World War II, this does not seem to have been the case, as individual creditors generally did not have a se-rious legal threat at their disposal that could have been used to extract full repayment (or a better settlement) after a debt restructuring agree-ment had been reached with a majority of creditors. Successful legal action was almost impossible due to full-blown sovereign immunity, and mobilizing political or economic sanctions required the joint pres-sure of many creditors and was hence outside the reach of holdouts by definition.

This began to change in the postwar period, and particularly after the codification of more restrictive sovereign immunity concepts in the United States and the United Kingdom in the late 1970s. Holdouts could now conceivably use the courts to extract a better deal than the settlement negotiated with the majority of creditors. The question is whether there is any evidence that creditor litigation was successful in this sense, and if so, whether it led to a systematic holdout problem. The answer is somewhat surprising: since the 1980s, there have been a large number of creditor suits (in the several hundreds), including sev-eral cases in which holdouts have in fact been able to secure better terms than average creditors. Yet holdout creditors do not so far seem to have posed a systemic obstacle to debt restructurings.

Fears that holdouts might create such an impediment go back to a well-known 1985 New York court decision, *Allied Bank International v. Banco Credito Agricola de Cartago.* In 1981, Costa Rica suspended debt payments to a thirty-nine-member bank syndicate. A restructuring agreement was subsequently reached with all creditors but one, Fidel-ity Union Trust of New Jersey, which sued through an agent, Allied

Bank, in U.S. courts. A lower court initially ruled in favor of Costa Rican banks that had acted on behalf of Costa Rica, accepting the defense's argument that Costa Rica's actions were protected by the act of state doctrine.

In 1984, an appeals court disagreed with this argument on the grounds that defaulting on foreign debt did not constitute an act of state. However, it initially upheld the lower court ruling on comity grounds, on the assumption that the U.S. executive branch was favorably disposed to Costa Rica's attempt to restructure its debts: "Costa Rica's prohibition of payments of its external debt is analogous to the reorganization of a business pursuant to Chapter 11 of our Bankruptcy Code. On that basis, Costa Rica's prohibition of payment of debt was not a repudiation of the debt but rather was merely a deferral of payments while it attempted in good faith to renegotiate its obligations" (United States Court of Appeals for the Second Circuit, 1984). Upon rehearing the case in March 1985, however, the court reversed itself after the U.S. Department of Justice argued that contrary to the court's initial assumptions, the U.S. government did not agree with "Costa Rica's attempted unilateral restructuring," concluding that "while parties may agree to renegotiate conditions of payment, the underlying obligations to pay nevertheless remain valid and enforceable" (United States Court of Appeals for the Second Circuit, 1985). According to Greenwood and Mercer (1995), this led to a settlement in which the U.S. government encouraged Fidelity Union to accept the package agreed by the rest of the bank syndicate.

The *Allied Bank* case was thus significant in several respects. It demonstrated that a holdout could be successful in the sense of obtaining a favorable judgment, and showed that two important legal principles— the act of state doctrine and international comity—did not necessarily protect sovereigns in the event of default (Power 1996). However, given the final outcome—Fidelity Union did no better than the creditors that had negotiated the earlier restructuring—the *Allied Bank* case can hardly be interpreted as illustrating the rewards of a holdout strategy. In a sense, Fidelity performed a free service for debt holders collectively, by helping to demonstrate the weakness of defenses that had been thought to protect sovereign debtors without achieving a financial advantage over creditors that had agreed to the previous restructuring. Indeed, the other creditors did not object to the litigation while it was ongoing; on the contrary, through the New York Clearing House Association, they filed a brief supporting Fidelity.

During the remainder of the 1980s, creditor litigation remained the exception, for two reasons. First, there were strong mechanisms, both contractual, and through informal institutions like the BAC process discussed in chapter 1, that encouraged collective action in resolving debt disputes and discouraged go-it-alone litigation. In particular, syndicated loan contracts, the main vehicle for private lending to developing countries during the 1970s and 1980s, typically contained "sharing clauses" that forced any member of the syndicate to share any payments extracted through litigation or settlement with the remaining members (Buchheit 1998b). Second, prior to the creation of the secondary debt market in the late 1980s, virtually all holders of distressed debt were banks, which had a regulatory incentive against declaring a creditor in default (in practice, a prerequisite for litigation), as this would have required them to write down their loans. Until the late 1980s, many creditor banks did not have sufficient reserves to do so. As observed by Power (1996), the "effect of these pressures was a de facto replication of the U.S. Bankruptcy Code's automatic stay of collection actions against a debtor. The banks were effectively unable to pursue their collection rights even though those rights were fully enforceable."

This situation began to change in the late 1980s, as creditor banks provisioned against loan losses and began writing off their loans, and the creation of a secondary market in securitized loans allowed new investors, including specialized firms that became known as "distressed debt funds" or "vulture funds," to buy defaulted debt at large discounts with a view to extracting the best possible settlement. The result was a sharp increase in holdout litigation following the Brady Plan restructurings of the early 1990s. A famous early case is *CIBC Bank and Trust Co. (Cayman) Ltd. v. Banco Central do Brazil* (Power 1996; Nolan 2001; Waibel 2003). In the early 1990s, the Dart family had accumulated $1.4 billion of Brazilian Multiyear Deposit Facility Agreement (MYDFA) debt at a large discount. The MYDFA was a 1988 debt restructuring agreement between Brazil and creditor banks that covered most of Brazil's outstanding debt. Brazil stopped servicing MYDFA debt in 1989, and eventually initiated negotiations leading to a 1993 restructuring under the Brady Plan that was accepted by all creditors except the Darts. Brazil restructured all debt except for $1.6 billion that were formally held by the Central Bank of Brazil; this prevented the Darts from becoming the majority debt holder with the right to accelerate outstanding principal and interest payments. In response, the

Darts, through CIBC as the holder of record of the debt, sued the Central Bank of Brazil in New York, claiming (1) past due interest under the MYDFA; and (2) the right to accelerate the entire principal and interest owed. In May 1995, the court ended up siding with the plaintiff on the first claim, but declined to allow the Darts to accelerate. The question of whether the Darts were entitled to recovering the full principal *at maturity* was not answered by the court since it was not the object of litigation, but in light of the *Allied Bank* case, there was a presumption that they would (Power 1996).

In March 1996, Brazil settled, paying the Darts $52 million in Eligible Interest Bonds covering past due interest until April 1994 (the settlement date of the Brady deal) and $25 million in cash covering accrued interest since April 1994. Hence, Brazil treated the remaining MYDFA as if it had been performing since April 1994, signaling that it would continue servicing the loan in the future. On that basis, the Darts managed effectively to sell their MYDFA holding by issuing $1.28 billion in Eurobonds secured by MYDFA debt in October 1996, at a modest spread over Brazilian sovereign debt with similar payment terms. Although the market value of this issue, at about $1.1 billion, fell short of the $1.4 billion that the Darts had initially demanded, this meant that the Darts came out much better than creditors that had accepted the Brady exchange.

From a legal point of view, several aspects of the *CIBC Bank* case are notable. First, Brazil did not invoke either sovereign immunity or the act of state doctrine in its defense, a recognition of the fact that these principles had lost their protective power in the context of sovereign debt litigation. Second, it tried to invoke two arguments designed specifically to fend off holdouts that had purchased distressed debt in the secondary market, namely, that assignment of the debt to CIBC was invalid under the terms of the original debt contract (in this case, the MYFDA), and that the Darts' suit violated New York's "law of Champerty," which prohibits litigating on a claim purchased exclusively for the purposes of filing a lawsuit. Both arguments were rejected by the court, establishing a precedent that was largely followed in subsequent court cases. The "Champerty defense" suffered from the problem of having to prove intent: claim holders could always argue that they had purchased the claim not with the intention to litigate but in order to get paid, and that the decision to litigate was merely a reaction to the sovereign's refusal to pay, and fully within their rights.

Finally, as in the *Allied Bank* case, the U.S. government filed a brief, but with the opposite thrust, urging the court to reject the Darts' claim for acceleration of principal on the grounds that holdouts that had purchased debt in the secondary market should not be allowed to take a free ride on debt workouts agreed by a majority of creditors: "The United States observed that its concern in *CIBC* was a 'mirror image' of its concern in *Allied* ten years earlier. In *Allied*, the United States had been concerned that a judgment for Costa Rica would encourage sovereign debtors to use the courts to extract better terms from creditors than they could obtain through negotiation. In *CIBC*, conversely, the United States was concerned that a judgment in favor of the Darts would encourage creditors to use the courts to gain unfair concessions from sovereign debtors" (Power 1996). The court ultimately agreed with the U.S. argument, so comity may have benefited the debtor in this aspect of the case.

By and large, the precedents set by the *CIBC Bank* case have been borne out in subsequent litigation. First, subsequent cases have confirmed a holdout's right to litigate on the basis of a claim acquired in the secondary market. The Champerty defense, in particular, was rejected in several instances, including by the English Court of Appeal in *Camdex International Limited v. Bank of Zambia* (1998), and on appeal by a New York court in *Elliott Associates v. Banco de la Nación* (1999). Second, courts generally paid some attention to the argument, made by the U.S. government in the *CIBC Bank* case, that holdout creditors should not be allowed to disrupt or undo debt restructuring agreements negotiated with a majority of creditors.

The desire to safeguard creditor rights as defined by the debt contract has tended to prevail whenever there has been a conflict between these two principles. For example, in *Pravin Banker v. Banco Popular del Peru* (1997), a New York court stayed Pravin's claims for full repayment by Peru on two occasions to avoid a disruption to the ongoing Brady deal negotiations, but ultimately decided in favor of Pravin. Similarly, in *Elliott & Associates v. Republic of Panama* (1997), Elliott obtained judgments covering the full claim, and subsequently settled for close to that amount, notwithstanding the fact that it had acquired the Panamanian debt at a substantial discount from Panama's original creditors. Elliott could extract full repayment because it was able to obtain an attachment order that could have inflicted serious harm on Panama, one directed against U.S. assets of the national telecommunications company which Panama was about to privatize, and one which would have interfered with a large new bond issue in New York. Although Panama paid in full, the amount paid ($71 million) was an order of magnitude smaller than both the value of the privatization deal and the proceeds received from the bond issue.

The famous 1999 case of *Elliott Associates v. Banco de la Nación* (Peru) constitutes an example of interference with future debt flows as a strategy for enforcing repayment. Following the by-now-familiar theme, Elliott Associates acquired nonperforming debt guaranteed by the Peruvian government, at a large discount, just prior to Peru's 1996 Brady deal. After Peru refused to repay in full, Elliott Associates sued in New York. A prejudgment attachment sought by Elliott Associates was initially denied on the grounds that it would have jeopardized the pending Brady restructuring, but in late 1999, Elliott obtained a prejudgment attachment order against Peruvian assets used for commercial purposes in the United States, and finally, in June 2000, a $57 million judgment against Peru. Based on this judgment, Elliott sought court orders in New York and various European countries that would either attach Peruvian assets or bar Peru from paying interest on its Brady bonds. It was eventually successful, convincing a Brussels appeals court to order the payments provider Euroclear on an emergency basis—namely, before arguments in opposition had been made—to suspend payment on Brady bond interest. Faced with an approaching payment deadline that would have brought its entire stock of Brady debt into default, Peru decided to settle with Elliott Associates for a reported sum of $56.3 million rather than continue the legal fight.

The *Elliott/Peru* case led to much consternation in policy circles because it appeared to open a powerful new channel for the enforcement of the claims of holdouts who had successfully obtained a judgment. Rather than engaging in the difficult and tedious process of attempting to attach debtor assets abroad, holdouts could ask courts to interfere with cross-border payments to mainstream creditors who had previously agreed to a debt restructuring. This seemed to be an almost foolproof enforcement channel, since it effectively gave holdouts a veto over the regularization of a country's relations with mainstream creditors, and hence over its return to international capital markets. Hence, *Elliott/Peru* appeared to catapult holdouts from their previous status of either a minor nuisance (at worst) or champions of creditor rights (at best) to a formidable obstacle to orderly sovereign debt restructurings.

However, interfering with payments to creditors that had accepted a restructuring offer did not turn out to be a very robust enforcement mechanism, for two reasons. First, its legal basis appeared questionable. Elliott Associates' motion to suspend payments to Peru's Brady bondholders rested on a broad interpretation of the pari passu clause in the debt contracts it had purchased, as giving it the right to receive a proportional share of any payments on external debt made by Peru (though arguably the Brussels court went further, effectively giving Elliott *priority* over the Brady bondholders). This contrasts with a more conventional interpretation of the pari passu clause stating that the claim in question does not have lower priority than other unsecured claims (Gulati and Klee 2001; Wood 2003; Buchheit and Pam 2004). By now, Elliott Associates' interpretation of the pari passu clause has been challenged not just by many legal commentators, but also (in the context of the Argentina case) by the U.S. government, the Federal Reserve Bank of New York, and the New York Clearing House Association.

Second, regardless of which interpretation of the pari passu clause is correct, practical and legal steps could be (and have been) undertaken to remove payments to mainstream creditors from the reach of holdouts. Most obviously, payments could be made in the debtor country, so that any cross-border transfer would involve creditor accounts only. In this case, holdouts would have to attempt to recover payments from other creditors, a legally difficult endeavor as long as explicit sharing clauses are absent from bond contracts (with such sharing clauses, however, holdouts could not hope to extract a better deal). Alternatively, international payments systems could be explicitly protected from judgment creditors through changes in national laws. Indeed, Belgium has recently adopted a law that prevents a judgment creditor from obtaining a court order that would preclude Euroclear from channeling payments from a sovereign debtor to its bondholders.

The possibility of structuring payment flows in ways that makes them difficult to attach cast doubt that Elliott Associates' strategy both in the Panama case (with respect to a new bond issue) and in the Peru case (with respect to payments to existing creditors) will continue to succeed in the future. Structuring international transactions so they are attachment-proof may, of course, impose costs; for example, if fear of attachment induces sovereigns to refrain from issuing new bonds abroad or investing reserves in international financial centers. To the extent that this is the case, it would give holdouts some leverage in settlement negotiations.

Several holdouts have attempted to mimic Elliott's legal strategy with respect to Peru, with limited success (Singh 2003; IMF 2004). In *LNC v. Nicaragua*, the Belgian Court of Appeals found that the contractual pari passu clause did not give LNC the right to attach payments channeled through Euroclear, since Euroclear was not a party to the contract in which the pari passu clause arose. In *Kensington v. Republic of Congo*, an English court also rejected enforcement based on the pari passu clause, on the grounds that reliance on this contractual clause was inconsistent with the fact that the plaintiff's claim had been reduced to a court judgment. Finally, in *Red Mountain Finance v. Democratic Republic of Congo*, the courts rejected the broad construction of the pari passu clause but issued an injunction with a similar effect, namely, preventing the debtor from making external debt payments unless proportionate payment was made to Red Mountain. The Democratic Republic of Congo (DRC) appealed the injunction, but settled with Red Mountain at about 37 percent of the value of the judgment claim before the appeal hearing, just ahead of an arrears-clearing payment to the IMF that allowed Congo to resume borrowing from official lenders after years of crisis and civil war.

In sum, changes in the legal environment since the late 1970s have made it much easier for holdout creditors to obtain judgment claims. In addition, there are several examples—most famously, *CIBC/Brazil*, *Elliott/Panama*, and *Elliott/Peru*—in which holdouts have been able to enforce those claims, or settle at substantially better terms than average creditors. These settlements seem to have occurred either because holdouts credibly threatened to attach sovereign assets or interfere with international transactions, or because of reputational concerns—debtor reluctance to defy court judgments at a time when they were regularizing their record as borrowers. This said, full repayment has remained the exception, and many holdouts have received nothing (table 3.1).

To conclude, holdouts currently enjoy some leverage—more than in previous decades and perhaps more than at any time in history. Nonetheless, this leverage remains limited, and attempts to exploit it are risky because of high legal costs and foregone debt service. Hence, holdout strategies may make sense only for highly specialized firms such as Elliott Associates. This may explain why actual or expected litigation from holdouts does not so far seem to have derailed any debt restructuring agreement. Holdout strategies may not be attractive for either retail bondholders or large investors with a broader commercial

Table 3.1
Sovereign litigation: Selected cases

Creditor	Domicile of creditor	Debtor	Original claim	Status	Year	Judgment for creditor (in millions of U.S. dollars)	Received (in percent)
Litigation with collective action problems[a]							
Dart and others[b]	US	Argentina	[c]	JTP	2002/2004	...[d]	—
Dart	US	Brazil	1400	JTP	1994	...[d]	100
Elliot Assoc.	US	Cote D'Ivoire	8	OCS	1994	...[d]	...[d]
Elliot Assoc.	US	Ecuador	6	OCS	1995	...[d]	100
LNC Investments	US	Nicaragua	26.3	JTP	1999	87.1	—
GP Hemisphere Assoc.		Nicaragua	30.9	JTP		126	—
Van Eck Emerg. Markets	US	Nicaragua	13	JTP		62.5	—
Elliot Assoc.	US	Panama	48	OCS	1998	78	100
Elliot Assoc.	US	Peru	64	OCS	1999	...[d]	100
Pravin Bankers Assoc.[e]	US	Peru	1.4	OCS	1996	...[d]	...[d]
Elliot Assoc.	US	Poland	SF 5	OCS	1995	...[d]	...[d]
Elliot Assoc.	US	Turkmenistan	3.8	OCS		...[d]	100
Litigation without collective action problems[a]							
Winslow Bank	Bahamas	Cameroon	8.9	JTP	1997	51.5	—
Del Favaro Spa	Italy	Cameroon	2.9	JTP	1998	4.9	<10[f]
EnergoInvest	Form. Yug.	Congo D.R.	55.8	JTP	1998	74.9	—
ITOH Middle East	Bahrain	Congo D.R.		JTP		...[d]	—
Equator Bank	UK	Congo	6.7	OCS	1994	...[d]	...[d]
Red Mountain	US	Congo	27	OCS	2001/2002	...[d]	30
Kintex	Bulgaria	Ethiopia	8.7	In arbitration		...[d]	—
Booker Plc.	UK	Guyana	6	Dropped case	2003	...[d]	—
Laboratorio Bago	Argentina	Honduras	1.45	Pending		...[d]	—
Yugoimport	Form. Yug.	Mozambique	10.9	Pending		...[d]	—

Table 3.1
(continued)

Creditor	Domicile of creditor	Debtor	Original claim	Status	Year	Judgment for creditor (in millions of U.S. dollars)	Received (in percent)
Export-Import Bank	Taiwan	Niger	60	JTP		72.3	—
J&S Franklin Ltd.	UK	Sierra Leone	1.2	JTP		2.7	74
UMARCO	France	Sierra Leone	0.6	Pending		...[d]	...[g]
Exec. Outcomes	US	Sierra Leone	19.5	Pending		...[d]	...[h]
Chatelet Inv. Ltd.	Sierra Leone	Sierra Leone	0.4	Pending		...[d]	—
Sancem Int.	Norway	Sierra Leone	3.7	OCS		...[d]	24
Banco Arabe Español	Spain	Uganda	1	JTP[i]		2.4	...[d]
Transroad Ltd.	UK	Uganda	3.9	JTP[i]	2003	8.3	30[j]
Ind. of Construction	Form. Yug.	Uganda	7	JTP[i]		8.9	—
Sours Fab. Famous	Form. Yug.	Uganda	0.3	JTP[i]		1.4	...[d]
Iraq Fund for Ext. Dev.	Iraq	Uganda	6	JTP[i]		6.4	—
Shelter Afrique	Kenya	Uganda	0.9	OCS		...[d]	11
Cardinal	Bahamas	Yemen	8.2	OCS	2001	...[d]	33
Camdex Int.	Bahamas	Zambia	40–45	JTP	1997	100	100

Source: Singh (2003), IMF (2004), and news reports. Original claim in millions of U.S. dollars unless otherwise stated.

Note: JTP denotes Judgment to Pay; OCS denotes Out of Court Settlement (including in cases when there was a JTP).

[a] Litigation with collective action problems refers to instances in which the plaintiff was one of many holders of the same instrument (or a similar debt instrument that was also defaulted).

[b] Others include Old Castle, Urban, Macrotechnic, NML, and so forth. Substantial litigation has also taken place in Germany and Italy, sometimes involving retail bondholders.

[c] Approximately US$1 billion in the United States, EUR64 million in Italy, EUR42.2 million in Germany. See 18-K filing presented to the SEC commission by the Argentine government.

[d] Indicates payments ongoing or settlement for an undisclosed amount.

[e] See Nolan (2001).

[f] Singh (2003) reports that GBP150,000 were attached in London.

[g] US$1 million paid so far.

[h] US$1.1 million paid so far.

[i] Ruling obtained in local courts.

[j] US$2.79 in legal fees were paid out. See http://fr.allafrica.com/stories/200412200466.html.

interest in the debtor countries. Agreeing to a reasonable debt restructuring offer—one that reflects the country's capacity to pay—may be the best option available to mainstream creditors, even if there is an expectation that there could be some successful holdouts. This is true, of course, only to the extent that payments to successful holdouts are expected to remain relatively small; otherwise, the country's capacity to honor its commitments to the majority could be undermined. However, the limited leverage of the holdouts should generally ensure that this is the case: holdouts will not be able to extract payments beyond their limited capacity to inflict direct or reputational damage to a country.

Pre-restructuring Litigation and the "Rush to the Courthouse"

In both law and economics, the possibility of destructive "creditor runs" began to attract attention in the early 1980s.[6] Among the first to raise the issue in the legal literature on sovereign debt were Barnett, Galvis, and Gouraige (1984), in the context of debt rescheduling agreements between commercial bank creditors and distressed sovereigns that had taken place since 1982, and had thus far stopped short of open defaults. Barnett, Galvis, and Gouraige argued that this was a fragile state of affairs. If an individual creditor decided not to participate in such an agreement and declared a default as the first step toward litigation, this would trigger cross-default clauses, resulting in a "race to the courthouse." This would result in an avalanche of creditor claims that could not possibly be met by the debtor. Moreover, the state of open default would further magnify the debtor's economic problems.

As it turned out, "races to the courthouse" did not happen during the 1980s. Based on the previous discussion, this is not surprising: a free rider problem may not, in fact, have existed. The rules of syndicated lending ensured that everyone who participated in a "race to the courthouse" arrived there at about the same time. And even if litigating creditors managed to attach payments ahead of others, they might have had to share these payments with other members of the syndicate. Barnett, Galvis, and Gouraige may have been right that "racing to the courthouse" would have triggered pandemonium. But under the rules of the 1980s, a creditor initiating the race stood to gain little, and might expect to suffer the same costs—in the form of an aggravation in the debtor's repayment capacity—as subsequent participants in the race. Hence, stability prevailed.

After the advent of secondary debt markets, these contractual restrictions began to lose their bite, either because new bond issues no longer had sharing provisions, or because distressed debt funds could acquire an entire loan (or a majority stake) at a discount, rendering sharing clauses irrelevant. Yet, there were relatively few cases of pre-restructuring litigation. The best known is *Pravin Banker v. Banco Popular del Peru*, which was mentioned previously. The argument that Pravin's suit might set off a race to the courthouse and disrupt Peru's ongoing restructuring negotiations was, in fact, made by the debtor, and the court initially accepted it, granting two stays of litigation. In the end, however, the court sided with Pravin, and no creditor stampede occurred. The reasons for this might be related to those discussed at the end of the previous section: for most creditors, a litigation strategy is not very attractive unless holdouts undermine the viability of a reasonable debt restructuring agreement. Pravin owned only $1.4 million of Peruvian debt: "Although irksome to both the country and its other creditors, it was not about to bankrupt the Peruvian treasury or scuttle the country's contemplated Brady deal" (Power 1996).

The only debt crisis of the postwar period (and perhaps in history) that has, in fact, witnessed massive pre-restructuring litigation is the most recent crisis in Argentina. By late 2004, almost 140 lawsuits, including 15 class action suits, a novel vehicle in the context of sovereign debt litigation, had been filed against Argentina in New York, Italy, and Germany, both by distressed debt funds holding Argentine claims and "retail investors."[7] Many of these suits have resulted in judgments in favor of the creditors, including a $725 million judgment in favor of one creditor (EML, a subsidiary of Dart Capital). In terms of sheer numbers, this looks very much like the "race to the courthouse" predicted by Barnett, Galvis, and Gouraige (1984).

The question is whether it also had any of the predicted effects. Barnett, Galvis, and Gouraige's main concern that a race to the courthouse would trigger a default is, of course, moot in this case, since Argentina had already declared default in December 2001. Moreover, in spite of the judgments obtained by EML and others, the avalanche of lawsuits has not, so far, weakened Argentina economically. Attempts actually to attach assets have so far turned out to be largely fruitless.[8]

The greatest harm that these lawsuits could have done to Argentina would have been to interfere with its debt exchange offer by creating legal obstacles to the debt exchange or its settlement, or by discouraging creditors from participating in the exchange. As far as creditor participation is concerned, this was, in fact, lower than in preceding exchanges (76 percent), but much higher than anticipated (chapter 8). Regarding legal obstacles, two class action litigants did, in fact, attempt to block the exchange offer, but a New York court ruled against them in November 2004, and the offer went ahead in January 2005.

This was followed by a further legal challenge in March 2005, shortly before the exchange was to settle. NML Capital (an offshore fund with ties to Elliott Associates) asked a New York court to attach a portion ($7 billion) of Argentina's defaulted bonds that had been turned in by consenting bondholders to the Bank of New York, in charge of carrying out the exchange, arguing that they had market value and hence could be sold to satisfy a future judgment. The court rejected this argument, on the grounds that until settlement, the bonds belonged to the creditors that had accepted the exchange, and that attaching them would jeopardize the exchange; however, it agreed to maintain a freeze pending appeal. In late May, an appeals court upheld this decision, arguing that the lower court "acted within its discretionary authority to vacate the remedies in order to avoid a substantial risk to the successful conclusion of the debt restructuring. That restructuring is obviously of critical importance to the economic health of a nation" (United States Court of Appeals for the Second Circuit 2005). While the court refused to rule on the legal issues disputed by the parties and hence did not set a precedent, one has to agree with Gelpern's (2005) observation that "if future judges use similar reasoning, preclosing challenges look increasingly remote."

Can Domestic Insolvency Procedures Be Mimicked Through Sovereign Bond Contracts?

A central theme of the discussion so far has been the tension between enforcing creditor rights, which is desirable from the perspective of efficient debt markets, and avoiding a holdout creditor problem, which is desirable from the perspective of an efficient resolution of debt crises. At the domestic level, this tension is resolved by bankruptcy legislation, which attempts to safeguard creditors' rights by giving creditors priority over equity holders and ensuring that the firm is restructured in a way that maximizes its capacity to repay while protecting majority creditors from holdouts (e.g., by imposing a stay of litigation pending the outcome of a reorganization, and making the outcome of a reorganization binding on all creditors). The question is whether the same objectives can be achieved by appropriately designing sovereign debt contracts, and relying on courts in the major issuing jurisdictions to enforce them. The consensus from a growing literature on that topic (Eichengreen and Portes 1995; Eichengreen 2000, 2002; Schwarcz 2000; Buchheit and Gulati 2002; Taylor 2002; Bolton 2003; Bolton and Skeel 2004; IMF 2002b, 2003b, d, e, f) appears to be, to some extent, but not completely.

Domestic bankruptcy procedures are often interpreted as serving three practical purposes: (1) eliminating free rider problems during and after the restructuring negotiations, particularly the holdout creditor problem; (2) ensuring that the firm has access to financing while it is being restructured ("debtor in possession" or "DIP" financing); and (3) enforcing a predetermined priority structure. Bond covenants currently deal with only the first of these, and do so to only a limited extent. Contractual innovations that could address the first purpose more completely and begin to address the second and third are not inconceivable, but are complicated and perhaps impracticable.

Consider first *free rider problems*. As argued in the last section, these can be divided into two groups: pre-restructuring litigation and problems caused by holdouts that litigate after a debt restructuring. As we have seen, most newly issued international bonds already contain some protections against these problems. With regard to pre-restructuring litigation, acceleration clauses ensure that a critical mass of creditors is necessary in order to accelerate repayment and that a majority of creditors can veto this decision. With regard to holdouts, majority amendment clauses can impose a restructuring agreed to by a supermajority of bondholders on a dissenting minority. However, the extent to which these clauses solve the free rider problem is limited. Even if the debtor had just one bond issue outstanding, a minority bondholder could obviously still block an agreement if he controlled a sufficiently large share of the issue. With multiple bond issues, this problem is aggravated by the need to coordinate creditors across these issues: many majority decisions are required, rather than just one, to amend bonds in a consistent way. Moreover, with public debt fractured into many issues, each of which may trade at large discounts in crisis times, it may be easy for distressed debt funds to acquire a controlling majority of one issue on the secondary market.

To deal with these problems, additional collective action clauses could be added to the standard acceleration, enforcement, and majority amendment clauses (Buchheit 1998a, b; Taylor 2002; IMF 2003e).

Bond-by-bond majority action clauses could be supplemented with "aggregation clauses" that would, in effect, allow a supermajority of bond holders *across* bond issues to amend the payments terms of all bonds even if the usual supermajority required for issue-by-issue amendments is not present. Moreover, proposals have been made to coordinate bondholder representation and discourage litigation by holdouts. These include adding sharing clauses to bond contracts that state that if any bondholder receives a payment disproportionate to that received by other bondholders, this must be shared with the remaining bondholders, and "collective representation clauses," which would delegate the authority to represent the bondholders in debt restructuring negotiations to an agent (though bondholder voting on a proposed restructuring would still be required). For example, bonds could be issued under a "trust indenture" (in U.S. law) or a "trust deed" (in English law); these give a trustee a limited monopoly over litigation and require it to share any proceeds among all holders of the same bond issue (Buchheit and Gulati 2002). Additional language in the bond contract would be required, however, to give the trustee the power to negotiate.

Bonds issued in recent debt restructurings have taken limited steps in these directions. In Uruguay's May 2003 exchange, all new external bonds were issued under a trust indenture, and included an aggregation clause to the effect that, if 85 percent of holders of bonds issued under the same indenture agreed to an amendment of the payment terms, then the supermajority level required for the amendment at the level of each individual bond was reduced from 75 percent to 66.66 percent. Argentina's 2005 exchange contains a similar clause, with the novel feature that aggregated voting would apply across bonds governed by different governing laws. These aggregation features are still very limited compared with a situation where all bondholders would make a supermajority decision "across" bonds, in the sense that they still give a 34 percent minority of holders of each individual bond issue the power to hold out, even if more than 85 percent of *all* bondholders desire a change. But in principle, they could be extended further.

Next, consider *DIP financing*. As we saw in chapter 1, the BAC process in the 1980s served this purpose, providing "new money" in the context of debt rescheduling agreements. In contrast, in the post–Brady era of debt exchanges, distressed borrowers have never been able to obtain new private financing either just before or at the time of a debt restructuring agreement. Instead, the role of the provision of "DIP financing" to countries has been assumed entirely by the official sector, particularly the IMF, although attempts were made, some of which were successful, in persuading private creditors to maintain or roll over their exposures in several crises that did not lead to a restructuring (see Roubini and Setser 2004, chap. 4). The question is whether legal innovations in bond contracts could make it easier for private sector DIP financing to come forward. A proposal in this direction has been made by Buchheit and Gulati (2002), who suggest that this could be achieved through an amendment in the pari passu clause in each bond that would legally subordinate the bond holders to new creditors that are willing to lend to the country during a preset period. In the event that the attempt to "rescue" the country through the infusion of new private funds fails, the new creditors would be paid off before the old creditors received any payments. However, the new infusion may also stave off a restructuring altogether and hence be in the interests of the existing creditors. As Buchheit and Gulati emphasize, an amendment of the pari passu clause would not affect the payment terms of the bond and hence could generally go forward with a simple majority of bondholder for bonds with U.S.-style amendment clauses.

Finally, consider the problem of *enforcing a preset priority structure* across claim holders. In sovereign bonds there generally is no such structure, arguably because it could not currently be enforced. However, as argued in a number of recent papers (Bolton and Skeel 2004; Bolton and Jeanne 2005; Borensztein et al. 2005; Gelpern 2004) a preset priority structure based on the time of first issuance—in other words, giving seniority to holders of earlier issues—could reduce incentives to overborrow and lower the cost of borrowing at low debt levels by removing the possibility of debt dilution (the reduction of the claims of earlier creditors on the recovery value of the debt through subsequent debt issuance). Senior creditors could, of course, still decide to give up their seniority in a crisis situation through an amendment as described by Buchheit and Gulati (2002). Borensztein et al. (2005) discuss some options for contractual enforcement of such a structure; these might be legally feasible, but they are complicated. The complication arises from the fact that existing creditors, rather than subordinating themselves, must somehow commit the debtor to negotiate future bond contracts such that *future* creditors are contractually subordinated to *present* creditors. This could possibly be achieved by defining the failure to do so as a default event, and giving creditors the power to accelerate their bonds in that event. In other words, current creditors could accelerate if they observed new bond issues that are not explicitly subordinated to currently outstanding issues. Whether this is a sufficiently strong incentive to induce debtors to negotiate a consistent priority structure based on time of issuance with successive generations of creditors is open to question.

The sense of the discussion so far is that introducing bankruptcy reorganization-like features in sovereign debt through bond contracts alone may be at best complicated and, at worst, impossible. This view has led several authors to propose mechanisms beyond contract law which might improve the debt restructuring process. A number of proposals since the 1980s have envisaged creating a formal legal regime for sovereign bankruptcy, through international treaty and/or amendments in national statutes (see Rogoff and Zettelmeyer 2002 for a survey). The best-known and most detailed of these is the IMF's recent proposal for a "Sovereign Debt Restructuring Mechanism" (Krueger 2002; IMF 2002b, 2003d; Hagan 2005), which was discussed by the IMF's Executive Board in 2002 and 2003, but ultimately failed to attract support from the requisite supermajority of the IMF's shareholders. In its final version, the IMF's proposal envisaged a majority action provision making a debt restructuring agreement binding on dissenting debt holders (including nonbond creditors, which cannot easily be dealt with through aggregation clauses), limited protection from pre-restructuring litigation, and a mechanism for DIP financing. A subsequent proposal by Bolton and Skeel (2004) went a step further in additionally proposing a mechanism for enforcing first-in-time seniority (see chapter 12).

A more limited alternative to a statutory sovereign bankruptcy regime, which would mainly address any remaining free rider problem, could be to use U.S. federal class action procedures as a basis for court-supervised restructurings involving sovereign debtors. According to Buchheit and Gulati (2002), sovereign debt restructurings satisfy the basic condition for initiating class action suit under federal procedures because creditors have a basic common ("class") interest, and separate legal actions by individual members of a class could harm that interest. In their strongest form ("mandatory class actions"), any eventual settlement reached in a class action will bind all members of the class, at least to the extent that the court has jurisdiction over the class members, hence essentially removing the holdout problem. A weaker form allows class members to opt out of the litigation proceedings. In either case, the proposed settlement must be approved by the court.

The mechanics of class action suits would be for one or several individual bondholders to bring a suit before a U.S. court asking the court to "certify" the creditors as a class (either mandatory or with an opt out). So far, there are ten cases on record in which U.S. courts have agreed to certify creditors of a sovereign as a class (*Hirshon v. Bolivia* in 1995, and nine cases involving Argentina, which were certified in 2004 and 2005). All have failed to meet the standard that would be required to deal effectively with holdout problems, as none of them constituted a mandatory class action. Moreover, in the cases involving Argentina, the classes were defined narrowly to comprise only the holders of one or two Argentine bond series issued under New York law, and the U.S. courts have denied certification requests involving broader class definitions.

In sum, for the foreseeable future, the prospects for applying domestic bankruptcy-like procedures to sovereigns are fairly dim. The application and coverage of collective action clauses has steadily grown in the last few years, but still falls far short of fully dealing with free rider problems. No attempt has been made to use bond clauses to subordinate existing creditors to new lenders in a crisis, or to create a systematic priority structure based on the time of issue. Mandatory class action suits have not been used as a vehicle to deal with the holdout problem, and court decisions in Argentina suggest that U.S. courts are unlikely to regard all bondholders (or even all creditors) as a "class," preferring much narrower class definitions that leave plenty of opportunities for independent litigation. Finally, the IMF's proposal to create a new body of sovereign bankruptcy law at the international level is on hold owing to lack of support from major creditor and debtor country governments. In the meantime, however, debt exchanges seem to have worked fairly well, and holdouts have not proven to be a significant obstacle to carrying out these exchanges. It remains to be seen whether this will continue to be the case in the future.

II The New Debt Crises, 1998–2005

Introduction

In the following chapters, we give an account of the main restructuring episodes involving privately held debt since "the" debt crisis of the 1980s. We could have selected our sample differently—for example, by picking episodes of debt distress, as defined by very high borrowing costs, or loss of access to international capital markets. Indeed, as explained in chapter 2, many of the empirical papers that analyze the causes of debt crises, or estimate "early warning models" to predict debt crises, take this broader approach. This is appropriate if the objective is to analyze *why* countries get into situations of debt distress, whether or not these are followed by a restructuring. But in this book, the emphasis is on documenting the history and mechanics of actual defaults and restructurings, and on their comparison with each other, rather than with crisis situations which ended differently. Focusing on these cases alone will not give a complete view; for this reason, the case studies presented here can only complement, but do not substitute for, the broader statistical analyses surveyed in chapter 2.

We focus on seven country cases: Russia, Ukraine, Pakistan, Ecuador, Argentina, Moldova, and Uruguay, in chronological order. This covers about half of the default or restructuring cases during 1998–2004 that are recorded in table 1.1.[1] We picked these cases for several reasons. First, we included all events that were important in the sense that substantial volumes of debt were involved and/or that the restructuring of privately held debt was the "main event" of the crisis. Second, we also included a few restructurings that involved relatively small amounts of privately held debt—both in dollar levels and as a share of total debt—but were unusual or innovative in some respect. For example, Pakistan's 1999 restructuring was the first to involve Eurobonds, and Moldova's restructuring was the first to fully rely on collective action clauses. Third, we gave bond restructurings, the hallmark of the debt crises of the 1990s relative to the 1980s, preference over a few restructurings that involved negotiations with banks.[2]

Most of the cases that we study are related to the "bust" phase in international capital markets that set in after the 1998 Russian crisis, but the onset of the crises had different origins in each case. Russia's problems were mostly domestic. Prior to its crisis, it had accumulated substantial debt (both from private sources and IFIs), of which an increasing share was short-term debt in domestic currency. High deficits combined with tight monetary policy and a strong real exchange rate led to high domestic interest rates, increasing difficulties in rolling over debt, and eventually a devaluation and debt crisis. Ukraine, which also had a weak fiscal position—though lower debt than Russia—suffered considerably from the Russian crisis, both through financial linkages and owing to strong trade links with its neighbor.

Pakistan started out with high debt levels, and was also affected by the collapse of capital flows to emerging markets in the aftermath of the Russian crisis. It differed from other cases, however, owing to its lower degree of integration into international capital markets, a different creditor structure with a much larger share of debt in the hands of official and domestic creditors, and a balance of payments crisis triggered in part by idiosyncratic shocks (including economic sanctions following a nuclear test). The 1999 commercial external debt restructuring was a relatively marginal event within a larger official debt restructuring deal. Moldova's 2002 restructuring was similar in that it was the last—quantitatively relatively minor—act in a protracted debt restructuring process which involved much larger amounts of official debt. This process, in turn, was triggered by a 1998 balance of payments crisis that was, in part, due to the repercussions of the crisis in Russia.

Ecuador suffered from substantial macroeconomic shocks during 1998 which led to a banking crisis, which in turn prompted a currency crisis. This combination made the debt crisis unavoidable. Argentina also suffered from a series of real shocks (the Brazilian devaluation and the dollar appreciation) to which it could not respond within the framework of its rigid fixed exchange rate regime. A protracted recession led to sustainability fears, which eventually triggered bank runs and a debt crisis that, in turn, led to a forced exit from the fixed exchange rate regime. The Argentine crisis, in turn, affected Uruguay, which also experienced a fall in economic activity, exchange rate depreciation, and a banking crisis. This combination eventually led to a debt crisis.

In each of the cases, our objective is (1) to give the background to the restructuring, providing a data-backed account of how the country got into a situation of debt distress; (2) to describe the modalities and terms of each debt restructuring deal; and (3) to describe the effects of the debt restructuring from both the debtor and investor perspectives.[3] For the investor, this involves estimating the losses that were associated with each exchange. For the debtor, it involves comparing the debt profile before and after the exchange, and briefly describing economic developments after the exchange.

We rely on two analytical tools that require a brief explanation: a "debt dynamics decomposition," and a specific approach to computing investor losses. Each of these is associated with a particular type of presentation, in table form. What follows is a minimal technical explanation necessary to read these tables (see the appendix for details).

Debt Dynamics

A debt dynamics decomposition is a way of "parsing out" the economic factors that pull—possibly in different directions—at the debt-to-GDP ratio over time. Start out with the basic debt $(D_t^\$)$ accumulation equation (with debt expressed in U.S. dollars):[4]

$$
\begin{aligned}
D_t^\$ - D_{t-1}^\$ &\equiv -\frac{P_t}{S_t} + \frac{I_t}{S_t} + \frac{D_{t-1}^d}{S_{t-1}^{eop}}\left[\frac{1/S_t^{eop}}{1/S_{t-1}^{eop}} - 1\right] \\
&\equiv -\frac{P_t}{S_t} + \frac{I_t}{S_t} + \alpha D_{t-1}^\$\left[\frac{S_{t-1}^{eop}}{S_t^{eop}} - 1\right],
\end{aligned}
\tag{II.1}
$$

where P_t and I_t are the local currency primary balance and interest bill, respectively, available from the fiscal accounts; D_t^d denotes debt denominated in local currency; α is the share of local currency denominated debt in total debt; the superscript "eop" denotes "end of period" (all variables not superscripted are period averages); and S_t is the exchange rate (local currency/U.S. dollar). Hence, the square bracket term measures the appreciation of the currency between periods $t-1$ and t. Equation (II.1) states that the debt in dollars increases one-for-one in response to a decrease in the primary balance (first term) or an increase in interest payments (second term), while it increases proportionally to an appreciation of the currency, with a proportionality factor that depends on the share α of domestic denominated debt in total debt. Thus, when α is zero (all debt is denominated in dollars), changes in the exchange rate have no impact on the dollar level of debt.

Next, divide both sides by dollar GDP $Y_t^\$(\equiv Y_t/S_t)$. In the appendix, we show that the resulting equation, after some manipulation, can be written as

$$d_t^\$ - d_{t-1}^\$ = -\frac{P_t}{Y_t} + \frac{d_{t-1}^\$}{(1+\pi_t^\$)(1+g_t)}$$

$$\times \left\{ (i_t^\$ - \pi_t^\$) - \left(\alpha \frac{s_t^e(1+e_t)}{1+s_t^e} - e_t \right) - g_t + i_t^\$ e - \pi_t^\$ g_t \right\}, \quad \text{(II.2)}$$

where $d_t^\$$ denotes debt as a share of GDP, $\pi_t^\$$ is U.S. inflation, $i_t^\$$ the average dollar interest rate on the public debt, g_t the real growth rate, and e_t the rate of *real* exchange rate depreciation. Equation (II.2) tells us that the change in the debt-to-GDP ratio can be decomposed into five terms: the primary balance as a share of GDP, as well as four other terms that each impact the debt-to-GDP ratio through the proportionality factor in front of the curly brackets:

· a "real interest contribution" $i_t^\$ - \pi_t^\$$;
· a "real growth contribution" (with a negative sign), g_t;
· a "real exchange contribution" $(\alpha(s_t^e(1+e_t)/(1+s_t^e)) - e_t)$;
· finally, a residual, sometimes called "theoretical discrepancy," which is the sum of the cross-terms on the right.

The "real exchange rate contribution" requires some interpretation. Suppose first that $\alpha = 0$, that is, that all debt is in dollars. Then, the real exchange contribution is proportional to the rate of real appreciation $-e_t$. What this says is simply that, if all debt is dollar-denominated, then a real appreciation of the currency translates into a proportional fall of the debt-to-GDP ratio. This effect is more attenuated, the higher the fraction of domestic currency debt α.

In the case studies we will use this decomposition to identify the sources of a rapid rise in a country's debt-to-GDP ratio, in particular, whether it resulted from an exchange rate depreciation in the presence of foreign currency debt, whether it was due to high real interest rates, or whether it was simply a result of large fiscal deficits.

Debt Restructurings and "Haircuts"

After we describe the background for each debt restructuring, we will describe the terms and outcome of each debt restructuring in some detail. This involves addressing the question of how big the "haircut" was that investors suffered in each deal. We do this by comparing the net present value of cash flows promised under the old and new debt instruments, using a common discount rate, namely, the yield that is implicit in the price of the new debt instruments traded immediately *after* the debt exchange (see Sturzenegger and Zettelmeyer 2005 for details on both the methodology and the actual computations).

Why is this a plausible way of computing realized investor losses? Consider a few alternatives. For example, an investor holding an instrument since the time of its emission or purchase may feel that he loses to the extent that the market value of the new debt instrument is lower than the market value of the old instrument at the time of its purchase; in effect comparing the net present value (NPV) of the original instrument discounted with precrisis yields to the NPV of the new instrument discounted with the yield prevailing after the exchange. This definition of investor losses is presumably too broad, since it includes any loss attributable to the deterioration of economic fundamentals prior to the crisis, rather than the loss attributable to the terms of the exchange. At the other extreme, it is unhelpful to compare the market value of the old instrument just prior to the exchange with the market value of the new instrument just after the exchange: in a world of perfect foresight, these should be equal. Any measured gain or loss will thus reflect the extent to which the result of the exchange was incorrectly anticipated, independently of the terms of the exchange.

We thus take the view that the cash flows promised under the new and old instruments should be compared using the same discount rate (except for minor adjustments reflecting differences in maturities). From the perspective of measuring *realized* losses the appropriate discount rate is the yield implicit in the market value of the new instrument immediately after the close of the exchange: this will reflect the results of the exchange (i.e., the participation rate) but not news about economic fundamentals that becomes available after the exchange, that is, after the results of the exchange are known. Thus, we compare the market value of the new instrument, plus any cash payment received, to the NPV of the payments remaining on the old instrument (inclusive of past due interest and principal), discounted using the yield of the new instruments (r_{new}). Note that in situations when no cash was paid, $NPV(new, r_{new})$ is just the price of the new bond:

$$H \equiv 1 - \frac{NPV(new, r_{new})}{NPV(old, r_{new})}. \tag{II.3}$$

Computing H for all original bonds allows us to compare the various restructuring in terms of their "harshness," and explore whether different classes of bondholders within a particular debt crisis fared about equally in terms of NPV losses or not. In addition, we also show how the value of a particular bondholder's claim would have evolved over time before and after the restructurings.

Our definition of haircuts is close to, but not quite identical, to a definition that is often used by market practitioners, which is to compare the market value of the new bonds to the *face value* of the old bonds, plus any accumulated past due interest:

$$\tilde{H} \equiv 1 - \frac{NPV(new, r_{new})}{100 + PDI}. \tag{II.4}$$

Because sovereign spreads in the aftermath of a restructuring tend to be higher than at the time when the old bond was originally issued, it is typically the case that $NPV(old, r_{new}) < 100 + PDI$ (the main exception in our sample was the 2005 Argentina restructuring, which happened in an environment where yields were so low that the net present value of the old instruments computed at those yields, inclusive of PDI, was generally larger than $100 + PDI$). As a result, our approach tends to give slightly lower haircuts than the practitioners' approach.

The practitioners' approach can be justified with the argument that in a default situation, the debt is accelerated (due immediately), so the net present value of the old claims is simply the face value (100). However, our objective is to compare the value of the new instruments to the value of the old debt in a situation in which the sovereign would not have defaulted. Hence it does not seem right to compute the value of the old instruments conditional on a change in the payment terms that is triggered by the decision to default (rather than the original terms). In addition, most debt exchanges studied in this paper (the exceptions being Argentina, Russia, and Ecuador) did in fact take place ahead of formal defaults, so that the debt was not, in fact, accelerated. This said, there is one important application in which the alternative definition based on the face value of the old instrument is in fact appropriate, namely, the estimation of recovery values in a default, which are quoted as a percent of outstanding principal. We take up this point in the appendix.

4   Russia

After the demise of Soviet planning in 1989, Russia went through a series of traumatic changes as it adjusted to the breakup of the Soviet Union and a new form of economic organization. Prices were freed on January 2, 1992, leading to a jump in consumer prices by 2,500 percent and a collapse of the real exchange rate. Inflation remained very high, with monthly rates in excess of 10 percent, until early 1995. Output plunged continuously through 1997, when it briefly rebounded, only to fall again following the debt crisis and devaluation in the second half of 1998 (table 4.1).[1]

The Soviet Union had accumulated large stocks of external assets, including loans to developing countries, real estate, and stocks of precious metals, as well as more than $100 billion in debts to Western governments, commercial banks, and former allies. As the Soviet Union began to disintegrate in 1991, most of these debts fell into arrears. After some failed attempts to establish collective responsibility for these debts, in April 1993 Russia declared itself responsible for the entire debt of the Soviet Union under the so-called zero option in which Russia would assume all external assets and liabilities of the former Soviet Union. In 1993, Russia issued five series of U.S. dollar-denominated "MinFin bonds" under domestic law, as a way of compensating foreign companies trading with the Soviet Union whose foreign currency accounts in Vneshekonombank, the former state foreign trade bank, had been frozen in 1991 (Duffie, Pedersen, and Singleton 2003; Santos 2003). Although the bonds were issued by Russia, they were regarded as Soviet-era debt because they securitized previously existing foreign currency accounts.

Russia hence started its transition with a relatively high public debt burden, on the order of about two-thirds of annual GDP in 1993. At the same time, fiscal deficits were high and output was falling. However, the effect of these factors on the debt dynamics were more

Table 4.1
Russian Federation: Selected economic indicators, 1993–2004

	1993	1994	1995	1996	1997	1998	1999	2000	2001	2002	2003	2004
Output and prices												
	(annual percentage changes)											
Real GDP	-8.7	-12.7	-4.1	-3.6	1.4	-5.3	6.3	10.0	5.1	4.7	7.3	7.2
Consumer prices (period average)	874.6	307.6	197.5	47.7	14.8	27.7	85.7	20.8	21.5	15.8	13.7	10.9
Rubles per U.S. dollar	350.8	120.9	108.1	12.3	13.0	67.8	153.7	14.3	3.7	9.0	-7.3	-5.8
Terms of trade (goods)	-1.7	16.4	-1.0	6.7	8.0	-14.9	4.4	35.9	-2.1	-4.1	4.4	12.2
World oil price (U.S. dollar per barrel)	-11.8	-5.0	7.9	18.4	-5.4	-32.1	37.5	57.0	-13.8	2.5	15.8	30.7
Public finances												
General government[a]						(in percent of GDP)						
Revenue	36.2	34.6	36.1	34.6	39.3	34.3	33.6	36.9	37.3	37.6	36.7	38.6
Expenditures	43.6	45.1	42.6	44.1	47.8	42.5	36.7	33.7	34.6	37.0	35.6	33.6
Noninterest	41.6	43.1	38.8	37.8	42.7	37.9	30.7	29.4	31.9	34.9	33.9	32.4
Interest	2.0	2.0	3.8	6.3	5.0	4.6	6.0	4.3	2.7	2.1	1.7	1.2
Primary balance	-5.4	-8.4	-2.7	-3.2	-3.5	-3.6	2.9	7.5	5.4	2.7	2.8	6.2
Overall balance	-7.4	-10.4	-6.5	-9.5	-8.5	-8.2	-3.1	3.1	2.7	0.6	1.1	5.0
Overall balance at constant oil price[b]	...	...	...	...	...	...	2.7	1.8	-0.3	-1.6	-1.3	-2.7
Federal government[a]												
Overall balance	-6.4	-11.4	-6.2	-8.9	-7.7	-6.0	-5.3	0.8	2.7	1.3	1.6	4.4
Primary balance	-4.5	-9.4	-2.4	-2.6	-2.6	-1.4	0.7	5.2	5.4	3.4	3.3	5.6
Government debt[c]	67.8	47.7	44.9	43.4	53.6	68.1	90.2	61.4	47.4	40.6	28.0	21.8
Foreign currency	66.2	45.7	40.9	34.7	33.2	58.6	79.3	53.8	41.6	34.3	23.0	17.3
Domestic currency	1.6	2.0	4.1	8.6	20.3	9.5	10.9	7.6	5.8	6.3	5.0	4.5

Money

					(annual percentage changes)							
Reserve money	...	203.5	107.8	27.3	27.6	28.1	65.6	67.2	29.1	31.2	54.1	24.4
Money market rate (percent)	...	...	190.4	47.7	21.0	50.6	14.8	7.1	10.1	8.2	3.8	3.3

External sector

			(in billions of U.S. dollars unless otherwise indicated)									
Total exports, fob	59.0	67.4	82.4	89.7	86.9	74.4	75.6	105.0	101.9	107.2	135.9	183.5
Total imports, fob	49.3	50.5	62.6	68.1	72.0	58.0	39.5	44.9	53.8	61.0	76.1	96.3
Current account	2.6	5.3	4.4	8.3	-2.6	-2.1	22.2	44.6	33.4	30.9	35.4	59.9
Current account (in percent of GDP)	1.5	1.9	1.4	2.1	-0.6	-0.8	11.3	17.2	10.9	9.1	7.9	9.9
Gross reserves	5.8	4.0	14.4	11.3	12.9	7.8	8.5	24.3	32.5	44.1	73.2	120.8

					(annual percentage changes)							
Export volumes	-2.1	4.9	7.7	5.4	-1.3	4.7	-0.6	8.6	2.8	7.2	6.1	9.7
Oil	11.0	6.6	16.4	7.7	-0.4	-3.1	-1.7	17.6	8.9	13.6	17.3	11.9
Non-oil	-7.0	4.2	3.7	4.1	-1.7	8.8	0.0	4.4	-0.4	3.5	-1.0	8.0
Import volumes	-9.4	9.4	8.1	12.3	16.3	-16.2	-30.3	20.4	24.3	10.7	9.0	15.4

Reference items:

Nominal GDP (in billions of rubles)	172	611	1,429	2,008	2,343	2,630	4,823	7,306	8,944	10,831	13,243	16,752
Exchange rate (rubles per U.S. dollar, period average)	1.0	2.2	4.6	5.1	5.8	9.7	24.6	28.1	29.2	31.8	29.5	27.7

Source: National authorities and IMF.

[a] On an accrual basis.

[b] At an oil price of $20 per barrel.

[c] Debt in U.S. dollars evaluated at end-period exchange rates, divided by current GDP in U.S. dollars.

Table 4.2
Russian Federation: Debt dynamics, 1993–2004 (in percent of GDP unless otherwise stated)

	1993	1994	1995	1996	1997	1998	1999	2000	2001	2002	2003	2004
Federal government debt[a]	67.8	47.7	44.9	43.4	53.6	68.1	90.2	61.4	47.4	40.6	28.0	21.8
Change in debt ratio attributable to…		−20.1	−2.8	−1.5	10.2	14.5	22.2	−28.9	−14.0	−6.8	−12.6	−6.2
Primary deficit[b]		9.4	2.4	2.6	2.6	1.4	−0.7	−5.2	−5.4	−3.4	−3.3	−5.6
Real interest rate		1.9	3.4	7.2	4.3	2.6	3.1	3.4	1.6	1.4	1.3	0.8
Real growth		9.7	2.0	1.6	−0.6	3.0	−4.0	−8.1	−2.9	−2.1	−2.7	−1.8
Real depreciation		−35.1	−7.2	−11.0	−1.2	16.2	28.4	−12.5	−5.5	−2.1	−6.2	−4.3
Cross-terms		−1.4	−0.5	−1.7	0.0	1.4	1.9	−1.0	−0.3	−0.1	−0.4	−0.3
Residual[c]		−4.7	−2.8	−0.3	5.0	−10.1	−6.5	−5.5	−1.5	−0.5	−1.3	5.0

[a] Debt in U.S. dollars using end-period exchange rates, divided by current GDP in U.S. dollars.
[b] Refers to federal government.
[c] Reflects debt stock adjustments, nondebt financing (including debt service arrears), and measurement error.

than offset by a rapid real exchange rate appreciation, following a pattern characteristic of all transition economies at the time (Krajnyak and Zettelmeyer 1998). As a result, the debt-to-GDP ratio fell, to just over 40 percent of GDP, by 1996 (table 4.2).

The macroeconomic situation began to improve after a Stand-by Arrangement with the IMF was agreed on in March 1995. The program relied on the exchange rate as nominal anchor and succeeded in stabilizing prices, with inflation rates falling to low levels by mid-1996. The standby was followed by a three-year Extended Fund Facility (EFF) in March 1996 that sought to consolidate inflation stabilization, reduce the fiscal deficit, and restart growth.

The 1995 and 1996 stabilization was achieved through strict limits on the money supply. Beginning in April 1995, the Central Bank of the Russian Federation (CBR) stopped extending loans to finance the federal budget deficit. The fiscal situation initially improved, with the federal deficit falling from over 11 percent of GDP to about 6 percent in 1995. However, this was not sustained, in part, due to easier policies ahead of the presidential election in June 1996. Without recourse to monetary financing, the government began to rely increasingly on the issue of short-term treasury bonds as a way of financing the deficit. As an agent of the Ministry of Finance, the CBR organized a ruble-denominated debt market in which two instruments, short-term treasury bills ("GKOs," which were discount instruments with maturities of up to twelve months) as well as longer-term (one to two years) coupon-bearing "OFZs" were traded. The stock of outstanding GKOs rose rapidly, from about 1.2 percent of GDP at end-1994 to over 12 percent at end-1997.

Local financial institutions purchased many of these bonds, which became one of the main sources of government finance (Robinson 2003a). Starting from a net debtor position in 1993, by August 1998 banks had accumulated net claims on the government on the order of 40 percent of GDP. On the eve of the crisis, government securities made up about 55 percent of the assets of state-owned Sberbank, which held about 75 percent of all deposits in the banking system. In parallel with this increasing exposure to government securities denominated in rubles, the liability side of the banking system became increasingly dollarized, as private banks began to borrow abroad, and the opening of the domestic debt market and stock markets to foreigners beginning in 1996 created a large demand for foreign currency derivatives which Russian banks were eager to supply.

In 1996, the government also began to take steps to normalize its access to international credit. The Paris Club agreed to restructure $40 billion of Soviet-era debt in April 1996. The Russian Federation also issued two additional MinFin bonds and, in November 1996, its first Eurobond. In 1997, the London Club, representing more than six hundred Western commercial lenders, agreed to restructure Soviet-era debt into two securities: $22 billion of "principal notes" (Prins) and $6 billion of "interest arrears notes" (IANs). The exchange, which required a 90 percent participation threshold, turned out to be a success, after more than a year of negotiations involving Vneshekonombank (the debtor) and a reconciliation office headed by Ernst and Young. On this basis, the Russian government successfully placed several additional Eurobonds during 1997 and 1998.

While debt financing was flowing easily, Russia's exchange rate-based stabilization became threatened in 1997, not only by continued weak fiscal performance but also by the collapse of oil prices (figure 4.1). The sharp fall in oil prices further weakened Russia's budget position as well as its current account, since oil made up a quarter of Russian exports at the time. This raised fears of a devaluation, leading to speculative attacks on the ruble in October 1997 and January 1998. International reserves declined sharply during this period (figure 4.2). At

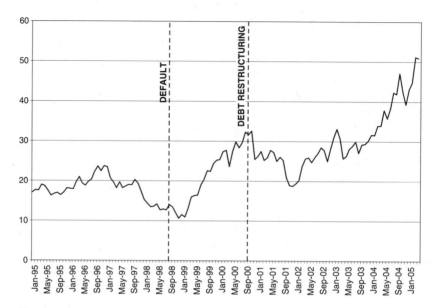

Figure 4.1
Price of oil (dollars per barrel)
Source: International Financial Statistics (IFS).

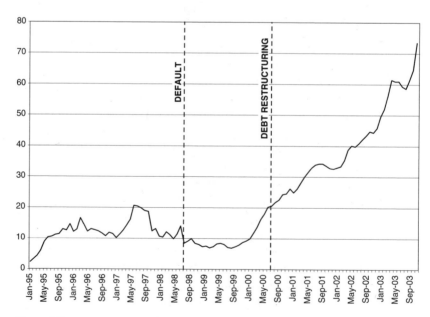

Figure 4.2
International reserves (in billions of U.S. dollars)
Source: IFS.

the same time, the favorable effects of real appreciation on the debt-to-GDP ratio subsided, and debt to GDP began to rise sharply, driven by fiscal deficits and rising interest rates (table 4.2). Faced with increasing difficulties in financing expenditures, the government began to accumulate wage and expenditure arrears.

As the economic situation deteriorated, a political crisis developed. In March, a young and fairly unknown technocrat, Sergei Kiriyenko, was chosen for the post of prime minister. However, a long row with the Duma, the Russian parliament, relating to his approval undermined his ability to straighten out the beleaguered Russian finances. After a series of mostly failed attempts at fiscal reform, sentiment had become increasingly pessimistic. At the same time, emerging market financing conditions deteriorated as a result of the political and economic crisis in Indonesia. With the ruble under heavy pressure, the CBR mounted an interest defense of the exchange rate band. Annualized GKO yields reached 50 percent and briefly peaked at over 100 percent at the end of the month. Growth projections for 1998 had been lowered to zero. With the inflation target set at 8 percent, and the real exchange rate projected to remain essentially flat, the debt dynamics looked increasingly unfavorable. In June, domestic borrowing came to a virtual halt, with the government making large net repayments. Moreover, $33 billion in GKO and OFZ debt were coming due between June and December. Unless confidence returned and interest rates fell, it would be very difficult to roll over this debt.

The June–July 1998 Rescue Attempt

In late June 1998, the government presented an "anticrisis" plan to the Duma, based on fiscal emergency measures, both on the expenditure and revenue side. Based on these measures, augmented by an agreement on the 1999 program budget and structural measures to boost growth, the government was able to negotiate a program augmentation with the IMF. On July 13, 1998, the IMF announced its intention to make an extra $11.2 billion available to Russia in 1998, with about half becoming available immediately after Board approval of the package on July 20, 1998. The strategy of the IMF-backed program was threefold: (1), fiscal adjustment to reduce the deficit by about 3 percentage points of GDP by 1999; (2), a defense of the exchange rate peg, in order to preserve stabilization gains and to prevent a collapse of the banking system in view of its foreign exchange exposures; and (3), a lengthening of the maturity structure of the debt, through a voluntary exchange of GKOs into seven- and twenty-year Eurobonds. Together with the new IMF financing, this was supposed to take care of the short-term debt rollover problem.

The initial market reaction to the IMF-backed package was favorable, with GKO yields declining sharply, from close to 200 percent in the week prior to the announcement to 54 percent on July 15, 1998. The GKO-Eurobond exchange was also a success, retiring a face value of about $4.4 billion GKOs—about in line with market expectations, and significantly above the assumption of the IMF-backed program ($3 billion).[2] Market commentary was upbeat, suggesting that the liquidity crisis had been overcome, and that the danger of a crisis within the next three to six months had passed. However, this success was very short-lived. Almost immediately after the IMF Board approval and the completion of the exchange on July 20, 1998, GKO yields resumed their rise. By early August they were back at 75 percent, rising steadily to 150 percent in mid-August. Finding yields unacceptably high, the government canceled new auctions. Gross domestic financing of the budget ground to a halt. At the same time, the run on the exchange rate picked up again, with the CBR selling $3.8 billion in the foreign exchange market between July 27 and August 14, 1998. Without new official financing, a default or devaluation had become unavoidable.

What had gone wrong? The reasons for the failure of the June–July 1998 rescue and the causes of the August 1998 crisis more generally, have been the subject of a heated debate. Because this debate is representative of views that are often exchanged in the aftermath of a failed rescue, it is worth a brief review. One influential view is that the June–July 1998 rescue was doomed to failure from the start (Kharas, Pinto, and Ulatov 2001; Williamson 2001). In this view, the strategy of "solving" the liquidity crisis by taking on large amounts of additional long-term debt—two Eurobonds with total face value of $3.75 billion issued in June 1998, IMF-led official disbursements totaling $5.5 billion in June and July 1998, and $6.4 billion in Eurobonds associated with the GKO exchange on July 24, 1998—was bound to backfire, because it made Russia's solvency problem worse, effectively subordinated GKO holders to the new debt, and hence increased the incentives of these debtholders to "get out" while the exchange rate band was still in place.

This view seems too extreme. If markets had been of the view that the strategy was counterproductive and detrimental to GKO holders, GKO yields should have gone up, not down, after the package was announced. Moreover, while public debt rose as a result of the June–

July 1998 strategy, it was sustainable, assuming interest rates came down and output decline did not continue for long (IMF 1998; Summers 2001). The critical question was whether either of these conditions *required* a devaluation. The Russian authorities and the IMF believed that this was not the case, and that the combination of short-term financing and fiscal/structural reforms had a fair chance at restoring confidence and restarting growth (Odling-Smee 2004). From a medium-term competitiveness perspective, it was not clear that the ruble was in fact overvalued (Krajnyak and Zettelmeyer 1998); and in the short term, it was clear that a devaluation would do more harm than good, given the foreign currency exposures of banks and non-exporting corporations.

However, while the package may have been consistent and enjoyed some chance of success, the impact on confidence was simply not large enough to achieve the improvement in the debt dynamics that would have been required to roll over the maturing GKOs without devaluing. Meeting in special session on July 15–17, 1998, the Duma rejected a portion of the fiscal proposals that were part of the IMF-backed program, casting doubt about the sustainability of the fiscal adjustment targeted by the government, and also leading to a reduction in the IMF disbursement that was made available immediately from an expected $5.6 billion to $4.8 billion. In addition, the GKO-Eurobond swap had unintended adverse effects. The new Eurobonds were issued at a substantial discount—at a spread of 940 basis points over U.S. Treasury bonds, up from 750 basis points in June 1998—depressing Eurobond prices and triggering margin calls on repurchase agreements entered into by Russian banks. In turn, this forced some banks to sell GKOs to raise liquidity (Kharas, Pinto, and Ulatov 2001).

During the week of August 10, 1998, trading on the Russian stock market was suspended twice as share prices crashed and uncertainty mounted. That same week, the flow of tax receipts dried up due to the growing crisis in the banking sector. The IMF made it clear that lending would be suspended unless the fiscal situation improved. But at this point there was no credible fiscal measure that might have contained the loss of confidence reflected in the increase in financing costs, and the crisis erupted.

Default and Devaluation

On August 17, 1998, unable to stem the run on reserves, the government decided to devalue the ruble, shifting and widening its band

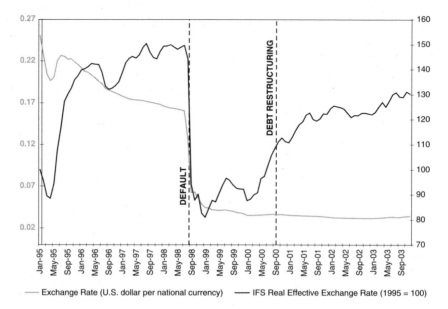

Figure 4.3
Nominal and real exchange rates
Source: IFS.

from 5.3–7.1 to 6.0–9.5 rubles per U.S. dollar (figure 4.3). At the same
time, the Russian authorities declared a moratorium on all ruble-
denominated public debt payments, pending negotiation of a restructuring agreement with creditors. This included the two main domestic
debt instruments, GKOs and OFZs. In addition, a ninety-day moratorium (prohibition to pay) was imposed on foreign currency liabilities
of Russian financial institutions, including derivative currency contracts, repayments of principal on loans from foreign lenders having a
term over 180 days, and insurance payments under credits secured by
pledges of securities such as repos. This measure was justified by the
need to compensate the banks for the impact of the devaluation
and the moratorium on debt payments. Together, these measures
amounted to a de facto Russian default on both domestic sovereign
debt and bank liabilities.[3]

On August 18, 1998, Moody's Investors Service downgraded its
ratings of all Russian corporate debt issuers. The dismissal of the
Kiriyenko government on August 23, 1998, triggered the collapse of
the negotiations with creditors, a panic by bank depositors,[4] and the
breakdown of the settlement system on domestic financial markets,

including the interbank money market. This was followed by an initial restructuring offer to holders of defaulted domestic debt on August 25, 1998. Bondholders were offered a choice of (1) receiving 5 percent of the nominal value in cash and redeeming the remainder in equal proportions of ruble-denominated securities maturing in three, four, and five years, yielding interest rates of 30 percent for the first three years, 25 percent in the fourth year, and 20 percent in the fifth year; or (2) swapping 20 percent of the nominal values of their existing ruble securities for dollar securities maturing in 2006 at a 5 percent interest rate, and receiving 80 percent in ruble bonds. All market participants reportedly rejected this offer.

In an attempt to deal with the crisis, President Yeltsin tried to reappoint former Prime Minister Viktor Chernomyrdin as prime minister. This led to a new struggle with the Duma. The stalemate triggered a further run on the ruble, which led to the abolishment of the exchange rate band on September 2, 1998. The ruble quickly plunged to twenty rubles per dollar before stabilizing at about fifteen rubles per dollar in the second half of September 1998 after Yevgeny Primakov had replaced Chernomyrdin. The new prime minister had to deal with what had by now become Russia's most immediate problem: a fullfledged banking crisis.

Banking Crisis

During the initial reform years, supervision of the banking sector had been poor.[5] Most deposits were held by Sberbank, whose majority owner was the CBR. Poor enforceability of creditor rights encouraged the development of major banks with close connections to large enterprises, and effectively acting as the financial arm of these enterprises, such as Gazprombank acting for Gazprom. In addition, there were a number of regional banks. In all, by the end of 1997 there were about one thousand and seven hundred banks operating in Russia (figure 4.4).

Due to the difficulties in assessing the risk of regular credit activities, Russian banks had accumulated large holdings of government debt, and returns from investment in government securities had become a major source of income, making up about 30 percent of total income in the first quarter of 1998 and above 20 percent in the second. This shift was also encouraged by the better liquidity provided by these instruments as well as their more favorable regulatory treatment (since government bonds were treated as low-risk assets).

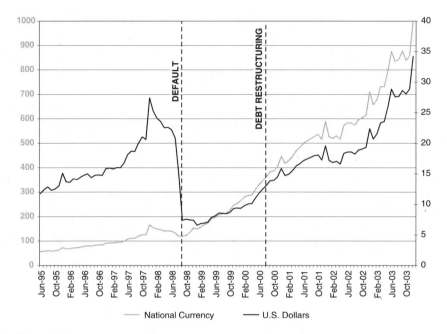

Figure 4.4
Deposits in Russia's financial sector (in billions)
Source: IFS.

Because deposits were mostly held by Sberbank, leading private banks had become highly dependent on external borrowing as a source of funds. At the end of 1997, banks' foreign currency denominated liabilities exceeded foreign currency denominated assets by at least $7 billion. In addition, the boom in capital inflows directed to the GKO and stock market led to an explosive growth in off-balance sheet foreign exchange contracts. In mid-1998, commercial banks' forward foreign currency obligations stood at an incredible $83 billion, or 150 percent of M2, making the system highly vulnerable to a devaluation.

The fragility of the system at the time of the crisis is stressed in Central Bank of the Russian Federation (1998), which reports that Russia's aggregate banking capital was about equal to the volume of the frozen GKOs and OFZs. Thus the default on domestic debt was equivalent to wiping out the entire financial sector. On top of this came the effects of the devaluation, which left banks with foreign currency obligations to foreign creditors that were either not matched by foreign currency claims, or were matched by claims that were mostly uncollectible. The combination of these factors made many of the large banks insolvent, though they could continue operating under Russian laws as long as they retained an ability to process payments. A CBR financial assessment of eighteen large Moscow-based banks after the crisis found that only three had positive capital.

After the August 17, 1998, announcement, lines of frightened depositors had started to appear at some banks. While depositors could, in principle, withdraw their funds, banks created administrative obstacles for doing so, eventually engaging in client-by-client bargaining over a settlement amount. Interbank transactions ceased, and over a period of about four weeks, the payments system effectively collapsed. In response, the CBR undertook a massive liquidity injection into the banking system, lowering reserve requirements, extending "rehabilitation loans" to systemically important banks in return for bank shares as collateral (since defaulted GKOs could no longer be used for this purpose), and making outright purchases of frozen GKOs from Sberbank to insure that it could meet deposit withdrawals (see Robinson 2003a for details). In addition, the CBR created a mechanism under which household deposits from Moscow-based commercial banks could be transferred to Sberbank; this led to the transfer of about 7.1 billion rubles by end-1998. These measures were successful at stopping the run and restarting the payments system, but also fueled a large depreciation of the ruble and a sharp surge in inflation, which averaged about 90 percent in 1999.

The authorities' response to bank insolvencies was more cautious and piecemeal. There was no general attempt to recapitalize the system. Instead, the authorities approached the problem through a mixture of regulatory forbearance—in effect, betting on a gradual strengthening of bank balance sheets as the economy recovered—and selective interventions. Among other steps, forbearance took the form of allowing banks to value their capital at precrisis levels for several months after the devaluation and default. At the same time, a review of the major Moscow-based banks were undertaken, which led to bankruptcy proceedings in three cases, while twelve other banks entered in voluntary restructuring agreements with ARCO, a bank restructuring agency established in November 1998. During 1999 the CBR withdrew the licenses of 127 banks, and ARCO initiated the restructuring of three major regional banks. The overall scope of bank restructuring remained modest, however, and setting up a new regulatory framework and better bankruptcy procedures turned out to be difficult. In the end, the strategy of effectively waiting for banks to recapitalize themselves seems to have worked, though at a slow pace and at the price of slow growth in real credit to the private sector. However, this does not seem to have held back the economic recovery, perhaps because the private sector was never very dependent on bank credit to begin with.

Defaults on External Debt, and Debt Restructurings

Although Russia did not initially default on its dollar-denominated debt, the devaluation led to a sharp rise in the share of debt to GDP and made it difficult to remain current on external debt payments (table 4.2). On December 2, 1998, Vneshekonombank missed a $362 million payment on its Prins, which had been issued the year before. On December 19, 1998, creditor banks voted not to call in their loans. One month later, after the grace period expired, rating agencies placed Russia in default on its external debt. However, Eurobonds issued by the Russian Federation continued to be serviced.

With a portion of its external debt in default, Russia began the task of normalizing its creditor relationships, beginning with the holders of domestic debt. In March 1999, the government finalized a restructuring agreement, known as "novation," with holders of GKOs and longer-term ruble-denominated OFZs, who had rejected the government's August 1998 exchange offer. Scheduled payments were first discounted to August 19, 1998, at a rate of 50 percent per annum. Based on this adjusted nominal claim, creditors would then receive a package of cash and very short-term instruments in addition to longer-term OFZs. The short-term component included a cash payment of 3.33 percent of the adjusted nominal value, 3.33 percent in three-month GKOs (these bonds had an issue date of December 15, 1998, so that they would mature shortly after the exchange), 3.33 percent in six-month GKOs (also with an issue date on December 15, 1998), and a "cash value" OFZ for 20 percent of nominal value that could be used at par to pay tax obligations or purchase newly issued shares of Russian banks. The remaining 70 percent was exchanged for OFZs with maturities ranging from four to five years with coupons of 30, 25, 20, 15, and 10 percent each year, respectively. Importantly, any receipts from selling these GKOs and OFZs had to be deposited in restricted ruble accounts that could be used to purchase selected Russian corporate bonds and equity securities, but allowed the withdrawal and repatriation of funds at market exchange rates only after one year.[6] Thus, the novation scheme in effect combined a standard debt restructuring with the imposition of capital controls.

Table 4.3 shows the losses investors suffered as a result of the GKO exchange. The upper part of the table focuses on the "pure" restructuring effect, ignoring the effect of capital controls. The main difficulty in computing the losses is how to discount the payment flows in view of the fact that the Russian domestic debt market was wiped out after the default, so there are no secondary market prices at which the new instruments could be valued, and no "exit yield" at which to discount the original instruments. To deal with this, we construct two alternative sets of discount rates, one as the sum of the sovereign default risk premium on external debt and the ninety-day interbank rate, and the other based on a declining path of discount rates in line with the actual future path in ninety-day interest rates. The table shows the "haircuts" received by investors who were able to obtain the shortest OFZ offered in the exchange; to the extent that investors received longer OFZs, haircuts would have been higher by about 6–10 percentage points (see Sturzenegger and Zettelmeyer 2005 for details). For brevity, we only show haircuts for four GKOs that would have matured prior to the exchange and four maturing after the exchange. The "haircuts" are computed, in percentage terms, by subtracting the total new value obtained from the present value of the old claim and dividing by the latter. The numbers indicate that—even ignoring the effect of withdrawal restrictions—nonresident investors lost at least 41–55 percent of the preexisting claim (depending on the discount rate applied and the GKO tendered).

Russian institutional holders, which were required to hold GKO/OFZs by law, received slightly different terms (10 percent cash, 10 percent in three-month GKOs, 10 percent in six-month GKOs, 20 percent in cash value OFZs and 50 percent in OFZs with maturities ranging from four to five years). The larger share of cash payments implied a slightly improved deal, by about 2–4 percent for investors receiving the shortest OFZ, depending again on the discount rate that is applied.

The lower half of the table shows the total losses suffered by nonresidents, including the effect of the repatriation restriction. This restriction took a relatively simple form, namely, that funds had to be deposited in noninterest bearing accounts for one year before they could be repatriated. In other words, ignoring the domestic uses of funds sitting in restricted ruble accounts, the effect of the repatriation restriction was equivalent to postponing payments by one year. Given

Table 4.3
Russian GKO exchange, March 1999: Haircuts (per 100 units of principal)

GKOs maturing on…	11/04/98	12/02/98	01/13/99	02/10/99	03/10/99	04/07/99	05/05/99	06/09/99
Present value on March 1, 1999	106.8	105.8	102.9	101.2	98.5	94.3	90.1	85.2
Compound or discount rate used (in percent)[a]	22.3	25.7	24.2	22.8	79.9	79.9	79.9	79.9
Values obtained and haircuts, not taking into account the effect of repatriation restrictions								
using downward sloping discount path:								
Value obtained[b]	62.7	60.7	58.0	56.2	54.4	52.7	51.1	49.2
Haircut	41.3	42.6	43.7	44.4	44.8	44.1	43.3	42.3
using constant discount rate of 79.9:								
Value obtained[b]	51.6	50.0	47.7	46.3	44.8	43.4	42.1	40.5
Haircut	51.7	52.8	53.6	54.2	54.6	53.9	53.3	52.5
Values obtained and haircuts, including the effect of repatriation restrictions								
using downward sloping discount path:								
Value obtained[b]	50.4	48.9	46.7	45.3	43.8	42.5	41.1	39.6
Haircut	52.8	53.8	54.7	55.3	55.6	55.0	54.3	53.5
using constant discount rate of 79.9:								
Value obtained[b]	35.6	34.5	32.9	31.9	30.9	29.9	29.0	27.9
Haircut	66.7	67.4	68.0	68.4	68.7	68.2	67.8	67.2

Source: Sturzenegger and Zettelmeyer (2005).
[a] For GKOs maturing prior to March 1, average ruble deposit rates were used for compounding. For those maturing after this date, the estimated post-restructuring GKO yield was used (see text).
[b] Assuming access to the shortest OFZ (longer dated ruble-denominated instrument) available in the exchange.

the prevailing interest rates, this raised haircuts by 8–15 percentage points above the figures shown in the upper half of the table.[7]

By the end of May 1999, about 95 percent of residents and 89 percent of nonresidents had agreed to the terms of the GKO-OFZ exchange. Nonresidents who decided not to participate were repaid in full, but had to place their proceeds in restricted accounts in combination with a five-year repatriation restriction. Given the high interest environment, this amounted to a "haircut" of similar magnitude as that suffered by investors that accepted the exchange.

In spite of the working agreement with GKO holders, a large amortization coming due in May 1999 prompted the government to miss the final repayment on yet another debt instrument, the Soviet-era, dollar-denominated, MinFin3. Furthermore, on June 2, 1999, Vneshekonombank missed a payment on the IANs issued as a result of the 1997 London Club restructuring of Soviet-era debt. However, at that point the IMF was back on board and negotiations were underway to restructure both Prins and IANs.

On July 28, 1999, the IMF approved a seventeen-month $4.5 billion Stand-by Arrangement to support the government's 1999–2000 economic program. This credit was to be released in seven equal disbursements of $640 million. The IMF praised the improvement in Russia's fiscal situation as the basis for its decision to resume lending. After the agreement with the IMF, in August 1999, the Paris Club rescheduled $8.1 billion in Soviet-era debts that was due between 1999 and 2000, allowing a repayment period of nineteen years with two years of grace.

In January 2000, the government began to restructure its defaulted dollar debt by offering to exchange the MinFin3 bond defaulted in May 1999 by either a new eight-year dollar-denominated bond with similar terms as the original instrument, or a four-year OFZ denominated in rubles. Based on the U.S. dollar option (the OFZ option reportedly attracted little interest), and using the yield of performing Russian external bonds at the time to discount the new payment flows, the implicit haircut was about 63 percent (see Sturzenegger and Zettelmeyer 2005 for details).

On February 11, 2000, this was followed by an offer to exchange Vneshekonombank's Prins and IANs for new Eurobonds of the Russian Federation. In exchange for their principal, bondholders were offered a 2030 Eurobond with a step-up (2.25–7.5 percent) coupon, after a face value reduction of 37.5 percent for the longer maturity Prins and 33 percent for the shorter maturity IANs. 9.5 percent of accumulated past due interest (PDI) was compensated in cash, while the remaining PDI was exchanged one-for-one by a 2010 Eurobond with a fixed 8.25 percent coupon.

The new instruments had a number of interesting features (JP Morgan 2000):

• There was an *upgrade in the obligor*. The Prins and IANs were technically debts of Vneshekonombank. Now Russia assumed that debt directly.

• The new bonds included *expanded cross-acceleration clauses* by which the Russian Federation committed to include in any *new* issues clauses to ensure equal status in the event of default/acceleration of the 2010 and 2030 bonds. The clauses would be symmetric, tying default on the 2010 and 2030 bonds to new issues of Russian Federation Eurobonds.

• Holders of both existing and new issues of the Russian Federation would *have the right to put back* to Russia at par those bonds, in the event of acceleration of the 2010 and 2030 bonds. This right would expire once Russia issued at least $US1 billion of new Eurobonds.

• Russia retained the right to *retap* the new bonds without prior notice.

A minimum threshold of 75 percent of bondholders was announced; if participation were to fall below that threshold, the exchange could still go forward but only with the consent of the creditors that had agreed to tender. No mention was made of the 95 and 98 percent collective action thresholds originally established in the terms and conditions of the Prins and IANs. This was considered a "voluntary" exchange, so collective action clauses were not invoked. In the end, participation was extremely high (about 99 percent). The deal was closed in August

Table 4.4
Russian Prins/IANs restructuring, 2/2000–8/2000: Haircuts (per 100 units of principal)

	Prins	IANs
Amount outstanding (in millions of U.S. dollars)	22,231	6,847
Due date	12/15/2020	12/15/2015
Present value at exchange	70.4	74.4
Discount rate used (in percent)[a]	16.4	16.2
Total new value obtained	33.7	34.1
Haircut	52.1	54.1

Source: Sturzenegger and Zettelmeyer (2005).
[a] Based on linear interpolation of outstanding Eurobond yields.

2000, with $21 billion of new instruments issued in exchange for the
original nominal value of US$31.8 billion.

Unlike the new instruments issued in the GKO and MinFin
exchanges, secondary market prices are available for the new Eurobonds issued immediately after the exchange, as well as for other performing Russian Federation Eurobonds that were trading at the time.
The methodology outlined in the introduction to part II can thus be applied without having to resort to constructed discount rates. Table 4.4
indicates holders of Prins and IANs lost over 50 percent in NPV terms,
discounted using Eurobond yields prevailing immediately after the
exchange. In contrast, Russian-era dollar-denominated bonds—both
MinFins and Eurobonds—were continually serviced throughout the
crisis (so were the "Soviet-era" MinFin 4 and 5). Hence, Russia managed to maintain its commitment to service Russian-era international
debt throughout the 1998–2000 default and restructuring episode,
while defaulting both on some Soviet-era debt (including the Prins
and IANs that had already been restructured once) and on domestic
debt. The overall effect of the restructurings was a substantial reduction in Russia's debt obligations through 2013 (figure 4.5). Figure 4.6
shows how investors fared prior and after the deal. The figure shows

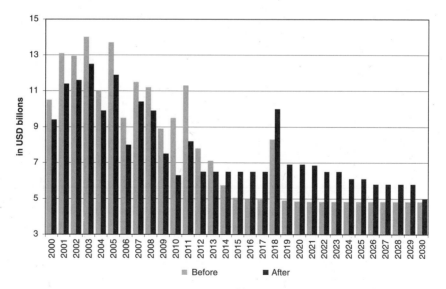

Figure 4.5
Total debt service before and after the exchange
Source: IMF (2000).

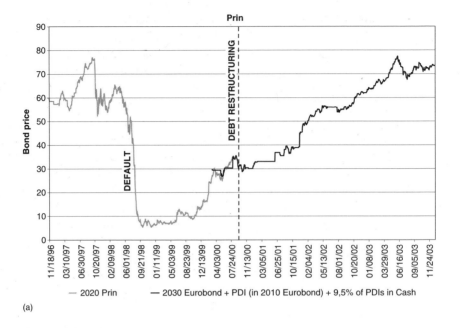

(a)

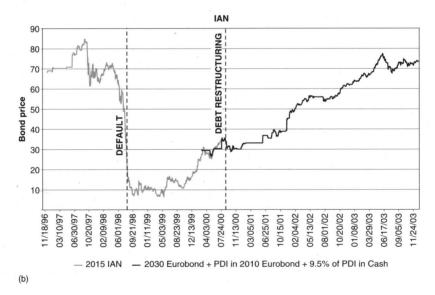

(b)

Figure 4.6
Bond prices before and after the exchange
Source: Bloomberg and authors' computations.

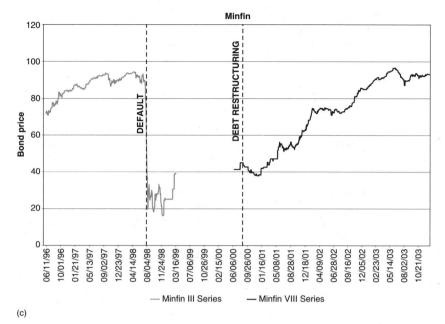

Figure 4.6
(continued)

the value of an original claim and the value of what was obtained in exchange. As expected, at the time of the exchange the market value of the original claim equaled the market value of what was offered by the government. Prior to the restructuring, defaulted debt allowed quick gains. At the height of pessimism, Prins and IANs traded below ten cents. Buying at the trough (eight cents) and holding until the exchange offer would have delivered a 400 percent gain.

Once the banking crisis had been overcome, the highly competitive exchange rate and a recovery in oil prices translated into a surge in exports and a sharp rebound in economy activity. Economic growth reached 6.3 percent in 1999 and 10 percent in 2000. Fiscal performance improved vastly, for reasons related to the increase in oil prices and the devaluation—as the price level rise reduced real expenditures, and an export tax offered an easy way to raise revenue—but also because a number of important fiscal structural reforms finally took hold in 1999 (Robinson 2003b). Ironically, the fiscal outturn in 1999 was significantly better than what the failed precrisis adjustment program of July 1998 had targeted. With an appreciating real exchange rate, this meant

Box 4.1
Chronology of Russia's crisis and debt restructuring

1989: End of Soviet planning.

1991: New government defaults on Soviet-era debt.

1992:

January: Prices are freed and consumer prices increase 2,500 percent.

1993:

April: Russian government declares itself responsible for Soviet debt.

May: Ministry of Finance issues $5-denominated MinFin bonds.

1995:

March: Stand-by Arrangement with IMF is approved. Inflation stabilization.

November: Agreement in principle is reached with London Club creditors on rescheduling of commercial bank debt defaulted in 1992.

1996:

Domestic (GKO/OFZ) ruble-denominated T-bill market is organized.

March: The IMF approves three-year Extended Fund Facility (EFF) program.

April: Paris Club agrees to restructure $40 billion of Soviet-era debt.

July 3: President Yeltsin wins second term in office after defeating Communist Party leader Gennady Zyuganov in a runoff election.

1997:

January–July: Sharp fall in oil prices.

December: Agreement with London Club is finalized. Soviet-era debt is restructured into two new securities: $22 billion of principal notes (Prins) and $6 billion of interest arrears notes (IANs).

1998:

March: Sergei Kiriyenko is appointed prime minister.

June: Market for GKOs dries up. Government announces "anticrisis" plan.

July 14–20: Voluntary GKO swap transforms $4.4 billion GKO into seven- and twenty-year Eurobonds.

July 20: IMF approves a crisis package, making available a first tranche of $4.8 billion.

August 17: Russia devalues and defaults on GKOs and OFZs. Ninety-day moratorium on external payments.

August 18: Moody's Investors Service downgrades its ratings on all Russian corporate debt issuers.

August 23: Yeltsin dismisses Prime Minister Sergei Kiriyenko, and negotiations to restructure public debt collapse. Bank depositors panic.

August 25: Government announces GKO restructuring plan. Proposal is rejected by the market.

September 2: Exchange rate band is abolished. The ruble plunges.

September 11: After rejecting Viktor Chernomyrdin on two occasions, the Duma accepts Yevgeny Primakov as prime minister.

December 2: Vneshekonombank misses a $362 million payment on its Prins.

Box 4.1
(continued)

1999:

March 1999: Defaulted GKO and OFZs are restructured under the "novation scheme."

May 14: Russia defaults on MinFin3.

June 2: Vneshekonombank misses a payment on the IANs.

July 28: IMF approves seventeen-month $4.5 billion Stand-by Arrangement.

August 1: Paris Club reschedules $8.1 billion Soviet-era debts due in 1999–2000.

December 31: Yeltsin resigns and is replaced by Vladimir Putin.

2000:

January: Open-ended restructuring offer is made for MinFin3.

February 11: Offers are made to exchange IANs and Prins for Russian Federation Eurobonds.

August: Exchange offer closes with 99 percent participation.

---

that all drivers of the debt dynamics turned positive (table 4.2). Combining these effects with the effects of the debt restructuring, 2000 alone witnessed a reduction in the debt-to-GDP ratio of close to 30 percent. The declining trend continued over the following years. As asset prices recovered, Russia became a star performer within the emerging market class. As shown in figure 4.6, investors recovered, albeit with a time lag, most of the money lost, even after factoring the nominal haircuts suffered in the restructuring. By 2005 Russia had fully repaid its debt to the IMF, as well as a substantial portion of its Paris Club obligations, which were fully repaid in 2006. In early 2006 its foreign exchange reserves topped $200 billion, making them the fourth largest among emerging market countries.

5   Ukraine

The collapse of the Soviet Union in 1991 reestablished Ukraine as an independent country, forcing its bureaucracy and political establishment to deal with unprecedented economic problems. Over the next years, Ukraine suffered a hyperinflation, and experienced output losses that were even worse than in neighboring Russia (table 5.1). As a newly independent country, Ukraine began its transition to a market economy without debts inherited from a previous regime.[1] However, as in Russia and other neighboring economies, economic liberalization was accompanied by fiscal imbalances that initially manifested themselves in high inflation and later in rapid debt accumulation. Table 5.2 shows how primary imbalances, output contraction, and interest costs pushed to increase the debt-to-GDP ratios, only partly compensated by a real exchange rate appreciation until about 1997.

As in Russia, monetary stabilization outpaced fiscal stabilization. In part, this was because of the sheer magnitude and stubbornness of the fiscal problem—including poor expenditure control, a culture of payments in noncash terms, and large subsidies to noncompetitive industries. In part, it was due to the continued drop in output. Although producer subsidies were substantially reduced in 1995 and 1996, large fiscal deficits remained, financed through a combination of borrowing from the CBR, assistance from international financial institutions, the accumulation of wage and pension arrears, and, since March 1995, a fledgling treasury bill (T-bill) market. As monetary financing and net borrowing from official creditors declined, the issue of Hryvnia-denominated T-bills to both domestic and international investors became more important as a source of financing.

Given its relatively low debt, Ukraine did not find it very difficult to tap financial markets. Major external investors included hedge funds

Table 5.1
Ukraine: Selected economic indicators, 1994–2004

	1994	1995	1996	1997	1998	1999	2000	2001	2002	2003	2004
Output and prices						(annual percentage changes)					
Real GDP	-22.9	-12.2	-10.0	-3.0	-1.9	-0.2	5.9	9.2	5.2	9.6	12.1
Consumer prices (period average)	891.2	376.7	80.3	15.9	10.6	22.7	28.2	12.0	0.8	5.2	9.0
Hryvnia per U.S. dollar (period average)	622.6	349.8	24.2	1.8	31.6	68.6	31.7	-2.6	0.6	0.0	-0.5
Terms of trade (goods)	-9.7	-8.2	-10.9	-0.3	4.7	9.2	-2.9	1.3	1.6	8.6	13.1
Public finances						(in percent of GDP)					
Revenue (including grants)	41.9	37.8	36.7	38.0	36.0	33.8	33.4	33.5	36.0	35.9	35.0
Expenditures	50.6	44.2	41.5	45.4	41.1	38.8	37.7	36.9	37.2	37.8	40.3
Noninterest	49.5	41.2	38.4	41.7	36.3	33.5	31.7	32.9	34.6	35.8	38.4
Interest	1.1	1.5	1.6	1.8	2.4	2.6	3.0	2.0	1.3	1.0	0.9
Primary balance	-7.6	-3.4	-1.6	-3.7	-0.4	0.2	1.7	0.6	1.4	0.1	-3.5
Overall balance	-8.7	-6.4	-4.8	-7.4	-5.1	-5.0	-4.3	-3.4	-1.2	-1.9	-5.3
Total public sector debt[a]	...	25.6	27.9	33.3	37.4	52.8	47.1	38.6	35.7	27.7	25.1
Foreign currency	...	23.0	20.1	19.2	26.5	39.5	33.1	26.3	24.1	21.6	19.2
Domestic currency	...	2.6	7.9	14.1	10.9	13.3	14.0	12.3	11.6	6.1	6.0
Money						(annual percentage changes)					
Reserve money	407.4	132.8	39.9	49.0	16.6	41.3	43.8	42.5	23.8	30.1	37.3
Refinancing rate (in percent)[b]	252.0	110.0	40.0	35.0	60.0	45.0	27.0	12.5	7.0	7.0	9.0
External sector						(in billions of U.S. dollars unless otherwise indicated)					
Total imports, fob	15.3	16.5	16.9	19.8	19.6	16.3	12.9	14.9	16.9	18.0	24.0
Total exports, fob	12.8	12.1	14.2	15.5	15.4	13.7	12.5	15.7	17.1	18.7	23.7

Current account	-1.4	-1.9	-1.2	-1.5	-1.3	0.8	1.5	1.4	3.2	2.9	6.8
Current account (in percent of GDP)	-3.8	-5.2	-2.7	-3.0	-3.1	2.6	4.7	3.6	7.5	5.8	10.4
Gross reserves	0.7	1.1	2.0	2.3	0.8	1.0	1.4	3.0	4.2	6.7	9.3
					(annual percentage changes)						
Export volumes	-14.0	4.9	9.4	-2.7	-12.4	-10.2	16.5	7.0	7.1	14.2	16.5
Import volumes	-11.7	-15.7	4.5	-3.2	-14.3	-14.3	3.5	12.8	5.9	30.4	15.7
Reference items:											
Nominal GDP (in billions of hryvnias)	12.0	54.5	81.5	93.4	102.6	130.4	170.1	204.2	225.8	267.3	345.9
Exchange rate (hryvnia per U.S. dollar, period average)	0.3	1.5	1.8	1.9	2.4	4.1	5.4	5.3	5.3	5.3	5.3

Source: National authorities and IMF.

[a] Overall public sector debt stock, including government guarantees and domestic arrears. Debt ratios refer to debt in U.S. dollars divided by GDP in U.S. dollars, using period average exchange rates. This differs from the way Ukraine's debt ratios are usually presented —namely, by converting all debt to local currency units, at end-period exchange rates, and dividing by GDP in local currency.

[b] Central bank policy rate.

Table 5.2
Ukraine: Debt dynamics, 1995–2004 (in percent of GDP unless otherwise stated)

	1995	1996	1997	1998	1999	2000	2001	2002	2003	2004
Total public sector debt[a]	25.6	27.9	33.3	37.4	52.8	47.1	38.6	35.7	27.7	25.1
Change in debt ratio attributable to...		2.3	5.4	4.1	15.4	−5.7	−8.5	−2.9	−8.0	−2.6
Primary deficit		1.6	3.7	0.4	−0.2	−1.7	−0.4	−1.8	−0.1	3.5
Real interest rate		1.5	1.6	1.6	1.4	1.7	1.2	0.7	0.4	0.4
Real growth		2.8	0.8	0.7	0.1	−2.9	−3.9	−1.9	−3.1	−2.9
Real depreciation		−7.0	−3.6	1.1	8.4	3.9	−3.6	−1.0	−1.8	−2.7
Cross-terms		−0.4	−0.2	0.4	0.7	0.2	−0.3	−0.1	−0.1	−0.2
Residual[b]		3.8	3.0	0.0	5.1	−6.9	−1.5	1.2	−3.3	−0.6

[a] Overall public sector debt stock, including government guarantees and domestic arrears. Debt ratios refer to debt in U.S. dollars divided by GDP in U.S. dollars, using period average exchange rates.
[b] Reflects debt stock adjustments (including debt restructurings in 1998 and 2000), nondebt financing such as privatization receipts, and measurement error.

and investment banks (among them Merrill Lynch, Warburg Dillon Read, ING Barings, and Credit Suisse First Boston). Until the fourth quarter of 1997, new T-bill issues were easily oversubscribed. OVDPs, as Ukraine's short-term (mostly 6- to 12-month) treasury instruments were known, had none of the foreign ownership restrictions that had complicated access to the Russian GKO market, and were one of the few ways to gain exposure to Ukrainian credit risk.

Notwithstanding Ukraine's lack of a credit rating and a history of external payment arrears related to energy imports, nonresidents rapidly absorbed OVDPs, to the tune of $1.5 billion in the course of 1997. At the end of the year, foreigners held almost half the outstanding stock of T-bills, while Ukrainian banks and the National Bank of Ukraine (NBU) held the remainder in roughly equal shares. At the same time, Ukraine began to borrow directly in external debt markets. In August 1997, it issued its first international bond, a one-year Eurobond that raised $396 million at a 12 percent interest rate. In October 1997, it raised $99 million through a one-year loan organized by Chase Manhattan at a 10 percent interest rate. While most of Ukraine's 1993 debt had been bilateral (mostly owed to the Russian Federation), by the end of 1997, bilateral debt amounted to just 40 percent of the total.

Borrowing conditions sharply deteriorated in the last quarter of 1997, in part, because of concerns about the slow pace of fiscal and structural reforms, and, in part, because of a change in investor sentiment following the Asian crisis. Yields in the domestic T-bill market more than doubled from about 22 percent in September to 45 percent in December. Nonresident purchases in the domestic T-bill market dried up in the first quarter of 1998 and were replaced by NBU T-bill purchases and new issues of external debt. In the first half of 1998, Ukraine raised $1.1 billion in international capital markets, at increasingly unfavorable terms. A three-year DM 750 million Eurobond at a 16 percent annual interest rate was issued in February 1998, a two-year Ecu 500 million Eurobond at 14.75 percent in March 1998, and a second 260 million tranche of the DM Eurobond in May 1998. Finally, to help repay the maturing $450 million Eurobond issued in August 1997, Ukraine obtained $155 million through a bond placement organized by ING Barings in early August 1998. This bond had a maturity of ten months, carried a hryvnia interest rate of 55 percent, and a guaranteed minimum dollar return of 17.5 percent.

The Russian Crisis and September Devaluation

Following the Russian financial crisis in August 1998, the market for government debt dried up altogether, at a time when large repayments on T-bills issued in the second half of 1997 began to come due. Ukraine's gross official reserves had more than halved from about $2.4 billion at the beginning of 1998 to about $1 billion in late August 1998, as T-bills held by foreigners and banks were not rolled over and the resulting monetary financing put pressure on the exchange rate (see Figures 5.1, 5.2, and 5.3).[2] Additionally, the deterioration of the essential Russian market weakened Ukrainian exports and put further pressure on the exchange rate (Russia absorbed about a quarter of Ukraine's exports).

On September 4, 1998, the reserves drain led the NBU to move the fluctuation band for the Hryvnia from 1.85–2.25 to 2.5–3.5 Hryvnia per U.S. dollar. Foreign exchange market restrictions were imposed as well. A 50 percent (increased to 75 percent three days later) obligation to surrender export proceeds was imposed and margins between the official exchange rate and the bank rate were not allowed to exceed 10 percent (decreased to 5 percent three days later). Advance payments on imports were forbidden. Banks lost their permission to give residents credits in foreign currency and their ability to purchase foreign currency was severely restricted. The NBU closed the interbank market for foreign exchange, forcing all transactions on the official market.

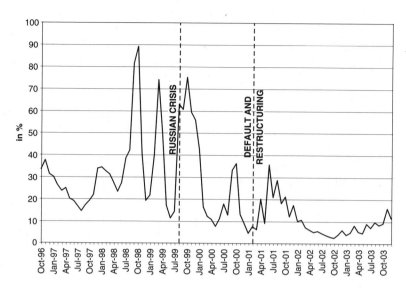

Figure 5.1
Money market interest rates
Source: IFS.

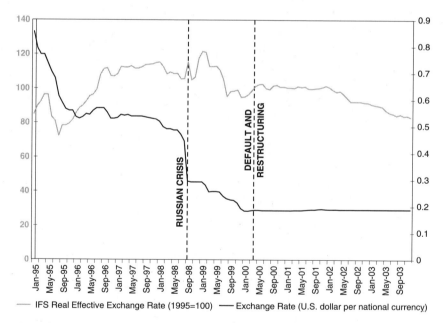

Figure 5.2
Nominal and real exchange rates
Source: IFS.

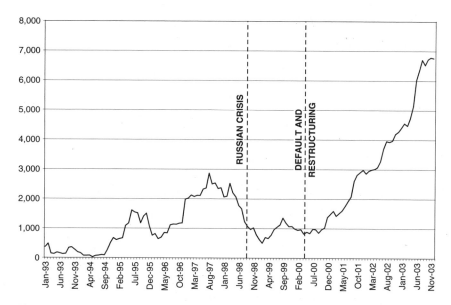

Figure 5.3
International reserves (in millions of U.S. dollars)
Source: IFS.

To help stabilize Ukraine, limit further contagion from the Russian crisis, and support a new round fiscal and structural reform efforts, the IMF approved a three-year $2.2 billion EFF on September 4, 1998. The World Bank also approved credits, worth about $900 million, tied to structural reforms and compliance with the requirements of the EFF. A key assumption of the EFF program was that Ukraine's debt would be restructured in a way that avoided use of IMF money to bail out private creditors.[3] At the same time, both the Ukrainian authorities and the IMF wanted to avoid an outright default.[4] Since Ukraine was at this point cut off from any new private financing, these objectives could be reconciled only by persuading creditors to agree to a debt exchange.

The Fall 1998 Debt Exchanges

Beginning in August 1998, the Ukrainian government began to negotiate debt exchanges with three groups of creditors: domestic commercial banks that were holders of treasury bills (OVDPs), nonresident holders of T-bills, and holders of the loan placed through Chase Manhattan in October 1997. A conversion scheme for treasury bills owned by domestic banks was announced on August 26, 1998. It offered to ex-change T-bills into longer-term hryvnia-denominated bonds of three to six years maturity. A range of exchange coefficients was determined in line with the present value of the T-bills at the time of the exchange, discounted at the prevailing T-bill rate of about 60 percent. The interest rate on the new bonds was set at 40 percent for the first year, and a floating coupon equal to the future six-month T-bill yield plus 1 per-centage point for the remainder of the period. The NBU indicated that all banks participating in the package would be given emergency short-term financing to guarantee liquidity if necessary, while banks that refused to participate would not be eligible to receive any emer-gency financing. According to the IMF (IMF Country Report No. 99/42, 43), commercial banks eventually agreed to exchange about Hrv 800 million, or about one-third of their portfolio.

Table 5.3 shows the haircuts for both a just issued and a just matured OVDP at the time of the exchange; because of the application of ex-change coefficients in line with present value, the haircuts of all other outstanding T-bills were very close.[5] The haircut appears to have been very mild, on the order of 5–10 percent for a domestic bondholder at the time of the exchange. The low value of the haircut derives from the fact that the government forced an interest rate reduction during the first year, but promised the market rate thereafter. This is consistent with the notion, advanced in market commentary at the time, that the Ukraine government was trying to avoid a harsh Russian-style default and restructuring, and instead was seeking to resolve a liquidity crisis mainly by extending maturities.

Foreign bondholders faced a similar conversion but on different terms. Holders could choose between a hryvnia-denominated bond with a 22 percent hedged annual yield or a two-year zero-coupon dollar-denominated Eurobond with a yield of 20 percent. Some holders that had purchased currency hedges—specifically, holders of nine- and twelve-month T-bills issued to nonresidents in December 1997 through Merrill Lynch—additionally received 20 percent of the present value of their principal in cash (hryvnia), exchanged into dollars at the market exchange rate of 2.94 prevailing on September 22, 1998. Table 5.3 shows the haircuts for four T-bills held by nonresidents: the two bills we examined previously, assuming that investors opted for the Euro-bond (as was reportedly the case for 97 percent of nonresident debt), and the two T-bills featuring guaranteed minimum dollar returns mar-keted through Merrill Lynch.

Table 5.3
Ukraine debt exchanges, 1998–1999: Haircuts (per 100 units of principal)

	OVDPs-residents 26-Aug-98		OVDPs-nonresidents 22-Sep-98				Chase loan 20-Oct-98	ING loan 20-Aug-99
	Maturing	Just issued	Unhedged		With $-hedge			
	(1)	(2)	(3)	(4)	(5)	(6)	(5)	(6)
Issue date	various	08/19/98	various	08/19/98	12/19/97	12/19/97	10/20/97	08/09/98
Amount issued and outstanding (in millions of U.S. dollars)	...	35.0	...	35.0	197.8	197.8	109.0	163.0
Due date	08/27/98	08/18/99	08/27/98	08/18/99	09/18/98	12/18/98	10/20/98	07/09/99
Present value at exchange	100.0	63.1	100.0	50.6	136.9	114.4	100.0	100.0
Discount rate used (in percent)	matured	60.0[a]	matured	112.6[b]	matured	74.1[c]	matured	matured
Total new value obtained	91.5	60.0	47.5	31.1	58.0	51.6	69.3	62.0
Haircut	8.5	5.0	52.5	38.4	57.6	54.9	30.7	38.0

Source: Sturzenegger and Zettelmeyer (2005).
[a] Illustrative; see text.
[b] Yield of 2001 DM Eurobond (adjusted for forward U.S. dollar per DM exchange rate) plus twelve-month consensus forecast change in UAH per U.S. dollar exchange rate.
[c] Yield of 2001 DM Eurobond (adjusted for forward U.S. dollar per DM exchange rate).

The main result is the much larger haircut suffered by nonresidents compared with the resident OVDP holders. What drives this is the low value of the new Eurobond, whose 20 percent coupon was much below the market yield (around 75 percent) of Ukraine's only foreign currency bond trading in secondary markets at the time (namely, a DM-denominated bond maturing in early 2001). Of the two T-bills shown, the longer T-bill suffered a smaller haircut, because the haircut computation assumes that the default risk that was implicit in the yield of the foreign currency bond would also have applied to the T-bill, depressing the value of the old instrument. Finally, holders who had purchased dollar hedges did significantly better in terms of values received than did unhedged OVDP holders, by virtue of the fact that they received about 20 percent of principal in cash.[6] However, their currency hedges also entitled them to a larger payment compared with unhedged investors. This much higher contractual entitlement was partly, but not fully, offset by the higher value received, resulting in a higher haircut (of around 55 percent) for the hedged instruments.

Table 5.3 suggests that resident holders of OVDPs were treated much better than nonresident holders, even those who had purchased currency hedges. How literally should one take this result? To this, two things can be said. First, the floating rate OVDPs offered to residents, which were attractive to the extent that they insured holders of restructured bonds against future increases in default risk, were not offered to nonresidents. In that sense, residents were, in fact, treated better. Second, nonresident investors worried about capital controls (see *International Financing Review*, no. 1251) because of the controls imposed in early September. The benefit of avoiding such controls in the future by receiving an instrument that paid in dollars is not reflected in our haircut calculations. In this respect, the exchanges discriminated in favor of nonresident investors, since only they were offered dollar instruments. This makes the packages received by resident and nonresident investors difficult to compare.

In addition to the OVDP restructurings, Ukraine also restructured the $109 million fiduciary loan issued through Chase Manhattan coming due on October 20, 1998. Holders received a 25 percent cash payment, while the remainder of their claim was restructured into a new amortizing loan with a dollar interest rate of 16.75 percent. Principal payment would be limited to $2 million per quarter during 1999; the balance would be paid in four equal installments in 2000. The penultimate column in table 5.3 shows the haircut on this restructuring. As the new loan did not trade, we again use the yield on Ukraine's DM Eurobond (adjusted to a dollar rate using the DM-US forward interest rate differential) for discounting. At around 30 percent, the haircut was lower than for the hedged OVDPs held by nonresidents, driven by the higher cash payment and somewhat faster amortization of the new Chase loan compared with the Merrill Lynch Eurobond.

The August 1999 Exchange

In February 1999, the NBU established a new official currency exchange band of 3.4–4.6 hryvnia per dollar. Although the NBU lifted most currency transaction restrictions between March and June 1999 (including the ban on advance payment on import contracts) and opened a foreign exchange interbank market, some restrictions remained (e.g., the mandatory sale of 50 percent of hard currency revenues).

In February and March 1999, debt service payments on the outstanding DM and euro Eurobonds were made punctually. In the face of a bunching of debt service in the second quarter—in particular, a maturing ten-month bond placed through ING Barings in August 1998 ($163 million including interest)—the government was again forced to seek a restructuring to avoid violating the reserves target set by the program with the IMF.

On May 18, 1999, the Ministry of Finance submitted to ING a debt conversion offer, according to which 20 percent would be repaid on time, with the remainder swapped for a new international bond with a three-year maturity. The ING bond was mostly held by one investor—Regent Pacific Group—which initially insisted on full repayment. Ukraine's first offer was rejected, and the original repayment date passed. On July 15, 1999, the Ministry of Finance and ING Barings finally reached an agreement according to which 20 percent of the bond would be repaid in cash, with the remainder exchanged for DM bonds that were to be added to the existing DM 1 billion Eurobond issued in 1998 and due in February 2001, with a coupon of 16 percent. The implicit present value loss to investors was about 38 percent (table 5.3, last column). On August 2, 1999, Ukraine made the 20 percent cash payment to ING Barings, and on August 20, it tagged the original 2001 DM Eurobond for the remainder.

In addition to the ING bondholders, holders of the restructured $500 million zero-coupon Eurobond issued through Merrill Lynch in the previous fall were invited to enter the exchange.[7] At the time of the announcement, the dollar-denominated zero-coupon bond was trading at 30 cents, while the DM bonds were trading at 75 cents. Following the announcement, the price of the DM bonds fell to 60 cents while the price of the zero coupon bonds rose to 40 cents. Thus, the exchange offer benefited holders of the Merrill Lynch Eurobond at the expense of incumbent holders of the DM bond. In the event, the offer received almost 50 percent acceptance among the Merrill Lynch bondholders.

The 2000 Restructuring

While the piecemeal restructurings of 1998–99 provided some immediate cash flow relief, they also created large payments obligations for 2000 and 2001. In addition, the debt burden had increased as a result of the depreciation of the real exchange rate. The debt-to-GDP ratio increased by about 15 percent in 1999, driven mostly by the larger burden of foreign-currency-denominated debt.

For 2000, Ukraine's debt service obligations were about $3 billion, of which about $1.1 billion were due to bondholders (principal and interest), $900 million to the IMF, and $250 million to Russia. About $1.2 billion were coming due in the first quarter, with payments of almost $800 million in February. Gross international reserves stood at only around $1 billion at the end of 1999. There was no hope for any significant amount of new borrowing, particularly since the program with the IMF had gone off track in the last quarter of 1999 as structural reforms were progressing poorly, and several fiscal targets had been missed. Consequently, Ukraine had no alternative but to seek a new restructuring. This time, however, it took a much more comprehensive approach, seeking to restructure all outstanding commercial bonds rather than just the closest maturing instrument, and aimed at significantly longer maturity extensions than had been achieved by the 1998–1999 exchanges.

On February 4, 2000, Ukraine offered to exchange its outstanding bonds—two Eurobonds issued in early 1998, the restructured Chase Manhattan bond, the remainder of the restructured Merrill Lynch Eurobond, and about $1 billion of "Gazprom bonds" falling due between March 2000 and March 2007—for two seven-year coupon amortization bonds denominated either in euros or U.S. dollars, to be issued under English law (table 5.4). For the euro-denominated bond, the coupon was set at 10 percent, while for the U.S. dollar-denominated bond it

Table 5.4
Ukraine external debt exchange, February–April 2000: Haircuts (per 100 units of principal)

	2000 US$ Eurobond	Chase Manhattan	Merrill-Lynch	2001 DM Eurobond	Gazprom bonds[a]
Issue date	3/1/98	10/20/98	10/1/98	26/02/1998	21/03/1995
Amount outstanding (in millions of U.S. dollars)[b]	493	74	258	756	1,015
Currency of denomination	Euro	US$	US$	DM	US$
Due date	3/1/00	10/20/00	10/1/00	2/26/01	3/21/07
Present value on 2/4/2000	112.4	73.6	84.8	90.4	63.8
Discount rate used (in percent)[c]	27.6	27.9	28.1	28.3	29.5
Total value obtained	73.5	65.6	55.7	75.7	50.0
Haircut based on choice of U.S. dollar bond	34.6	33.4	34.3	28.9	21.7

Source: Sturzenegger and Zettelmeyer (2005).
[a] Simple average, that is, synthetic instrument consiting of all twenty-nine outstanding Gazprom bonds in equal parts.
[b] Evaluated using February 4, 2000, market exchange rates.
[c] Yield to maturity of new bond of corresponding currency, with minor maturity adjustment based on U.S. yield curve.

was set at 11 percent.[8] The exchange was to take place at full face value except for the zero coupon Merrill Lynch Eurobond, where 95 cents of new debt principal were offered for each dollar of old principal, and for the "Gazprom bonds," where declining exchange coefficients between 1 and 0.67 were to be applied, depending on the maturity date. Accrued interest was to be paid in full and in cash to accepting investors after the completion of the exchange. The exchange offer was conditional on a minimum participation of 85 percent among the holders of bonds maturing in 2000–2001 (all Eurobond holders and the holders of $280 million Gazprom bonds maturing in 2000–2001).

To deter holdouts, Ukraine decided not to make two principal payments falling due in January 2000 and a coupon payment falling due on another bond issue in February 2000. After the original exchange deadline was extended from March 15 to April 7, 2000, Ukraine also missed the principal repayment of the euro 500 million Eurobond, which matured on March 17. According to the IMF (2001), these payments were missed for "intercreditor equity" reasons, namely, to avoid paying some investors in full during or immediately before a debt restructuring offer. During the period in which the exchange offer was open, Ukraine was thus temporarily in default, and exposed to the risk of litigation.

In the event, no litigation took place either before or after the exchange. Two of Ukraine's international bonds (the restructured Chase Manhattan and Merrill Lynch bonds) were held by a relatively limited number of investment banks and hedge funds. Thus, the government could establish a dialogue to gauge what conditions would be acceptable to creditors, and the proposal of one fund manager to use litigation did not attract the support of other investors. Moreover, all bonds except for the 2001 DM Eurobond included collective action clauses allowing investors holding a qualified majority of the principal to modify the payment terms.

Collective action clauses (CACs) were in fact invoked preemptively, as follows. According to the terms of the exchange, accepting holders of CAC bonds were required to hand their votes to an exchange agent who would act as their proxy at a bondholders' meeting. The calling of such meetings was predicated upon the receipt of proxy votes reflecting at least 75 percent of outstanding principal; this threshold was met in all cases. At the meeting, the payments terms of the bonds were then modified so they were exactly the same as the payments terms of the new bonds (but different with regard to their nonpayment terms, which were not modified). Following the meeting, bondholders tendered these modified instruments in exchange for the new issues with the same payment terms and a consistent documentation. Any dissenting bondholder would hence be left with a modified instrument that had identical payment terms as the new issues but different documentation, and was therefore illiquid. Thus, dissenting bondholders could not only be forced to accept the new payment terms, they could be punished for having dissented.

The DM bond was governed by German law and did not include collective action clauses. Moreover, principal holdings were widely dispersed among retail investors, making negotiations more difficult. Even in this case, however, acceptance was high. The terms of the exchange were apparently sufficiently attractive to convince even debtors who could have held out and litigated based on the original claim. Market commentary cited the fact that there was no reduction in principal, and that accrued interest (in total, $220 million) was repaid in cash, as key reasons for the high participation. Because the terms of the exchange were considered favorable by most investors, the DM bond traded at a fairly high price soon after the terms of the exchange offer were announced (about 70 cents on the dollar, up from 55 cents on the dollar just prior to the announcement), so that the upside to holding out—or buying the bonds specifically for the purpose of litigation—was small. Another contributing factor may have been the use of several co-lead managers (Commerzbank AG, Credit Suisse First Boston, and Salomon Smith Barney) in addition to the lead manager, ING Barings. These banks were supposed to identify and convince continental European retail investors, and were paid fees based on the face value of bonds they brought into the exchange.

Table 5.4 confirms that the terms of the 2000 restructuring were indeed much milder, from an investor perspective, than those of the Russian external restructuring that was being carried out at the same time, and similar to those of the Pakistan Eurobond restructuring that had just been completed a few months earlier (see chapter 6). Present value losses varied from about 22 to 35 percent. Not surprisingly, the haircut did not depend much on which of the two *new* bonds was chosen by investors. However, it varied across the old bonds: bonds with shorter life suffered somewhat larger haircuts than bonds with longer life (this can be observed both for the bonds shown and within the class of Gazprom bonds). In a mechanical sense, the explanation for this is that all international bonds were exchanged for new bonds of more or less the same value (with no face value haircut, except the small haircut suffered by the Merrill Lynch issue) although the present value of the longer dated old bonds was smaller. Hence, the reduction in present value was not as high for the longer bonds as for the shorter bonds. The longer dated Gazprom bonds did in fact receive larger nominal haircuts than the shorter dated Gazprom bonds, but this was not enough to offset the smaller present values of the longer bonds at the discount rates applied in our calculations.

After the Exchange

The 2000 exchange significantly smoothed Ukraine's debt service profile (figure 5.4). Additionally, there was progress in the implementation of structural reforms during 2000, and the fiscal situation markedly improved. Growth turned positive, reaching about 6 percent. On this basis, IMF lending under the three-year EFF program resumed in December 2000. The macroeconomic situation strengthened further in 2001, with growth accelerating to 9 percent and annual

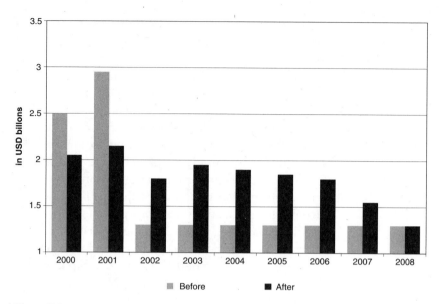

Figure 5.4
Total debt service profile before and after the exchange
Source: IMF 2000.

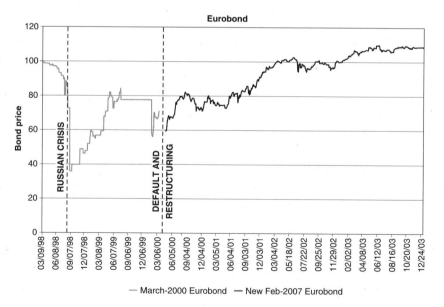

Figure 5.5
Bond prices before and after the exchange
Source: Bloomberg and authors' computations.

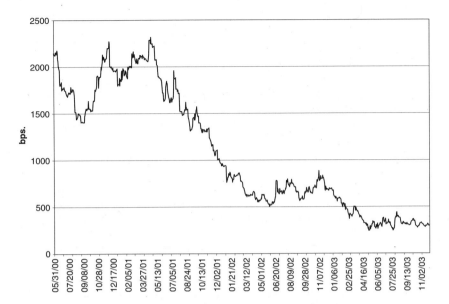

Figure 5.6
EMBI spread on Ukrainian bonds
Source: JP Morgan.

inflation declining sharply. Debt dynamics turned around fairly quickly with reductions in the debt-to-GDP ratios after 2000. High growth, reasonable fiscal performance, and some real exchange rate appreciation against the dollar were the main contributing factors.

As a result of these developments, bond prices strengthened soon after the exchange (figure 5.5) and two years after the restructuring the holder of a Ukraine bond had recovered the nominal value of his capital. Ukraine's 2000 bond issues were sufficiently liquid and large that they became part of the EMBI Global bond index. Figure 5.6 shows the reduction in spreads on Ukraine debt in the wake of the restructuring. By late 2003, spreads were below 300 basis points.

On July 13, 2001, Paris Club members agreed to a debt restructuring, rescheduling $580 million due on loans contracted by Ukraine before December 1998 on standard nonconcessional terms. Rescheduled credits are to be repaid over twelve years, with three years of grace, in eighteen equal and successive semiannual payments. Since then, there have been no further restructurings, and Ukraine has remained current on all its payments.

Box 5.1
Chronology of Ukraine's crisis and debt restructuring

1991: Soviet Union collapses.

1995:

March: Domestic T-bill market is created.

1996:

May: First Stand-by Arrangement with IMF is approved. Stabilization from high inflation occurs.

September: A new currency, the hryvnia, is introduced.

1997:

April: Unofficial exchange rate band is set at 1.7–1.9 hryvnia per dollar.

August: First Eurobond issue (face value $450 million) occurs. Second Stand-by Arrangement with the IMF is approved.

September: Exchange rate band is formalized.

October: Fiduciary loan is issued through Chase Manhattan (face value $109 million).

1998:

January: IMF supported program goes offtrack. First devaluation, with new band at 1.8–2.25 hryvnia per dollar.

February: Ukraine issues three-year DM 750 million Eurobond.

March: Ukraine issues two-year Ecu 500 million Eurobond.

May: Second tranche of DM Eurobond (DM 260 million).

Early August: $155 million is raised through ten-month T-bills placed by ING Barings. $450 million Eurobond is repaid to its lead manager, Nomura International.

August 17: Russian default and devaluation. Market for government debt dries up.

August 26: Conversion scheme for T-bills held by domestic banks.

September 4: Second devaluation, with new official exchange band at 2.5–3.5 hryvnia per dollar. Exchange restrictions are imposed. IMF approves three-year $2.2 billion EFF.

September–October: Bond exchange program targeted at nonresident T-bill holders achieves about 82 percent participation, leading to issuance of new $500 million zero-coupon bond maturing in September 2000.

October 20: $109 million of debt issued originally through Chase Manhattan is exchanged for new 16.75 percent coupon bond maturing in October 2000.

1999:

February 9: NBU announces a new official currency exchange band range of 3.4–4.6 hryvnia per dollar.

March–June: NBU lifts most currency transaction restrictions and allows exchange rate to be determined on a foreign exchange interbank market.

May 18: Ministry of Finance submits to ING a debt conversion offer for $163 million coming due in June.

July 15: Debt exchange deal is made with ING Barings.

Box 5.1
(continued)

August 20: $538 million added to outstanding 2001 DM Eurobond is used to exchange ING Barings bond as well as about half of the outstanding $500 million zero-coupon bond maturing in September 2000.

October: Program with IMF goes offtrack.

November: President Leonid Kuchma is reelected. The exchange rate comes under pressure.

December 22: Reformer Victor Yuschenko is appointed prime minister.

2000:

January: Ukraine misses debt payments due on "Gazprom bond" and October 2000 16.75 percent bond.

February 4: Ukraine launches a comprehensive exchange offer involving all outstanding commercial debt (Eurobonds and Gazprom bonds).

February 8: IMF Deputy Managing Director Stanley Fischer issues statement supporting the exchange.

February–March: Ukraine misses interest payments on 2001 DM Eurobond and principal payment on March 2000 euro Eurobond.

March 15: Initial deadline of exchange offer is extended to April 7 after about 90 percent of investors agree.

April 14: Exchange is completed with 99 percent participation among holders of bonds maturing in 2000–2001 and 76 percent among holders of Gazprom bonds maturing in 2002–2007.

December: EFF program with IMF resumes.

2001:

July 13: Paris Club members agree to a debt restructuring on standard terms.

6   Pakistan

In spite of significant GDP growth, primary fiscal deficits during the 1980s and early 1990s led to a gradual rise in Pakistan's public debt ratio. From 1975 until 1992, public debt rose by about 25 percentage points of GDP, to about 75 percent.[1] Aided by declining primary deficits, the public debt ratio subsequently stabilized (tables 6.1 and 6.2).[2] However, the interest burden continued rising, driven by sharply rising interest rates on domestic debt associated with financial liberalization. Between 1995 and 1998, interest payments rose from 34 to 47 percent of tax revenues, and although the primary fiscal deficit declined to close to zero, the overall fiscal deficit continued to be large (6–7 percent of GDP, see table 6.1). Moreover, about half of the public debt was denominated in foreign currency, making the public sector vulnerable to a sudden depreciation of the exchange rate.

In the early 1990s, Pakistan had significantly liberalized foreign exchange controls. The rupee had become fully convertible, and both individuals and firms were allowed to hold foreign currency bank accounts and freely move foreign currency into and out of the country. This led to a surge of privately issued external debt, which more than doubled as a share of GDP, from about 5 percent in 1992 to over 11 percent in 1997. Most of these external debt inflows came in the form of (short-term) foreign currency deposits—a tax-privileged instrument introduced in the early 1970s to provide Pakistani nationals working abroad with a savings opportunity in Pakistan—which was opened to institutional investors in 1985. Commercial banks and other foreign exchange dealers accepting these deposits had to surrender the foreign exchange to the State Bank of Pakistan (SBP) but could purchase foreign exchange cover from the SBP.

Pakistan's current account deficits sharply widened in the mid-1990s, financed by a large increase in nonresident's foreign currency

Table 6.1
Pakistan: Selected economic indicators, 1993–2004

	1993	1994	1995	1996	1997	1998	1999	2000	2001	2002	2003	2004
Output and prices					(annual percentage changes)							
Real GDP at factor costs	2.1	4.4	5.1	6.6	1.7	3.5	4.2	3.9	1.8	3.1	4.8	6.4
Consumer prices (period average)	9.8	11.3	13.0	10.8	11.8	7.8	5.7	3.6	4.4	2.5	3.1	4.6
Pakistani rupees per U.S. dollar (period average)	4.5	16.2	2.3	8.8	16.2	10.7	17.0	3.0	12.8	5.2	−4.7	−1.5
Terms of trade (period average)	−1.4	5.6	−0.2	−7.3	0.3	6.0	2.2	−7.5	−1.6	−0.5	−0.9	0.9
Public finances					(in percent of GDP)							
Revenue (including grants)	14.9	14.3	13.7	14.5	13.4	13.1	13.8	14.4	14.3	16.1	17.4	14.9
Expenditure	21.7	19.9	19.2	21.0	19.0	19.5	18.4	18.9	17.6	19.7	18.7	16.7
Noninterest	17.3	14.9	15.0	15.9	13.6	13.4	12.4	12.5	12.0	14.1	14.4	13.1
Interest	4.4	5.0	4.3	5.1	5.4	6.1	6.0	6.5	5.6	5.6	4.3	3.5
Primary balance (including grants)	−2.4	−0.6	−1.3	−1.4	−0.2	−0.3	1.4	1.9	2.3	2.0	2.9	1.8
Overall balance (including grants)	−6.8	−5.5	−5.6	−6.5	−5.6	−6.4	−4.6	−4.6	−3.3	−3.6	−1.4	−1.8
Total government debt[a]	79.4	79.2	73.9	74.0	74.8	76.8	81.7	83.8	88.8	80.2	74.3	67.8
External government debt	39.1	41.3	38.5	38.2	38.4	39.5	40.7	40.3	45.6	39.8	35.0	31.5
Domestic government debt	40.3	37.9	35.4	35.8	36.3	37.3	41.0	43.4	43.3	40.4	39.3	36.3
					(in percent)							
Implicit interest rate on government debt[b]	6.6	7.4	6.5	7.9	8.3	9.0	8.6	8.5	7.4	6.6	5.9	5.5
Six-month T-bill rate (period average)	12.3	12.5	11.7	12.8	15.6	15.1	12.9	8.6	10.4	8.1	4.1	1.6
External sector					(in percent of GDP)							
Merchandise trade balance												
Merchandise exports	10.9	10.7	10.6	10.8	10.7	11.2	10.7	11.2	12.5	12.7	13.2	12.9
Merchandise imports	16.1	13.8	14.0	15.7	14.9	13.7	13.6	13.1	14.3	13.1	13.7	14.1

Current account excluding official transfers	-5.9	-3.0	-3.7	-6.3	-5.1	-2.6	-3.8	-2.9	-2.7	0.1	3.8	1.4
Current account including official transfers	-5.3	-2.5	-3.3	-6.0	-4.7	-2.3	-3.0	-1.6	-1.6	2.2	5.1	2.0
Gross reserves (in billions of U.S. dollars)[c]	0.5	2.3	2.7	2.1	1.1	0.9	1.7	0.9	1.7	4.3	10.3	10.6
in percent of short-term external public debt[d]	22	105	113	69	35	25	39	19	42	104	258	216
Reference items:												
GDP at market prices (in billions of rupees)	1607	1882	2249	2556	2927	3228	3542	3793	4163	4402	4823	5533
Exchange rate (rupees per U.S. dollar, period averages)	25.8	29.9	30.6	33.3	38.7	42.9	50.1	51.6	58.3	61.3	58.4	57.5

Sources: National authorities and IMF.

Note: On a fiscal year basis, for example, 1993 refers to period from July 1992 to June 1993.

[a] Debt ratios refer to debt in U.S. dollars divided by GDP in U.S. dollars, using period average exchange rates. This differs from the way Pakistan's debt ratios are usually computed, namely, by converting all debt to local currency units at end-period exchange rates and dividing by GDP in local currency.

[b] Calculated as interest payments in percent of the end-of-period debt stock of the previous year.

[c] End of period; excluding gold, foreign deposits held with the SBP, and net of outstanding forward contracts.

[d] On a remaining maturity basis.

Table 6.2
Pakistan: Debt dynamics, 1975–2004 (in percent of GDP unless otherwise stated)

	1975–1992 (av.)	1993	1994	1995	1996	1997	1998	1999	2000	2001	2002	2003	2004
General government debt[a]		75.5	77.6	73.2	70.4	71.7	71.7	79.7	83.1	81.0	82.0	75.2	67.1
Change in debt ratio attributable to...	1.0	2.8	2.1	−4.4	−2.8	1.3	0.0	8.0	3.4	−2.1	1.0	−6.8	−8.1
Primary deficit	4.0	2.4	0.6	1.3	1.4	0.2	0.3	−1.4	−1.9	−2.3	−2.0	−2.9	−1.8
Real interest rate	−0.2	3.0	3.2	3.1	3.7	3.9	4.9	4.5	5.0	3.4	3.7	3.2	2.2
Real growth	−3.4	−1.2	−2.7	−3.6	−3.3	−0.7	−1.8	−2.5	−3.2	−1.5	−2.5	−3.8	−4.4
Real depreciation	−0.2	−3.8	−0.4	−6.4	−2.3	−1.7	−1.2	4.0	1.1	−2.0	6.5	−4.0	−4.8
Cross-terms	−0.1	−0.1	0.2	−0.5	0.1	0.2	0.2	0.6	0.1	0.3	0.2	−0.4	−0.4
Residual[b]	0.9	2.6	1.2	1.6	−2.2	−0.8	−2.4	2.8	2.4	−0.1	−4.9	1.1	1.0

Note: On a fiscal year basis, for example, 1993 refers to the period between July 1992 and June 1993.
[a] Debt expressed in local currency units divided by nominal GDP in local currency.
[b] Reflects debt relief and other debt stock adjustments, nondebt budgetary financing, and measurement error.

deposits. In the fourth quarter of 1997, however, private capital inflows collapsed, reflecting both spillovers from the Asia crisis and a political crisis that resulted in the sacking of the chief justice and the resignation of the president in December of that year. As the SBP intervened to maintain the exchange rate peg of forty-four rupees to the dollar, foreign exchange reserves declined rapidly (figure 6.1). By the end of April 1998, the SBP had an uncovered foreign exchange position on the order of $10 billion (16 percent of 1998 GDP).

From the 1998 Crisis to the January 1999 Paris Club Deal

Pakistan was hence already in a vulnerable position when a full blown balance of payments crisis erupted at the end of May 1998, triggered by the international repercussions of a series of nuclear tests. The United States and Japan imposed economic sanctions, and following an agreement by the G-8, all bilateral official lending was suspended. Private transfers collapsed, and capital flows suffered a sharp reversal. Withdrawals in foreign currency from deposits amounted to close to $3 billion over the following months. In the face of rapidly declining reserves, the government took a series of emergency measures. With-

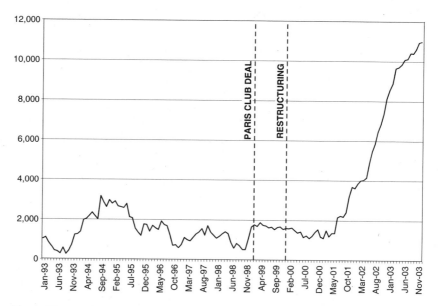

Figure 6.1
International reserves (in millions of U.S. dollars)
Source: IFS.

drawals were restricted to be made in local currency at the official exchange rate, which was devalued to PR46 per U.S. dollar in June (figure 6.2). Some foreign currency deposits were converted into five- to ten-year dollar bonds. Exchange restrictions on current account transactions were also introduced, while external debt service payments to official bilateral creditors and commercial banks were suspended.

On July 14, 1998, Standard and Poor's (S&P) lowered Pakistan's long-term foreign currency issuer rating from B- to CCC. On July 22, the government introduced a two-tier exchange rate mechanism comprising the official rate and the more depreciated floating interbank rate (FIBR). Suppliers into the FIBR market included exporters, remittances from overseas workers, and invisible flows; the demand included "nonessential" imports and other current transactions that did not have access to the official rate. Notwithstanding these measures, official reserves continued to fall. By late November 1998, reserves stood at less than $500 million while external arrears had risen to $1.6 billion. Because of these arrears, Pakistan was further downgraded by S&P in December 1998 and January 1999, when it was rated "selective default." Except for some payment delays, however,

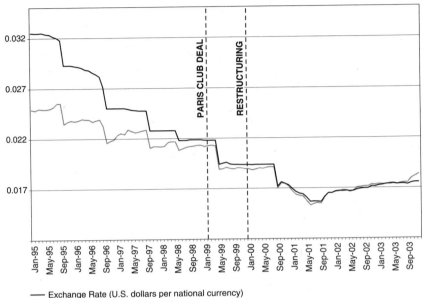

Figure 6.2
Nominal and real exchange rates
Source: IFS.

Pakistan continued to service its international bonds and IFI debt, as well its very large domestic debt.[3]

Pakistan turned the corner in early 1999 thanks to the lifting of most U.S. sanctions in November 1998, the revival of an IMF program that had been suspended in May 1998, and the negotiation of a debt rescheduling agreement with the Paris Club at the end of January 1999. About $3.3 billion of debt contracted prior to September 1997 and falling due between January 1, 1999, and December 31, 2000, was rescheduled. The rescheduling took place on somewhat concessional "Houston terms." Official development assistance (ODA) loans were rescheduled over twenty years with ten years of grace, while other loans were rescheduled over eighteen years with a three-year grace period.

Although the combination of Paris Club debt relief, the lifting of sanctions, and the IMF-supported program might have put Pakistan in a position to pay its Eurobonds, the Paris Club imposed the requirement that Pakistan should look for a similar debt relief from private investors, including, in particular, the restructuring of its international bond on comparable terms. This requirement was viewed as a watershed in international financial markets. For the first time, the official sector seemed to be sweeping aside the seniority that international bonds had de facto enjoyed for many decades. As a Moody's headline put it, "Pakistan's Paris Club Arrangement Implies New Official Strategy Regarding Seniority of Sovereign Eurobonds." Emerging market bond prices reacted accordingly. According to McBrady and Seasholes (2000), "Pakistan's rescheduling agreement with the Paris Club raised *other* countries' borrowing costs by 25 bp to 95 bp—even those countries with no trade links to Pakistan."

The November 1999 Bond Exchange

After the Paris Club deal and the revival of the multilateral lending, Pakistan's reserves quickly recovered to over $1.6 billion. On May 19, 1999, the exchange rate was unified and the surrender requirement for foreign exchange earnings was eliminated. The government also entered into negotiations with commercial banks, which lead to a rescheduling agreement on July 6, 1999, covering about $900 million in commercial loans. However, it initially held off on restructuring the Eurobonds. The Paris Club deal gave it flexibility on the timing of the bond restructuring, requiring only signs of "progress" in negotiations with bondholders by the end of 1999. No principal repayments were coming due until the end of the year, and the amounts involved were relatively small ($450 million between December 1999 and May 2000). Loath to further damage Pakistan's reputation in financial markets, the government may have hoped to renegotiate its commitment to the Paris Club and repay in full. In the event, however, no renegotiation took place, and on November 15, 1999, Pakistan finally launched a debt exchange offer in line with its commitments.

The exchange involved swapping three bonds: a $150 million, 11.5 percent Eurobond due in December 1999; a $158 million, 6 percent exchangeable note due in February 2002 with a put option in February 2000; and a $300 million LIBOR-plus 3.95 percent floating rate note due in May 2000. All three were to be exchanged for a new amortizing bond with an overall maturity of six years, three-year grace period, paying a 10 percent coupon (table 6.3).

There was some discussion as to whether Pakistan would invoke CACs in order to secure success in the exchange, but they were not used. In the end virtually all bondholders—99 percent, with the

Table 6.3
Pakistan Eurobond exchange, November–December 1999: Haircuts (per 100 units of principal)

	12/1999 Eurobond	2/2002 Eurobond with 2000 put option	5/2000 Eurobond
Issue date	12/22/94	2/26/97	5/30/97
Amount outstanding (in millions of U.S. dollars)	150	160	300
Due date[a]	12/22/99	2/26/02	5/30/00
Present value on 12/13/1999[b]	105.3	104.3	97.0
Discount rate used (in percent)[c]	21.4	21.4	21.4
Total new value obtained	70.3	72.0	68.1
Haircut	33.3	31.0	29.8

Source: Sturzenegger and Zettelmeyer (2005).
[a] 2002 bond had put option in February 2000.
[b] For puttable 2002 bond, we assume that the option to put would have been used for the entire outstanding amount in February 2000.
[c] Yield to maturity on new 2005 Eurobond, with a minor maturity correction based on the U.S. yield curve.

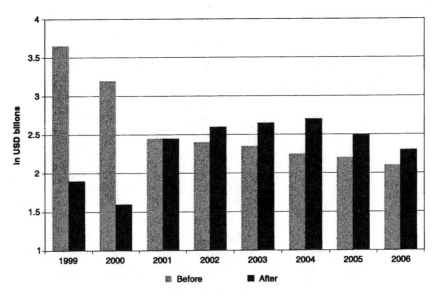

Figure 6.3
Total debt service before and after the exchange
Source: IMF 2000.

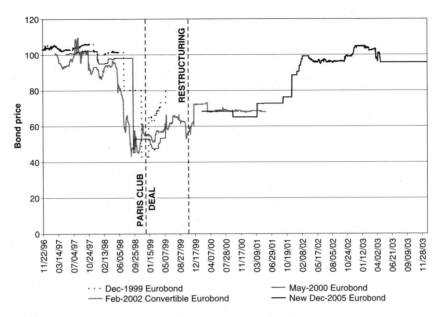

Figure 6.4
Bond prices before and after the exchange
Source: Bloomberg and authors' computations.

remainder too small to trigger cross-default clauses—tendered. Figure 6.3 shows the impact on the debt profile.

The exchange was successful for several reasons. Because of the conditions attached to the January Paris Club deal, the threat of default was credible, and the terms offered were fairly attractive. There was no write-down in principal, and in two cases investors did in fact receive a few more units of principal of the new bond than were owed under the old bond, as unpaid interest between launch of the exchange offer and the maturity of the old bonds was rolled into the new principal. In addition, the new bond would be more liquid than the tendered ones. The fact that the number of bondholders was rather limited was also a critical factor in assuring the success of the exchange, and support from the IMF and a substantial upgrade by S&P also contributed. The results for bondholders are described in table 6.3 and figure 6.4. We find that investors lost around 30 percent in NPV, using the relatively high launch yield of the 2005 Eurobond (21 percent) to discount old and new cash flows. Since there were no nominal haircuts and the coupon on the new bonds was about in line, or slightly higher, than that of the old bonds, this NPV reduction is attributable entirely to the maturity extension.

The 2001 Paris Club Deals and Beyond

The joint effect of the January 1999 Paris Club deal, the July 1999 agreement with commercial banks, and the November–December bond exchange was to create temporary payments relief during 1999–2000 (see figure 6.3). As a more permanent solution to Pakistan's debt problem, however, they were too small, barely denting the overall burden. Moreover, after the program with the IMF went offtrack in the second half of 1999 and the discovery of problems with the way fiscal data had been reported to the IMF, not all of the official debt relief promised in January was actually delivered. As a result, by the end of November 2000, Pakistan had again accumulated arrears worth about US$800 million to official creditors. In addition, the window for official debt relief promised in January 1999 expired at the end of 2000, and major repayments were coming up in 2001.

In the event, these problems were addressed, in two steps. At the end of November 2000, the IMF approved a new Stand-by Arrangement in an amount equivalent to about $600 million. This paved the way for a new Paris Club deal in which creditors rescheduled about $1.8 billion of debt (as before, under "Houston terms"), comprising both the arrears and debt falling due between December 2000 and September 2001. Second, following the successful completion of the Stand-by Arrangement—Pakistan's first IMF supported program since the late 1980s to be fully disbursed—the IMF approved a $1.3 billion three-year program under the Poverty Reduction and Growth Facility, which opened the door for new bilateral debt relief through the Paris Club in December 2001.

Aided by a more favorable political environment following the September 11, 2001, terrorist attacks in the United States, Pakistan's new Paris Club deal was both more concessional and comprehensive than its predecessors, covering about $12.5 billion in debt service, corresponding to almost the entire stock of outstanding bilateral debt. ODA loans—about two-thirds of the bilateral debt—were rescheduled for thirty-eight years with a fifteen-year grace period, while the remaining debt was rescheduled for twenty-three years with five years of grace. Under these terms—which fell somewhere in between the "Houston Terms" under which previous reschedulings had been conducted and the far more concessional "Naples terms" reserved for very poor countries—Pakistan saved about $3 billion in debt service payments through 2004.

Box 6.1
Chronology of Pakistan's crisis and debt restructuring

1997

October 20: Capital outflows occur as a result of the Asian crisis and domestic political crisis. IMF approves a three-year IMF ESAF/EFF program.

1998

May 28: After nuclear testing capital flows dry up, sanctions are imposed, and bilateral and IMF lending is suspended. Foreign Currency Accounts (FCAs) are frozen.

June: Devaluation of the rupee.

July 14: Pakistan's long-term foreign currency credit rating is downgraded by Standard & Poor from B− to CCC.

July 22: Government introduces a multiple exchange rate system comprising an official rate, a floating interbank rate (FIBR), and a composite rate. The official exchange rate continues to tie the rupee to the dollar.

July: New FCAs are permitted with fresh foreign exchange inflows. Pakistan's government begins accumulating arrears on official bilateral debt and commercial loans.

November: Lifting of most U.S. sanctions.

December: S&P downgrades Pakistan to selective default (SD).

1999

January 15: Revival of the IMF ESAF/EFF program.

January 30: Agreement with Paris Club reschedules $3.3 billion in debt payments to bilateral creditors coming due in 1999 and 2000, under "Houston terms." Paris Club requires Pakistan to restructure both its commercial loans and its international bonds on comparable terms.

May 19: Government unifies the exchange rate.

July 6: Agreement is reached on rescheduling of $877 million in commercial bank loans.

October 12: New military government takes office.

November 15: Pakistan launches an offer to exchange three Eurobonds due between December 1999 and February 2002 (total face value $608 million) for a new amortizing bond with an overall maturity of six years, with a three-year grace period. Ninety-nine percent of all bondholders tender.

2000

November 29: IMF approves a Stand-by Arrangement for $596 million. Unlike its predecessors, this program is fully disbursed and does not suffer interruptions.

2001

January 23: Paris Club reschedules $1.8 billion in debt under Houston terms.

December 6: IMF approves new three-year program for $1.3 billion.

December 14: Paris Club approves concessional rescheduling of $12.5 billion in bilateral debt.

At the same time, Pakistan has pursued a structural reform agenda focused on tax administration, expenditure management, the financial sector and energy (IMF Country Report No. 04/411). As a result of these reforms as well as the improved external environment, Pakistan has maintained a positive primary fiscal balance, the current account (excluding official transfers) has been in surplus, and real GDP has grown by an average of about 5 percent per annum (see Lorie and Iqbal 2005, for an analysis of Pakistan's macroeconomic adjustment and the sources of growth between 1999 and 2004). While total public debt remains high, it has sharply fallen from its peak in 2000–2001 and stood at about 68 percent of GDP at the end of the 2004 fiscal year (2003–2004). Gross reserves increased from about $1.6 billion in 2000–2001 to almost $11 billion at the end of 2003–2004, implicit interest rates on government debt fell, and so did spreads on international debt issues. Since 2003, Pakistan's Emerging Markets Bond Index Global (EMBIG) spread has hovered between 200 and 400 basis points, about the same as Mexico's. In February 2004, Pakistan reaccessed international bond markets for the first time since the 1998–1999 crisis, issuing a $500 million Eurobond at a spread of 370 basis points.

7   Ecuador

Ecuador's 1999 crisis began in 1998 as a slow-moving banking crisis, compounded by external shocks, and developed into a systemic financial crisis in early 1999. By January 2000 it had resulted in a currency crisis, default, official dollarization, and the ousting of the president. GDP fell by over 6 percent in 1999, and the fiscal costs of the banking crisis amounted to about 20 percent of GDP, according to IMF estimates (table 7.1).[1]

In the first half of the 1990s, Ecuador's economic prospects had looked quite promising. After a decade of poor economic performance following the debt crisis of the early 1980s, output growth had recovered to almost 4 percent per annum on average between 1990 and 1994. With tight fiscal policy and a preannounced crawling exchange rate band, inflation was steadily reduced from high levels to just over 20 percent by 1995. The early 1990s were also a period of significant structural and institutional reforms, culminating in a new central bank charter in 1992 and the 1994 Law of Financial Institutions. These reforms ended directed credit, liberalized interest rates, reduced and rationalized reserve requirements, eliminated foreign exchange surrender requirements, and allowed banks to both take deposits and provide loans in U.S. dollars and conduct offshore operations. In addition, Ecuador negotiated debt restructuring deals with the Paris Club in 1992 and 1994 and a Brady deal with commercial banks in early 1995.[2] Table 7.2 shows how this debt restructuring improved Ecuador's debt picture, with sizable debt to GDP reductions in 1993 through 1995 fueled both by real exchange rate appreciation (1993 and 1994) and debt relief in 1995.

However, Ecuador emerged from this period with substantial vulnerabilities. While the 1992–1995 debt restructurings had reduced Ecuador's external public debt burden to a level that was perhaps sustainable in normal times (about 68 percent of GDP), it was almost

Table 7.1
Ecuador: Selected economic indicators, 1993–2004

	1993	1994	1995	1996	1997	1998	1999	2000	2001	2002	2003	2004
Output and prices						(annual percentage changes)						
Real GDP	2.0	4.7	1.7	2.4	4.1	2.1	-6.3	2.8	5.1	3.4	2.7	6.9
Consumer prices (period averages)	45.0	27.4	22.9	24.4	30.6	36.1	52.2	96.1	37.7	12.5	7.9	2.7
Sucres per U.S. dollar (period averages)	25.1	14.5	16.7	24.4	25.4	36.2	116.4	112.0	0.0	0.0	0.0	0.0
Terms of trade (goods)	-7.7	4.1	-4.7	4.0	27.6	-6.1	13.4	18.9	-3.8	10.8	4.9	10.1
World oil price (U.S. dollars per barrel)	-11.8	-5.0	7.9	18.4	-5.4	-32.1	37.5	57.0	-13.8	2.5	15.8	30.7
Public finances						(in percent of GDP)						
Revenue	26.1	24.5	25.6	24.2	23.6	20.3	22.5	27.6	24.7	26.0	25.4	27.0
Expenditures	25.6	24.3	27.8	27.1	25.2	25.7	27.2	26.5	25.1	25.0	23.7	24.7
Noninterest	22.2	20.6	23.7	23.1	20.9	21.5	19.1	19.9	20.4	21.5	20.7	22.0
Interest	3.4	3.7	4.1	4.0	4.3	4.2	8.1	6.6	4.7	3.5	3.0	2.7
Primary balance	3.9	3.9	1.9	1.1	2.7	-1.2	3.4	7.7	4.3	4.5	4.7	5.0
Overall balance	0.5	0.2	-2.2	-2.9	-1.6	-5.4	-4.7	1.0	-0.5	1.0	1.7	2.3
Total public debt[a]	89.2	81.8	68.6	68.1	62.1	66.7	101.2	91.4	70.2	58.2	52.6	46.4
External	86.5	74.1	61.3	59.3	53.2	56.9	82.5	72.0	54.5	46.9	42.2	36.4
Domestically issued[b]	2.7	7.7	7.3	8.8	8.9	9.8	18.7	19.4	15.7	11.3	10.4	10.0
External sector					(in billions of U.S. dollars unless otherwise indicated)							
Total imports, fob	-2.3	-3.0	-4.1	-4.0	-4.7	-5.2	-3.0	-3.6	-5.1	-6.2	-6.2	-7.5
Total exports, fob	3.0	3.6	4.4	4.9	5.3	4.2	4.5	4.9	4.7	5.0	6.0	7.9
Current account balance	-0.7	-0.8	-0.7	-0.2	-0.7	-2.2	0.8	0.8	-0.7	-1.2	-0.5	0.0
Current account (in percent of GDP)	-4.4	-4.4	-3.6	-0.7	-3.0	-9.3	4.6	5.3	-3.3	-4.9	-1.8	0.0
Gross reserves (excluding gold)	1.4	1.8	1.6	1.9	2.1	1.6	1.6	0.9	0.8	0.7	0.8	1.1

					(annual percentage changes)						
Import volumes	20.7	29.3	16.2	-9.4	46.4	24.1	-38.3	24.1	51.5	21.3	-3.6	13.0
Export volumes	13.4	13.8	11.4	-0.8	4.5	-5.3	1.3	-5.8	5.6	-1.6	8.3	12.4
Oil	6.3	9.5	10.9	-3.9	-7.3	-12.7	16.6	5.1	-9.7	5.8	9.2	32.6
Non-oil	21.6	18.2	11.8	2.1	15.0	0.0	-8.3	-14.5	20.6	-7.0	7.6	-4.7
Reference items:												
Nominal GDP (in billions of U.S. dollars)	15.1	18.6	20.2	21.3	23.6	23.3	16.7	15.9	21.0	24.3	27.2	30.3
Exchange rate (sucres per U.S. dollar, period average)[c]	1919	2197	2564	3189	3998	5447	11787	24988	...	...	...	...

Source: National authorities and IMF.

[a] Debt expressed in U.S. dollars using end-period exchange rates, divided by current GDP in U.S. dollars.

[b] Mostly denominated in U.S. dollars or dollar-linked (even before official dollarization in 2000).

[c] U.S. dollar became national currency in 2000, at a conversion rate of 25,000 sucres per U.S. dollar.

Table 7.2
Ecuador: Debt dynamics, 1993–2004 (in percent of GDP unless otherwise stated)

	1993	1994	1995	1996	1997	1998	1999	2000	2001	2002	2003	2004
Total public debt[a]	89.2	81.8	68.6	68.1	62.1	66.7	101.2	91.4	70.2	58.2	52.6	46.4
Change in debt ratio attributable to...	−9.5	−7.4	−13.2	−0.5	−6.0	4.6	34.5	−9.8	−21.2	−12.0	−5.6	−6.2
Primary deficit	−3.9	−3.9	−1.9	−1.1	−2.7	1.2	−3.4	−7.7	−4.3	−4.5	−4.7	−5.0
Real interest rate	1.6	2.5	2.6	2.8	3.4	3.3	5.1	3.9	3.7	2.6	2.1	1.4
Real growth	−1.9	−3.9	−1.4	−1.6	−2.6	−1.3	4.4	−2.7	−4.3	−2.3	−1.5	−3.3
Real depreciation	−10.3	−11.3	−4.1	−1.0	−3.4	2.3	21.0	9.0	−15.6	−6.0	−3.5	−0.7
Cross-terms	−0.4	−0.6	−0.2	−0.1	−0.3	0.2	2.1	0.5	−1.2	−0.4	−0.2	−0.1
Residual[b]	5.5	9.9	−8.3	0.5	−0.5	−1.2	5.3	−13.0	0.5	−1.5	2.2	1.5

[a] Debt in U.S. dollars evaluated at end-period exchange rates, divided by current GDP in U.S. dollars.
[b] Reflects debt stock adjustments (debt restructurings in 1995 and 2000), nondebt financing (including interest arrears), and measurement error.

entirely denominated in foreign currency, making the government finances vulnerable to a real depreciation. Second, the combination of exchange rate based stabilization and financial liberalization created a large credit boom in 1993 and 1994 and a rapid growth in the number of banks, without a corresponding strengthening of prudential supervision, in particular, with regard to the banks' offshore operations. At the same time, Ecuador's financial safety net did not have crisis resolution instruments beyond central bank emergency assistance, creating a moral hazard problem. The result was a bias toward risky lending practices, setting the system up for a rapid deterioration in credit quality in the event of adverse shocks.

Unfortunately, several large adverse shocks did in fact materialize in the first half of 1995: a sharp reduction in capital inflows triggered by the currency crisis in Mexico, a border conflict with Peru, and drought-related power shortages. The central bank's reaction was to defend the exchange rate, which succeeded at the cost of a liquidity crunch that led to the failure of two banks but avoided a systemic crisis. However, the political situation remained unstable, leading to the resignation of the proreform vice-president in October 1995. Structural and fiscal reforms stalled, growth stagnated, and the fiscal balance remained in deficit, financed largely by domestic debt. An IMF program that had gone off track in the second half of 1995 could not be revived in spite of several attempts. With macroeconomic policy credibility low and inflation edging up to 30 percent per annum, financial dollarization accelerated. By late 1997, about 45 percent of bank loans were in foreign currency, compounding the economy-wide currency mismatch.

The 1998–1999 Banking Crisis

In this vulnerable situation, the economy was hit in 1998 by three major shocks: the decline in the price of oil, which caused a decline in public sector resources of 3.5 percent of GDP, floods related to El Niño (with damages of about $2.6 billion, or 13 percent of GDP), and finally the sudden stop in emerging market capital flows following the Russian crisis in August. These shocks put pressure on the banking system through two channels: the quality of bank assets, both through the direct effects of El Niño in the coastal areas and the depreciating sucre, and a sharp reduction in foreign credit lines after the Russian crisis. They also sharply aggravated the authorities' fiscal situation and thus their scope for dealing effectively with the crisis.

It is beyond the scope of this chapter to give a full account of the banking crisis that unfolded as a result of these shocks (see Jácome 2004 for an excellent recent analysis). In sum, four phases can be distinguished (see also figures 7.1–7.5).

• After the closure of a small bank in April 1998 triggered deposit runs on several other banks, the Central Bank of Ecuador tried to contain the crisis with the only instrument at its disposal at the time (other than further bank closings), namely sucre liquidity support. At the same time, the process of financial dollarization accelerated, with deposits shifting from sucres to dollars, and in spite of efforts to sterilize the increase in liquidity, the sucre lost about 25 percent of its value in the last quarter of 1998.

• A new law was passed in December 1998 to provide a legal basis for "purchase and assumption operations" of insolvent banks by other banks as an alternative to either closing down the bank or providing liquidity support. This included a blanket guarantee on bank deposits (previously, only small deposits had been guaranteed) and imposed a one percent tax on financial transactions to shore up the public finances. However, the bank resolution instruments provided in the law were ultimately not used,[3] the financials transactions tax

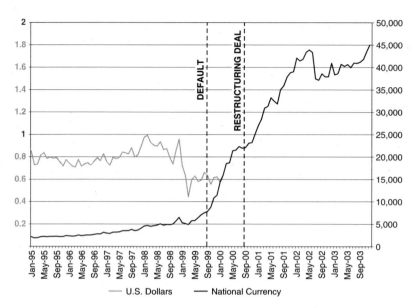

Figure 7.1
Deposits in Ecuador's financial sector (in billions)
Source: IFS.

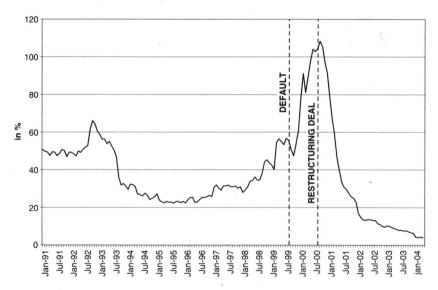

Figure 7.2
CPI inflation (accumulated in the last twelve months)
Source: IFS.

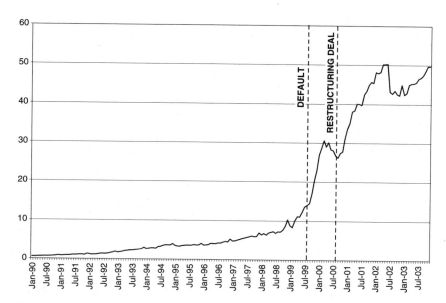

Figure 7.3
Money supply (in millions of sucres)
Source: IFS.

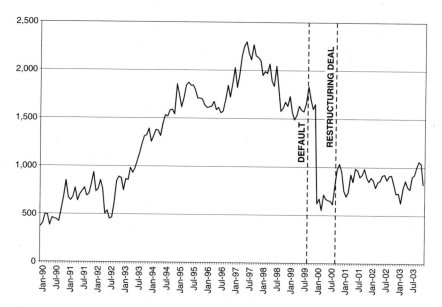

Figure 7.4
International reserves (in millions of U.S. dollars)
Source: IFS.

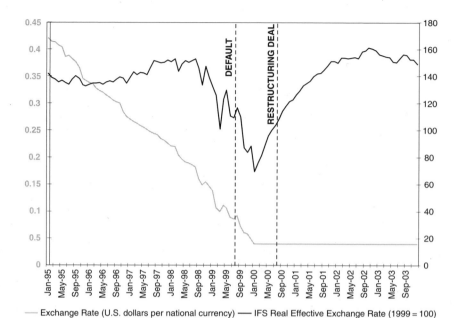

Figure 7.5
Nominal and real exchange rates
Source: IFS.

encouraged further withdrawal of deposits, and the blanket guarantee also failed to calm depositors, in view of delays in compensating depositors and the rapidly depreciating sucre, which was floated in February 1999.

• When the country's second largest bank began to experience liquidity problems in March 1999, the government declared a general deposit freeze. This temporarily halted the fall of the sucre, but at the expense of impairing the payments system, thus contributing to the output loss. In the meantime, international auditors where hired to identify solvent banks and several insolvent banks were shut down.

• Under heavy political and economic pressure, the government began unlocking deposits, including those of unviable banks, in mid-1999. Absent clear signals of stabilization, this led to a renewed general run on deposits which triggered further bank failures, rapid monetization, a new currency crisis, a default on external debt payments, and accelerating inflation.

Default and Dollarization

By mid-1999, it was clear that without IMF support, Ecuador's prospects of servicing its public debt over the near term were dim.[4] Net international reserves stood at about US$1.3 billion, against upcoming debt service of about $550 million on Brady and Eurobonds during the remainder of 1999 and 2000, and maturing domestic debt on the order of US$500 million. In turn, the IMF insisted on some degree of "private sector bail-in" both to help close the financing gap and to return debt to sustainable levels.

Against this background, on August 25, 1999, Ecuador announced that it would suspend coupon payments on discount and PDI Brady bonds scheduled for August 28, 1999. The original intention was to take advantage of the thirty-day grace period on coupon payments to negotiate some reduction in the debt service obligations immediately ahead, while avoiding a general default. Ecuador's preferred option was a debt exchange limited to Brady bonds; this would have preserved a clean debt service record on Eurobonds, which were to be the vehicle for a return to capital markets after the crisis. Not surprisingly, this idea was rejected by Brady bondholders—ostensibly, because it would not have significantly improved Ecuador's cash flow, casting doubts on Ecuador's ability to service even the restructured instruments (Peterson 1999).

Ecuador next tried to persuade the holders of discount bonds to agree to a release of the collateral securing the interest on these bonds, while offering to service the PDI bonds (which were not secured by such collateral) in full. The effect of this would have been to allow Ecuador to suspend servicing its discount bonds for up to one year.[5] Again, this was rejected by discount bondholders, who disliked the unequal treatment (the fact that it was thought to favor Ecuadorian residents, who were more heavily invested in PDI than in discount bonds, may have played a role). The thirty-day deadline lapsed without payments on either of the two bonds.

On October 22, 1999, the finance minister announced Ecuador's intention to restructure its entire external public debt except that owed to multilateral institutions, plus a portion of its domestic debt, and suspended payments on its remaining Brady bonds and Eurobonds. The default on these bonds was viewed as extraordinary because the Brady bonds, in particular, had been regarded as "inviolable": any change in the payment terms required the unanimous agreement of bondholders, and cross-default and acceleration clauses made it particularly easy for a minority of bondholders to inflict damage on the debtor. In the event, however, only one bond was accelerated (the Brady discount bond) and no litigation took place.

The domestic portion of the debt restructuring announced on October 22, 1999, affected about $500 million out of about $2 billion in domestic debt, and was carried out within a week. It included all dollar-denominated domestic debt coming due between October 28, 1999, and December 31, 2000. Sucre-denominated debt, including debt linked to the U.S. dollar, was not restructured, and neither was longer-term domestic dollar-denominated debt. The restructured debt was reportedly largely in the hands of local banks. Debt holders received new seven-year debt that was to pay an annual interest of LIBOR plus 200 basis points (the old instruments had been carrying interest rates ranging from 12 to 19 percent), with biannual amortizations after a two-year grace period.

Based on the crisis yields that were prevailing at the time—external bonds were trading at yields of 40–52 percent—this long maturity extension at noncrisis coupons implied a large haircut. For example, assuming a 50 percent discount rate, the value of the bonds maturing on October 28, 2006, would have been about 32 cents on the dollar, implying a haircut of 68 percent. This discount rate may be too high, of course, since it is based on yields of bond that were expected to be restructured in the near future, while the new domestic bonds were post-restructuring instruments.[6] Assuming a discount rate in line with the *post*-exchange yield prevailing at the time of the 2000 external restructuring (i.e., about 23 percent) results in a haircut of just under 40 percent, in line with the haircut suffered later by the holders of the shorter external instruments (table 7.3).[7] On this basis, it is fair to say that restructured domestic and external bonds received about the same treatment, although it is important to remember that about three-quarters of domestic debt was not restructured at all.

As the default triggered a new currency crisis and the banking crisis continued, President Mahuad announced his intention to officially dollarize the economy—to adopt the U.S. dollar as legal tender—on January 9, 2000. This finally stabilized inflation and the run on the banks. For him, however, the announcement came too late; on January 21, 2000, Mahuad was ousted by a civilian-military coup. The new administration of President Noboa (formerly Mahuad's vice-president) de-

Table 7.3
Ecuador exchange, July–August 2000: Haircuts (per 100 units of principal)

	Pars	Discounts	PDIs	IEs	2004 Euro	2002 Euro
Issue date	2/28/95	2/28/95	2/28/95	12/21/94	4/25/97	4/25/97
Amount outstanding (in millions of U.S. dollars)	1,655	1,435	2,781	143	150	350
Due date	2/28/25	2/28/25	2/27/15	12/21/04	4/25/04	4/25/02
Present value of cash flow on 8/23/00	48.5	65.7	44.9	75.2	78.3	89.0
Discount rate used (in percent)[a]	21.6	22.0	22.4	23.4	23.3	23.5
Past due principal (PDP)	0.0	0.0	0.0	10.0	0.0	0.0
Past due interest (PDI)	4.1	4.7	2.0	7.3	11.3	12.1
Present value including PDI and PDP	52.6	70.4	46.9	92.5	89.5	101.1
Total new value obtained	42.6	51.3	33.4	57.3	52.7	53.4
Haircut	18.9	27.1	28.9	38.1	41.2	47.2

Source: Sturzenegger and Zettelmeyer (2005).
[a] Based on linear interpolation of outstanding Eurobond yields. For collateralized pars and discounts, principal and first twelve months of interest were discounted using a U.S. long rate (5.81 percent).

cided to continue with dollarization supported by fiscal reforms. This was achieved by the *Economic Transformation Law*, enacted in March 2000, that prohibited currency issues in sucre, established a conversion obligation of sucres for U.S. dollars at a fixed exchange rate of 25,000 sucres per dollar as well as a mechanism for converting sucre loans and deposits into dollars at lower interest rates, and contained new fiscal rules and financial sector reform steps.

The 2000 Debt Exchange

On April 19, 2000, the IMF approved a twelve-month Stand-by Arrangement in the amount of $304 million on the understanding that Ecuador would undertake a debt exchange of both its Bradys and Eurobonds "aimed at restoring medium-term fiscal and external sustainability."[8]

The first procedural decision confronting the Ecuadorian government was whether it would convene a formal creditor committee. Ecuador decided against that, in order to avoid long negotiations and because creating a representative creditor committee in view of widely diverging creditor characteristics and interests was believed to be difficult. However, in late 1999, it convened a consultative group of eight representative institutional creditors. This group was not offered any details on the characteristics of the proposed deal, but rather information about Ecuador's economic and financial position, which was made available to all market participants through the Emerging Markets Traders Association (EMTA) in New York. Only two meetings were held, with mixed results (see Buchheit 2000). Salomon Smith Barney was hired as a manager for the future exchange; JP Morgan was later added as co-manager.

On July 27, 2000, with IMF backing, Ecuador launched an offer to exchange its defaulted Brady bonds and Eurobonds for new uncollateralized bonds maturing in 2030 with a step-up coupon starting at 4 percent and rising to 10 percent, in 1 percent steps, by 2006. For each type of defaulted bond, an exchange ratio was set in line with "stripped" secondary market prices; thus, the idea was to treat each bond equally based on their predefault prices. The shortest instruments (Eurobonds and Brady interest equalization bonds) were exchanged at par, while longer dated Brady bonds were exchanged at 1:0.78 (PDI bonds), 1:0.58 (discount bonds) and 1:0.40 (pars). Holders of par and discount bonds also received a cash payment equal to the present value of their U.S. collateral. Past due interest and principal were repaid in cash, while accrued interest (interest owed since the last scheduled coupon payment) was exchanged, at par, for a new Republic bond with a fixed coupon of 12 percent, maturing in 2012. Bondholders could also elect to exchange their principal for this shorter bond rather than the 2030 bond at the cost of a further 35 percent discount. The aggregate amount of 2012 bonds was limited to $1.25 billion, and holders of Eurobonds and shorter dated Brady bonds were given priority in the allocation of the 2012 bonds.

The new bonds contained two novel features meant to minimize the chances of a new debt restructuring in the foreseeable future and protect the interests of bondholders. A "mandatory debt management" provision committed Ecuador to retiring—through cash buybacks or debt-equity swaps—a minimum proportion of the face value of each of the new bonds outstanding every year, beginning in year 6 in the case of the 2012 bonds and in year 13 in the case of the 2030 bonds. This was meant to reduce the bullet repayment due at maturity and the likelihood of a crisis related to the refinancing of that payment, while "allowing Ecuador to benefit from the market discounts available on the bonds over time" (Buchheit 2000). Failure to meet the reduction targets in any year would trigger a mandatory partial redemption of the relevant bond, at par, in an amount equal to the shortfall, as in the case of an amortizing bond. Furthermore, a "principal reinstatement provision" stipulated that a payment default occurring in the first ten years would automatically result in the issuance of additional 2030 bonds to the holders (30 percent if the default event occurred during the first four years after issuance, 20 during the next three years, and 10 during the last three years). The effect of this was to offer a (limited) protection of bondholders against the dilution of their claims by new debt holders in the event of default.

Ecuador had committed to the exchange if 85 percent or more of the principal amount of the eligible debts chose to participate. By the time the exchange was finalized on August 23, 2000, 98 percent of the eligible bonds had agreed to tender. The transaction resulted in a reduction in the face value of the debt stock of 40 percent and cash flow savings of about $1.5 billion over the first five years. Figure 7.6 shows the reprofiling of the debt service. Table 7.3 shows the losses that the

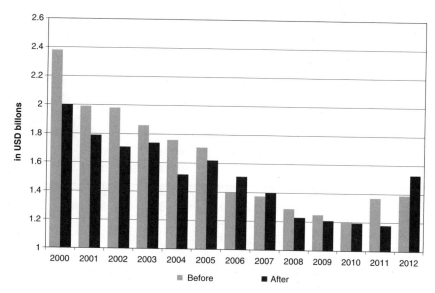

Figure 7.6
Total debt service before and after the exchange
Source: IMF 2000 and authors' computations.

restructuring inflicted on investors, using the yield prevailing immediately after the exchange (around 22 percent) to discount old and new cash flows.[9] As expected, the shorter 2012 bond delivered a slightly higher value, and thus was rationed. There were substantial differences in the haircuts across instruments, ranging between 19 and 47 percent. As in the case of Ukraine, the bonds with the longest remaining average life tended to suffer the smallest NPV haircuts (in the 20–30 percent range), while the largest haircuts were associated with the shortest instruments, notwithstanding the fact that the longer instruments were subjected to larger reductions in face value. Ex post, these reductions were insufficient to equalize the NPV haircuts; consequently, there is a negative correlation between NPV haircuts and nominal haircuts.

What explains the high acceptance rate in the Ecuadorian exchange, in spite of the relatively high haircut suffered by some bonds, and the fact that it was viewed as coercive and "unpalatable" by many investors at the time? The answer must be that the alternative—to hold out—looked even less attractive. In part, this was due to the new and imaginative use of "exit amendments." These exploited the fact that New York law bonds, while precluding amendments to the payment terms of bonds without unanimous consent of all bondholders, allowed most *nonpayment* provisions of the bond to be amended with a simple majority. As part of the exchange, Ecuador solicited the consent of existing bondholders to amend some of these nonpayment terms, in particular: the covenant to maintain the listing of the defaulted instruments on the Luxembourg Stock Exchange, the cross-default clause, the so-called exit covenant by which Ecuador had promised in 1995 never to seek a further restructuring of the Brady bonds, and the negative pledge clause restricting the issuance of collateralized debt. By tendering their bonds, participants were voting in favor of these amendments, with the effect of reducing the liquidity of nontendered bonds and stripping them from various creditor protections. This made them unattractive, even if Ecuador were eventually to decide to pay holdouts according to the original payment terms. It also made it more difficult for holdouts to litigate in the event of nonpayment.

The successful August 2000 debt exchange was quickly followed by a Paris Club rescheduling. On September 15, 2000, Ecuador renegotiated $880 million with the Paris Club under Houston terms. Non-ODA

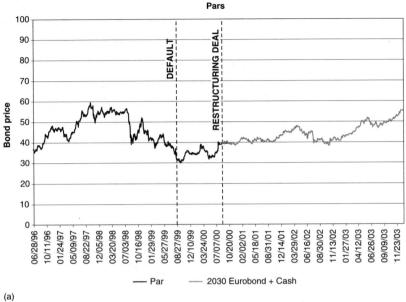

(a)

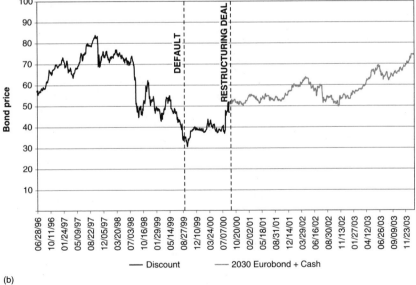

(b)

Figure 7.7
Bond prices before and after the exchange
Source: Bloomberg and authors' computations.

162   Chapter 7

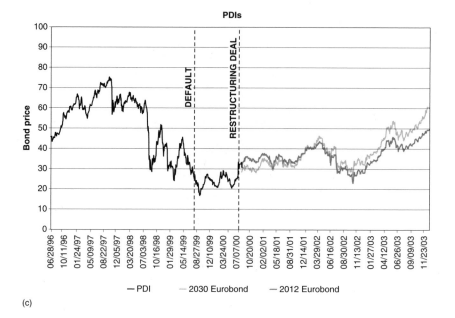

(c)

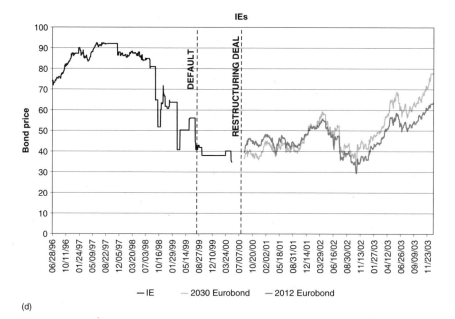

(d)

Figure 7.7
(continued)

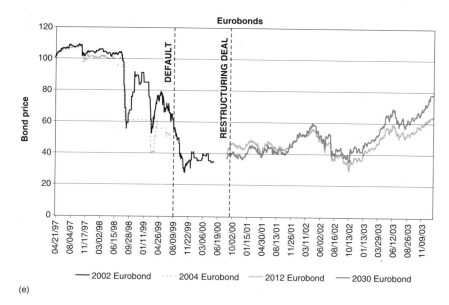

Figure 7.7
(continued)

credits would be repaid over eighteen years with three years of grace at the appropriate market rate while ODA credits would be repaid over twenty years with ten years of grace.

A relatively strong budget allowed for a substantial normalization of the macroeconomic environment, after mid-2000. As country risk declined, deposits in the financial sector recovered, and the demand shock achieved through the exchange rate depreciation allowed for a steady recovery of output. The fiscal situation greatly improved, reflecting a sharp recovery in oil prices and fiscal adjustment. Bond prices recovered, suffered a second downturn in the aftermath of the Argentine default and uncertainty related to Brazilian elections in mid-2002, and recovered again (figure 7.7). Driven by positive primary balances, the recovery in real output, and a real exchange rate appreciation following the undershooting in 1999 and 2000, total and external debt fell to less than 60 percent of GDP by 2002, and less than 50 percent by 2004.

Box 7.1
Chronology of Ecuador's crisis and debt restructuring

1992:

January 20: Paris Club agreement.

1994:

Standby Arrangement with the IMF is approved.

June 27: Paris Club agreement.

1995:

January 26–March 30: Border war with Peru.

February 28: Brady Plan restructures $7.8 billion external commercial bank debt.

1996:

July 7: Abdala Bucaram is elected president. Ecuador fails to meet the targets of an IMF-monitored program.

December: Chase Manhattan gives $300 million bridging loan.

1997:

February 6: Ecuador's National Congress removes Abdala Bucaram from office.

March: El Niño-related devastation begins (total cost about 13 percent of GDP).

1998:

April: Closure of Solbanco sparks deposit runs on other banks.

August: President Jamil Mahuad takes office. Russian crisis. The insolvent Banco de Prestamos is closed.

October: Peace treaty with Peru.

December: A blanket deposit guarantee is created by law, and a Deposit Insurance Agency (AGD) is established to administer the guarantee and to manage the disposal of assets in closed banks. AGD takes over Filanbanco.

1999:

February: First currency crisis. Floating of the sucre.

March 11: Deposit freeze.

August 25: President Mahuad announces suspension of Brady bond payments.

September: Second currency crisis.

October 28: Default on Eurobonds and unilateral rescheduling of domestic dollar-denominated debt.

2000:

January 9: Dollarization.

January 21: Mahuad is ousted in civilian-military coup.

April 19: IMF approves twelve-month standby credit of $304 million.

July 27–August 23: $6.5 billion in Brady and Eurobonds is exchanged for a combination of thirty- and twelve-year global bonds. Ninety-eight percent participation rate.

September 15: Paris Club agreement renegotiating $880 million under Houston terms.

8 Argentina

Among all crises described in this book, Argentina's 2001–2005 debt crisis and restructuring stands out in many respects. Its 2001 default was by far the largest, involving more than $100 billion of privately held debt, plus official bilateral debt. It led to at least four large restructurings: the June 2001 "mega swap" (a voluntary rescheduling operation), the November 2001 "Phase 1" restructuring directed at domestic residents, the March 2002 "pesification," and finally the January–February 2005 exchange. It was also by far the most protracted, taking almost three-and-a-half years between the default and the closing of the restructuring deal. And it extracted by far the highest economic cost, with output collapsing between the first quarter of 2001 and the first quarter of 2002 by a staggering 16.3 percent.

Background

The roots of the 2001 crisis go back at least to the Convertibility Plan of 1991, an exchange-rate-based stabilization program that ended forty-five years of high inflation in Argentina. The Argentine peso was pegged to the U.S. dollar at 1:1, and the Central Bank of the Republic of Argentina (BCRA) was required to back at least two-thirds of its monetary base with hard currency reserves. While convertibility became the signpost of the reform process, the initial success of Argentina's transformation during the 1990s was the result of the simultaneous implementation of significant structural reforms (deregulation, trade liberalization, and privatization), as well as the reopening of its access to capital markets after the signing of the Brady deal in April 1992, which had left Argentina with manageable debt levels on the order of 30 percent of GDP (table 8.1).

Table 8.1
Argentina: Selected economic indicators, 1994–2005

	1994	1995	1996	1997	1998	1999	2000	2001	2002	2003	2004	2005 (est.)
Output and prices												
Real GDP	5.8	-2.8	5.5	8.1	3.9	-3.4	-0.8	-4.4	-10.9	8.8	9.0	9.2
					(annual percentage changes)							
Consumer prices (period average)	4.2	3.4	0.2	0.5	0.9	-1.2	-0.9	-1.1	25.9	13.4	4.4	9.6
Arg$ per U.S. dollar (period average)	0.0	0.1	0.0	0.0	0.0	0.0	0.0	0.0	206.5	-5.3	0.8	-0.7
Terms of trade (goods)	17.3	0.1	7.4	-2.1	-5.8	-6.2	10.0	-0.5	-0.5	8.7	1.5	-2.2
Public finances												
General government						*(in percent of GDP)*						
Revenue	24.2	23.2	22.2	23.2	23.8	24.3	24.6	23.7	23.0	25.9	28.9	29.4
Expenditures	25.4	25.5	25.4	25.3	25.9	28.5	28.2	29.6	24.8	24.8	25.2	27.0
Noninterest	24.1	23.7	23.3	22.9	23.3	25.1	24.2	25.0	22.4	22.8	23.9	25.0
Interest payments (cash)	1.3	1.9	2.1	2.3	2.6	3.4	4.1	4.6	2.4	1.9	1.4	2.0
Primary balance	0.2	-0.4	-1.1	0.3	0.5	-0.8	0.4	-1.3	0.6	3.0	5.0	4.4
Overall balance (cash)	-1.2	-2.3	-3.2	-2.1	-2.1	-4.2	-3.6	-5.9	-1.8	1.1	3.7	2.4
Federal government												
Revenue	19.4	18.6	17.6	18.5	19.0	19.4	19.5	18.8	18.2	20.5	23.4	23.7
Expenditures	19.9	19.6	20.1	20.1	20.3	21.9	22.0	22.4	19.4	20.0	20.8	21.9
Noninterest	18.6	18.0	18.4	18.1	18.0	19.0	18.6	18.6	17.2	18.2	19.6	20.0
Interest payments (cash)	1.3	1.6	1.7	2.0	2.2	2.9	3.4	3.8	2.2	1.8	1.3	1.9
Primary balance	0.8	0.6	-0.8	0.4	0.9	0.4	1.0	0.2	0.9	2.3	3.9	3.7
Overall balance (cash)	-0.5	-0.9	-2.5	-1.6	-1.3	-2.5	-2.4	-3.6	-1.2	0.5	2.6	1.8
Debt[a]	31.3	33.7	35.7	34.5	37.6	43.0	45.0	53.7	149.9	138.0	124.9	74.0
of which: domestic currency debt	3.5	2.4	3.1	3.5	2.8	2.9	2.0	1.7	35.4	33.2	30.5	35.0

(in billions of U.S. dollars unless otherwise indicated)

External sector

Total exports, fob	16.0	21.2	24.0	26.4	26.4	23.3	26.4	26.6	26.2	30.0	34.7	40.0
Total imports, fob	20.2	18.8	22.3	28.6	29.6	24.1	23.9	19.2	9.2	13.9	22.5	28.7
Current account	−11.1	−5.1	−6.8	−12.2	−14.5	−11.9	−9.0	−3.3	8.7	8.0	3.3	3.5
Current account (in percent of GDP)	−4.3	−2.0	−2.5	−4.2	−4.9	−4.2	−3.2	−1.4	8.4	5.7	2.0	1.9
Gross reserves	14.3	14.3	18.1	22.3	24.8	26.3	25.1	14.6	10.5	14.2	19.7	28.1

(annual percentage changes)

Export volumes	17.4	25.1	6.6	15.0	11.6	−0.7	2.7	4.3	0.7	5.0	6.6	14.2
Import volumes	26.9	−11.6	19.4	31.2	8.7	−13.9	−0.9	−17.4	−54.1	53.2	50.4	23.2

Reference item:

Nominal GDP (in billions of Arg$)	257	258	272	293	299	284	284	269	313	376	448	532
Exchange rate (Arg$ per U.S. dollar, period average)	1.00	1.00	1.00	1.00	1.00	1.00	1.00	1.00	3.06	2.90	2.92	2.90

Source: National authorities, IFS, and IMF Country report No. 05/236.

[a] Debt in U.S. dollars evaluated at end-period exchange rates, divided by current GDP in U.S. dollars. For 2005, arrears to creditors that did not participate in the debt exchange are evaluated at the terms of the exchange. Including arrears at face value would result in a debt-to-GDP ratio of 82.9 percent. Excluding them would result in a debt-to-GDP ratio of 70.1 percent.

In the ensuing years, Argentina grew significantly, and improvements in tax collection and privatization revenues allowed it to balance the budget. Capital inflows were briefly interrupted during the tequila crisis, but an effective fiscal tightening and support from the IFIs allowed convertibility to be preserved and strengthened the view that Argentina was on a sound reform path. In the aftermath of the tequila crisis, FDI poured into the country, fueling high growth. However, starting in the second half of 1994, after a brief period of fiscal surpluses, budget deficits reemerged, mainly financed through debt. After the 1995 election, government spending increased, both at the level of the federal government (the president was hoping for a third term) and in the provinces. In addition, a 1994 social security reform reduced contributions to the pay as you go system while the government still needed to pay the current generation of beneficiaries, creating a financing gap that reached almost 3 percent of GDP by the late 1990s. Debt issues by subnational jurisdictions added to the overall debt problem, and recorded debt also increased due to new issues used to cancel previous unregistered liabilities.[1]

In spite of these developments, Argentina's debt-to-GDP ratio stayed below 40 percent until the 1998 Russian default, which increased sovereign spreads and financing costs for all emerging market countries, and led to the January 1999 devaluation of the Brazilian real. These two shocks put substantial pressure on Argentina's exchange rate regime. At this point, many analysts believed that Argentina was trapped in an unsustainable policy mix, fixing its exchange rate to the dollar while pursuing trade integration with Brazil through the trade agreement known as Mercosur. Along with the direct effects of the "sudden stop" of capital flows to emerging market countries, this pessimism, shared by the local business community, led to a slowdown in investment, and a worsening of a recession that had started at the outset of the Russian crisis. The recession in turn reduced revenue, and the deficit increased in 1998 and 1999, for both national and provincial governments. At the same time, restructured debt that had been issued on low-interest terms in the early 1990s was coming due and had to be replaced by market debt at much higher interest rates. These factors increased the primary surpluses that were needed to maintain debt ratios in check, at a time when the economy was in recession. A stream of successive fiscal adjustment packages barely managed to keep up with the increase in the interest bill, delivering no real improvement in the overall deficit situation.

Table 8.2
Argentina: Debt dynamics, 1994–2005 (in percent of GDP unless otherwise stated)

	1994	1995	1996	1997	1998	1999	2000	2001	2002	2003	2004	2005
Federal government debt[a]	31.3	33.7	35.7	34.5	37.6	43.0	45.0	53.7	149.9	138.0	124.9	74.0
Change in debt ratio attributable to...		2.4	1.9	−1.2	3.1	5.4	2.1	8.7	96.2	−11.9	−13.1	−51.0
Primary deficit		−0.6	0.8	−0.4	−0.9	−0.4	−1.0	−0.2	−0.9	−2.3	−3.9	−3.7
Real interest rate[b]		1.0	1.1	1.4	1.8	2.3	2.4	2.6	−0.1	−0.6	−1.9	−1.1
Real growth		0.9	−1.7	−2.6	−1.3	1.3	0.3	2.0	6.5	−11.9	−11.1	−10.2
Real depreciation		−0.3	0.6	0.7	0.9	1.3	0.5	1.6	58.4	−12.9	−7.1	−8.2
Cross-terms		0.0	0.0	0.0	0.0	0.1	0.0	0.2	1.4	−0.5	−0.4	−0.4
Residual		1.5	1.2	−0.2	2.5	0.8	−0.3	2.5	31.0	16.4	11.3	−27.4
of which:												
debt stock operations[c]		0.0	0.0	0.0	0.0	0.0	0.0	0.0	24.7	2.7	0.0	−22.3
interest arrears		0.0	0.0	0.0	0.0	0.0	0.0	0.0	6.5	5.1	4.3	−12.1

[a] Debt expressed in U.S. dollars (local currency debt evaluated at end-period exchange rates), divided by current GDP in U.S. dollars. Debt stock during 2002–2004 includes accumulated interest arrears. 2005 debt stock assumes full participation in the exchange, that is, eligible debt not tendered is reflected as if it had participated.
[b] Computed on a cash basis for 2001–2005, that is, excluding interest arrears.
[c] Includes US$11 billion of provincial debt assumed by federal government in 2002 (10.8 percent of 2002 GDP), US$17.66 billion in compensation "Bodens" to banks (US$14.2 billion in 2002 and US$3.46 billion in 2003), and US$38.3 billion in estimated debt stock reduction as a result of 2005 exchange (assumes full participation).

Table 8.2 allows one to track the sources of changes in the debt-to-GDP ratio from 1994 until the eve of the crisis. The debt-to-GDP ratio remained low—around 35 percent, or a bit less—until about 1997, as interest costs and generally positive residuals, reflecting mainly official recognition of previously unrecorded debt, were offset by real growth, with the primary deficit close to zero. Between 1997 and 2000, the debt-to-GDP ratio rose by about 10 percentage points, as growth stopped and turned negative, and real interest rates rose. The federal primary balance went into a slight surplus, between 0 and 1 percent, but this effect was not large enough to offset the factors pulling up the debt to GDP ratio. Finally, there was a sharp rise in debt in 2001 attributable mainly to high real interest rates and negative growth. The debt ratio exploded after the devaluation in early 2002.

The Crisis Begins

In late 1999, Fernando De La Rúa, a centrist from the Radical Party, was elected after ten years of Peronist administration. De La Rua made fiscal responsibility his main priority. However, his finance minister, Jose Luis Machinea, president of the BCRA during the hyperinflation of 1989, failed to create the confidence needed to turn around the economy. By mid-2000, expectations turned very negative, and analysts began arguing that Argentina, given its stagnant growth rate, was embarked on an unsustainable debt path. These worries increased after the resignation of the vice-president over an alleged bribery scandal, which substantially weakened the government.

In spite of significant tax increases and some expenditure cuts (including public sector wage reductions), the federal fiscal deficit remained almost unchanged at around Arg$7 billion (about 2.5 percent of GDP) in 2000. The resilience of the fiscal imbalance triggered a run on the bond market, with country spreads skyrocketing to close to 1,000 points in late 2000, before the Ministry of Finance was able to put together a program with the aim of covering Argentina's financing needs for the period 2001–2002. The program, known as the "blindaje," was announced on December 18, 2000, and released a substantial line of credit from multilaterals, totaling close to $20 billion.[2] In an attempt to jump-start the economy, the package also relaxed the limits imposed by the "fiscal responsibility law" approved in 1999, which had imposed quantitative targets for the budget and was supposed to constrain government deficits. The package brought relief in the short run, and country risk fell from about 1,000 to 700 basis points in just a few days (figure 8.1). However, this improvement turned out to be short-lived.

One aim of the blindaje was to make the fiscal program incentive compatible, by maintaining fiscal pressure on local authorities. This was achieved by not covering all of Argentina's financial needs in either year. As a result, the government faced combined rollover needs of the order of $4 billion in April and May 2001. By early March, market rumors pointed to the fact that such financing would not be forthcoming unless radical fiscal consolidation could be implemented. Once the fiscal numbers for the first quarter showed that the IMF fiscal targets had been missed by close to $1 billion (with a deficit of $3 billion in the first quarter alone), the minister realized that he had no chance of securing the financing, and resigned. Ricardo Lopez Murphy, a respected orthodox economist, was appointed to the post.

The new finance minister attempted an expenditure cut of about $2 billion (about 3.7 percent of federal noninterest expenditure in 2000). While this was a quantitatively modest objective, it would have been sufficient at the time to put the IMF-backed program back on track. However, the expenditure cuts met fierce political opposition. The minister lost the support of the president and decided to resign only two weeks after being appointed. He was replaced by Domingo Cavallo, the architect of the 1991 Convertibility Plan, who was widely credited with taming Argentina's inflation and engineering the economic miracle of the early 1990s.

Cavallo argued that Argentina's problem was not fiscal disequilibria but the lack of growth. To stimulate growth, he slashed taxes in some labor-intensive sectors, replacing the proceeds with a tax on financial transactions. In spite of the heterodox rhetoric, this new tax allowed the fiscal deficit to fall in line with the targets of the ongoing program with the IMF (figure 8.2). To deliver a more stable trade-weighted real exchange rate—the strength of the dollar relative to the euro had hurt Argentina's competitiveness in European markets—Cavallo also proposed to change the convertibility arrangement by shifting from a dollar peg to pegging to an average of the euro and the dollar. To avoid a devaluation, the policy would become effective only when the euro reached parity with the dollar. While the dollar remained strong, the government instituted a "convergence factor" that would tax imports and subsidize exports in the amount of the difference between the ongoing exchange rate and that implied by the new basket peg. This was widely viewed as a hidden devaluation, and convinced many analysts that an exit from convertibility was near. In addition, disagreements between the finance minister and the president of the central bank led to the resignation of the latter. The combination of these events shattered confidence in Argentina's exchange rate system, increasing interest rates and halting a surge in consumer confidence—as indicated, for example, by a brief rise in retail sales—that had taken place in the initial weeks of Cavallo's tenure.

The financing needs of April and May 2001 were covered by issuing a bond to local financial institutions, with a regulatory incentive that allowed banks to integrate liquidity requirements with the new instrument. Banks drew from their liquid reserves abroad (which previous regulation had encouraged with the intention of providing liquidity in times of need). Later in the year the government also exerted moral suasion on the banks, particularly to roll over provincial debt. As a

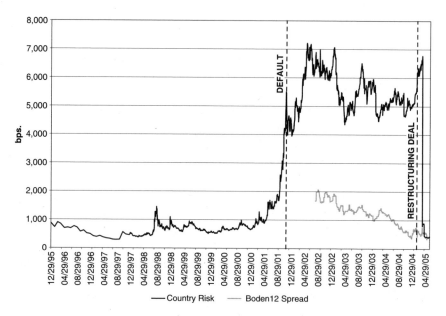

Figure 8.1
Country risk
Source: JP Morgan.

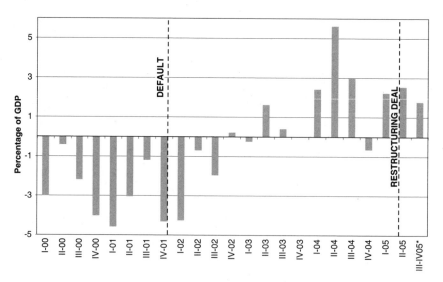

Figure 8.2
Quarterly deficits before and after the crisis
Source: Argentine Ministry of Economy.

result, bank exposure to government paper increased somewhat during the year, in spite of the fact that some banks were attempting (unsuccessfully) to reduce their exposure to the public sector. However, banking system exposure to the government remained moderate compared with other sovereign debt crises studied in this book, on the order of 25 percent of assets, and the banking system remained reasonably capitalized. Instead, a more immediate concern was liquidity, driven by deposit outflows, which accelerated in April 2001.

With low international confidence in Cavallo's recovery plan and lower international reserves of the Argentine banking system as a result of the April–May 2001 government financing operation, international debt markets remained closed for Argentina. Local markets also seemed to dry up, forcing a cancellation of a short-term T-bill auction scheduled for April 24. Many Wall Street analysts argued that Argentina would devalue or default, and some even contended that Argentina should do so as quickly as possible.

The Mega Swap

In a final attempt to stave off default, the government offered a debt swap to lengthen the maturity of its debt and reduce its financing needs in the short run. The exchange was expected to be larger than any previous attempt and included a number of special characteristics. First, it would cover a very large range of bonds, including short-, medium-, and long-term, and a total nominal value of debt of $65 billion. The government stressed that the exchange was strictly "voluntary" in order to avoid any suggestion that it was looking at restructuring its debt. As the exchange was taking place at a moment in which risk spreads were extremely high, the extension of maturity could potentially be very expensive. In light of this, the exchange was structured in "buckets" according to maturity: short-term debt could only be transformed into relatively short instruments (though obviously longer than the original); medium-term instruments could be exchanged for similar medium range instruments; and long instruments exchanged for longer instruments with substantial short-run capitalization of interests. The coupon structure was changed to provide substantial debt relief in the initial years.

The operation was implemented through a syndicate of banks with JP Morgan and Credit Suisse First Boston (CSFB) as lead managers, and Deutsche Bank, Salomon Smith Barney, and a set of local institutions as co-managers.[3] The offers could be placed either in a competitive or noncompetitive segment, with noncompetitive offers accepting any cutoff price (over a threshold announced in advance). Competitive offers risked being left out of the exchange.

Under the operation, short-term local debt was exchanged for another local bond (under Argentine law) with maturity in 2006, six semester amortization bullets, interest capitalization in the first two years, and an interest rate linked to local rates after two years. New York-denominated bonds were exchanged for three global bonds (also under New York law) maturing in 2008, 2018, and 2031. The 2008 global had an interest rate of 7 percent during the first three years and 15.50 percent for the remaining years and amortized in six semester bullets at the end of its life; the 2018 five years of interest capitalization with a 12.25 percent interest rate after the first year and amortized in five semester bullets; and the 2031 five years of interest capitalization, an interest coupon of 12 percent in ensuing years, and an amortization in only one bullet after thirty years. "Competitive" participants in each market segment announced the price at which they were willing to part with their old bonds in exchange for the new bond to be issued. The government chose its cutoff price so as to to balance participation, short-term debt relief, and cost.

Out of a total eligible debt of $65 billion, offers were received for $32.8 billion. In the end, $29 billion of debt was exchanged, reducing debt service obligations by close to $16 billion in the initial five years. The cost of the exchange was 35 basis points, based on comparing the yield of the debt retired and the cost of new issues of similar maturity. Maturities, however, were extended at a cost, given medium-term market interest rates of about 16 percent. In other words, debt service obligations in the short run were reduced at the expense of higher debt service in the medium and long run (figure 8.3).

While the government insisted that the debt exchange was not the priority of its economic program, and that sustained recovery could only come from a fiscal improvement, the debt exchange allowed for a short-lived reduction in secondary market spreads. However, the economic recovery remained elusive. Furthermore, in July 2001, several provinces started showing significant refinancing difficulties. The provinces had relied on bond issues as well as on bank loans to finance their increasing deficits, backed by a tax guarantee by which taxes collected by the federal government but owned by the provinces were

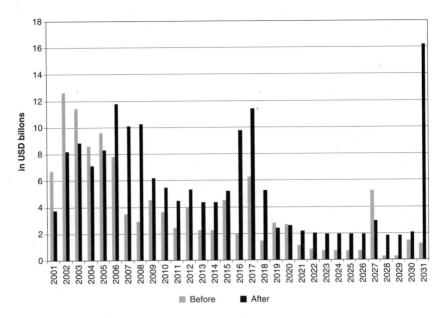

Figure 8.3
Total debt service and amortizations before and after the exchange
Source: Argentine Ministry of Economy.

first assigned to a fiduciary which honored debt payments prior to transferring the remainder of the resources to the provinces. However, by early July many provinces had run up so much debt that the residual resources after debt payments were dangerously low. This uncertainty triggered a new run on the bond markets. Spreads that had fallen to less than 800 basis points after the debt exchange increased to 1,000 two weeks later. Faced with a new run, Cavallo launched the idea of implementing a zero deficit fiscal rule. A change in the financial administration law was enacted, which legally committed the secretary of the treasury to cut wages and pensions if resources were not sufficient to balance the budget. The initial cut was 13 percent to be applied to the third quarter, ensuring a zero deficit on an accrual basis (a deficit of $800 million remained on a cash basis).

The zero deficit law, passed on July 29, was met with substantial market skepticism. In spite of implementing an expenditure cut of about $4 billion per year (about 1.4 percent of GDP), it induced a massive sell-off of Argentine debt with spreads increasing by about 400 basis points immediately after the announcement. It is not entirely clear why the markets reacted so negatively to a fiscal adjustment they

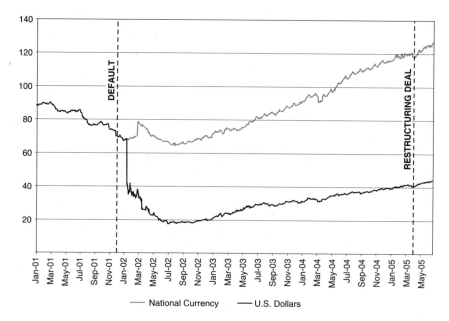

Figure 8.4
Deposits in Argentina's financial sector (in billions)
Source: IFS.

had been demanding for so long. One possibility is that the zero deficit rule was interpreted as a recognition by the government that it had been cut off from credit market markets, leaving it only with a radical, procyclical fiscal measure which would be very difficult to sustain. At the same time, worries about an impending public debt crisis spilled over into the financial sector, whose exposure to the public sector had grown in the course of 2001 as a result of the government's difficulties in placing new debt in international markets. The result was a substantial outflow of deposits and loss of reserves (figure 8.4). As money poured out of the financial sector and out of Argentina, the economic implosion accelerated.

At this point, the only alternative to default was to obtain additional support from the IMF. After much debate within the IMF and among its major shareholders, the IMF decided to extend its support, in part in recognition of the substantial fiscal effort the administration had undertaken throughout the year. A $4 billion credit line to prop up the reserves of the central bank was made immediately available (figure 8.5). About $1 billion was transferred to the government. Some addi-

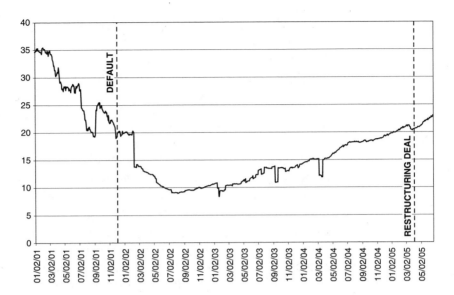

Figure 8.5
International reserves (in billions)
Source: IFS.

tional private financing was also mobilized by triggering a contingent repo line with private banks in the amount of about $2 billion.[4] At about the same time, the U.S. Treasury took the view that some IMF money should be used to reduce Argentina's debt burden directly, by buying back high-interest debt, or guaranteeing new debt issues at a lower cost.[5] However, the money allocated by the IMF for this purpose (about $3 billion, to be disbursed in the next year) was relatively small, and no other financing sources were readily available. Hence, the main effect of the U.S. Treasury initiative may have been to bolster market views that Argentina's debt problem could not be resolved without some kind of debt restructuring, undermining the authorities' efforts to weather the crisis through a combination of new financing and additional fiscal austerity.

The November 2001 Phase 1 Exchange

Tax collection in September 2001 fell substantially, once again forcing additional fiscal measures. Unable to convince governors to cut provincial spending, Cavallo announced that he would seek debt relief through a "voluntary" exchange in two phases, initially with local bondholders, and in a second stage with foreigners. The announcement created substantial uncertainty, with bond prices plummeting in the days following the announcement. In the event, only "Phase 1" materialized, as the government was ousted shortly after the exchange.

The strategy of Phase 1 was to offer local holders of Argentina's bonds a "guaranteed" loan, governed by Argentine law, in exchange for their bonds. The guarantee of the loan was to be the revenue collected through the financial transactions tax. Moreover, bondholders were given the option of recovering the original bonds if any terms or conditions of the guaranteed loans were changed in the future. In exchange for the granting of the guarantee, interest payments would be reduced and maturities extended. Depending on the bond tendered, investors were given up to three exchange options. One option was a fixed rate bond in which interest rates would be reduced by 30 percent relative to the original rate, with a cap at 7 percent per annum. Maturities were also extended on shorter term instruments and interest payments made monthly, in order to match interest payments with the collection of the financial transaction tax. For floating rate bonds similar conditions were imposed, the cap being set at LIBOR plus 300 basis points. Finally, a third option was to convert into a capitalizing bond with maturity in 2011. Only a few bonds were offered this alternative.

Several incentives for participation were offered, including a regulatory benefit for participating banks and pension funds, namely, that the new instrument could be valued at par rather than marked to market. However, the main incentive was the threat of an involuntary restructuring at worse terms if the exchange was not accepted.[6] The exchange offer was considered a technical default by rating agencies and S&P moved Argentina to the selective default (SD) category.

The bond exchange was successful in the sense that almost all debt in the hands of banks, local pension funds, and local residents was tendered. In all, $41.7 billion of debt instruments were tendered, implying a reduction of $2.35 billion in interest, and $2.5 billion in amortizations in 2002 alone. Financing needs were reduced by $26.2 billion in the first five years (figure 8.6).

How harsh was the Phase 1 exchange from an investor perspective? Table 8.3 contains haircut calculations for most of the exchanged instruments, using maturity adjusted yields derived from either the November 2001 yields on the old, mostly externally issued instruments ("upper bound" estimates) or yields calculated from postdefault debt prices ("lower bound" estimates).[7] Argentina had remained current on

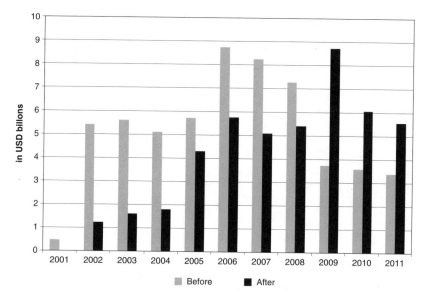

Figure 8.6
Total debt service and amortizations before and after the exchange
Source: Argentine Ministry of Economy.

its payments until the exchange, so there was no PDI or past due principal, and there were no cash payments associated with the exchange. Based on Option 1, which was given to all instruments and which was generally the most favorable, almost all "lower bound" estimates exceed 25 percent while most "upper bound" estimates are below 60 percent. The average haircut was about 40 percent, somewhat higher than for the Ecuador, Ukraine, and Pakistan exchanges, but below those suffered by Russia's creditors in 1999 and 2000.

In spite of the improvement in the government's cash flow, Argentina deficit continued to overshoot the targets convened with the IMF in August 2001, and by late November, it was clear that new IMF disbursements would, at a minimum, be delayed. As a result, deposit withdrawals from the financial sector accelerated in the last week of November, forcing the government to announce an exchange market holiday and a deposit freeze in order to avoid the collapse of the two largest public banks (Banco de la Nación and Banco Provincia). The deposit freeze led to a popular uprising that ended with the resignation of Cavallo on December 19, 2001, and one day later, of the president.

Table 8.3
Argentina Phase 1 exchange, November 2001: Haircuts (per 100 units of principal)

Old instrument	Outstanding (millions of U.S. dollars)	Due date	Haircuts					
			Upper bound[a]			Lower bound[b]		
			Option 1: Fixed rate	Option 2: Floating	Option 3: Capitalizing	Option 1: Fixed rate	Option 2: Floating	Option 3: Capitalizing
Bonte 02	2,201	5/9/02	42.1	44.2	...	23.4	24.1	...
Bonte 03F	260	7/21/03	40.5	51.0	...	29.3	29.6	...
Bonte 03	1,695	5/21/03	41.4	51.7	77.7	28.4	28.7	49.8
Bonte 04	1,358	5/24/04	45.7	64.5	77.6	30.1	32.2	47.7
Bonte 05	1,727	5/21/05	46.6	50.9	78.7	27.0	25.8	47.5
Bonte 06	856	5/15/06	39.1	45.4	73.9	27.3	25.4	45.2
FRB	2,310	3/29/05	71.3	...	...	18.1	...	...
FRN 04	231	4/6/04	61.9	...	...	22.5	...	...
GD03D	1,843	12/20/03	53.4	54.7	...	25.0	25.3	...
GD05D	862	12/4/05	45.5	49.7	76.7	24.5	22.6	43.9
GD06D	1,213	10/9/06	31.2	36.6	70.6	21.4	17.1	39.7
Global 08	11,096	12/19/08	37.6	64.4	71.8	29.1	52.0	43.9
Global 09	1,413	4/7/09	41.5	59.8	71.1	32.3	28.5	43.3
Global 10	860	3/15/10	42.9	60.3	70.9	32.6	28.3	42.0
Global 12	923	2/21/12	42.4	66.2	...	33.5	16.7	...
Global 15	903	6/15/15	46.3	62.3	...	37.7	17.2	...
Global 17	2,503	1/30/17	41.9	63.0	...	35.2	29.3	...
Global 18	7,060	6/19/18	66.0	83.5	...	47.7	17.3	...
Global 19	176	2/25/19	46.0	60.9	...	39.6	32.9	...
Global 20	158	2/1/20	44.3	63.7	...	38.8	32.4	...
Global 27	995	9/19/27	32.8	63.2	...	30.3	20.4	...
Global 30	241	7/21/30	37.6	61.6	...	33.9	25.2	...
Global 31	15	1/31/31	46.9	63.6	...	43.0	35.5	...

Global 31 mega	9,219	6/19/31	52.5	85.2	…	50.9	38.5	…
PRE 3	73	9/1/02	56.9	…	…	35.2	…	…
PRE 4	648	9/1/02	64.7	…	…	38.6	…	…
PRO1	658	4/1/07	50.5	…	…	27.9	…	…
PRO2	520	4/1/07	69.1	…	…	38.9	…	…
PRO3	6	12/28/10	48.7	…	…	26.2	…	…
PRO4	1,144	12/28/10	71.8	…	…	47.5	…	…
PRO6	1,033	4/15/07	57.9	…	…	18.8	…	…
Hidro	20	12/2/08	75.1	…	…	42.1	…	…
Bonex 92	177	9/15/02	58.2	…	…	90.0	…	…
Bonte 27	98	9/19/27	32.5	63.2	…	41.8	34.2	…
Span 02	135	11/30/02	46.1	61.2	83.8	30.5	31.3	53.0
FRAN	456	4/10/05	66.1	68.8	86.5	28.4	27.2	48.5
RA $02	113	7/10/02	49.5	…	…	22.1	…	…
RA $07	80	2/12/07	45.4	…	…	41.2	…	…
RA $08	931	9/19/08	40.7	…	70.4	37.8	…	45.0
Global 29	125	3/1/29	42.1	60.3	…	39.6	38.6	…
PRE 5	0	1/1/10	10.1	…	…	23.6	…	…
Pre 6	76	1/1/10	55.2	…	…	24.9	…	…
PRO5	289	4/15/07	44.7	…	…	26.5	…	…
PRO8	10	1/1/16	35.1	…	…	19.3	…	…
PRO9	101	4/15/07	38.6	…	…	27.9	…	…
Radar 1	380	4/24/03	45.3	…	75.2	23.9	…	46.6
Radar 2	380	5/28/03	46.9	…	75.7	25.0	…	47.4
Radar 3	400	7/24/06	17.7	…	60.5	15.7	…	38.2
Radar 4	250	8/8/06	16.3	…	43.6	18.8	…	23.4
Celtic 2	300	9/4/07	40.1	…	59.9	13.4	…	33.8

Source: Sturzenegger and Zettelmeyer (2005).

[a] Based on the yield of old instruments trading in the market on November 7, 2001.

[b] Based on the yield of postdefault bonds trading in September 2002 (see text).

Default and Pesification

A new interim president, Adolfo Rodríguez Saá, decided to default outright on all debt. In a brief communiqué on December 24, 2001, Argentina announced that it was suspending all debt service, though the status of some debt instruments remained uncertain. Multilateral lending remained current, and guaranteed loans, which capitalized interest through April, were left in a gray area pending definition. This default was unique in that all claims were declared in default, even before payments were actually missed. The default was also unique in that it was celebrated in Congress as a victory, in spite of the fact that an estimated 60 percent of the defaulted debt was held by Argentines themselves (a larger fraction than in our previous case studies).

Only ten days into his tenure, Rodríguez Saá lost the support of his party and was forced to resign. The new president, Eduardo Duhalde, quickly decided to devalue the peso, and in early February 2002 announced the forced "pesification"—conversion into local currency at nonmarket exchange rates—of dollar-denominated assets and liabilities in the financial sector. Pesification was to occur in an asymmetric fashion: dollar deposits and loans to the public sector would be pesified at a rate of 1:1.4, while loans to private sector debtors would be pesified at 1:1. Given that the exchange rate was close to two pesos per dollar and rapidly depreciating (figure 8.7), asymmetric pesification hence involved a transfer from banks to both public and particularly private debtors. Depositors were also hurt, but since they were pesified at a more appreciated rate than bank loans to private creditors, the net effect was to make the banking system insolvent, requiring a government bailout. Bank withdrawal restrictions remained in place, and all time deposits above a small threshold were restructured into long ten-year inflation-indexed peso- or dollar-denominated bonds.

Details of the pesification of government debt were spelled out in government decree 471, issued on March 8, 2002. Domestically issued government debt instruments would first be pesified at 1.40 pesos per dollar, and then indexed to a local inflation index. Bonds would keep their payment schedule and original maturities, but would pay an interest of only 2 percent beginning in February 2002. The only exception was the guaranteed loans that would accrue 3–5 percent depending on maturity; guaranteed loans with five-year capitaliza-

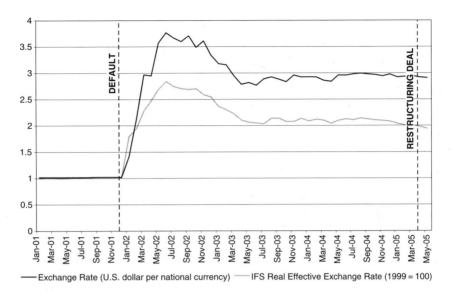

Figure 8.7
Nominal and real exchange rates
Source: IFS.

tion of interest would accrue at a rate of 5.5 percent. There was no exchange—the terms of domestic law instruments were simply changed by fiat—except that investors were given the choice to return to the defaulted foreign currency bonds they had tendered in Phase 1. It is estimated that holders of about $3.65 billion "pesified loans" made use of this option. In addition, creditors holding about $16.3 billion pesified loans—mostly pension funds—rejected both alternatives, and took legal action against the government; their loans were eventually "redollarized" by decree in August 2003. In contrast, banks decided not to sue, expecting a direct compensation from the government for their losses, and the government eventually announced the issuance of compensation bonds (Bodens) amounting to about $9 billion.

Table 8.4 shows the creditor losses resulting from the discrepancy between the conversion rate and the market exchange rate, as well as the reduction in interest payments. For brevity, we show only the options available to the bonds that had exchanged at least $500 million in the Phase 1 exchange (see Sturzenegger and Zettelmeyer 2005 for a more complete listing and details). We discount the original

Table 8.4
Argentina pesification, February 2002: Haircuts (per 100 units of principal)

Bond	Due date	Haircut[a]	Bond	Due date	Haircut[a]
Bonex 92	9/15/02	25.6	PG TV FRN 04	4/6/07	37.3
Bonte 02	5/9/02	27.5	PG TV GL 03	12/20/06	35.6
Bonte 03	5/21/03	35.8	PG TV GL 05	12/4/08	42.4
Bonte 03F	7/21/03	38.7	PG TV GL 06	10/9/09	42.6
Bonte 04	5/24/04	40.7	PG TV GL 08	12/19/11	46.9
Bonte 05	5/21/05	47.0	PG TV GL 09	5/7/12	45.0
Bonte 06	5/15/06	51.0	PG TV GL 30	7/21/30	61.0
Bonte 27	9/19/27	84.2	PG TV GL 31	1/31/31	61.2
Hidro	12/2/08	29.1	PG TV GL 31 mega	6/19/31	71.3
PG 2009 7%	6/19/09	42.4	PG TV Hexagon 2	11/30/05	35.5
PG 2011 GL 08	11/6/11	36.9	PG TV Hexagon 3	12/23/05	35.8
PG TF API	3/15/16	39.4	PG TV Hexagon 4	9/27/08	41.6
PG TF BP E+400/02	7/21/06	36.9	PG TV Radar 1	4/24/06	37.1
PG TF Bonte 02	5/9/05	33.1	PG TV Radar 2	5/28/06	37.4
PG TF Bonte 03	5/21/06	36.4	PG TV Radar 3	7/24/09	44.0
PG TF Bonte 04	5/24/07	35.5	PG TV Radar 4	8/8/09	44.2
PG TF Bonte 05	5/21/08	37.7	PG TV SPAN	11/30/05	35.5
PG TF Bonte 06	5/15/09	39.8	PGTF GL10	3/15/13	40.1
PG TF Bonte 27	9/19/27	51.0	PGTF GL12	2/21/12	38.7
PG TF Capitalizable 2020	6/29/20	54.1	PGTF GL15	6/15/15	43.4
PG TF Cert. Cap BNA 2018	12/30/18	51.4	PGTF GL17	1/30/17	44.3
PG TF FRAN	4/10/08	37.5	PGTF GL18	7/19/18	49.8
PG TF GL 03	12/20/06	33.7	PGTF GL19	2/25/19	46.1
PG TF GL 05	12/4/08	38.9	PGTF GL20	2/1/20	46.4
PG TF GL 06	10/9/09	40.5	PGTF GL27	9/19/27	50.0
PG TF GL 08	12/19/11	42.4	PGTF GL29	3/1/32	40.2
PG TF GL 09	5/7/12	38.9	PGTF RA$08	9/19/11	44.4
PG TF GL 30	7/21/30	52.4	PGTV GL10	3/15/13	46.6
PG TF GL 31	1/31/31	52.6	PGTV GL12	2/21/12	42.1
PG TF GL 31 mega	6/19/31	60.8	PGTV GL15	6/15/15	51.1
PG TF SPAN	11/30/05	35.0	PGTV GL17	1/30/17	52.0
PG TV API	3/15/16	44.2	PGTV GL18	7/19/18	60.4
PG TV BONEX 92	9/15/05	32.8	PGTV GL19	2/25/19	54.5
PG TV BP Act./02	8/7/05	34.4	PGTV GL20	2/1/20	54.4

Table 8.4
(continued)

Bond	Due date	Haircut[a]	Bond	Due date	Haircut[a]
PG TV BP E+300/02	8/7/05	34.4	PGTV GL27	9/19/27	59.3
PG TV BP E+330/02	8/22/05	33.2	PGTV GL29	3/1/32	50.3
PG TV BP E+400/02	4/24/05	33.1	PGTV Hidro$	12/2/11	29.7
PG TV BP E+435/02	2/16/07	36.9	PGTV Pre4	9/1/05	32.6
PG TV BP E+580 mega/02	6/19/09	43.8	PGTV Pre4	1/1/13	46.8
PG TV BP E+580/02	7/21/06	38.1	PGTV Pro10	4/15/10	30.1
PG TV BP E+580/02	8/7/05	34.4	PGTV Pro2	4/1/10	37.4
PG TV Bono YPF	2/3/09	36.9	PGTV Pro4	12/28/13	34.9
PG TV Bonte 02	5/9/05	33.3	PGTV Pro6	4/15/10	28.0
PG TV Bonte 03	5/21/06	37.4	PGTV Pro8	1/1/19	46.1
PG TV Bonte 03 F	7/21/06	38.1	PRE 4	9/1/02	35.7
PG TV Bonte 04	5/24/07	37.6	PRO2	4/1/07	31.4
PG TV Bonte 05	5/21/08	40.6	PRO4	12/28/10	34.6
PG TV Bonte 06	5/15/09	43.5	PRO6	4/15/07	29.9
PG TV Bonte 27	9/19/27	59.7	PRO8	1/1/16	69.8
PG TV Celtic I	9/23/10	47.1	Pre 6	1/1/10	65.2
PG TV Celtic II	9/4/10	47.1	Radar 1	4/24/03	29.2
PG TV FRAN	4/10/08	40.4	Radar 2	5/28/03	29.6
PG TV FRB	3/31/08	45.4	Radar 3	7/24/06	35.7

Source: Sturzenegger and Zettelmeyer (2005).
[a] Using yields on performing domestic U.S. dollar and peso-indexed bonds to discount payment streams of old and new instruments, respectively, and an exchange rate 1.9 pesos per U.S. dollar to express the resulting NPVs in the same currency.

dollar-denominated instruments by the yield of dollar-denominated instruments at the time, while the cash flow of the new instruments are discounted by the yield on indexed peso bonds. The final step is to convert the peso NPVs into dollars using the current exchange rate of one point nine pesos per U.S. dollar, so they can be compared with the present value of the old instruments. Haircuts were in the 30–60 percent range, and the average haircut was about 42 percent.

The pesification of guaranteed loans led to a wave of depositor litigation and court orders directed against the government and the banking system. In January 2002 the Supreme Court had ruled in a case related to the deposit freeze, *Smith v. Poder Ejecutivo*, finding that an "economic emergency" justified a transitory suspension of property rights but not the arbitrary or permanent denial of such rights. Following pesification, this ruling gave depositors a legal basis for obtaining court orders ("amparos") that required banks to pay out U.S. dollar-denominated deposits at the prevailing market exchange rate rather than the Arg$1.40 per U.S. dollar at which they had been pesified. As a result of these deposit leakages, the BCRA was forced to inject liquidity into an increasing number of banks, fueling a run on the currency, which led the BCRA to sharply raise interest rates on peso deposits to almost 100 percent in early April. The authorities eventually declared a weeklong bank holiday in late April, and further tightened deposit and exchange restrictions.

Although many of these emergency measures were overturned by the Argentine congress or the judiciary, deposit outflows abated at the end of the second quarter, reflecting high domestic interest rates, expectations that the Supreme Court would overturn pesification and the fact that depositors were effectively given full protection in cases of bank closures. At the same time, the government exercised regulatory forbearance to allow banks to continue operating, including special valuation rules for debt under default, and renewed liquidity assistance that had been granted during the crisis. Liquidity improved, and withdrawal restrictions on sight deposits were lifted on December 2, 2002. However, credit recovery was very slow, as banks preferred to hoard liquidity in light of the liabilities they could face if courts insisted on returning deposits in dollars, as well as uncertainty about the ultimate outcome of the external debt restructuring.[8]

By mid-2002, the crisis had bottomed out. The large real depreciation stimulated strong import substitution and thus a recovery of employment, reducing social tensions. A reduction in capital outflows also provided some stimulus to the economy. The government moved to stabilize the exchange rate at 3.5 pesos to the dollar, further contributing to a sense of relief, and called elections for May 2003, helping to reduce political uncertainty. By the end of the year the economy was growing strongly. Prices had jumped in the initial part of the year but then stabilized. By the second half of the year it was clear that a hyperinflation had been avoided. At the same time, the increase in tax revenues that went hand in hand with the increase in price levels allowed a strong improvement in the fiscal position. Pesified "guaranteed loans" were serviced, and the government used its reserves to repay about $4 billion to multilaterals. In early 2003, a temporary lending package was agreed with the IMF, ahead of a longer-term arrangement after the May elections.

From the Dubai Guidelines to the 2005 Debt Restructuring

In May 2003, Nestor Kirchner, a left-wing candidate from the Peronist party, was elected President. By mid-September, a new medium-term agreement was negotiated with the IMF, which envisaged no additional funds but implied that the IMF's claims would effectively be rolled over during the next three years.

In September 2003, the government presented an initial debt restructuring strategy known as the "Dubai guidelines" focused on the objective of attaining a haircut of 75 percent in nominal terms. In contrast to previous practice, past due interest would not be recognized. Initial computations put the NPV loss implied by the proposal on the order of 90 percent. Not surprisingly, the proposal met fierce resistance from creditors and unleashed a wave of litigation both in Europe and New York (see chapter 3). In one of the more notable cases, a U.S. federal court in New York granted a $700 million judgment against Argentina in favor of EM Ltd., a subsidiary of Dart Capital, but, at the same time, granted a stay on enforcement to give Argentina time to make a restructuring offer. The stay expired on January 30, 2004, but enforcement efforts remained unsuccessful, as judgment creditors found it difficult to find attachable assets.

In late 2003, the government held a series of meetings with "consultative groups" which the government's financial advisors had set up in mid-2003 to facilitate contacts with creditors. At about the same time, regional creditor groups began to organize. In January 2004, a Global Committee of Argentine Bondholders (GCAB) claiming to represent at least $37 billion of defaulted debt (about 45 percent of the nominal debt stock to be restructured, and about two-thirds of the externally held debt) was established; this was comprised of U.S. bondholder representatives (Argentine Bondholders Committee, or ABC); Italian and Japanese banks, and the Argentina Bond Restructuring Agency, a special-purpose vehicle representing German, Austrian, and Italian retail bondholders. After initially declining to negotiate with GCAB, the government committed to talks with a long list of external creditor groups, including GCAB, in its March 2004 letter of intent to the IMF.[9] A meeting took place on April 16, 2004, but was not followed by any further negotiations before the government presented its exchange offer. That in itself was not particularly unusual: unlike the BAC process of the 1980s, most bond exchanges described in this book were not preceded by substantive negotiations (see chapter 1 and

Rieffel 2003). But because it occurred in the context of a the government's contentious Dubai debt resolution strategy, and because the March letter of intent to the IMF may have raised expectations, the lack of negotiations triggered bitter reactions from creditor representatives.

On June 1, 2004, the government presented a tentative restructuring plan based on the Dubai guidelines that became known as the "Dubai Plus" or "Buenos Aires proposal." The offer would comprise a "menu" of three securities—a par bond with no face value reduction, a discount bond with a high face value reduction, and a "quasipar" bond in between—to be issued in a range of currencies. Furthermore, all instruments would include a detachable "GDP warrant" with payments tied to GDP growth. Details of the proposal emerged in the following weeks and months in the context of various government filings with the U.S. Securities and Exchange Commission. On November 1, 2004, the government published its final offer.

Par and discount bonds would be offered in four currencies: U.S. dollars, euros, yens, and CPI-indexed pesos. Existing debt securities denominated in U.S. dollars, euros, or yen could be exchanged for new debt securities denominated in the original debt security currency, in U.S. dollars or in indexed pesos; other international currency debt could be changed for debt in pesos, dollars, or euros (a featured geared mostly to the Italian retail market that had large holdings of Italian lira denominated bonds). Owners of peso bonds were required to stay in peso indexed bonds. Par bonds would have a maturity of thirty-five years, pay low but increasing coupons (see table 8.5), and amortize in nineteen half-year installments starting in September 2029. Discount bonds would have a maturity of thirty years and amortize in twenty equal payments beginning in June 2024; they would be exchanged at 33.7 percent of the original face value but pay a high constant coupon: 8.28 percent for the dollar instrument or 5.83 percent in indexed pesos (part of this capitalized during the first ten years). Because the real exchange rate of the Argentine peso with respect to the major currencies was expected to appreciate following the exchange, indexed peso coupons were set lower than dollar, yen, or euro coupons, by about 2.5 percentage points. However, at the time of the exchange the difference between dollar rates and peso-indexed yields of performing bonds in both currencies was closer to 3.5 points; this provided an incentive to choose local currency CPI-indexed bonds.

The "quasipar" bond had a maturity of forty-two years, was exchanged at 69.6 percent of face value, had an interest rate of 3.31

Table 8.5
Argentina: Characteristics of 2005 bonds

	Par bond			"Quasi par" bond	Discount bond		
Currency	Pesos	Dollars	Euros	Pesos	Pesos	Dollars	Euros
Issue date	12/31/03	12/31/03	12/31/03	12/31/03	12/31/03	12/31/03	12/31/03
Due date	12/31/38	12/31/38	12/31/38	12/31/45	12/31/33	12/31/33	12/31/33
Maturity	35 years	35 years	35 years	42 years	30 years	30 years	30 years
Face value discount	0	0	0	30.1	66.3	66.3	66.3
Coupon (in percent)	Year 1–5: 0.63 Year 6–15: 1.18 Year 16–25: 1.77 Remainder: 2.48	Year 1–5: 1.33 Year 6–15: 2.50 Year 16–25: 3.75 Remainder: 5.25	Year 1–5: 1.20 Year 6–15: 2.26 Year 16–25: 3.38 Remainder: 4.74	3.31 (capitalizes during first 10 years)	Year 1–5: 2.79 in cash, 3.04 capitalizing; Year 6–10: 4.06 cash, 1.77 capitalizing; Year 11–30: 5.83	Year 1–5: 3.97 in cash, 4.31 capitalizing; Year 6–10: 5.77 cash, 2.51 capitalizing; Year 11–30: 8.28	Year 1–5: 3.75 in cash, 4.07 capitalizing; Year 6–10: 5.45 cash, 2.37 capitalizing; Year 11–30: 7.82
Amortization	19 biannual payments (March and September) beginning on 09/30/29 and one final quarterly payment on 12/31/38; Principal linked to CPI	19 biannual payments (March and September) beginning on 09/30/29 and one final quarterly payment on 12/31/38		20 equal payments (June and December), beginning on 06/30/36	20 equal payments (June and December), beginning on 06/30/24; Principal linked to CPI	20 equal payments (June and December), beginning on 06/30/24	
Applicable law	Argentina	New York or Argentina	United Kingdom	Argentina	Argentina	New York or Argentina	United Kingdom

that capitalized during the first ten years, and amortized in twenty se-mester payments starting in 2036. This bond was issued in indexed pesos only, and targeted specifically to local pension funds. A mini-mum of $350,000 was required to bid for this bond, imposing a con-straint on retail investors. In contrast, a maximum of $50,000 per holder of each issue was set for the par bond, as a way of forcing larger holders to the discount bond, which with a nominal haircut of 66.3 per-cent provided the largest debt relief in terms of face value. No restric-tions were placed on the discount bond. The currency conversion was to take place at the exchange rate prevailing on December 31, 2003, the formal issue date of the bond. The new bonds would pay interest be-ginning at this date, which was paid in cash at settlement. Unpaid and accrued interest through the default date of December 31, 2001, would also be included. There was no recognition, however, for unpaid inter-est due between December 2001 and December 2003—the only in-stance, among the debt restructurings covered in this paper, when PDI was not recognized in some form.

All bonds tendered would share equally in a GDP "kicker." This fa-cility would distribute the equivalent of 5 percent of the excess of GDP beyond a stipulated trend (initially slightly higher than 3 percent per year and then stabilizing at that rate) on December 15 of every year starting in 2006. Payments were tied to three conditions: GDP had to be higher than the stipulated trend; growth in the previous year had to be larger than 3 percent; and the total payments made by the facility could never be larger than 48 cents on the dollar. According to the official presentation, at a 10 percent discount such a kicker had an NPV of $6.4 billion for a GDP growth rate of 3.5 percent, or close to eight cents on the dollar. In contrast, market estimates initially placed the value of the "kicker" at about two cents on the dollar. Analysts later valued the facility in a wide range, from as low as $1 billion (1.2 cents on the dollar) to $6 billion (7.4 cents on the dollar) and beyond (Pernice and López Fagúndez 2005; Ceballos 2005). As the economy recovered and discount rates decreased, net present value estimates for the facility increased accordingly. By early 2006 it was trading above the original government valuation.

As a final incentive to encourage participation, the government com-mitted to buying back outstanding *performing* debt (i.e., excluding defaulted bonds not tendered in the exchange) in the amount of the "annual excess payment capacity" resulting from the difference between debt service if participation in the debt exchange had been

100 percent and the actual debt service, until 2009. Furthermore, in the event that GDP exceeded the baseline path defined in the GDP warrant, the government also committed to using 5 percent of "excess GDP" toward purchasing outstanding bonds issued in the exchange.

The new bonds also carried a number of novel contractual features. The one that attracted most attention was the "most favored creditor clause," which gave bondholders the right to participate in any future exchange offer, as a way of reassuring participating creditors that holdouts would not get a better deal. A similar clause had been used in the 2001 Phase 1 restructuring (and was in fact honored in the 2005 exchange) and in some English law Brady bonds issued in the 1990s (Buchheit 2002), but this was the first time that a most favored creditor clause was used in New York law sovereign bonds. Furthermore, following the example set by several emerging market issuers in 2003, collective action clauses were included in all new bonds, allowing changes in the payment terms with a 75 percent majority of bondholders. Finally, following the example of the Uruguay exchange (see chapter 10), "aggregation clauses" allowed amending the terms of multiple bond issues with the consent of 85 percent of the *aggregate* principal outstanding across all issues, as long as at least two-thirds of the bondholders of each specific issue supported the amendment (see Gelpern 2005 for details).

On October 8, 2004, just a few weeks before the final details of the public exchange offer were announced, the government reached a deal with eleven local pension funds, who agreed to tender $16.2 billion in bonds, giving the government a head start (about 20 percent of the outstanding principal) in its effort to maximize creditor participation in the upcoming exchange. About $13.6 billion of the tendered debt was to be swapped for the new quasipar bonds. The remainder was swapped for ten-year domestic bonds (Bodens). As a result, the pension funds obtained somewhat better terms than were accessible to other creditors, prompting protests from international creditor groups. The government also agreed to allow pension funds to value the new bonds at face value, protecting them against sharp accounting losses. In exchange, the pension funds agreed to drop their lawsuits against the government.

Although the November 1, 2004, offer contained a notable improvement compared to earlier versions—namely, moving back the official issue date of the new bonds from June 30, 2004, to December 31, 2003, and hence making an extra coupon payment available to bondholders immediately upon settlement[10]—creditor reactions to the deal were generally not favorable (see, e.g., *The Economist*, November 6, 2004). GCAB denounced the offer, and filed a "friend of the court" brief supporting a motion by the plaintiffs of the class action suit *Urban v. Republic of Argentina* to prevent Argentina from going forward with the exchange (chapter 3). This and other legal attempts to block the exchange were unsuccessful (see IMF 2005a for details). After a delay related to regulatory approvals in Italy and the United States and the temporary withdrawal of the Bank of New York as Argentina's exchange agent, the offer finally opened on January 12, 2005, and closed on February 25.

The offer period comprised two subperiods: before and after February 2, 2005. A guaranteed subscription of $50,000 of par bonds was allowed only during the first period. These subperiods turned out to be relatively unimportant as most investors were opting for the discount bond, which was expected to carry higher liquidity in the aftermath of the exchange. Local pension funds subscribed to the exchange on the first day and absorbed all "quasipar" bonds, which were allocated on a "first come first serve" basis.

Participation was something of a cliff-hanger. A survey taken in late September—at a time when the terms of the offer were largely known—among members of the Emerging Markets Creditors Association suggested that at least 65 percent of external creditors would reject the offer, even if incremental improvements lifted its net present value to 32 cents per unit of face value (which turned out to be more or less the value of the final offer). Following the publication of the final offer—which did not set any minimum participation threshold—and its rejection by GCAB, market reports put expected acceptance between 50 and 65 percent, on the assumption that most GCAB members would not take the offer. In the end, however, collective action problems seem to have worked in favor rather than against Argentina. Final participation reached 76.15 percent; reflecting about two-thirds participation outside Argentina (with estimated participation of about 63 percent among foreigners and 90 percent among Argentine citizens) and 98 percent inside Argentina (100 percent for pension funds, banks, and other institutional investors, and about 91 percent for retail bondholders). One factor that seems to have boosted participation among foreigners was the passing of a law, on February 9,

2005, prohibiting the government not only from making future exchange offers to holdouts, but also from entering into any type of settlement with holdouts, whether judicial, extrajudicial or private (see IMF 2005a for details). In effect, the law plugged a loophole that had been left open by the "most favored creditor clause" included in the new bonds (although new legislation could of course amend or overturn this law).

The debt restructuring retired $62.3 billion out of the eligible $81.8 billion debt, and resulted in $35.3 billion in new debt issues: $15 billion in par bonds, $11.9 billion in discount bonds, and Arg$24.3 billion (about $8.3 billion) in quasipar bonds. Forty-four percent of the new debt was denominated in indexed pesos. Settlement was originally expected to begin on April 1, 2005, but was delayed by litigation that attempted to attach tendered bonds that were temporarily held at the Bank of New York, Argentina's exchange agent (see chapter 3 for details). After an initial ruling in favor of Argentina (later upheld by an appeals court), settlement finally took place in early June 2005. However, a gray "when and if" market promising to deliver the new bonds after settlement sprung into existence immediately after preliminary exchange results were announced on March 3, 2005. Using the prices and yields in this market as well as the yields of other performing postdefault debt, it is possible to calculate haircuts in the usual way. In table 8.6, we show the results for sixty-six US$- and Arg$- denominated instruments (we do not show haircuts for instruments denominated in other currencies because of the symmetric treatment offered to Euro and U.S. dollar bonds).[11]

The main finding is that average haircuts (weighted by the face value of original instruments tendered) were 71–75 percent: around 71 percent for the par, 75 percent for the discount, and 73 percent for the quasipar. The higher haircut for the discount bond is the result of a relatively low secondary market price of this bond compared with the par bond, as indicated by higher yields of the discount bonds relative to their par counterparts. Except for two outliers (see Sturzenegger and Zettelmeyer 2005), haircuts across instruments varied between 64 and 82 percent. The high end of this range is constituted by bonds issued during the June 2001 "megaswap," such as the Global 18 or Global 31 "mega." Because they were long-term and carried high coupon rates (having been issued in near-crisis circumstances), the present value of these bonds was relatively high, and hence the haircut in our definition

Table 8.6
Argentina 2005 exchange: Haircuts (per 100 units of principal)

	Outstanding (millions of U.S. dollars)	Due date	Original currency	Value of old instrument[a]	Haircuts[a]					
					Par, US$	Par, AR$	Discount, US$	Discount, AR$	Quasi-par	Average
Bonte 02	1,513.4	5/9/02	US$	108.1	63.3	62.4	69.0	66.1	64.1	64.9
Bonte 03	732.9	5/21/03	US$	120.5	67.1	66.3	72.1	69.6	67.7	68.5
Bonte 03F	143.1	7/21/03	US$	114.0	64.7	63.8	70.1	67.4	65.4	66.2
Bonte 04	508.7	5/24/04	US$	129.8	69.5	68.7	74.2	71.8	70.1	70.8
Bonte 05	759.5	5/21/05	US$	142.0	72.1	71.4	76.3	74.2	72.6	73.2
Bonte 06	225.2	5/15/06	US$	144.9	72.6	71.9	76.8	74.7	73.1	73.7
Bonte 27	3.4	9/19/27	US$	150.0	73.2	72.5	77.3	75.2	73.7	74.3
FRAN	383.5	4/10/05	US$	311.4	86.7	86.4	88.7	87.7	87.0	87.3
FRN 04	225.9	4/6/04	US$	120.0	66.7	65.9	71.8	69.3	67.4	68.1
Global 03	1,794.4	12/20/03	US$	118.8	66.9	66.1	72.0	69.5	67.6	68.3
Global 05	821.6	12/4/05	US$	139.1	71.6	70.9	76.0	73.8	72.2	72.8
Global 06	1,185.4	10/9/06	US$	143.8	72.1	71.4	76.4	74.2	72.6	73.3
Global 08	5,024.7	12/19/08	US$	147.8	73.4	72.8	77.5	75.5	74.0	74.5
Global 09	1,197.0	4/7/09	US$	155.9	74.2	73.6	78.2	76.2	74.7	75.3
Global 10	775.0	3/15/10	US$	156.7	74.2	73.5	78.1	76.1	74.7	75.2
Global 12	465.3	2/21/12	US$	174.5	76.6	76.0	80.1	78.3	77.0	77.5
Global 15	718.2	6/15/15	US$	166.7	76.4	75.8	80.0	78.2	76.9	77.4
Global 17	1,903.7	1/30/17	US$	169.3	75.8	75.2	79.5	77.6	76.3	76.8
Global 18	104.6	6/19/18	US$	216.8	80.8	80.3	83.7	82.2	81.1	81.6
Global 19	146.8	2/25/19	US$	178.8	77.2	76.6	80.7	78.9	77.6	78.1
Global 20	121.7	2/1/20	US$	178.0	76.9	76.3	80.4	78.7	77.4	77.9
Global 27	809.5	9/19/27	US$	147.4	72.7	72.0	76.9	74.8	73.3	73.8
Global 29	125.0	3/1/29	US$	138.0	70.8	70.1	75.3	73.0	71.4	72.0
Global 30	166.0	7/21/30	US$	154.0	73.4	72.8	77.5	75.4	73.9	74.5
Global 31	13.2	1/31/31	US$	178.7	77.0	76.4	80.5	78.7	77.5	78.0
Global 31M	8,595.2	6/19/31	US$	214.5	80.6	80.1	83.5	82.1	81.0	81.4
PRE 4	259.9	9/1/02	US$	26.4	74.8	74.2	78.7	76.8	75.4	75.9
Pre 6	73.5	1/1/10	US$	107.4	59.5	58.5	65.7	62.6	60.3	61.2
PRO2	332.6	4/1/07	US$	73.3	64.1	63.3	69.6	66.9	64.9	65.6
PRO4	452.3	12/28/10	US$	126.9	61.6	60.7	67.5	64.6	62.4	63.2
PRO6	527.6	4/15/07	US$	91.5	63.9	63.0	69.4	66.6	64.6	65.4
PRO8	14.7	1/1/16	US$	101.2	57.0	56.0	63.6	60.3	57.9	58.8
PRO10	51.5	4/15/07	US$	103.6	62.0	61.1	67.8	64.9	62.8	63.6
Hidro	18.2	12/2/08	US$	96.3	63.0	62.1	68.7	65.8	63.7	64.6
Bonex 92	150.0	9/15/02	US$	13.3	62.7	61.8	68.5	65.6	63.5	64.3
Radar 1	349.5	4/24/03	US$	112.3	64.1	63.2	69.6	66.8	64.8	65.6

Table 8.6
(continued)

	Outstand-ing (mil-lions of U.S. dollars)	Due date	Orig-inal cur-rency	Value of old instru-ment[a]	Haircuts[a]					
					Par, US$	Par, AR$	Dis-count, US$	Dis-count, AR$	Quasi-par	Aver-age
Radar 2	351.7	5/28/03	US$	115.9	65.7	64.9	71.0	68.3	66.4	67.2
Radar 3	361.9	7/24/06	US$	117.5	65.8	64.9	71.0	68.4	66.5	67.2
Radar 4	232.0	8/8/06	US$	115.5	65.1	64.3	70.5	67.8	65.8	66.6
Celtic 2	279.1	9/4/07	US$	112.9	64.3	63.4	69.7	67.0	65.0	65.8
Span 02	130.1	11/30/02	US$	117.7	66.3	65.5	71.5	68.9	67.0	67.7
Letras T90	448.5	3/15/02	US$	103.8	62.3	61.4	68.1	65.2	63.0	63.9
Letras T105	119.7	2/15/02	US$	103.9	62.3	61.4	68.1	65.2	63.1	63.9
Letras T106	116.8	3/8/02	US$	103.8	62.3	61.4	68.1	65.2	63.0	63.9
Letras T108	25.0	2/22/02	US$	103.9	62.3	61.4	68.1	65.2	63.1	63.9
Letras T109	30.8	3/22/02	US$	103.8	62.3	61.4	68.1	65.2	63.0	63.9
RML	561.8	4/16/02	US$	108.4	63.2	62.3	68.8	66.0	63.9	64.7
Pagare III	4.0	4/24/02	US$	107.6	62.5	61.6	68.2	65.4	63.3	64.1
Pagare IV	11.3	8/22/02	US$	110.3	63.4	62.5	69.0	66.2	64.2	64.9
Pagare V	1.4	10/30/02	US$	112.4	64.6	63.7	70.0	67.3	65.3	66.1
Pagare VI	20.7	2/16/04	US$	126.8	68.9	68.1	73.6	71.2	69.5	70.2
Pagare A	197.8	8/7/02	US$	111.9	64.6	63.7	70.0	67.3	65.3	66.1
Pagare B	130.0	8/7/02	US$	107.6	63.1	62.2	68.8	65.9	63.9	64.7
Pagare C	75.0	8/7/02	US$	106.1	62.6	61.6	68.3	65.4	63.3	64.1
Pagare 2006	15.0	6/19/06	US$	144.7	71.9	71.2	76.2	74.1	72.5	73.1
Global F	181.6	10/15/04	US$	100.5	71.0	70.3	75.5	73.3	71.6	72.3
FRB	1,637.2	3/29/05	US$	59.5	62.8	61.9	68.5	65.7	63.6	64.4
RA $02	20.3	7/10/02	ARS	40.8	...	64.9	...	68.3	66.4	66.4
RA $07	5.8	2/12/07	ARS	48.1	...	70.1	...	73.1	71.4	71.4
RA $08	248.6	9/19/08	ARS	44.3	...	68.1	...	71.2	69.5	69.5
PRE 3	9.9	9/1/02	ARS	9.1	...	75.9	...	78.2	76.9	76.9
PRO1	39.2	4/1/07	ARS	20.7	...	53.5	...	58.1	55.5	55.5
PRO3	1.0	12/28/10	ARS	33.6	...	56.1	...	60.4	58.0	58.0
PRO5	96.9			32.8	...	64.6	...	68.1	66.1	66.1
PRO9	30.3			36.7	...	62.3	...	66.0	63.9	63.9
Discount	800.5			99.6	...	...	38.5	37.1	...	37.8

Source: Sturzenegger and Zettelmeyer (2005).
[a] Discounted based on yields in "when and if" market, early March 2005.

was high as well. The lower end corresponds to bonds that derived from previous debt consolidations and carried a low interest rate and high degree of capitalization; hence, these bonds had low market value.

An unusual feature of the Argentine exchange compared with most other exchanges described in this book is the fact that it was undertaken and carried out without the explicit or implicit support of the IMF. Although the IMF was supportive of the idea of a comprehensive restructuring that would restore Argentina's debt sustainability, it was uncomfortable with the aggressive approach that Argentina had taken toward its private creditors. In part for this reason, both sides agreed, in August 2004, to suspend the IMF program pending the outcome of the debt restructuring. Argentina continued repaying the IMF on schedule. Following the exchange, the IMF referred to the debt exchange as "an important step" but at the same time urged the Argentine government, in light of its opposition to engage in any negotiation with holdouts, to "formulate a realistic strategy to address the issue of the remaining arrears." Discussions with the IMF were restarted after the exchange, but did not lead to a new program.[12] In January 2006, following a similar early repayment by Brazil, Argentina repaid its entire outstanding debt to the IMF (about $10 billion) ahead of schedule.

After the Exchange

The main reason why the losses suffered by investors were significantly lower than implied by the 2003 "Dubai guidelines" were the low interest rates prevailing at settlement. These rates had fallen both due to an extremely favorable international liquidity environment, and the high primary surpluses obtained by the Argentine government after the crisis (2004 ended with an unprecedented consolidated primary surplus of about 5 percent of GDP). Figure 8.1 shows the EMBI spread as well as the spreads on the Boden 12 bond, a postdefault instrument that started trading in the second half of 2002. Spreads on Argentine bonds fell steadily from about 2,000 basis points to closer to 500 basis points at the time of the exchange (the large drop in the country spread following the exchange reflects JP Morgan's redefinition of the index, eliminating the defaulted bonds and including the restructured ones). Trade conditions also changed for the better. Commodity prices, including those of oil and soybean increased substantially, while world and regional growth resumed at a healthy pace. After a large increase in the aftermath of the crisis, inflation stabilized at low values in 2003 and 2004. The more stable macroeconomic environment stimulated a strong recovery of economic activity. Real GDP recovered rapidly after bottoming out in the second quarter of 2002 with annual growth rates of 8.8 percent in 2003 and 9.0 percent in 2004. In the second quarter of 2005, Argentine GDP exceeded its precrisis maximum (attained in the second quarter of 1998) for the first time, and the year ended with growth of 9.2 percent.

The strong fiscal numbers as well as a strong current account created substantial appreciation pressure on the currency. This was resisted by the monetary authorities through purchases of foreign currency (initially unsterilized and later on increasingly sterilized). The successful completion of the debt exchange triggered a wave of capital inflows that put additional pressure on the currency. The government reacted with increased intervention and the imposition of taxes on capital inflows. Bond prices rallied (figure 8.8), particularly on peso-indexed bonds, as inflation fears increased in mid-2005. Six months after their launch the peso-indexed par bond reached a dollar equivalent of 50 cents on the dollar, while the discount reached 45 cents on the dollar, up from an implicit valuation (obtained from the price of defaulted bonds) of 30–33 cents on the dollar just prior to the exchange.

The last column of table 4.2 shows the large drop in the debt ratio achieved as a result of the debt exchange.[13] Notwithstanding the large amount of debt relief achieved, however, the 2005 exchange leaves Argentina with a large debt burden: close to 80 percent of GDP (though this may be more manageable than it seems, as the net present value burden of this debt stock is lower by at least 10 percentage points as a result of the long maturities and low coupons of the restructured debt). Table 4.2 also shows that the "negative residual" attributable to the 2005 exchange is balanced by "positive residuals" due to interest arrears accumulation, compensation bond issues to banks, and assumption of provincial debt between 2002 and 2004. In U.S. dollar terms, the reduction in the face value of external debt attributable to the exchange—about $38 billion, assuming full participation—exceeded fiscalized crisis losses—about $30 billion in new debt issued between 2002 and 2004—but not by very much.

As of early 2006, the bilateral official debts of Argentina remained in default. Furthermore, there remains substantial uncertainty as to what will happen with the relatively large fraction of bondholders that decided to hold out. By the time the exchange went to settlement, around

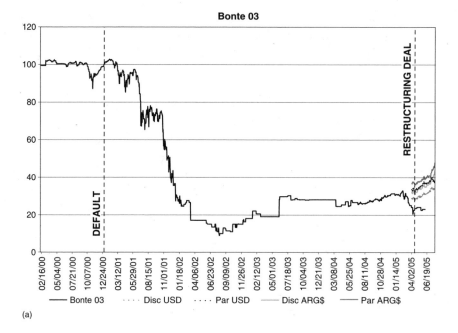

(a)

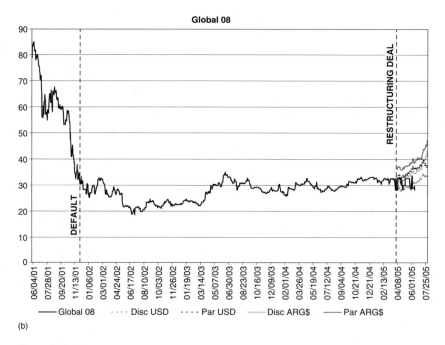

(b)

Figure 8.8
Bond prices before and after the exchange
Source: Bloomberg and authors' computations.

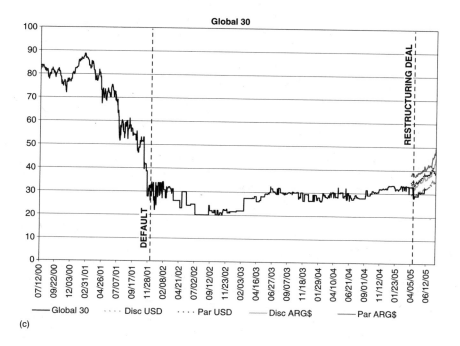

(c)

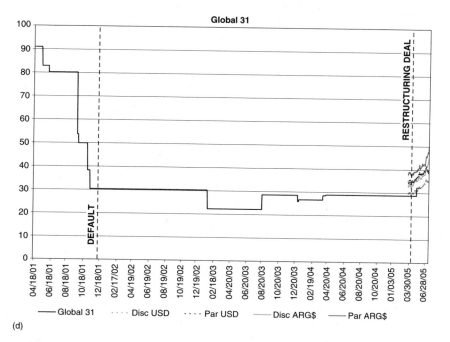

(d)

Figure 8.8
(continued)

Box 8.1
Chronology of Argentina's crisis and debt restructuring

1999:

January: Brazil's real is devalued.

October 24: Fernando De La Rúa, a moderate centrist from the Radical Party, is elected president after ten years of Peronist administration.

2000:

October: Resignation of the vice-president.

December: Country spreads skyrocket to close to 1,000 points.

December 18: The "blindaje" is announced, and a substantial line of credit from multilaterals totaling close to $20 billion is released. Country risk falls to 700 points in just a few days.

2001:

March 2: Machinea, the finance minister, resigns. Ricardo Lopez Murphy is appointed to the post.

March 19: Lopez Murphy announces a tight fiscal program that fails to gain the support of the president. He resigns and is replaced by Domingo Cavallo. Financial transactions tax imposed to improve fiscal accounts.

April and May: Rollover financing needs are covered with the issue of a bond sold to local financial institutions. Weakening of the convertibility ratios. President of the Central Bank is removed. New peg to a basket of euro and dollar is established but will become effective only when the euro is on par with the dollar.

April 24: A short-term T-bill auction scheduled for that day is canceled.

June: Successful comprehensive voluntary debt exchange extends maturities for $29 billion.

July: Several provinces start showing significant refinancing difficulties. Uncertainty triggers a new run on the bond markets. Spreads that had fallen to less than 800 points after the debt exchange increase to 1,000 two weeks later.

July 29: Zero deficit law passed, cutting spending by 1.5 percent of GDP. Sell-off of Argentine debt, with spreads increasing about 400 bps points shortly after the announcement.

August 22: $8 billion IMF support program. $5 billion is disbursed. Contigent repo line with private banks is tapped for close to $2 billion.

October: Cavallo announces that he will seek debt relief in a voluntary fashion. Bond prices plummet.

November 23: Domestic bond exchange commences. It is considered a technical default by rating agencies, and S&P moves Argentina to the SD category. Exchange is completed with $41.7 billion of debt restructured.

November 30: Bank run intensifies.

December 1: Cavallo announces a deposit freeze and an exchange rate holiday.

December 5: IMF announces that $1.25 billion disbursement scheduled for December will not be made.

December 19: Cavallo resigns.

December 20: De La Rúa resigns.

Box 8.1
(continued)

December 23: Legislative Assembly names Adolfo Rodríguez Saá, a Peronist, as the new interim president.

December 24: Argentina announces the suspension of all payments on all debt instruments. The default is celebrated in Congress.

2002:

January 2: Adolfo Rodríguez Saá loses the support of his own party and is forced to resign. The new president, Eduardo Duhalde, decides immediately on a devaluation of the peso, and pesifies the financial sector.

March 8: Pesification of government debt and of assets and liabilities in the financial sector. Sixty-five percent of bondholders participate with dissenting creditors litigating against the government.

June 25: The exchange rate reaches a maximum of 3.86 pesos to the dollar.

Second semester: the exchange rate is stabilized at 3.5. BCRA starts accumulating reserves.

2003:

May: President Kirchner sworn in.

September 22: Dubai proposal.

2004:

June 1: Buenos Aires proposal.

August 2004: Program with IMF suspended. Argentina continues to pay to the fund.

November 1: Final debt exchange proposal is announced.

2005:

January 12: Offer opens.

February 25: Offer closes, with participation of 76 percent.

March 3: Results are announced and bonds start trading in *when-and-if* market.

March: NML requests attachment of bondholding by Bank of New York, the bank in charge of the exchange. U.S. courts withhold the bonds and block the exchange.

May: U.S. courts rule in favor of Argentina freeing the collateral. Shortly after, bonds are exchanged and trading starts.

December 15: Argentina announces early repayment of all its debt to IMF.

---

forty lawsuits against Argentina had been filed in New York and over one hundred in Italy and Germany. Italian courts have also issued judgments in favor of bondholders against Italian financial institutions that had advised the purchase of Argentine bonds. None of the holdouts that have obtained judgment claims against Argentina has so far been able to enforce. However, the presence of these claims could complicate future Argentine attempts to issue debt abroad.

9　Moldova

Like most other economies emerging from the ruins of the Soviet Union, the Moldovan economy suffered a large fall in measured output following independence in 1991. However, Moldova's collapse was extreme even by the standards of former Soviet Union countries, and it was unusually long. Table 9.1 shows that growth was negative in every year until 2000. By 1999, the measured economy had collapsed to about one-third of its 1989 size. In addition to the standard transitional recession, Moldova had suffered a war with the breakaway region of Transnistria (1992) and a large terms-of-trade shock as traditional supply links to Russia and other republics of the former Soviet Union were disrupted and/or implicit subsidies were reduced (particularly with respect to energy). Moreover, there was a severe drought in 1994. Widespread corruption and hesitant economic reforms slowed new private sector growth. Finally, the 1998 crises in Russia and Ukraine had a large adverse impact on export demand and made the current account deficit skyrocket to almost 20 percent of GDP in 1998.

Levels of public debt increased sharply in the same period, from nearly zero to about 70 percent of GDP on the eve of the 1998 crisis. Until 1997, these sharp rises were driven mainly by the combination of large primary fiscal deficits and the output decline (table 9.2). In effect, both the government and the country as a whole were borrowing heavily in anticipation of a growth turnaround that did not arrive until much later. In this sense, Moldova's experience is similar to the mid-1990s experience of Russia and Ukraine. What made Moldova different is that it financed its deficits overwhelmingly through official debt. Though some borrowing from private external sources occurred—including a five-year, $75 million Eurobond issue in 1997 carrying a fixed coupon of 9.875 percent per annum—over half of Moldova's $1 billion public external debt at end-1998 (excluding energy payment arrears) was owed to multilateral institutions, and a further 21 percent to

Table 9.1
Moldova: Selected economic indicators, 1993–2004

	1995	1996	1997	1998	1999	2000	2001	2002	2003	2004
Output and prices				(annual percentage changes)						
Real GDP	−1.4	−5.9	1.6	−6.5	−3.4	2.1	6.1	7.8	6.6	7.3
Consumer prices (period average)	30.2	23.5	11.8	7.7	39.3	31.3	9.8	5.3	11.7	12.5
Lei per U.S. dollar (period average)	10.0	2.2	0.4	16.5	95.5	18.2	3.5	5.5	2.7	−11.6
Terms of trade (goods)	5.1	−2.7	1.3	0.3	−1.0	−4.5	−2.6	−0.2	−9.2	−5.5
Public finances[a]				(in percent of GDP)						
Revenue	39.4	35.9	38.5	37.6	30.4	31.0	29.4	29.8	34.0	35.4
Expenditures	45.2	43.9	49.6	44.9	37.6	34.5	29.4	31.5	33.3	34.7
Noninterest	41.1	40.7	45.4	40.3	30.6	28.1	25.2	29.4	31.2	32.8
Interest	4.1	3.1	4.2	4.6	7.0	6.4	4.2	2.2	2.1	1.9
Primary balance	−1.7	−4.9	−6.9	−2.7	−0.2	2.9	4.1	0.4	2.8	2.6
Overall balance	−5.8	−8.0	−11.1	−7.3	−7.2	−3.5	−0.1	−1.8	0.7	0.7
Government debt[b]	53.7	56.5	63.0	70.2	93.9	93.9	78.7	73.4	63.6	46.9
Foreign currency[c]	46.3	47.1	52.1	59.0	79.8	81.2	66.4	61.1	52.5	35.4
Domestic currency	7.4	9.3	10.9	11.1	14.1	12.7	12.4	12.3	11.2	11.5
Money			(annual percent change unless otherwise indicated)							
Reserve money	41.5	9.3	31.5	−5.5	41.4	29.8	27.9	31.1	16.6	39.7
Money market rate, percent	...	...	28.1	30.9	32.6	20.8	11.0	5.1	11.5	13.2
External sector			(in billions of U.S. dollars unless otherwise indicated)							
Total exports, fob	0.9	0.9	1.0	0.8	0.6	0.6	0.7	0.9	1.1	1.3
Total imports, fob	1.0	1.3	1.4	1.2	0.8	1.0	1.1	1.3	1.7	2.1
Current account	−0.1	−0.2	−0.3	−0.3	−0.1	−0.1	0.0	−0.1	−0.1	−0.1
Current account (in percent of GDP)	−8.0	−11.1	−13.9	−19.7	−6.7	−8.4	−2.4	−4.4	−6.6	−4.4
Gross reserves	0.2	0.2	0.2	0.1	0.2	0.2	0.2	0.3	0.3	0.5
Export volumes	13.9	14.4	5.4	3.6	16.1	−2.0	17.0	6.2	16.6	24.8
Import volumes	22.2	15.9	1.1	2.4	−3.5	26.1	10.2	9.1	30.8	23.6
Reference items:										
Nominal GDP (in billions of lei)	6.5	7.8	8.9	9.1	12.3	16.0	19.1	22.6	27.6	32.0
Exchange rate (Lei per U.S. dollar, period average)	4.5	4.6	4.6	5.4	10.5	12.4	12.9	13.6	13.9	12.3

Source: National authorities and IMF.

[a] Refers to general government, on a cash basis.

[b] Debt ratios refer to debt in U.S. dollars divided by GDP in U.S. dollars, using period average exchange rates. This differs from the way Moldova's debt ratios are usually computed—namely, converting all debt to local currency units at end-period exchange rates, and dividing by GDP in local currency.

[c] Excludes energy arrears.

Table 9.2
Moldova: Debt dynamics, 1994–2004 (in percent of GDP unless otherwise stated)

	1994	1995	1996	1997	1998	1999	2000	2001	2002	2003	2004
General government debt[a]	39.7	53.7	56.5	63.0	70.2	93.9	93.9	78.7	73.4	63.6	46.9
Change in debt ratio attributable to…		14.0	2.8	6.5	7.2	23.7	0.0	−15.2	−5.3	−9.8	−16.7
Primary deficit[b]		1.7	4.9	6.9	2.7	0.2	−2.9	−4.1	−0.4	−2.8	−2.6
Real interest rate		3.3	2.8	3.7	3.6	3.9	4.8	2.4	1.0	0.9	0.8
Real growth		0.6	3.3	−0.9	4.4	2.4	−1.9	−5.3	−5.6	−4.5	−4.2
Real depreciation		0.0	−10.6	−5.1	0.0	25.7	−5.4	−5.4	−2.3	−5.4	−8.5
Cross-terms		0.0	−0.6	−0.4	0.4	2.1	−0.4	−0.4	−0.1	−0.3	−0.5
Residual[b]		8.4	3.1	2.3	−3.8	−10.6	5.8	−2.4	2.1	2.2	−1.7

[a] Debt expressed in U.S. dollars using end-period exchange rates, divided by current GDP in U.S. dollars.
[b] Refers to general government.
[c] Reflects debt stock adjustments, nondebt financing (including debt service arrears), and measurement error.

bilateral creditors. As a result, Moldova's external debt carried longer maturities and lower interest rates on average than that of the other crisis countries examined in this book.

Moldova was hence in a position to borrow well beyond debt levels that would have triggered servicing difficulties if its debt had been mainly on commercial terms. By the time of the 1998 crisis, its total indebtedness as a share of GDP was much higher than Ukraine's, or even Russia's. In spite of its brief access to international bond markets, Moldova's debt structure and level resembled that of a highly indebted poor country more than that of an emerging markets economy.[1] Moldova's debt service situation became untenable after the devaluation of the leu by about 50 percent in late 1998, which added almost twenty-five points to Moldova's debt-to-GDP ratio. Including the country's sizable energy arrears—about $400 million by 1999, of which about 60 percent, according to IMF estimates, were contingent government liabilities—implied a public debt-to-GDP ratio of well over 100 percent. Public debt service rose to more than 40 percent of government revenues. At the same time, Moldova not only lost access to new private financing, but official flows slowed to a trickle because of the country's poor track record of economic reforms. This forced Moldova into a combination of sharp fiscal adjustment—with the primary balance swinging from a large deficit until 1998 to a large surplus in 2000—and debt restructuring.

In 2000, Moldova began to restructure its external debt in several steps. In March, an agreement was reached regarding US$137 million of arrears to the Russian energy company Gazprom. This was settled through the issue of a promissory note for US$90 million with a seven-year maturity, two-year grace period and 7.5 percent interest, in addition to a debt equity swap in which Gazprom acquired 51 percent of Moldovagas, the state gas company. A comprehensive agreement with the Russian Federation followed in April; this was followed by rescheduling agreements with China (September 2000), Romania (July 2001), and Germany (April 2002). Moldova was also able to conclude rescheduling agreements with several commercial suppliers and creditors (see IMF Country Report No. 02/190, appendix I, for details). In addition, during 2001 Moldova bought back, at a price of about 71 cents on the dollar, about $35.5 million (out of $75 million) of outstanding Eurobond principal falling due in June 2002.

Economic conditions improved in 2001, largely as a result of the recovery in Russia and rising workers' remittances. Following an incipient recovery in 2000, growth accelerated to 6 percent, but even so it was clear that Moldova would not obtain the financing it needed to roll over its maturing Eurobond and make payments due on the Gazprom bonds issued in 2000. In July 2001, interest payments on the Eurobond were made two days before a twenty-one-day grade period expired (Moldova had failed to settle with investors on the due date of June 13, 2001). Mariana Durlesteanu, the first deputy minister of finance in charge of debt management, was quoted by Bloomberg as saying, "The payment was made yesterday of $3.7 million. Payment of the bond next year will be difficult if we don't get any external finance. We have a very big problem."

In June 2002, faced with imminent default, Moldova began restructuring negotiations with its largest creditor, TCW Asset Management Company (TAMCO), which held 78 percent of the outstanding Eurobond. On June 21, 2002, an initial agreement was reached to extend the maturity of the bond by five months while negotiations continued, and on August 8, 2002, a restructuring agreement was reached in principle which was ratified by bondholders and the Moldovan parliament in October 2002. Collective action clauses contained in the original bonds (which had been issued under English law) were used to bind any dissenting creditors. Under the agreement, 10 percent of the outstanding principal was repaid in cash upon implementation of the agreement (on October 29, 2002), while the remaining principal would amortize in several steps over the next seven years, with interest payments occurring semiannually at LIBOR plus 462.5 basis points. In addition, creditors received interest on the full outstanding principal, at the original interest rate of 9.875 percent per annum, for the period between the original maturity date (June 13, 2002) and the implementation date of the agreement (October 29, 2002). Hence, there was no face value reduction, and except for the transfer of interest rate risk from creditors to the debtor, the interest rate terms of the modified bond were also close to the original bond. Any reduction in NPV came mostly from the seven-year maturity extension.

Computing the "haircut" that investors suffered in this debt exchange is complicated by the fact that because of the small face value of the issue and its concentrated ownership, no secondary market prices are available following the exchange. Hence exit yields cannot be computed, nor can they be inferred from other debt instruments since Moldova had issued no other foreign currency market debt. However, we can compute a range for the implicit haircut using exit yields obtained at other exchanges as discount rates. Comparing old and new cash flows using a 14 percent discount rate—toward the low end of what was observed elsewhere—would imply a haircut of 20 percent, while discounting at 28 percent—the highest exit yield, observed only in the case of Ukraine—would deliver a haircut of about 47 percent. This places the Moldovan haircut in the same territory as that of the Ecuador, Pakistan, and Ukraine exchanges, and somewhat below that of the 2000 Russian external exchange.

For Gazprom, the offer was expected to envisage a 5 percent rate, ten-year maturity with an eighteen-month grace period. However, this agreement never materialized, and Moldova remained in default to that creditor until June 2004, when Moldova finally bought back its outstanding debt, with face value of $114.5 million, for $50 million. Hence, the overall impact of the 2002 restructuring was small: it applied to such a small share of the debt that it barely affected the debt dynamics. Moreover, Moldova's financing situation did not improve after the restructuring. Due to poor policy implementation, programs with the IMF and the World Bank expired without additional disbursements, and so the tap was closed on most new official lending, let alone new international bond issues.

As a result, Moldova continued to face debt service difficulties, and in August 2003, it also suspended payments to bilateral creditors (while continuing to pay multilaterals and Eurobond holders). Ironically,

Box 9.1
Chronology of Moldova's crisis and debt restructuring

1991: Soviet Union collapses. Moldova becomes independent.

1992: War with breakaway region of Transnistria.

1995:

March 22: IMF approves a twelve-month Stand-by Arrangement.

1996:

May 20: IMF approves a three-year credit under EFF.

1997: Five-year, $75 million. Eurobond issue.

1998:

Russian default and devaluation. Devaluation of the lei by about 50 percent.

1999: Energy arrears reach about $400 million.

2000: Start of Moldova's external debt restructuring.

March: Agreement is reached regarding $137 million in arrears to the Russian energy company Gazprom.

April: Comprehensive agreement with the Russian Federation is reached.

September: Rescheduling agreement with China.

December 21: The IMF approves three-year loan under the Poverty Reduction and Growth Facility (PGRF).

2001:

Buyback of about $35.5 million (out of the $75 million) of outstanding Eurobond principal falling due in June 2002.

July: Rescheduling agreement with Romania.

2002:

April: Rescheduling agreement with Germany.

June: Faced with imminent default, Moldova begins restructuring negotiations with its largest creditor (TAMCO), which holds 78 percent of the outstanding Eurobond.

August 8: Restructuring agreement is reached with TAMCO, then ratified by bondholders and the Moldovan parliament in October.

2003:

August: Moldova suspends payment to bilateral creditors (while continuing to pay multilaterals and Eurobond holders).

2004:

June: Moldova buys back outstanding debt toward Gazprom, for $50 million (with face value of $114.5 million).

however, this lack of new debt financing—combined with continued growth rates in the range of 6–8 percent, and a recovering leu, buoyed by workers' remittances—seems to have had a positive impact on Moldova's underlying solvency situation, as the government had little choice but to continue running substantial primary surpluses. By end-2003, Moldova's public debt-to-GDP ratio was back to its 1997 level, and it has since declined to less than 50 percent.

Moldova's case shows some similarities with that of Pakistan, in that its restructuring of commercial debt was somewhat of a sideshow of economic developments, in general, and its more important problems with official debt, in particular. It also does not seem to have had major economic costs, at least in the short run. With the exception of its one international bond issue, Moldova had no access to private capital markets, so the restructuring did not have much of an impact on its ability to borrow. The muted impact of Moldova's restructuring was also related to Moldova's relatively small financial sector. In mid-2000, banking sector assets stood at only about 20 percent of GDP, and government loans at a paltry 10 percent of GDP. Banks were not exposed to the restructured debt and were thus fairly isolated from the restructuring process. This has been changing as of late, with the financial sector growing, particularly in foreign currency, so that Moldova is only now developing the characteristics of some of the other crisis countries covered in this book. This could make a future debt restructuring episode substantially more costly.

Moldova's debt restructuring is unusual in two further respects. Unlike all other debt restructurings described in this book, the Moldovan restructuring did not take the form of a bond exchange but consisted in amending the terms of the original bond, after invoking collective action clauses. This was partly because the restructured debt consisted of a single English law bond held largely by one creditor, so that collective action was not an issue. Second, its debt restructuring with external commercial debtors was not comprehensive. Moldova restructured its Eurobond but did not manage to restructure its Gazprom debts until much later (e.g., unlike Ukraine). Failure to agree with the holders of Gazprom promissory notes does not seem to have created a "holdout problem" that obstructed the Eurobond restructuring. The Moldovan authorities seem to have been successful in convincing TAMCO that the Gazprom notes would not receive better treatment than the Eurobonds; in the end, they did in fact settle at somewhat less favorable terms than the Eurobonds.

10 Uruguay

Uruguay is a small open economy closely linked to its two large and crisis-prone neighbors, Brazil and Argentina, making it vulnerable to macroeconomic instability in the region. In recent years, this potential vulnerability has been enhanced through increasing integration via the trade agreement Mercosur.

The Uruguayan economy is also characterized by an aging population, a comparatively large welfare state, and public skepticism with respect to major reforms. For example, in two referendum initiatives, voters turned down the privatization of the telephone company in 1992 and the opening up of the state oil monopoly to foreign investment in 2003. At the same time, Uruguay established a track record of sound macroeconomic management. Except for a brief recession at the time of the 1995 tequila crisis, growth was healthy until 1998, in part reflecting a favorable external environment, including the economic strength of Argentina (table 10.1). As a result, Uruguay enjoyed an investment grade rating through most of the decade.

However, two problems in Uruguay's financial system made it highly vulnerable to external shocks. First, financial dollarization: by the end of the 1990s, over 90 percent of deposits and over 70 percent of bank lending were denominated in dollars, but only about half of this lending was to borrowers with foreign currency earnings. In addition, the public debt was almost entirely denominated in dollars, compounding the economy-wide balance sheet mismatch. Second, over 40 percent of deposits were held by nonresidents, mainly from Argentina. Traditionally, this had not been a source of instability; on the contrary, crises in its neighboring countries typically benefited the Uruguayan financial system as a "safe haven." However, there was one conceivable exception: a crisis so cataclysmic that the need for cash would trump the desire of nonresident depositors to take their

Table 10.1
Uruguay: Selected economic indicators, 1994–2005

	1994	1995	1996	1997	1998	1999	2000	2001	2002	2003	2004	2005
Output and prices					*(annual percentage changes)*							
Real GDP	7.3	-1.4	5.6	4.9	4.7	-2.8	-1.4	-3.4	-11.0	2.2	12.3	6.6
Consumer prices (period average)	44.7	42.2	28.3	19.8	10.8	5.7	4.8	4.4	14.0	19.4	9.2	4.7
Ur$ per U.S. dollar (period average)	28.0	25.9	25.6	18.4	10.9	8.3	6.7	10.1	62.1	30.4	1.5	-14.8
Terms of trade (goods)	...	...	...	...	...	-4.7	-6.6	-0.7	4.3	2.9	-3.1	-9.7
Public finances					*(in percent of GDP)*							
Revenue	30.0	30.2	29.8	30.2	32.7	32.2	31.2	32.7	31.0	31.1	30.0	31.8
Expenditures	33.0	31.6	31.2	31.6	33.7	36.3	35.3	36.5	35.6	34.4	32.2	32.5
Noninterest	31.0	29.5	29.3	29.7	31.7	34.2	32.7	33.6	30.9	28.4	26.3	27.9
Interest payments	2.0	2.1	1.9	2.0	1.9	2.1	2.6	2.9	4.6	6.0	6.0	4.6
Primary balance	-1.0	0.7	0.5	0.5	0.9	-2.0	-1.5	-1.3	0.0	2.7	3.8	3.9
Overall balance	-2.9	-1.4	-1.5	-1.4	-1.0	-4.1	-4.1	-4.2	-4.6	-3.2	-2.2	-0.7
Public sector debt[a]	32.6	30.9	30.3	32.1	35.5	40.8	45.5	53.8	94.2	108.6	100.5	83.0
of which: domestic currency debt	...	...	...	...	...	3.8	3.2	9.3	3.8	6.2	9.9	10.5
External sector					*(in billions of U.S. dollars unless otherwise indicated)*							
Total exports, fob	1.9	2.1	2.4	2.8	2.8	2.3	2.4	2.1	1.9	2.3	3.1	3.8
Total imports, fob	2.6	2.7	3.1	3.5	3.6	3.2	3.3	2.9	1.9	2.1	3.0	3.8
Current account	-0.4	-0.2	-0.2	-0.3	-0.5	-0.5	-0.6	-0.5	0.4	-0.1	0.0	-0.1
Current account (in percent of GDP)	-2.5	-1.1	-1.1	-1.3	-2.1	-2.4	-2.8	-2.8	3.2	-0.5	0.3	-0.5
Gross reserves	0.2	0.2	0.2	0.2	2.6	2.6	2.8	3.1	0.8	2.1	2.5	3.4
					(annual percentage changes)							
Export volumes	...	...	...	...	2.4	-7.3	6.5	-7.8	-2.1	9.4	28.7	16.2
Import volumes	...	...	...	...	9.4	-3.5	-0.4	-10.4	-26.9	6.2	29.1	9.4
Reference items:												
Nominal GDP (in billions of Ur$)	88.1	122.5	163.5	204.6	234.3	237.1	243.0	249.2	261.0	315.4	379.3	411.0
Exchange rate (period average)	5.0	6.3	8.0	9.4	10.5	11.3	12.1	13.3	21.6	28.2	28.6	24.5

Source: National authorities, IFS, and authors' calculations. Definition of series changes in 1999; pre-1999 numbers exclude (small) stock of domestic currency debt.
[a] Total public debt (including central bank). Debt expressed in U.S. dollars (local currency debt evaluated at end-year exchange rate), divided by current GDP in U.S. dollars.

Table 10.2
Uruguay: Debt dynamics, 1999–2005 (in percent of GDP unless otherwise stated)

	1999	2000	2001	2002	2003	2004	2005
Total public debt[a]	40.8	45.5	53.8	94.2	108.6	100.5	83.0
Change in debt ratio attributable to...		4.7	8.4	40.4	14.4	−8.1	−17.8
Primary deficit		1.5	1.3	0.0	−2.7	−3.8	−3.9
Real interest rate		1.6	1.6	2.3	3.5	3.7	2.8
Real growth		0.6	1.6	6.6	−2.0	−11.6	−6.0
Real depreciation		1.8	1.6	22.3	10.9	−1.5	−11.8
Cross-terms		0.1	0.2	1.4	0.6	−0.5	−0.9
Residual[b]		−0.9	2.1	7.8	4.1	5.6	2.1

[a] Total public debt (including central bank). Debt in U.S. dollars evaluated at end-period exchange rates, divided by current GDP in U.S. dollars.
[b] Reflects debt stock adjustments (in particular, compensation bonds to issued to banks in 2002), nondebt financing, and measurement error.

cash to Uruguay, triggering a sudden withdrawal of deposits. Unfortunately, just this type of crisis materialized in Argentina in 2001.

Table 10.1 shows that debt as a share of GDP remained below 40 percent until the late 1990s. After 1998, however, the debt ratio began to creep up, driven by higher deficits, negative growth resulting from the reversal of capital flows to the region and the 1999 Brazilian devaluation, and some real exchange rate depreciation under Uruguay's crawling band system, which had been in place since the early 1990s (table 10.2). Macroeconomic difficulties in Argentina further contributed to economic stagnation, and output continued to decline in 2000 and 2001. In June 2001, the government decided to widen the exchange rate band and doubled the rate of depreciation to 15 percent per annum. However, confidence was not restored, and interest costs continued to creep up as a share of GDP.

The Banking Crisis

In this already weak situation, Uruguay was faced with Argentina's currency crisis, deposit freeze, and finally default in December 2001. Cash-starved Argentine residents began to draw down their deposits in Uruguay, putting pressure both on Uruguay's banking system and its balance of payments. A further change in the exchange rate band was implemented in January 2002, when the band was doubled from 6

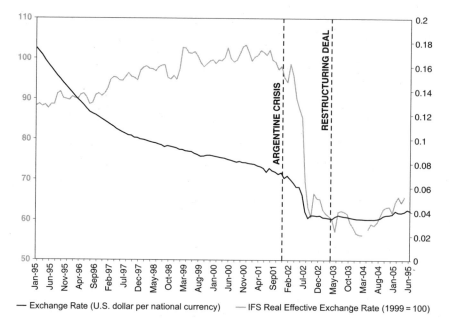

Figure 10.1
Nominal and real exchange rates
Source: IFS.

to 12 percent, and the rate of depreciation moved to 30 percent on an annual basis (figure 10.1).

As liquidity pressures and reserve losses mounted, the largest domestically owned banks began to experience runs. Rating agencies downgraded Uruguay below investment grade, further fueling the crisis. The central bank's attempt to provide liquidity assistance led to a quick depletion of international reserves. On June 19, 2002, the government decided to float the currency. A 50 percent exchange rate depreciation followed, leading to a large increase in the debt-to-GDP ratio, which undermined the government's ability to rescue distressed banks. As a result, pressures on the banking system continued, which the government initially attempted to stem without deposit freezes or direct controls, by creating a Fund for Fortifying the System of Banks financed through borrowing from the IMF. However, this proved insufficient, forcing the government to declare a bank holiday at the end of July 2002 (figure 10.2).

The exit from the bank holiday was different from that implemented in Argentina, and turned out to be more successful. The basic strategy,

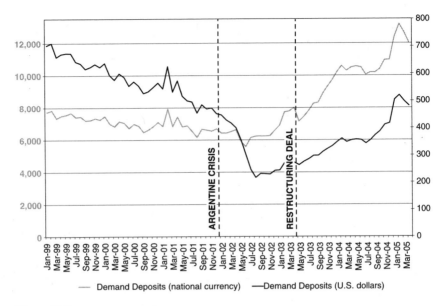

Figure 10.2
Deposits in Uruguay's financial sector (in millions)
Source: IFS.

supported by IMF financing, was to refrain from an Argentina-style freeze on sight deposits, which would have threatened the payments system, while creating a new lender-of-last resort facility called Fund for the Stability of the Banking Sector (FSBS) which fully backed unrestricted dollar deposits at a core set of domestic banks. Withdrawal restrictions at these core banks were limited to time deposits. In addition, maturities were extended on time deposits at two large public banks, and four insolvent private banks were suspended. Foreign banks were allowed to continue operating normally, without access to the FSBS, thus forcing them to put their reputation on the line. The authorities correctly assumed that given the relatively small size of the Uruguayan financial sector, large foreign banks would support their local branches.

The combination of a full backing of sight deposits, limited withdrawal restrictions, and normal foreign bank operations quickly halted the run. By October 2002, deposits were recovering. However, the large depreciation and credit contraction associated with the crisis had taken its toll on output and the fiscal accounts. Output fell by close to 11 percent and the budget deficit climbed further to close to 5 percent of GDP, driven by sharply higher interest payments. Furthermore, the debt-to-GDP ratio had almost doubled as a result of the depreciation, casting doubt on Uruguay's ability to service its debt.

The Debt Exchange

Faced with high and rising debt service obligations—about 16 percent of GDP in 2003 alone, rising to over 21 percent of GDP in 2006—the government reluctantly decided to offer a debt exchange. Although the debt-to-GDP ratio stood at close to 100 percent of GDP, the objective of the exchange was not debt reduction as such, but achieving debt service relief in as investor-friendly a way as possible. There were two reasons behind this approach: first, the authorities wanted to minimize the reputational impact of the restructuring in order to return to investment grade as quickly as possible; second, there was a fear that if the offer did not attract high participation, this could precipitate a second run on the banks. Hence, the exchange was not modeled after Ecuador's 2000 exchange or Argentina's November 2001 Phase 1 exchange, but was closer to Argentina's megaswap of June 2001, which had been a pure maturity-extending operation (see chapter 8). However, unlike that exchange, the maturity extension took place not at market rates, but at the original interest rates at which the bonds had been issued. Since Uruguay had previously benefited from investment grade status, this implied that the refinancing was implemented at precrisis rates, and hence contained an element of NPV debt reduction when evaluated at postexchange yields, as we see later in this chapter.

The exchange targeted all market debt (about half of total debt). Eligible securities comprised (1) forty-six domestically issued bonds and treasury bills, accounting for US$1.6 billion in principal; (2) eighteen international bonds issued under foreign law, accounting for US$3.5 billion; and (3) one "Samurai" bond issued in Japan, accounting for US$250 million. Domestic-law bonds could be exchanged through a custodian or broker, or directly at the central bank. Foreign law bonds could be exchanged by submitting applications to an internet site maintained by Citigroup. The Samurai bond's terms were to be changed at a bondholder's meeting.

The authorities communicated closely with bondholders prior to the exchange and developed the exchange offer through these consultations. After the initial launch on April 10, 2003, the government organized a second roadshow to explain the details, with explicit support from the IMF. With regard to the treatment of holdouts, the authorities indicated that, although they remained committed to servicing all their debt in full if possible, they would direct their funds to pay the new bonds in preference of the old bonds.

The offer originally expired on May 14, 2003, for the domestically issued bonds and on May 15 for the international offer, but it was extended for one week, and settlement took place on May 29. On June 10, the central bank announced that it would continue to accept domestic bonds that had not yet been submitted.

Most bondholders were offered a choice between two options.[1] Under a "maturity extension option," each bond could be exchanged by a new one with similar coupon and extended maturity (in general, five years longer than the original), mixed in some cases with a thirty-year bond that capitalized part of the interest earned over the first four years. Alternatively, investors could opt for a "benchmark bond option," involving one of a smaller number of new bonds, that were generally longer dated than the maturity extension bond but more liquid (also mixed with a thirty-year bond). Three external and four domestic benchmark bonds were introduced, with maturities ranging from seven to thirty years. Some of these bonds, geared to investors trading out of floating rate bonds, had step-up coupons that matched the expected increase in the floating rate that would have determined coupon payments under the old bonds. The benchmark bonds were designed to be attractive not only to institutional investors but also to index-tracking funds, on the premise that the new issues would be large enough to be included in international indices.

In addition, some bondholders were offered small upfront cash payments to compensate for accrued interest on the old bonds (there was no past due interest or principal). Holders of two collateralized Brady bonds (the 2021 par "Series A" and "Series B" bonds) also received the present value of the principal repayment in cash. With a minor exception, the sum of cash and new face value received per one hundred units of old principal was one hundred (or even slightly more); hence, there were no reductions in face value. Brady bondholders received seventy units of new bonds in addition to 38 percent in cash, that is, one hundred and eight units per one hundred of old principal. This implied a significantly higher value than that received by other bondholders, not so much because of the small "negative haircut" in face value terms, but because a much higher share of the units were in cash rather than in new bonds.

The authorities committed to going forward with the exchange if participation in the three concurrent exchange offers was larger than 90 percent. They retained discretion to move ahead if participation was larger than 80 percent. To maximize participation, exit amendments were used that eliminated the ability of holders of the old bonds to attach payments made on new bonds, deleted all cross-default and cross-acceleration provisions, and removed the listing requirements on the old bonds.[2] These exit consents were generally viewed as limited or "defensive" in the sense that their main objective was to protect the new bonds from holdout litigation, rather than to make the old bonds as unattractive as possible. The exchange also included the right of withdrawal prior to the May 15, 2003, deadline (but not after). This rule was included to encourage early participation, but most participating investors nevertheless waited until the last few days to accept the offer.

The new bonds, issued under New York law, included debt management provisions, which spread the payment of principal over several years prior to maturity, and a number of collective action clauses. In addition to a majority action clause allowing changes in the payment terms of any individual bond series with the consent of investors representing at least 75 percent of outstanding principal of that series, the new bonds included a novel "aggregation clause" that lowered the required supermajority threshold to only two-thirds provided that at least 85 percent of all affected series approved the change.

Participation of domestic financial institutions was encouraged through regulatory incentives. The superintendency of banks announced that the old bonds would become nontradable securities due to the suspension of stock exchange quotations. As a result, the old bonds would become subject to a 100 percent risk weighting in banks capital adequacy ratios. In addition, reduced provisioning requirements or higher credit ceilings would no longer be allowed when the old bonds were used as collateral. A provisioning requirement of at least 50 percent was announced for bonds rated in default or selective default. The central bank also said that it would not accept old bonds as collateral for liquidity assistance.

The announcement to delist the old bonds acted as a strong incentive for the participation of pension funds. In addition, a special rule allowing pension funds to value the old Global 2027 at purchase price, rather than mark-to-market was transferred to the new benchmark 2033 bond. The Chilean regulatory authorities also facilitated the participation of two Chilean peso-denominated bonds, by allowing the funds to "exchange" the bonds rather than "acquiring" the bonds, since Chilean regulation would have prevented them from purchasing speculative grade investments.

In the event, participation reached 89 percent for internationally issued bonds, 99 percent for domestically issued bonds, and 100 percent for the Samurai bonds, whose terms were changed with the consent of over 99 percent of bondholder votes. Though participation among the international bonds was high on average, it varied considerably from bond to bond; in particular, Brady bond participation was much lower than the average (see IMF Country Report No. 03/247, appendix II, for details).

Table 10.3 shows the haircuts for the eighteen exchanged international bonds. As in the case of the Argentina Phase 1 exchange, the computations are complicated by the large number of bonds and options offered, and the fact that secondary market prices are not available for some of the new bonds that were part of the menu (either because they were illiquid or because they were in fact not issued due to lack of interest). However, prices and hence exit yields are available for all fixed coupon U.S. dollar-denominated and for the two euro-denominated bonds. Using these, table 10.3 computes the haircuts for each old instrument and each of the two exchange options, under two alternative approaches. First, using the yield of the new instrument actually received to discount the old cash flows, regardless of differences in maturity; second, using a yield corresponding to the remaining life of the old instrument interpolated from the available yields of the new U.S. dollar bonds, with a maturity correction based on the U.S. yield curve at the short-end. The latter can be used for all dollar-denominated old bonds, while the use of the former depends on whether secondary market prices were available for the new instruments. Since this was always the case under the "benchmark option" but not necessarily under the "extension option," our haircut estimates for the latter are somewhat less complete.

The main result is that the haircuts for the Uruguay exchange were substantially lower than in any of the other large exchanges studied in this book, namely in the range of 5–20 percent, with a few outliers above and below. Based on the computations that do not make maturity adjustments (i.e., where old and new cash flows are discounted at the same rate) the weighted average haircut is about 13 percent.

Table 10.3
Uruguay international bonds exchange, April–May 2003: Haircuts (in 100 units of face value)

Old instrument	Maturity	Amount outstanding (millions of U.S. dollars)	Extension option			Benchmark option		
			Maturity	Haircut, computed using… Yield of bond received	Yield curve of new U.S. bonds	Maturity	Haircut, computed using… Yield of bond received	Yield curve of new U.S. bonds
US$ 7.875 2003	Nov-03	191	Nov-08	30.0	31.2	Feb-11	7.4	6.4
US$ New Money	Feb-06	26	July-09	…	29.0	Feb-12	13.5	11.2
US$ Conv. 91	Feb-07	55	Jan-10	…	28.0	Feb-13	11.1	8.0
US$ Conv. 02	April-07	150	April-12	…	…	Feb-14	4.9	-0.6
US$ 8.375 2006	Sep-06	97	Sep-11	15.6	15.2	Feb-15	10.7	5.4
US$ 7.0 2008	April-08	240	April-13	14.1	8.4	March-15	10.9	2.9
US$ 7.875 2009	March-09	248	March-14	13.9	8.5	March-16	11.7	3.6
US$ 7.25 2009	May-09	241	May-14	13.1	7.0	March-17	11.6	3.2
US$ 8.75 2010	Jun-10	274	June-15	16.2	11.6	March-18	14.4	6.6
US$ 7.625 2012	Jan-12	410	Jan-17	14.9	9.7	March-19	13.3	5.1
US$ 6.75 ParA	Feb-21	250	May-33	10.5	9.5	May-33	10.5	9.5
US$ 6.75 ParB	March-21	30	May-33	8.8	7.9	May-33	8.8	7.9
US$ 7.875 2027	July-27	510	May-33	9.8	12.8	May-33	9.8	12.8
Euro 7 2005	Sep-05	264	Sep-12	17.4	…	Feb-15	18.7	…
Euro 7 2011	June-11	237	June-19	17.1	…	March-15	23.2	…
Pound Conv. 91	Feb-07	39	Jan-10	…	…	Feb-15	14.7	…
Chilean Pesos 7.0 2007	May-07	118	May-12	…	…	March-15	18.0	…
Chilean Pesos 6.375 2011	March-11	127	March-16	…	…	May-33	17.9	…

Source: Sturzenegger and Zettelmeyer (2005).

Figure 10.3 shows how holders of two specific Eurobonds tendered at the exchange, maturing in 2003 and 2005, fared prior and after the exchange. Investor losses were short-lived, as prices recovered to pre-crisis values fairly quickly. The graph also provides interesting evidence on how holdouts fared, as we know that holdouts' claims have so far been honored in full. In the case of the 2003 bond, investors fared better by holding the benchmark bond, which had much higher liquidity after the exchange. For this bond, participation led to better terms than keeping the original instrument in spite of the fact that entering the exchange entailed a NPV haircut. For the 2005 bond the story is different. Due to its size, the bond retained liquidity after the exchange and holdouts performed better than investors that participated in the exchange. The initial differences, however, were eliminated fairly quickly.

Table 10.4 shows the results of a similar restructuring applied to all (dollar-denominated) Uruguayan domestic bonds—forty-six in total. They can be divided into three groups: T-bills coming due within the next twelve months; medium- and long-term variable rate bonds indexed to LIBOR, and five fixed-rate government bonds (including a relatively large, $300 million issue, and two "previsionales" associated with the social security system) coming due between 2005 and 2012. Floating rate bonds were equipped with a put option that allowed bondholders to ask for early repayment of up to 10 percent of principal on each annual anniversary of the issue date. The present value for these instruments shown in table 10.4 takes into account the value of these options; that is, it assumes, given the discount rate of about 14 percent at the time, that the put options would have been exercised in full.

T-bill holders received 15 percent in cash, with the remainder traded either into a 5.25 percent fixed rate bond maturing in 2006, or a step-up coupon bond maturing in 2010 (benchmark option). To keep the table manageable, we only show the first T-bill maturing in any month in which a T-bill was restructured. Floating rate bonds could be exchanged either for a floating rate "extension bond" indexed to LIBOR with a maturity extension of generally five years, or a slightly longer dated benchmark bond with step-up coupon. Bonds maturing in 2003 received some cash payments, but those maturing in 2004 or later did not. Finally, fixed rate bond holders generally had a choice between a fixed 7.5 coupon bond and a step-up coupon bond, with maturity extensions of five to ten years.

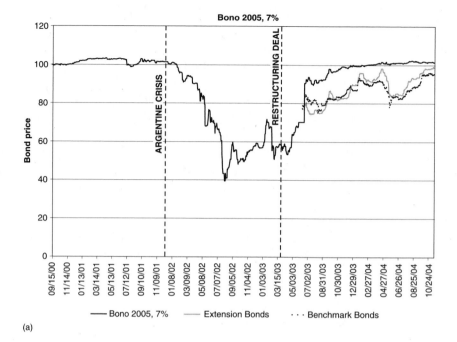

(a)

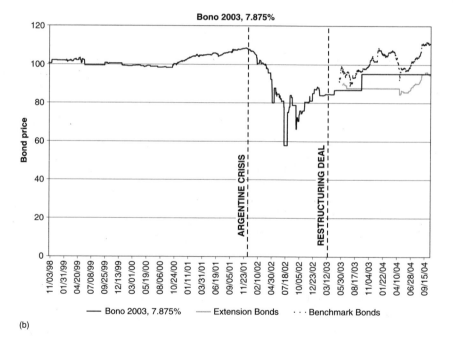

(b)

Figure 10.3
Bond prices before and after the exchange
Source: Bloomberg and authors' computations.

Table 10.4
Uruguay domestic law bonds exchange, April–May 2003: Haircuts (per 100 units of principal)

Old instruments	Amount outstanding (millions of U.S. dollars)	Maturity date	Extension option Maturity	Haircut[a]	Benchmark option Maturity	Haircut[a]
Letras 10121	5.3	May-03	Sep-06	15.5	Jun-10	30.1
Letras 10123	5.3	Jun-03	Sep-06	14.5	Jun-10	29.3
Letras 10127	5.3	Jul-03	Sep-06	13.5	Jun-10	28.4
Letras 10132	5.3	Aug-03	Sep-06	12.5	Jun-10	27.6
Letras 10137	5.3	Sep-03	Sep-06	11.5	Jun-10	26.8
Letras 10201	5.3	Mar-04	Sep-06	5.3	Jun-10	21.6
32a. TV	39.2	Jun-03	Sep-06	15.8	Jun-10	30.3
33a. TV	37.9	Sep-03	Dec-08	28.5	Jun-10	29.7
34a. TV	40.1	Dec-03	Dec-08	29.0	Jun-10	30.2
35a. TV	40.4	Mar-04	Dec-08	27.6	Jun-10	29.0
36a. TV	25.5	Jun-04	Nov-09	31.9	Jun-10	29.4
37a. TV	29.6	Sep-04	Nov-09	29.9	Jun-10	27.3
38a. TV	12.2	Nov-04	Nov-09	28.4	Jun-10	25.7
39a. TV	29.1	Dec-04	Nov-09	29.0	Jun-10	26.4
40a. TV	35.0	Mar-05	Nov-09	26.4	Jun-10	23.7
41a. TV	53.9	Jun-05	Sep-10	29.6	May-13	29.9
42a. TV	31.3	Sep-05	Sep-10	29.5	May-13	29.8
43a. TV	25.6	Dec-05	Sep-10	27.7	May-13	27.9
44a. TV	35.1	Apr-06	Sep-10	24.5	May-13	24.8
45a. TV	50.7	Jun-06	Aug-11	29.3	May-13	27.2
46a. TV	129.1	Aug-06	Aug-11	28.6	May-13	26.6
47a. TV	48.7	Dec-06	Aug-11	27.9	May-13	25.9
48a. TV	32.3	May-09	Jun-17	33.0	Apr-18	25.4
49a. TV	48.0	Jun-12	Jun-17	42.0	Apr-18	35.5
51a. TV	34.3	Sep-12	Jun-17	43.2	Apr-18	36.8
52a. TV	82.8	Feb-10	Jun-17	32.0	Apr-18	24.3
50a. TV	28.4	Aug-12	Jun-17	43.1	Apr-18	36.7
53a. TV	10.9	Mar-11	Apr-18	26.7	Apr-18	27.0
54a. TV	105.5	May-13	Apr-18	31.5	Apr-18	31.7
29a. TF	25.0	Dec-05	Dec-10	19.3	Jun-10	24.1
30a. TF	299.1	Mar-11	...	...	Mar-19	9.6
31a. TF	40.0	Feb-12	Feb-20	3.0	Mar-19	10.0
A.P. 3a.	46.2	Feb-10	Feb-18	10.7	Mar-19	11.0
A.P. 2a.	108.5	Mar-07	Mar-12	14.9	May-13	20.6
Letras 10122	5.3	May-03	Sep-06	15.5	Jun-10	30.1
Letras 10124	5.3	Jun-03	Sep-06	14.5	Jun-10	29.3

Table 10.4
(continued)

Old instruments	Amount outstanding (millions of U.S. dollars)	Maturity date	Extension option		Benchmark option	
			Maturity	Haircut[a]	Maturity	Haircut[a]
Letras 10125	5.3	Jun-03	Sep-06	14.5	Jun-10	29.3
Letras 10128	5.3	Jul-03	Sep-06	13.5	Jun-10	28.4
Letras 10129	5.3	Jul-03	Sep-06	13.5	Jun-10	28.4
Letras 10130	5.3	Jul-03	Sep-06	13.5	Jun-10	28.4
Letras 10131	5.3	Jul-03	Sep-06	13.5	Jun-10	28.4
Letras 10133	5.3	Aug-03	Sep-06	12.5	Jun-10	27.6
Letras 10134	5.3	Aug-03	Sep-06	12.5	Jun-10	27.6
Letras 10135	5.3	Aug-03	Sep-06	12.5	Jun-10	27.6
Letras 10138	5.3	Sep-03	Sep-06	11.5	Jun-10	26.8
Letras 10139	5.3	Sep-03	Sep-06	11.5	Jun-10	26.8

Source: Sturzenegger and Zettelmeyer (2005).
[a] Discount factor based on yield curve for international bonds trading after the exchange.

The result is that for the floating rate bonds, haircuts appear to have been in the 20–35 percent range, and for the short-dated T-bills, in the 15–30 percent range. Hence, it appears that the short-dated and variable rate domestic treasury bonds and bills suffered a somewhat higher haircut than Uruguay's international bonds. In contrast, the long-dated fixed rate domestic bonds and "previsionales" seem to have been subjected to about the same haircut as the international bonds.

After the Exchange

By the time Uruguay had completed its exchange, the international environment was changing significantly in favor of the Uruguayan economy. Commodity prices recovered, and growth in both Brazil and Argentina turned positive. Argentina's fast recovery, with average annual real growth around 9 percent between mid-2002 and 2006, as well as a real appreciation of the Argentine peso, led to a significant recovery in tourism inflows from its main neighbor. Substantial liquidity in international markets and Uruguay's friendly attitude toward international investors during the exchange also led to a quick fall in bond spreads. By November 2004 they had fallen to less than 400 basis points, compared with 2,000 basis points at the height of the crisis. The

Box 10.1
Chronology of Uruguay's crisis and debt restructuring

1995:

January: Launching of Mercosur.

1999:

January: Devaluation of the real.

November: Jorge Batlle is elected president.

2001:

June: Widening of exchange rate band in response to worsening crisis in Argentina.

December 24: Argentina defaults on its debt and shortly after devalues the peso.

2002:

January 4: Further widening of exchange rate band.

February 14: S&P downgrades Uruguay below investment grade.

April 26: Banco Comercial gets government assistance and is recapitalized by shareholders.

May 28: IMF and IDB announce augmentations of financial assistance.

June 19: Move to a floating exchange rate regime.

June 21: Central bank intervenes Banco Montevideo and Banco La Caja Obrera.

July 23: Minister of Finance and members of the Board of the central bank resign.

July 30: Bank holiday and suspension of Banco Montevideo and Banco La Caja Obrera for sixty days, and Banco Comercial and Banco de Credito for thirty days. Time deposits of public banks are reprogrammed with a three-year schedule.

2003:

April 10: Launch of debt exchange offer.

May 29: Closing of debt exchange offer with 89 percent participation of international investors and 99 percent participation of domestic investors.

2004:

November: Left-wing Tabaré Vázquez is elected president.

---

combination of all these factors led to a spectacular recovery, with GDP growth on the order of 12 percent in 2004. In 2005, GDP was expected to exceed its precrisis maximum (attained in 1998) for the first time.

While Uruguay's debt exchange was a great success in resolving the country's public debt service difficulties in a nonconfrontational way, the flip-side of Uruguay's investor-friendly approach was that it did not achieve much debt relief. Because no face value reductions were attempted, Uruguay's restructuring had no impact on the headline debt to GDP number (in fact, this went up in 2003, as "skeletons" were discovered ahead of the exchange), and, depending on the discount rate that is applied, it may have had either a positive or a small negative effect on the net present value of the debt burden (see chapter 11). The debt-to-GDP ratio dropped rapidly in 2004 and 2005 as a result of fast growth, real appreciation, and a primary surplus of almost 4 percent, but gross public debt was still expected to stand at over 80 percent of GDP at the end of 2005. As a result, the country is likely to need high primary fiscal surpluses over several years—government targets remain around 4 percent—if the debt-to-GDP ratio is to remain on a declining path.

Afterword: The Dominican Republic

In mid-2005, the Dominican Republic became the most recent Latin American country to restructure its sovereign debt. The origins of the crisis were somewhat idiosyncratic, but the debt exchange followed a by now familiar pattern. In this afterword, we briefly summarize the background and outcome of the debt restructuring without going into the same detail as in our previous country studies.

The Dominican Republic enjoyed a decade of substantial growth following significant structural reforms and an opening of the economy to trade and foreign investment. In 2002, the economy slowed somewhat as a result of a reduction in tourism flows following September 11, 2001. A full-fledged crisis erupted in 2003 after the uncovering of bank fraud in the context of weak supervision (several attempts to strengthen prudential regulation in the 1990s had failed). The resulting banking crisis led to the closing of one of the major banks and a jump in the debt-to-GDP ratio, as losses in the banking sector were converted into public debt. Furthermore the liquidity issued by the central bank to protect the payments system lead to a substantial depreciation of the exchange rate, coupled with rising inflation. The combination of debt issued in connection with the banking crisis and the reduction of dollar GDP as a result of the depreciation led to a more than doubling of the debt-to-GDP ratio from around 26 percent in 2002 to 54 percent at the end of 2003.

Fiscal slippages continued to compromise stability in early 2004, and inflation remained high, while spreads on external debt moved well above 1,000 basis points. Confidence returned after a new president took office in August 2004, leading to reductions in spreads, a recovery of the exchange rate, accumulation of reserves, and declining inflation.

In the context of a stabilizing economy and recovering growth, the Dominican Republic authorities decided on a debt strategy that entailed a restructuring of external commercial banks and suppliers debt, a Paris Club rescheduling, the renegotiation of a Standby Arrangement with the IMF, and a restructuring of privately held external bonds, which stood at close to US$1.2 billion and were beginning to come due in 2006. The government insisted that the exchange would be voluntary, implicitly guaranteeing full payment to holdouts and hence committing to a transaction with a minimal haircut, if any at all. A minimum participation threshold of 85 percent was announced, but this threshold was nonbinding, in the sense that while the authorities committed to go forward if participation exceeded 85 percent, they reserved the right to do so even if participation fell short of this threshold. The reason for this was that a bondholder committee representing about 20–25 percent of holders had formed, and the government was worried that setting a tight participation threshold might give this group excessive bargaining power.

The debt was exchanged through two exchange offers made to holders of the Dominican Republic's 2006 and 2013 bonds: an initial offer that closed on May 11, 2005, and a reopening that closed on July 20, 2005. Participation after the first exchange exceeded 93 percent. After rising secondary market debt prices over the next few months effectively improved the value of the initial offer, the exchange was reopened to give the initial holdouts a chance to change their minds and allow the government to achieve further cash flow relief. Over half of the initial holdouts accepted the offer during this second round, resulting in a final participation rate of about 97 percent.

As in the case of Pakistan, the restructuring served the purpose of fulfilling a pledge to the Paris Club and the IMF that the government would seek to obtain comparability of treatment from its other creditors. A lone coupon that matured during the period when the offer was open and that could not have been rolled into the exchange offer without falling into default was paid punctually. A restructuring agreement with commercial banks was reached at about the same time as the bond exchange, rescheduling about US$200 million in principal falling due in 2005–2005.

The exchange offers invited holders of the 9.50 percent bonds due in 2006 to exchange for new 9.50 percent amortizing bonds due in 2011, and holders of the 9.04 percent bonds due in 2013 to exchange for new 9.04 percent amortizing bonds due in 2018. Although the new bonds had the same coupon as the old ones, they partially capitalized interest payments due in 2005 and 2006. As under Uruguay's extension option, the exchange extended the maturities of the Dominican Republic's out-standing bonds by five years. The legal features were also virtually the same as those used in Uruguay; in particular, New York law bonds including collective action clauses and an aggregate voting feature were issued under a trust indenture, and "defensive" exit amendments were used to protect new bondholders from potential litigation (see IMF 2005b for details). In this sense, the basic terms of the exchange were identical to those of Uruguay's exchange. But given that emerging market spreads had declined further since Uruguay's exchange, the implied haircut was even lower than in the case of Uruguay, as anticipated by market reports when the exchange was being planned in late 2004.

Using the yields on the "new" bonds prevailing after the closing of the May 2005 exchange—about 10 percent for the 2018 and 9.10 percent for the 2011—to discount old and new cash flows results in minimal haircuts, of 0.14 percent for a holder of a 2006 bond and 2.67 percent for a holder of the 2013. This makes the Dominican Republic exchange the most investor-friendly distressed debt exchange among all studied in this book. Since yields declined by about 130 basis points between May and July 2005, the haircut would have been even lower (zero, or slightly negative) at the time of the July exchange.

Shortly after closing the exchange, the authorities announced that they would honor the claims of bondholders that had not participated.

III   Policy

11 Debt Crises from the Perspective of an Emerging Market Economy Policymaker

This chapter discusses how domestic policymakers can best prevent, prepare for, and, if necessary, manage a sovereign debt crisis. As the preceding chapters have shown, several of the debt crises of the last decade—Argentina, Ecuador, and Russia, in particular—have had very high economic and social costs. Moreover, these costs appear to have gone far beyond the costs of default suggested in the traditional sovereign debt literature, with sharp aggregate output costs, large redistributions of wealth and periods of significant political change and instability. In contrast, in other cases of sovereign debt restructurings, such as Pakistan and Moldova, the costs appear to have been much smaller. Presumably, these differences were related to differences in the size of the default and in the underlying economic problems, which were in part a consequence of how the economies were managed ahead of the crisis. In addition, the management of the crisis itself is likely to have had some impact on the eventual outturn.

The remainder of this chapter is devoted to studying the link between economic management and crisis costs more closely. We distinguish three phases. First, we look at policies in "tranquil" times, namely, well before a crisis has erupted. These involve both reducing the chances that the economy will face a debt crisis, and preparing it so that its costs will be lower if such an event were to happen. Second, we examine what to do when the country is already suffering a capital flow reversal and a debt crisis appears imminent. In this case, the policymaker faces the tough decision of either attempting to overcome the crisis without a default—at the risk of having to default later under more adverse circumstances—or to preempt a default by trying to engineer a relatively smooth restructuring. Finally, we study the challenges faced by the policymaker that has to undertake a debt restructuring. In this phase, the main concern is to minimize the costs of the restructuring (in the broadest sense), and obtain sufficient debt relief to put the economy on a sustainable debt path.

Policymaking during Tranquil Times

Long before a debt crisis becomes evident, the policies in place have an influence on both the likelihood and potential cost of such an event. In other words, the policymaker has to decide on issues that relate to *crisis prevention*, that is, how to minimize the probability of actually experiencing a crisis, as well as how to prepare the economy for such an event, something that we refer to as *crisis preparation*. Consider an automotive analogy. Crisis prevention would be equivalent to insuring that the car has well-functioning brakes, allowing one to stay clear of a dangerous situation. Crisis preparation could be compared with having a good set of airbags, that is, a defensive mechanism in case one cannot avoid a crash. We now review policy issues arising in both areas.

Crisis Prevention

To discuss crisis prevention, it is useful to recall the discussion in chapter 2 on the causes of debt crises. Three main sources of debt crises were analyzed: debt runs, balance sheet effects in the face of large devaluations, and overborrowing. Moreover, as we have seen in the country chapters, there are important interactions between sovereign debt and the private financial sector that affect both the likelihood and depth of a crisis, either because implicit guarantees give quasipublic status to some private debts, or because the costs of sovereign debt crises depend on whether these trigger banking crises or not (a subject to be taken up in the next section).

Hence, policies for debt crisis prevention can be discussed in terms of four or five categories: debt levels, debt structures, international reserves and other forms of country insurance, and financial sector regulation and supervision. It is easy to define in general terms what a "safe" country would look like in terms of these categories. It would have low debt, a smooth repayment profile, a low share of short-term debt on a residual maturity basis, a currency structure that matches the currency denomination of receipts (with a low share of foreign currency debt except for sovereigns that rely mainly on commodity exports), sufficient reserves to cover rollover risk and perhaps reduce real exchange rate volatility, and equity-like indexed liabilities or other forms of insurance to buffer the country from solvency shocks (see also chapter 12). In addition, it would have sound financial sector institutions that insure that the private financial sector is not overindebted, has prudent balance sheet structures, and sufficient liquidity.

However, there are two problems with simply advising countries to move closer to the safe ideal. First, what should be considered safe in one category depends in part on whether or not the country is vulnerable in another category. Second, crisis prevention is not free. Holding liquid foreign currency reserves is obviously costly. Even more important, emerging market countries may face significant incentives that push them toward "dangerous debt," since long-term borrowing in local currency may be much more expensive (or even impossible) than short-term borrowing in foreign currency. As argued in chapters 2 and 12, dangerous debt structures may be a reflection of deeper incentives, credibility, and information problems. If that is so, how much scope do domestic policymakers really have? In what follows, we summarize what can be said about sensible choices regarding total debt levels, debt structures, reserve levels, and other forms of insurance, based on recent crisis experiences and research in these areas.

Regarding *debt levels*, it has recently been argued that indebtedness thresholds that might be considered "safe" depend on the country's debt history, the quality of its institutions, the level of reserves, and its debt structure. At a general level, this must be true; for example, the quality of institutions and the stability of the political system will determine the fiscal adjustment that a country might be able to deliver in a crisis, and hence imply safe debt levels of different size. Some industrial countries, such as Japan and Italy, have debt to GDP ratios several times larger than those in most developing countries without raising much of a concern. Debt structure also determines what may be considered a safe threshold. A 30 percent debt-to-GDP ratio that could double to 60 percent at a moment's notice in the event of a currency crisis is clearly less safe than a 40 percent debt to GDP ratio with the debt-denominated in domestic currency. And of course the terms of lending also matter: countries with large amounts of multilateral or concessional lending may be much safer in spite of much higher debt levels.

What do these interactions imply in terms of actual "safe" thresholds? This is an empirical question, and a difficult one to answer. Some recent work in this area attempts to give a sense of the orders of magnitude. For example, based on empirical work inspired by Kraay and Nehru (2004), the IMF and the World Bank have recently argued that in developing countries whose "institutional strength and quality of policies" are rated "poor," sustainable debt-to-GDP ratios (in NPV terms) are 30 percent or less, while in countries whose institutions are rated "strong" they can be as high as 60 percent (IMF and IDA 2004). Manasse and Roubini (2005) identify "safe zones" in which safe debt levels depend on a host of other indicators, particularly the country's ratio of short-term debt to reserves and indicators of macroeconomic solvency and political stability. They identify a maximum debt ratio of about 50 percent of GDP as "safe" for emerging market countries that have stable macroeconomic indicators and do reasonably well in terms of liquidity and debt structure (i.e., have low short-term debt compared with reserves—a ratio of less than 1.3 is identified as safe in this regard).

At any rate, these are of course "soft" thresholds that could be trespassed on occasions. The analysis of the debt dynamics is as important as the debt level. A devaluation or a real shock may bring a country above the threshold level, but if authorities respond so that the debt dynamics point downward this should not be an immediate cause for concern. In fact, financial markets do approach public debt in this way, with the debt dynamics becoming the main focus as soon as debt levels become large.

Whether or not a debt level is safe will also depend on the *repayment profile*. Debt levels are usually computed as the ratio of debt outstanding to GDP, even if this debt is due far in the future and pays concessional rates. In these cases, the debt ratio by itself does not convey much information about either the debt burden or its vulnerability to sudden increases in financing needs. Given the political economy constraints that typically face fiscal policy, a smooth interest and amortization profile is safer than a lumpy profile, because it creates the permanent need to assign some budget resources for the purpose of servicing the debt. Once the budget fight to obtain the resources has been won, no substantial changes to the status quo are required later on. In contrast, bullet repayments imply significant exposure to market risk: if refinancing is not feasible, the required fiscal adjustment may be impossibly large. For example, Ukraine's 1998 restructurings left the country with a manageable debt to GDP ratio (less than 40 percent), but an uncomfortably large fraction of this debt was maturing in 2000. When 2000 came along and markets were not providing the financing, fiscal adjustment would have had to increase dramatically, making the restructuring inevitable. Although a smooth repayment profile may require the government to tap the market more often, a temporary rollover problem need not automatically spiral into a debt crisis because it can be dealt with through a mixture of fiscal adjustment, international reserves, and possibly international official lending.

A related question is how countries can move to safer *public debt structures*—that is, longer maturities that reduce rollover risk, and domestic currency debt that reduces the vulnerability of a sovereign to a currency crisis.[1] An important strand of the literature argues that the inability of many emerging market countries to issue long-term debt domestically in domestic currency is a reflection of lack of monetary and fiscal policy credibility (see Borensztein et al. 2005 for an overview).[2] Countries with a history of high inflation and weak fiscal and monetary institutions will find it prohibitively expensive to issue long-term debt in their own currency. However, experiences in countries such as Chile, Mexico, Israel, Poland, Peru, and most recently Brazil, also suggest that countries can overcome this stigma relatively quickly after stabilizing their currencies and reforming their monetary policy frameworks (e.g., making their central banks independent or introducing inflation-targeting regimes). Once some credibility is established, policy steps that can help dedollarize public debt at an acceptable cost include lengthening maturities gradually and issuing inflation-indexed debt as an intermediate step. Policies that encourage the development of a domestic investor base, such as a move to a fully funded pension system, can also be useful in this context, by creating a demand for CPI-indexed instruments. Of course, this assumes that credible CPI-indexed instruments are offered by the government.[3]

Improving unsafe *liability structures in the private financial sector* is arguably harder (Levy-Yeyati 2003; Ize and Levy-Yeyati 2003; Ize and Powell 2004). Again, the root of the problem is often a lack of macroeconomic credibility: in spite of having enjoyed currency stability for a while, depositors and firms may still worry that high inflation and/ or a sharp devaluation might happen in the future. This need not be driven by "long memories" of hyperinflation, but could reflect a fragile fiscal situation, or more generally a broad lack of faith in the society's "institutions of conflict management"—a lack of confidence that the political system could handle a major disruption without resorting to desperate measures (Rajan 2004a). This encourages simple forms of contracts that are the most conflict-immune, including, in the financial system, demand deposits denominated in dollars.

Hence, improving fiscal and monetary institutions is a necessary first step to financial dedollarization, as are steps towards *public* sector debt dedollarization, as a means of developing a financial market in local currency instruments. Regulatory measures, such as higher liquidity requirements on dollar deposits and higher capital requirements on dollar loans, may also help, and can be independently justified as prudential measures that help reduce the risk of living with a dollarized financial system. Finally, the most radical approach would be to directly forbid the holdings of foreign currency deposits. This is likely to induce some capital flight and lead to a smaller financial sector, but as long as interest rates are allowed to move freely (so that financial repression does not arise), capital flight will be relatively contained and its costs might be compensated by the positive externalities of a less fragile financial sector.

The appropriate *level of foreign currency reserves* will depend on the level and currency composition of short-term public debt, as well as the extent to which financial sector liabilities are dollarized. With large currency mismatches in the aggregate private financial sector (including corporations), monetary policy could lose its effectiveness, and large reserve levels may become necessary if the central bank is to play its traditional role of safeguarding the financial system (Jeanne and Wyplosz 2001). Indeed, some highly dollarized countries, such as Bolivia, have developed dollar-based interventions in financial markets into an art form. The problem is that, by definition, international reserves need to be held in liquid form which is remunerated at low interest rates. This puts a limit on the reserves that a country can afford, and raises the question of what the optimal level of reserves is. Bussiere and Mulder (1999) and Wijnholds and Kapteyn (2001) argue that the "Greenspan-Guidotti rule" that countries should hold reserves that cover at least their short-term foreign currency debt is useful as a starting point, based on evidence suggesting that countries that meet the rule are less prone to suffer from contagion-related crises.[4] This is broadly consistent with Manasse and Roubini (2005), who find that a ratio of short-term debt to reserves of 1.3 is an upper bound for the purpose of avoiding a debt crisis.

However, reserves as an insurance device have two important shortcomings, which have spurred a discussion on *new mechanisms for country insurance*. First, reserves are an inefficient form of insurance in the sense that they force a country to pay a carrying cost all the time, although they may only really be needed when market access is lost.[5]

Second, reserves insure a country only against liquidity shocks, not shocks to GDP or net worth. Holding reserves is analogous to receiving an official *loan* in the event of a crisis, as opposed to a contingent *transfer*. To deal with these shortcomings, countries could more aggressively issue contingent debt, or buy derivatives that have insurance-like properties. Several proposals have recently been made in this context, ranging from GDP or CPI-indexed bonds (Borensztein and Mauro 2004; Borensztein et al. 2005), to hedging instruments based on financial indices that are correlated with "sudden stops" in emerging markets (Caballero and Panageas 2004).

The main problem with these forms of insurance—and perhaps a reason why they have only been sporadically adopted in the past[6]—is that they tend to be expensive when markets for particular derivatives or contingent claims are new and shallow, while their benefits in terms of crisis avoidance accrues only if they are issued en masse. Hence, while policymakers would do well to explore issuing or purchasing instruments of this type, a breakthrough in this area may require a coordinated effort at the international level. We return to this topic in chapter 12.

Crisis Preparation

Economic variables that matter for crisis prevention are mostly relevant from the perspective of "crisis preparation" as well. The most obvious example is that the level of debt matters for both: large debts not only make defaults more likely, but also messier. Market-friendly restructurings become more difficult, a longer period between default and restructuring may elapse, and many categories of debt may be affected—all factors that have been associated with larger output costs of crises. Another example is debt structure: Guidotti, Sturzenegger, and Villar (2004) study the output response of countries suffering a sudden stop, and find that balance sheet effects are relevant in explaining negative output performance in the aftermath of a current account reversal. Dedollarized economies recover faster. They also find that open economies seem to enjoy higher growth in the aftermath of the crisis.

However, policies for crisis preparation can and should go beyond policies for crisis prevention. As we saw in our case studies, debt problems are magnified by links between currency crises, banking crises, and debt crises. Weak output performance reduces tax collection and leads to a widening fiscal deficit. At the same time, nonperforming loans rise and bank balance sheets deteriorate. Banking crises strain fiscal resources by requiring bailouts financed by public bonds. A debt crisis, in turn, can destroy the balance sheets of banks to the extent that they hold public bonds and trigger a devaluation via a surge in capital flight. A devaluation of the exchange rate increases the real value of dollar linked debts and worsens both the fiscal situation and the balance sheet of the private financial sector. Conversely, the provision of liquidity required to keep healthy banks afloat can fuel a run on the currency. Containing crises must involve weakening these links.

Several of these mechanisms could be observed during the actual crises studied in this book. In the case of Russia, persistent weak fiscal performance led to a rollover problem which forced a default on short-term local currency denominated debt. At the same time, there was a reserve drain as creditors attempted to repatriate funds; this triggered a devaluation. The increased dollar value of debts forced a default on a portion of the external debt. Both the government default on T-bills and the devaluation triggered a banking crisis, as banks were heavily exposed to government debt and major banks had accumulated extensive foreign currency liabilities during 1995–1997. The pattern in Ukraine was similar (with the added effect of the external shock implied by the Russian devaluation and default), except that no domestic financial crisis erupted because of the relatively small banking sector. In the case of Pakistan, an external shock triggered a banking crisis that led to substantial capital flight, devaluation, higher interest rates, and debt payment difficulties. In Ecuador, sizable real shocks associated with the El Niño storms led to a banking crisis that required bailouts and liquidity support which in turn fueled a run on the currency and a large depreciation of the exchange rate. This depreciation made it unfeasible to pay the external debt. In the case of Argentina, a long and protracted recession created fears of an exit from the fixed exchange rate regime, a series of bank runs, and a fall in revenues. This resulted in sharp deteriorations in borrowing conditions, leading to a default on debt payments that in turn triggered a devaluation. Uruguay suffered a banking crisis as a result of contagion from the crisis in Argentina, which required liquidity support in dollars, as bank deposits were dollar-denominated. Dwindling reserves led to doubts about the sustainability of the exchange rate band, a run on the currency, and eventually a sharp depreciation that made a rescheduling of debt payments inevitable.

What would it take to separate the three crises? The link between currency crises and debt and banking crises can be broken by reducing currency mismatches in private and public balance sheets, as discussed previously. The link between banking and currency crises can be weakened by creating mechanisms that expedite the resolution of banking sector problems, identifying and shutting down (or absorbing) problem banks rather than providing open-ended liquidity support. The link between banking and debt crises can be mitigated through an effective deposit insurance mechanism, though it cannot be eliminated completely: a systemic financial sector crisis is always a liability for the government. Hence, the best way the public sector can protect itself from a banking crisis is probably through prevention, by providing adequate banking regulation and supervision in tranquil times. Finally, the link between debt crises and banking crises can be mitigated by limiting the exposure of the banking system to government debt. Note that this may require a departure from the standard Basel rules for capital adequacy, which favor the holding of government paper relative to other risky assets.

The most direct way of isolating the financial sector from either currency or debt crisis is through regulation. As discussed previously, regulation could be part of a more comprehensive dedollarization strategy. Similarly, the government could forbid banks to hold government paper, or limit government bond holdings to investment banks, which would not be allowed to hold deposits. In this way, commercial bank balance sheets would be completely free of government bonds. This is akin to "narrow banking" rules splitting the assets of banking activities in high and low risk assets and matching deposits with low risk assets. A run would force the "investment/high risk" part of the bank to go bankrupt, while transaction accounts would remain protected (Dujovne and Guidotti 2001). Uruguay implemented a de facto mechanism of this kind ex post by freeing and backing all transaction accounts but restructuring longer term deposits.

Another way to make the financial sector more crisis resistant is to "internationalize" it by allowing the entry of foreign banks.[7] The idea is that a run in one country should not threaten the solvency of a regional or global bank with assets in many countries, and that global institutions will not risk the reputation loss of allowing the activity in one of the countries to go bankrupt. This strategy worked successfully in Uruguay. After a brief deposit freeze, foreign banks were forced to deal with the bank run without government support, and responded by delivering the funds required by depositors to their Uruguayan branches. Argentina, on the other hand, by imposing an across the board protracted freeze on the deposits of all banks basically released the banks from the reputation cost of not honoring their deposits. While it is open to question whether Uruguay's approach would have worked as well in a larger economy such as Argentina, the strategy of internationalization remains attractive.[8]

The Policymaker Facing the Crisis

To Fight or Not to Fight?

At some point, tranquil times may give way to a process that risks taking the economy into a debt crisis. Policymakers may face a choice between taking measures that could avert the crisis, at the risk of merely postponing it and perhaps ending up with an uncontrollable situation, or preempting it by attempting a debt restructuring ahead of an overt default. How should he or she decide?

To clarify the tradeoffs involved, consider the following setup. Imagine that the decision to restructure the debt now delivers an expected utility of U_{D_1}. Delay, on the other hand, requires implementing adjustment or reform measures at cost c and then obtaining an expected utility of $pU_{ND} + (1 - p)U_{D_2}$, where the subscript ND refers to the outcome in case a debt restructuring can be avoided entirely, and the subscript D_2 refers to the utility if the debt restructuring or default happens at a later date.[9] p denotes the probability of avoiding the default conditional on a reform effort. We assume that the utility of avoiding a default is larger than the utility of restructuring the debt in the first period and that this, in turn, is larger than the utility of defaulting in the second period: $U_{ND} > U_{D_1} > U_{D_2}$.

The policymaker will choose to implement the reform if the expected utility from attempting to avoid the default is larger than the utility of defaulting today:

$$pU_{ND} + (1 - p)U_{D_2} - c > U_{D_1}, \tag{11.1}$$

or, alternatively,

$$p(U_{ND} - U_{D_1}) > c + (1 - p)(U_{D_1} - U_{D_2}). \tag{11.2}$$

This just says that the policymaker is better off trying to fight the default if the expected gains of avoiding the default, which is the utility gain relative to defaulting today $(U_{ND} - U_{D_1})$ times the probability that the default is averted, are larger than the expected costs of fighting the default, namely, the sum of the adjustment costs c and the expected utility loss resulting from merely delaying the crisis. Hence, the decision to fight or not fight the default depends on three factors: the effectiveness of the reform tools available in reducing the probability of default, how much there is to gain by avoiding the default, and how costly it is to wait.

What can be said about the plausible relative magnitude of these variables? As far as the cost of delay is concerned, it is often argued that the attempt to survive the crisis may imply the need to roll over debt at very high interest rates, a substantial drain of reserves, and further loss of economic activity. But it is important to keep in mind that what is relevant is the potential *increase* in crisis cost owing to a default *at a later moment in time*. In particular, if output costs come mostly from the default per se, this cost cannot be avoided by defaulting earlier. Similarly, an increase in the debt burden resulting from an attempt to stave off a default does not have a direct impact on the costs of delay, since it will burden the economy only if no default takes place in the end. An example is provided by Argentina's megaswap debt exchange of July 2001. While it entailed a rollover at high interest rates, in the event of default all these payments were restructured again.

This leaves two candidates that might be driving a wedge between U_{D_1} and U_{D_2}: reserve losses in the process of staving off the run (at least to the extent that these are not transfers from the public to private residents), and the possible capital market repercussions of having to default on a bigger nominal debt.[10] The Argentine default again provides useful illustrations. Argentina lost about $6.5 billion in gross reserves between June and December 2001. A portion of these losses presumably benefited residents, so this number can be viewed as an upper bound to the national reserves cost of the delay. As far as capital market repercussions are concerned, there is a plausible link between the size of Argentina's restructuring and its exceptionally harsh terms. Defaulting in June rather than December 2001 might have led to a haircut in a more conventional range, and hence less creditor resentment. The question is how this resentment impacts domestic welfare. Only a few months after its harsh restructuring, Argentina's sovereign spread seemed to be about the same as that of neighboring countries that avoided a default—in line with evidence surveyed in chapter 2 suggesting that the effect of default histories on borrowing costs, if it exists at all, appears to be small.[11] Hence, it is hard to argue that an earlier and smaller default would have led to more favorable borrowing conditions after the restructuring. This leaves one potential cost of the later and harsher default, namely, the presence of a large and hostile group of holdout creditors. As argued in chapter 3, there are some ways in which these creditors could hurt Argentina, in particular, by blocking future sovereign debt issues in international markets. It is difficult to say how large the associated welfare cost might be. In our view, it is probably not very large.[12]

These costs of delay must be compared with the expected gain from avoiding the default altogether. The potential magnitude of this gain depends significantly on *how much* of the crisis can be avoided by staving off a default. If the economy has not collapsed yet there are large potential benefits. Among the cases discussed in this book, this was plausibly the case for Russia and Ukraine, as well as Argentina from the perspective of June 2001, none of which had suffered prior crisis-driven output declines. But if the economic collapse has already materialized then there is not much to be lost by actually defaulting, a situation that loosely fits the experience of Argentina in December 2001, as well as Ecuador, Uruguay, and Moldova, in which currency and/or banking crises preceded the default.

Finally, the most difficult parameter to gauge in our cost-benefit calculation is p, the probability of success. The problem here is not only that the success of adjustment and reform efforts is uncertain, but that the eventual outcome depends on external factors over which the policymaker has no control: the financing environment of emerging markets, output growth of major trading partners, and the terms of trade. Examples for such external developments that played a critical role in contributing to the debt crises studied in this book include the low price of oil for Russia, the Russian crisis for Ukraine, the El Niño storms in Ecuador, the U.S. dollar appreciation and Brazil's real depreciation for Argentina, and the Argentine crisis for Uruguay. Some of these shocks were permanent, but others were transitory or, at least, mean-reverting. In fact, it is quite striking that for the countries studied in this volume we found that after default most external conditions improved, sometimes dramatically. In part, this reflects the endogeneity of the crisis: debt crises tend to happen when everything has turned wrong—a fairly rare occurance. Hence, betting on a reversal may not be unreasonable.

At any rate, if $(U_{ND} - U_{D_1})$ exceeds $(U_{D_1} - U_{D_2})$ by an order of magnitude—as may be the case in situations where no sharp output drop has yet occurred—the likelihood of success does not have to be very high to make fighting the default worthwhile. For example, in the case of Argentina, the cumulative output drop during the crisis— computed as sum of the 2002 and 2003 output gaps relative to 2001 GDP, measured at purchasing power parity exchange rates—was about $60 billion dollars (this assumes a zero growth scenario as the relevant alternative in case of no default). Ignoring the adjustment cost c, a back-of-the-envelope calculation suggests that a success probability of as low as 11 percent (6.5/60) might have been enough to justify the decision not to seek a comprehensive debt restructuring in June 2001, and instead opt for a combination of IMF support and a pure maturity extension. This stabilization attempt failed, and the crisis rapidly deepened in the second half of 2001. By late 2001, the gains from further attempts to delay the default had shrunk dramatically, as much of the decline in output was sunk at this point (about two-thirds of the total output decline attributable to the crisis occurred in the second half of 2001). In hindsight, it would have been better if Argentina had defaulted or comprehensively restructured six months earlier than it did, but the odds in June arguably did not point in that direction.

While this book has concentrated on crises which led to debt restructurings or defaults, it is important to bear in mind that there were other important recent crises with similar causes and characteristics in which defaults were averted. These include Mexico (1994–1995), Korea (1997), Brazil (1998–1999 and 2002), and Turkey (2000–2001). While these countries suffered currency crises and, in some cases, banking crises, all avoided national defaults by betting on the temporary relief offered by large-scale official crisis lending in combination with domestic adjustment and reform. Most crises led to significant output losses (the main exception being Brazil), but the recoveries were fairly swift. Brazil in 2002 is a particularly dramatic illustration of default-fighting: with high and growing debt ratios, political uncertainty, and a relatively difficult international environment, market spreads surpassed 2,000 basis points in July 2002. It took substantial fiscal effort, further help from the IFIs, and a new policy track record before the crisis subsided and spreads fell. In spite of the great ex ante risks to this strategy—and continued high debt levels after the crisis—this and most other cases previously named are viewed as successes.

This is not to suggest that policymakers who make a decision to fight a default inevitably do the right thing from a social welfare perspective. A default may entail bigger private utility loss for a policymaker than for the average citizen, since policymakers typically lose their jobs (and, in some cases, have been subjected to criminal prosecution) after a default. In four of the seven cases studied in this book, the default led to the ousting of the finance minister and/or prime minister; in two instances (Argentina and Ecuador) it led to the resignation of the head of state. Hence, if p is sufficiently low, resisting the default might not make sense from a social perspective while it may still make sense for a politician, who "gambles for redemption."

Moreover, there could be situations when politicians choose to fight a crisis even when the probability of success is zero. In the framework of inequality (1), this would be the case if the cost of resisting the crisis, c, is a social cost that is not borne by the politician, and if (contrary to societal preference) $U_{D_2} > U_{D_1}$ from the politician's perspective. One might call this a pure case of procrastination: the politician knows that the crisis cannot be avoided, but he would rather have it arrive later than sooner, and since he does not bear the costs of fighting it, his preferred course of action is to postpone. To use a World War II analogy, Hitler's decision to continue fighting the war after the catastrophic defeat at Stalingrad in 1943 could perhaps be interpreted as a gamble for redemption. But his 1945 decision to declare Berlin a "fortress" and order his troops to offer bloody resistance until the last minute can no longer be rationalized in this way. The probability of avoiding defeat was zero at this point. It was a pure case of procrastination, and obviously senseless from a societal point of view.

In the context of sovereign debt crises, are there ever such pure cases of procrastination? They are certainly conceivable. Suppose, for example, that a country faces a short-term rollover problem of such magnitude that addressing it would require new long-term borrowing (or a debt exchange) at terms that would blow up the country's debt to unsustainable proportions (because the new debt would have to be issued at a heavy discount). In that case, the country may be able to choose between a "liquidity crisis" and a "solvency crisis," but the crisis itself can no longer be avoided.[13] Assuming that there is a cost to postponing (e.g., in the form of reserve outflows), politicians who choose the second strategy as a means of buying time would be guilty of procrastination. Are there examples for this type of behavior among the crises studied in this book? Kharas, Pinto, and Ulatov (2001) have argued that the Russian government's attempt, in June–July 1998, to fight a devaluation based on fresh long-term borrowing and a debt exchange operation made the August 1998 crisis unavoidable (see chapter 4 and Summers 2001). A similar argument is sometimes made with respect to the June 2001 Argentine megaswap and adjustment package. But to the extent that these policy actions were part of a plausible crisis aversion strategy, as we argued earlier, one has to disagree with these claims. The fact that these strategies failed ex post does not imply that the probability that they would succeed was zero ex ante. Moreover, spreads narrowed after their implementation, suggesting that markets believed they had increased the chance of averting the default.

In sum, gambles for redemption and procrastination are reasons why policymakers might be (even) less inclined than society as a whole to choose an early default or devaluation over a strategy of fighting the crisis. However, observing a government fight a default in the face of a low probability of success is not sufficient reason to conclude that the government's actions conflict with the interests of society. Moreover, the fact that policymakers may have a strong private incentive to avoid defaults cuts both ways. Faced with the choice of defaulting or delaying, politicians might choose a suboptimal delay, but they will also want to avoid such unappetizing alternatives in the first place, by seeking solutions, including early restructurings, that do not trigger the same sanction as a default. Our overall sense is that conflicts between the social good and politicians' interests are far more likely to arise at the stage of debt accumulation than when countries are facing a crisis.

Policymaking under Pressure

Having argued that it may sometimes make sense to attempt to avoid a default even when the chances of success are modest, it is also clear that policy options become increasingly unpleasant as the crisis deepens. How should monetary policy react to pressure on the currency? If there are currency mismatches in either public or private sector balance sheets—with future income streams mostly in local currency, but debt mostly in foreign currency—there is no easy answer. Defending the exchange rate by raising interest rates will depress the present value of future domestic currency income. Letting it go will blow up the domestic currency value of liabilities. Either action might lead to insolvency and default. This is one situation where international crisis lending can help. By lending the central bank the hard currency it needs to guarantee the dollar liabilities of banks that are normally solvent, it could prevent a bank run and hence break a critical link in the vicious circle that fuels the currency crisis and may lead to a default (Jeanne and Wyplosz 2001; Jeanne and Zettelmeyer 2005a). Without either ample reserves or outside help, however, there may not be much that monetary policy can do, except choosing the damage-minimizing policy stance (which depending on balance sheets could be either to raise interest notes or to lower them).

A similar trade-off may confront policymakers who are trying to stop a bank run, even if bank deposits are denominated in local currency. If the government reduces liquidity requirements or extends direct liquidity support, it risks fueling the run on the currency, with pernicious consequences if there are currency mismatches in either government or corporate balance sheets. But refusing support may force financial institutions into bankruptcy at a time when the market is extremely sensitive to bad news about the financial sector. Some observers have suggested the use of deposit freezes as a temporary means of reducing the costs of the banking crisis (IMF 2002c). If the run is a pure panic, a deposit freeze or bank holiday may indeed be called for. However, such a freeze may strongly hinder the normal payments operation of the economy and, if so, may plunge the economy into a crisis (this was the case of Argentina in December 2001). Thus, a deposit freeze cannot be more than a temporary solution while other measures are undertaken (for example, the resolution of problem banks coupled with a deposit guarantee for the remaining banks, or the announcement of fiscal measures) that reassure the public.

Another example refers to debt management. Should the country move to short-term debt or, on the contrary, attempt to lengthen maturity? Going short exposes the country to a liquidity crunch, but it may also send a signal that the government is committed to staying on course—since any failure to live up to policy commitments will immediately trigger a rollover crisis—and hence provide interest rate relief. The decision is not obvious. The choice may, in part, depend on the characteristics of the local financial sector. Brazil, for example, moved to short-term debt at the height of its crisis, as it considered it relatively safe to assume that financial institutions would roll over their claims. Not having such assurances, neighboring Argentina opted to go long, paying a higher debt service cost.

Fiscal policy during this period is another area in which there are no easy choices. As the crisis unfolds, output will be falling, so that further fiscal adjustment risks adding to the contraction. Ordinarily, this effect would be partly offset by reduced crowding out of private demand—as the government absorbs fewer scarce resources from the local financial sector—but in crisis circumstances, freeing up those resources might only fuel capital flight, increasing the pressure on the currency and the financial system. Continued deficits, on the other hand, may further increase the risk of default, send a poor signal to international investors, and fuel external pressures on the currency and the bond markets. A possible solution is to focus on measures that increase the intertemporal solvency of the public sector, without requiring reductions in government spending or increases in taxes today; in other words, measures that maximize the signaling effect of fiscal policy for a given fiscal contraction today. Measures along this line include, for example, a reform of the pension system that focuses on reducing future liabilities of the government (as implemented, e.g., by Brazil in 2003).

The Policymaker Who Implements the Default

At some point, the default decision has been made and the restructuring phase begins. The policymaker (probably a different one from the one making the decisions in the previous stages of the crisis) faces several new challenges. First and foremost, he or she needs to minimize the costs of the default, both present and future. Minimizing the costs in the short-run implies containing the spillovers to the banking and corporate sector and minimizing disruptions to economic and social institutions (including contracts). Minimizing the costs in the longer term implies putting together a debt restructuring package that ensures sustainability and that does not hinder medium-term economic growth. This involves deciding on how much debt relief the country should ask for, how it should ask for it—namely, how an exchange offer should be designed in order to make it as palatable as possible and ensure its success—and what the structure of the new debt should be in terms of currency composition, maturity composition, and possible indexation.

Keeping the Economy Going

The country experiences discussed in earlier chapters show that most default episodes were associated with significant output loss. In some

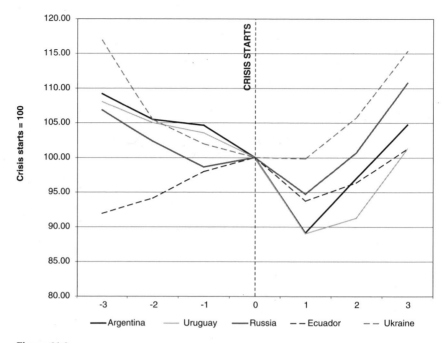

Figure 11.1
GDP performance surrounding default episodes
Source: Authors' computation on IFS data. Year 0 corresponds to 1998 for Russia, Ecuador, and Ukraine, and 2001 for Argentina and Uruguay.

cases, the large output fall occurs right after the default, in other cases before; in these cases, it tends to coincide with a predefault currency and/or banking crisis. In all cases defaults were associated with a large turnaround of the current account, reflecting the large capital outflows associated with the institutional, financial, and reputational consequences of a default. Figure 11.1 shows the V-shaped output profile, indicating that following the default, all economies recovered reasonably quickly (though sometimes after some additional output reduction). Figures 11.2 and 11.3 indicate two other regularities: both fiscal accounts and the current account experience massive improvements during the process. What are the lessons for fiscal and exchange rate policy, as well as for dealing with the financial crisis, in a context that entails a large devaluation, political change, and possibly an institutional breakdown?

Regarding fiscal policy, the experiences studied teach us that once the crisis scenario hits, the political game changes radically. Societies often conclude that the previous regime had been unsustainable, lead-

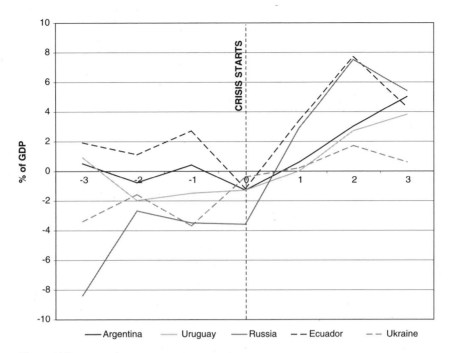

Figure 11.2
Fiscal balance surrounding default episodes
Source: Authors' computation on IFS data. Year 0 corresponds to 1998 for Russia, Ecuador, and Ukraine, and 2001 for Argentina and Uruguay.

ing to a large and potentially costly crisis. By generating large swings in asset prices, the crisis often produces big winners and big losers, a situation that is typically viewed as divisive and undesirable. Thus, politicians often have leeway, in the aftermath of the crisis, to pursue strong fiscal consolidations and fiscal-structural reforms. The fact that crises operate as catalysts for reform is well known in the political economy literature, particularly in connection with hyperinflation experiences (Drazen 2000, chap. 10). Default experiences seem to be similar in this respect.

Armed with the political strength that comes from having to deal with the crisis, fiscal consolidation can take place mostly through two channels. One is a reduction of public sector real wages and pensions. In the aftermath of a devaluation there is always some inflation, and as public sector wages lag behind the inflation rate, fiscal accounts quickly recover. The second mechanism is extraordinary taxation. In the aftermath of the crisis, the real exchange rate depreciates, in some cases strongly overshooting its long-run equilibrium level. In those

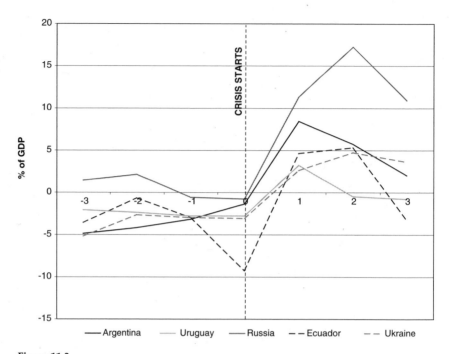

Figure 11.3
Current account performance surrounding default episodes
Source: Authors' computation on IFS data. Year 0 corresponds to 1998 for Russia, Ecuador, and Ukraine, and 2001 for Argentina and Uruguay.

cases, temporary export taxes serve the purpose of containing the domestic impact of the devaluation on the price level, as well as generating significant government resources. Countries have relied and should rely on these instruments to some extent, though it is important to keep them at levels that maintain the relative price effect of the devaluation on producers' incentives.

One problem that governments—particularly of countries with large concentrations of urban poor—may need to contend with is a significant surge in poverty (Fallon and Lucas 2002; Agenor 2004). Because the incomes of the urban poor are tied to services, but a significant share of their consumption basket is in tradable items such as food, they tend to be hard-hit by large real depreciations. This comes on top of the vulnerability of the poor to any economic downturn, regardless of its source, and to any rise in cyclical unemployment, which comes mostly at the expense of unskilled labor. Governments must therefore be prepared to structure the fiscal consolidation in a way that protects the poorest in society, particularly if the exchange rate is allowed to adjust freely in the aftermath of a default.

How should macroeconomic policy deal with real exchange rate overshooting after a default? On the upside, this overshooting will stimulate export growth and hence accelerate the recovery through this channel, as well as increase the domestic currency value of the central bank's reserves, thus naturally delivering a cushion that can be used in the critical initial moments of the crisis. Furthermore, a large devaluation of the currency, if coupled with a consolidation of fiscal results, quickly generates the expectation of an appreciation of the domestic currency. At that point, the central bank may find itself *buying* foreign currency, while interest rates plummet in anticipation of the appreciation.

On the downside, the main worry is that plummeting exchange rates could bankrupt corporate and financial sector institutions, including institutions that may well be solvent when exchange rates return to their long run equilibrium level. One possible reaction is to resist the freefall of the exchange rate through a mixture of capital controls and tight monetary policy. However, in countries which face a generalized loss of confidence, these measures may not be very effective, and as argued previously, there are some desirable effects associated with a temporary overshooting. A better, or, at any rate, more realistic approach, may hence be to allow the exchange rate to run its course and find its equilibrium level, while attempting to contain the adverse effects on private sector balance sheets using other policy instruments. Depending on whether private sector institutions are "conditionally solvent" or not, this can involve either restructuring banks and corporations, or giving them breathing space until confidence returns and the exchange rate recovers. The former may be unavoidable for financial institutions whose solvency is compromised because of previous exposure to government debt (as was the case in Russia, Ukraine, and Argentina, among others).

Measures that give banks time to overcome confidence crises and deal with exchange rate overshooting include bank holidays, some degree of regulatory forbearance, and limited deposit guarantees. As argued earlier, bank holidays need to be kept short if they are to be part of the solution rather than become a problem themselves, and the removal of the bank holiday has to be carefully worked out. Foreign banks should be among the first to have their restrictions lifted. Foreign banks usually claim to be backed by an international asset base (and because of that often pay lower interest rates on deposits), so they may have incentives to live up to their reputation for safety. Other banks that feel secure enough to face the aftermath should also be allowed to reopen. For banks that are unsure but that are considered viable, it is important to normalize their transactions accounts quickly, if necessary, by providing an explicit guarantee up to certain deposit limits. Longer-term deposits may be restructured to the medium-term at some predetermined conditions, as was done by Uruguay, or be left for the interested parties to renegotiate, as was done in Russia. Both options worked reasonably well.

Banks that clearly become insolvent in the aftermath of the crisis need to be restructured. If the regulatory framework allows, reasonably sound assets and deposits should be auctioned off to other banks, with the remainder of the other assets moved to a bankruptcy procedure. If the regulatory framework does not allow for this, the bank may be intervened, the transactions account normalized as much as possible, and the remaining assets liquidated. At any rate, while this has to be done, it does not need to be done at the outset of the crisis, when uncertainty runs high, and when closing down financial institutions may fuel additional runs on the financial sector.

Government debt on the balance sheets of the banks may require designing the debt restructuring so that it maintains the viability of the financial sector. In Russia and Ukraine, for example, the restructuring of short-term debt instruments held mostly in the domestic financial sector was done faster, and entailed somewhat lower "haircuts" than the external debt restructuring. In Argentina, pension funds were offered a slightly better deal ahead of the general debt exchange offer. Alternatively, the government could opt for a fast, uniform restructuring that subjects domestic bank creditors and external creditors to the same treatment, while selectively intervening or recapitalizing systemically important banks that become insolvent as a result of the government debt restructuring.

Finally, to contain the adverse impact of a devaluation and the collapse of domestic demand on the corporate sector, the government can impose a payments moratorium until the economy stabilizes and firms work out renegotiation packages with their creditors. These standstills were imposed in Russia, Ukraine, and Argentina, and work-outs were gradually implemented with relatively little government intervention. Corporate access to credit from abroad will depend on whether foreign creditors expect to have stable access to the foreign currency market. Hence, avoiding capital controls even during tough times can critically contribute to a smooth continuation of credit flows to corporations, particularly trade credit. Allowing markets to continue operating freely will accelerate the recovery.

Most countries studied here followed some combination of these recommendations. The main exception was Argentina in the immediate aftermath of its default. After the default and the devaluation, the government decided to change the currency of denomination of the contracts, converting claims denominated in dollars into peso claims. This dramatically increased the demand for foreign exchange as the population realized that its holdings of dollars had been wiped out. As people tried to recompose their dollar portfolios, the exchange rate collapsed. While we argued that dedollarization is desirable, and that regulatory measures can be used to achieve it, these measures should be taken at the margin, and not by breaking current contracts, which generates uncertainty and casts doubt on the basic rules of the economic system. In the case of Argentina, this effect was aggravated by the fact that the government decided to "pesify" assets, including bank deposits, at a more appreciated rate than loans. This led to massive litigation, triggered demands for compensation by the banks (whose net worth had been significantly reduced as a result of the operation), and released branches of foreign banks from liability in foreign courts. Additionally, it generated a major redistribution of income that was widely viewed as arbitrary, with severe adverse consequences for the reputation of policymakers and institutions.

Working Out a Debt Deal

Once a default has occurred, the policymaker has to decide between a wide range of alternatives, from outright repudiation (i.e., a refusal to repay even part of the debt) to a quick restructuring deal that minimizes the reputational costs of default in international credit markets. Some authors have recently argued that a growth strategy based on national savings (as opposed to one based on foreign savings) delivers a more stable growth path (Prasad et al. 2003) and that the welfare gains that are to be expected from access to international capital markets via allocative efficiency effects are small (Jeanne and Gourinchas 2004). However, the country experiences discussed in our historical review and in the country chapters summarized in table 11.1 indicate that a majority of countries seem to value access to international capital

Table 11.1
Summary of debt restructurings, 1998–2005

	Were payments missed prior to restructuring?[a]	Classes of debt restructured[b]	Were bondholders treated differently?	Relations with official creditors and IMF
Pakistan (1999)	No	Foreign currency deposits at banks (1998), international bonds, loans from commercial banks, bilateral official debt.	No. All bondholders face similar NPV haircuts.	Eurobond restructuring triggered by Paris Club demand for comparable of treatment.
Russia (1998–2000)	Yes, initially for domestic debt, six months later for restructured Soviet era international debt. No default on Russian era international debt. Debt deal came two years after initial default	Domestic currency treasury bills and bonds, foreign currency bonds representing restructured Soviet era debt, bilateral official debt. New foreign currency bonds issued by the Russian federation were not restructured.	Yes. Some bonds were not defaulted; and haircuts varied both across exchanges and within the GKO exchange. Domestic institutional creditors received better terms in the GKO exchange.	Four weeks before the default, the IMF provided a financial package in an attempt to stave off the crisis, but did not provide additional financing when this package failed. A year later, the IMF negotiated a new Standby Arrangement and lent into arrears as the government was negotiating its debt restructuring.
Ukraine (1998–2000)	Several debt restructurings, without default prior to 2000 restructuring. One principal payment missed just before 2000 exchange offer.	Domestic currency treasury bills, foreign currency loans from commercial banks, international bonds, bilateral official debt.	In domestic debt restructurings domestic holders obtained better terms but face capital controls. In the 2000 international restructuring NPV haircuts were fairly similar (slightly lower on longer term bonds).	In 1998, new IMF financing was made contingent on a debt restructuring. 2000 restructuring occurred while Ukraine had an IMF supported government (though this was off track for unrelated reasons), and IMF supported exchange.

Relation with creditors	Holdouts and litigation	Exit consents	CACs	De-dollarization
No formal negotiations, but communications with small group of bondholders.	No holdouts (few creditors).	Not used.	All three outstanding bonds contained CACs, but not used.	No
Negotiations with foreign banks. 2000 restructuring was negotiated with a Bank Advisory Committee ("London Club").	1 percent holdouts, paid in full (refers to PRINs/IANs exchange).	Not used.	Not used.	Debt dollarized further.
No formal negotiations.	2 percent holdouts, paid in full.	Used.	In the three bonds that contained CACs, used pre-emptively in conjunction with exit consents to back exchange offer.	No

Table 11.1
(continued)

	Were payments missed prior to restructuring?[a]	Classes of debt restructured[b]	Were bondholders treated differently?	Relations with official creditors and IMF
Ecuador (1999–2000)	Yes. Defaulted on international bonds and some domestic debt about one year prior to debt exchange.	International bonds, dollar denominated domestic bonds coming due in the next fourteen months, and bilateral official debt. Domestic currency denominated debt and medium term dollar denominated domestic debt was not restructured.	NPV haircuts lower on longer term bonds. Treatment of holders of domestic dollar debt and shorter term international debt broadly similar.	1999 default was related in part to IMF decision not to lend unless Ecuador restructured its debts. IMF lent into arrears prior to 2000 debt exchange, and supported the exchange.
Moldova (2002)	No. Debt negotiations started at the time of maturity of old bond with an initial rescheduling agreement while final deal was negotiated.	International bond, bilateral official debt, debt to energy supplier Gazprom.	No. Only one bond restructured; haircut received by second commercial creditor (Gazprom) about the same.	Lending from multilaterals had stopped in 2001 for unrelated reasons. Following the decision to restructure, IMF made one more disbursement before program went off track again.
Uruguay (2003)	No	All foreign currency bonds and bills, both international and domestically issued. No restructuring of any other debt class (including domestic currency public debt) except for bank deposits at state-owned banks (2002).	Haircuts were relatively small and similar for externally issued debt and long term domestically issued debt. Short term domestically issued debt suffered somewhat higher haircuts.	Debt restructuring occurred in the context of an IMF-supported program, and the IMF supported the exchange.

Relation with creditors	Holdouts and litigation	Exit consents	CACs	De-dollarization
No formal negotiations, but convened a consultative group of institutional creditors.	2 percent holdouts, paid in full.	Used.	Outstanding bonds did not have CACs, new bonds do not have them.	No
Restructuring negotiated with a single creditor holding 78 percent of the bond that was restructured.	No holdouts (collective action clause invoked).	Not used (negotiated deal).	Used to bind minority Eurobond holders.	No
No formal negotiations, but government stressed the importance of communication with bondholders and conducted two "road shows."	7 percent holdouts, paid in full.	Used.	Used in the case of one (Samurai) bond. New bonds contain both CACs and an aggregation provision lowering the CAC voting threshold depending on support across bonds.	No

Table 11.1
(continued)

	Were payments missed prior to restructuring?[a]	Classes of debt restructured[b]	Were bondholders treated differently?	Relations with official creditors and IMF
Argentina (2001–2005)	Yes. No payments missed prior to November 2001 "Phase 1" exchange, but general default on public debt shortly thereafter, in December 2001. 2005 debt exchange three years after default.	International bonds, domestically issued bonds and loans, bilateral official debt. Temporary arrears to some multilateral creditors.	Yes, both across exchanges, and within, particularly within the Phase 1 and Pesification exchanges. In the 2005 exchange local pension funds obtained a slightly better deal.	IMF supported Argentina prior to 2001 default, and the default was partly triggered by the IMF's decision to suspend lending. IMF lent into arrears between January 2003 and March of 2004, but suspended its lending in mid-2004, in part because it disagreed with the authorities' approach to the restructuring.
Dominican Republic (2005)	No	International bonds, bilateral official debt.	No. Haircuts were close to zero for both bonds.	Debt restructuring occurred in the context of an IMF-supported program, and the IMF supported the exchange.

[a] Only refers to debt service on privately held debt that was eventually restructured.
[b] Refers to all restructurings prompted by the same debt crisis. This may include restructurings that happened outside the time frame of the restructurings of privately held debt on which we focus.

markets, making efforts to maintain working relationships with debt holders and restructure and normalize their debt payments. We hence take the country's desire to normalize relations with both external and domestic creditors as a given in the remainder of the chapter, and focus this section on how this can be reconciled with the objectives of lowering the debt burden to sustainable levels and making the debt safer.

The principal trade-off governing the design of a debt exchange offer is obviously the conflict of interest between future taxpayers and current bondholders. The higher the haircut, the smaller the burden will

Relation with creditors	Holdouts and litigation	Exit consents	CACs	De-dollarization
No formal negotiations, but contacts with consultative groups established by the government, and several self-declared creditor committees.	23.85 percent holdouts, which have not been paid nor offered any alternative at time of writing. February 2005 Law prevents government from settling with these creditors.	Not used.	Some outstanding bonds contained CACs, but they were not invoked. New bonds issued in 2005 exchange contain both CACs and an aggregation provision lowering the CAC voting threshold depending on support across bonds.	Extensive de-dollarization through the issue of bonds in indexed pesos.
No formal negotiations but authorities stressed the importance of this being a voluntary exchange.	3 percent, paid in full.	Used.	New bonds contain both CACs and an aggregation provision lowering the CAC voting threshold depending on the support across bonds.	No

be for future taxpayers and the higher the loss for current bondholders. Current bondholders, in turn, may include both local holders and international holders. Given the experience in the debt restructurings summarized in table 11.1, we will assume that it is possible to discriminate, though imperfectly, between local and foreign bondholders. In that case, the domestic policymakers' problem boils down to maximizing debt relief while maintaining or restoring a satisfactory relationship with external creditors.

But what exactly is the "satisfactory" standard that countries should be advised to meet? The literature surveyed in chapter 2 suggests that countries that defaulted in the past may be faced with somewhat higher future borrowing costs over extended periods, but there is no evidence to suggest that countries that negotiated higher haircuts were more severely punished. Hence, the main reason why countries should stop short of seeking very large haircuts is not so much the incremental effect of such a write-down on future borrowing costs, but that it may impede a successful debt restructuring—namely, one that achieves high creditor participation rate—and hence jeopardize the objective of normalizing creditor relations.

Hence, the question is how a debt restructuring offer can be designed to maximize debt relief from the country perspective for a *given* haircut from an investor perspective. The reason why there may be scope for doing so is that investors and country social planners will probably want to discount the post-restructuring debt profiles at different rates. Investors are interested in *expected* repayment; hence, it makes sense for them to evaluate a debt exchange offer based on an interest rate that embodies the perceived likelihood that repayment will actually happen. Since this likelihood depends on the success of the debt exchange, a good candidate for such a risky rate is the "exit yield": the observed secondary market interest rate after the debt exchange results have become known. In contrast, the social planner should be discounting at the interest rates at which the country will be borrowing and saving financial assets in the future, because these are the interest rates that are relevant from the perspective of matching future liabilities and income streams. Hence, discount rates for the purposes of computing post-restructuring debt burdens, and thus debt relief, should be in the interval between the international risk-free rate (the lower bound of interest rates at which the country can transfer financial resources into the future) and future borrowing rates, that is, borrowing rates in noncrisis times. This will generally be lower than the "exit yield" at which investors evaluate haircuts, because the latter is often still a near-crisis rate.

In general, the interval of acceptable discount rates for the purposes of computing debt relief will hence be country and time specific (since it depends on international interest rates, which fluctuate over time). However, for illustrative purposes, we have computed what the debt relief would look like if discount rates between 4 and 10 percent were applied to the restructurings studied in earlier chapters. The former approximates an international risk-free rate; the latter an emerging market noncrisis borrowing rate.[14]

Table 11.2 shows that debt relief computed using the lower rate will generally be smaller than the haircut suffered by investors. Because debt relief from a country perspective and "haircuts" from an investors perspective are not the same thing, the design of the exchange offer can

Table 11.2
NPV haircuts compared to debt relief (in percent)

	Average haircut[a]	Debt relief, using discount rate of	
		4 percent	10 percent
Restructurings involving mainly external creditors:			
Russian GKO-OFZ nonresidents	61.1	42.2	46.7
Russian Prin/IAN	52.6	37.8	48.2
Russian MinFin3	63.2	9.4	36.3
Ukraine OVDPs-nonresidents	56.3	9.3	17.2
Ukraine Chase Manhattan Loan	30.7	−14.0	−7.4
Ukraine ING Loan	38.0	−8.5	−2.0
Pakistan 1999	31.0	−21.4	0.3
Ecuador 2000	28.6	4.0	21.0
Ukraine 2000	28.9	−9.2	2.2
Argentina 2005	75.0	37.0	77.8
Uruguay external debt, extension option	15.1	−12.3	8.9
Uruguay external debt, benchmark option	12.9	−14.7	7.8
Dominican Republic	1.5	−9.2	1.6
Restructurings involving mainly domestic creditors:[b]			
Russian GKO-OFZ domestic investors	48.3	24.7	30.4
Ecuador domestic debt	38.0	−19.5	4.7
Argentina Phase 1	40.5	37.0	48.5
Argentina pesification	42.4	37.9	39.4
Uruguay domestic debt, extension option	38.1	1.5	15.2
Uruguay domestic debt, benchmark option	24.0	−8.1	15.7

[a] Generally uses bond yields observed immediately after exchange to compare old and new flows.
[b] Calculations ignore effects of exchange restrictions and devaluations (if any).

help reconcile the interests of investors and future taxpayers. For any given haircut, debt relief can be maximized by front-loading payments under a debt exchange offer as much as possible. For example, suppose that a country has just defaulted on debt coming due today, and offers to exchange each unit of debt for a zero coupon five-year bond, with no reduction in face value. Assuming an exit yield of 20 percent, similar to what we found in several of our case studies, this implies a value of $100/(1.2)^5 = 40$ cents on the dollar, namely, a 60 percent haircut. Assuming that the social planner discounts the same bond by the borrowing rate in normal times, which is expected to be 10 percent, the same bond implies a social burden of $100/(1.1)^5 = 62$ cents, namely, debt relief of only 38 percent. From a domestic taxpayer perspective, the government can do better than that by offering the investor cash combined with a face value haircut. The debt-burden minimizing offer consistent with a 60 percent haircut is simply to repay investors 40 percent of their face value in cash, implying debt relief of 60 percent.

Complete front-loading is usually impossible, because the government faces a liquidity problem after a default and not just a solvency problem. Indeed, as we saw in the case studies, defaults are sometimes triggered by a liquidity problem, so some extension in maturities is necessary. But the previous argument implies that to the extent that the country's liquidity situation allows it, cash "sweeteners" in exchange for lower debt payments down the road are a good idea. More generally, maturities should not be extended more than necessary from a liquidity perspective. Further extensions are inefficient in the sense that a better deal exists for both the creditor and debtors. In addition, standard debt management considerations apply: the resulting debt profile should be smooth, avoiding promises of lumpy repayments in the distant future.

Apart from the objective of maximizing debt relief for given investor losses, a second principal objective of a debt restructuring might be to design it in a way that minimizes the "collateral damage" that the default imposes on the economy. As described in chapter 2 and in the country case studies, this damage appears to have mainly two sources. First, "secondary runs" as capital (foreign and domestic) flees the financial system and the country; second, the direct impact of the restructuring on the domestic financial sector, leading to insolvencies and possibly a breakdown in the payments system. In previous sections, we discussed how the policymaker might react to such an economic emergency using financial sector intervention and macroeconomic tools, but the question is whether he or she can also attempt to limit the extent of the emergency through the design of the debt restructuring offer itself. Again, there are difficult trade-offs involved.

Part of the reason why a default could trigger secondary runs is that it may be viewed as a signal of (even) worse things to come: confiscatory measures, hyperinflation, perhaps a political crisis—in short, as the beginning of a period in which normal contractual relationships, both formal contracts and informal trust relationships, particularly with regard to public institutions, no longer apply (Cole and Kehoe 1998). How the debt restructuring proposal is designed and implemented may have consequences for whether or not this is the case. A quick, transparent restructuring showing concern for fairness, including intercreditor equity, and seeking some degree of dialogue with creditors is likely to have milder reputational repercussions, for example, than a protracted show of defiance with special deals for particular creditors and populist and nationalist overtones (though the show of defiance may be an effective negotiating tactic to extract a better deal).

In contrast, minimizing the direct impact of a default on the financial system may require, at least prima facie, some degree of discrimination in favor of domestic creditors. In principle, this could happen in two ways: by giving domestic and foreign residents different deals, as was the case, for example, in Russia and Ukraine, or by allowing all creditors access to the same menu, but endowing some instruments with certain advantages that apply only to either external or domestic holders. For example, Argentina offered somewhat better deals, in NPV terms, on peso-indexed instruments, which were less attractive to foreign bondholders because of their currency denomination. From the perspective of maintaining fairness, and hence minimizing reputational damage, the second approach is clearly superior to the first. Moreover, as discussed earlier, policymakers may have other instruments at their disposal, including selectively intervening and/or recapitalizing specific financial institutions that face insolvency, to make an evenhanded approach seem preferable.

A further key concern of domestic policymakers is often whether a debt deal will give rise to harmful litigation. Based on the evidence discussed in chapter 3, this does not seem a great threat, at least not in debt exchanges that achieved high participation rates. Though there are some counterexamples, such as post-Brady litigation involving Panama and Peru, which led to credible attachment orders targeting debtor assets outside the country even after successful restructuring deals with a large majority, these were exceptions (see chapter 3). Still, conditional on offering an exchange of a particular value, sovereigns should be concerned with maximizing acceptance and minimizing the number of holdouts. What tools could help in this regard?

The experiences of Ecuador and Uruguay show that *exit amendments* of nonpayment features of the old bonds, particularly amendments that have the effect of protecting the new bondholders from legal action by holdouts, could be useful in this respect. Indeed, in the case of Uruguay changes in these nonpayment terms had the effect that some of the old bonds traded at lower prices than the new bonds, even though they were being serviced in full and the new bonds had much longer maturity (see chapter 10). However, other exchanges have reached similar, or even higher, participation rates without the use of exit consents. As argued in chapter 1, defining a high *minimum acceptance threshold* may have been helpful. Suppose there are two classes of potential holdouts: specialized funds that may hold out regardless of the acceptance rate, and mainstream creditors that are in principle willing to take the offer, but only if the acceptance is sufficiently high that it does indeed reduce the debt burden to sustainable levels. The latter can lead to coordination failure: mainstream creditors may be worried that acceptance might not be high, and hence choose not to accept. This possibility is eliminated if the offer is made contingent on high participation. Mainstream creditors can take the offer with the comfort that they will receive their old claims back if the threshold is not met.

Where the threshold should be set exactly depends on how many "notorious holdouts" are expected to be in the market. As table 11.1 shows, with the exception of Argentina—which set no minimum threshold—the share of holdouts has been in the range of 0–7 percent, suggesting that a 90 percent threshold may be reasonable. This said, actual threshold levels have been somewhat lower, in the 80–90 percent range, and the decision for each exchange must, of course, be made on the basis of specifics of each case.

Characteristics of the Debt to Be Issued

As argued at the beginning of this chapter, debt should also be structured in a way that avoids big spikes in interest and principal payments. In principle, the payments profile throughout the life of the bond should be matched to the revenue stream of government resources; this may justify mildly increasing debt payments. However, sharply increasing payment streams should be avoided, for two reasons. First, they conflict with the principle discussed previously, that the new payments stream should be frontloaded within limits set by reasonable liquidity management. Second, if the payment stream increases too quickly, this may create a very unfavorable political dynamic if growth and revenues stagnate, as the increasing coupon stream will force the country to engage in successive tighter fiscal adjustment programs. In contrast, a decreasing debt burden becomes increasingly easy to service. Given that societies tend to accept fiscal adjustment more easily at the beginning of a debt restructuring, we would recommend a *declining* fiscal adjustment profile as much as possible.

A debt restructuring may offer a significant opportunity to dedollarize debt by including a domestic currency indexed bond in the "menu" offered to bondholders (as demonstrated by the recent Argentine restructuring). Given heightened inflation risk after a default, the government may want to opt for a CPI-indexed bond. Offering such a bond may also be a way of enhancing the relative value of the exchange for domestic bondholders. Financial institutions and pension funds could be encouraged through regulatory advantages to switch into these types of bonds.

By the same token, a debt exchange may be a way to introduce more state-contingent instruments. It is sometimes argued that it is difficult to introduce these types of bonds at the margin, because they have the disadvantage of being novel and perhaps illiquid while their main advantage—reducing the risk of future debt crises—only materializes if they constitute a sufficiently large share of the country's debt. Hence, if countries want to issue these instruments at all, they may want to issue them en masse, and a debt restructuring may be an opportunity to do so. Indeed, Argentina did include "growth clauses" in all bonds offered in its most recent exchange, which promise higher payments if output growth exceeds a certain level. However, the link to GDP is asymmetric in the sense that coupon payments cannot fall below a minimum, even when growth collapses; hence, these bonds do not have very strong stabilizing debt service properties. In the event, they received a cold reception, in the sense that the "upside" offered by these bonds was initially not valued very much by the market. After trading started, a liquid market in the new GDP market quickly developed increasing their value. Following this experience, it is conceivable that future attempts to introduce GDP-indexed or other contingent bonds in the context of a debt exchange will be more successful, particularly if they are designed symmetrically and introduced in sufficient quantity to improve significantly the risk characteristics of the public debt (see chapter 12).

Another route which a debtor can take to enhance the attractiveness of an exchange offer and hence obtain a better deal is to include contractual features that improve creditor rights and similar enhancements. Examples include a creditor upgrade by which the quality of the debtor is increased (this was the case when the Russian Federation took over debt initially issued by Vneshekonombank); guarantees (examples include the Brady bonds); regulatory enhancements which refer to tax, accounting, liquidity, or jurisdiction benefits and regulatory prerogatives, such as rediscount window privileges, reserve requirement integration, and tax cancellation properties (most of these enhancements were used in some of the several restructurings in Ukraine and Argentina); puts and acceleration clauses as described in the context of the Russian exchange; and principal reinstatement rules, aimed at assuring creditors that they will not be subject to future renegotiations on weaker terms than those from which they started (see chapter 7).[15] A related but much more radical step in this regard would be to introduce bond clauses, perhaps backed by legislation, which give restructured bondholders legal seniority over subsequent bond issues, hence giving them assurances that they will be repaid *first* in the event of a new default ("first in time seniority"; see Borensztein et al. 2005). If this is credible, it could significantly add to the value of an exchange offer and lower the country's financing costs. However, contractual constructs implementing "first in time" priority remain unexplored at this point, and may be infeasible without legal or institutional changes at the international level.

Finally, in recent restructurings, some countries have introduced collective action clauses, including majority decision clauses and aggregation clauses (chapter 3). It is not clear how much markets value or punish the introduction of this feature: by making it easier to restructure debt down the road, they provide for a more efficient restructuring process (which benefits both creditors and debtors and would tend to lower risk premia), but may also make it more tempting to restructure (which would tend increase risk premia). Empirical research based on the comparison of English law bonds with New York law bonds (Eichengreen and Mody 2004; Becker, Richards, and Thaicharoen 2003) and experience with new debt issues introducing collective action clauses in New York law bonds suggest that collective action clauses generally do not make debt more expensive. Hence, it is a good idea to introduce such clauses: they are very unlikely to do harm, and might do some good.

In the case studies discussed in this book, all exchanges took place through the mechanism of a bond exchange. The policymaker will have to obtain first-rate legal counsel in order to use the many legal alternatives discussed in chapter 3, as well as good financial advice to sound out the market's disposition towards a particular offer, and carry out the paperwork (submission requirements in foreign jurisdictions, setting up the booking of the deal, etc.). However, a portion of the exchange operation—for example, with respect to domestic or large creditors—can be handled by the government itself.[16]

12 International Financial Architecture

In chapter 11, we argued that debt crisis prevention and mitigation are very much within the scope of domestic policymaking. However, the occurrence and depth of such crises are obviously also influenced by circumstances outside the control of policymakers. For example, almost all crises described in part II were related (sometimes indirectly) to the sudden stop in international capital flows to emerging markets that took place in 1998. In addition, a country's international environment, including international capital markets and the policies guiding international institutions, can constrain domestic policymaking, and influence policy outcomes. For these reasons, the "international financial architecture," defined broadly as the institutional and legal framework outside the control of the domestic policymaker that influences the behavior of international capital flows, plays a critical role in determining whether debt crises occur and how they are resolved.

This chapter focuses on the question whether changes in the international financial architecture could eliminate or significantly reduce the incidence of costly defaults. We address this question selectively, focusing on a handful of ideas motivated by the most recent crises and grounded in a new economics literature. Hence, this chapter is not a survey of policy proposals on reforming the international financial architecture; these are well covered by a number of recent monographs and articles.[1] Instead, we present some ways of thinking about the deep causes of debt crises, based both by the experience of the last decade and by the academic literature surveyed in chapter 2, and use these to motivate a small number of proposals.

Two Views on Financial Architecture

Any proposal for reforming the international financial architecture with the objective of avoiding costly debt crises is based on two premises. The first is that costly crises are inefficient, in the sense that they do not simply just constitute a punishment for the debtor that translates into a corresponding gain to another party (as would be the case, for example, if defaulting debtors were fined, and the fine were handed over to creditors, or used for a productive purpose). The cases studied in this book leave little doubt that debt crises are indeed something of a lose-lose situation: there is a "deadweight loss" in the sense that value is destroyed without an offsetting benefit. If this were not the case, reforming the international financial architecture in ways that creates gains would be impossible. Hence, any "reformer" must implicitly accept this premise.

The second shared premise is that the deadweight costs of defaults are ultimately related to the institutions and legal arrangements that govern the relationship between creditors and debtors. Although runs, financial system collapses, and exclusion from international capital markets may be the proximate reason why debt crises are costly, they depend on the institutions and rules that govern capital flows, and are hence amenable to changes in the financial architecture.

The question then arises of *why* these institutions and legal frameworks are currently such that they give rise to deadweight costs of default. It is here where the answers differ. With some degree of caricature, it is possible to distinguish two views.

The first view argues that institutions and contractual arrangements are imperfect because change is slow and difficult. Suppose—as we have every reason to believe—that international financial markets are constantly evolving along with the world economy. As a result, institutions that were created decades ago, or contracts that were perhaps adapted from other markets, need not be a perfect fit for today's problems. For example, sovereign bonds issued in a particular jurisdiction may not have contained collective action clauses because *corporate* bonds in the same jurisdiction were barred from having them, and for a long time, sovereign bonds simply followed that template (chapter 3). The reason why improvements may not occur by themselves is that they involve externalities—for example, first movers benefit the parties that follow, without internalizing this benefit—and hence require coordination. But coordination is not easy, and may require special institutions, or official intervention. This view has been articulated for some time in the context of financial contracts, under the heading "barriers to financial innovation" (Allen and Gale 1994). One can extend the idea to slow institutional change, which may require political effort and coordination among countries.

More recently, a second view—driven by developments in economic contract theory and its applications to corporate finance and sovereign debt—has gained traction. This view, which we later refer to as the "deep distortions view," argues that institutions and, particularly, contractual arrangements may *look* imperfect, but are in fact "constrained optimal" responses to deeper problems. Perhaps the most significant such problem is debtor moral hazard—incomplete or unverifiable information by the creditor about actions of the debtor that matter for the creditor—or more generally, the inability to write contracts that condition on all relevant actions of the debtor.[2]

Because of this "incomplete contracts" problem, creditors prefer debt contracts that make them as immune as possible from actions that the debtor might take at their expense. One way in which this can be achieved is by keeping maturities short so that creditors have the option of not rolling over their debt if policies have deteriorated, and benefit from higher risk premia if they do roll over. Another way is foreign currency debt, which protects creditors against domestic inflation and depreciation. Finally, creditors can choose debt forms that are hard to restructure, as a way to acquire effective seniority: if a restructuring must occur, the debtor will first attempt to restructure other debt forms. These debt contracts are all optimal responses to the underlying distortion in the sense that they protect creditors and hence allow sovereign borrowing at relatively low cost to debtors; moreover, they mitigate the underlying moral hazard problem by exposing debtors to market discipline—rollover crises, currency crises, or painful restructurings—as a "punishment" for bad behavior. However, the flipside is that these "punishments" will take effect even if crises arise as a result of shocks outside the control of the debtor. This is why contracts of this type are only *constrained* efficient—conditioning on the inability of writing truly "complete" contracts, in which debt service payments would simply be lowered in line with the debtor's payment capacity following a bad shock, and offset by higher payments in good times. Such equity-like contracts would be superior to debt contracts in which the debtor bears all the risk of bad shocks because they avoid the deadweight losses of default.[3]

In short, in this view, the answer to the question "Why are there costly debt crises?" is the impossibility of writing contracts that are first best in the sense that they both provide the right incentives to the debtor and share exogenous risk efficiently. If such contracts existed— either explicitly or implicitly, in the form of quick renegotiations and continued access to capital when defaults are "excusable"—costly debt crises would not arise. In turn, the difficulty of writing such contracts must have to do either with lack of verifiable information or lack of institutions that could enforce such contracts.[4]

Which view is right? We are not aware of any empirical literature that attempts to test one against the other. Both views certainly have their appeal. The appealing feature of the "deep distortions" view is that contracting parties do not irrationally pick suboptimal debt contracts but rather that risky debt may reflect deeper problems. The appeal of the "barriers to innovation" view is its emphasis on contractual and institutional inertia, which implies that contracts and institutions need not be optimal all the time. The history of financial innovations certainly seems to back that view (Borensztein et al. 2005). Importantly, although the previous discussion has emphasized the intellectual tension between the two views, the problems that they conjure may, in fact, coexist in practice, in the sense that there may be *both* deep distortions motivating contracts and institutions, and barriers to innovation that imply that some of these contracts and institutions could be suboptimal (i.e., not even "constrained optimal"). Assuming that there is some degree of truth to both views is attractive because it leads to complementary standards of intellectual discipline that helps detect the potential pitfalls of various reform proposals. Because costly crises may be symptoms of underlying problems, proposed contractual or institutional solutions should be required to either state how they address the underlying distortion, or convince us that there is, in fact, no deeper problem in the particular case in question, so that the symptom *is* the problem. Furthermore, ideas for contractual improvements must explain what barriers kept those improvements from being adopted in the past, and how they propose to get around those barriers in the future.

In the remainder of this chapter, we evaluate a number of proposals with these criteria in mind. We first discuss proposals for new institutions or institutional reform, beginning with comprehensive but perhaps unrealistic ideas, and ending with more limited proposals that build on existing institutions. We then review some ideas for financial or contractual innovation.

New Institutions and Institutional Reform

A Crisis Insurance Fund

Suppose that it is possible, on a country by country basis, to define a set of "good policies" that would ordinarily prevent a crisis but impossible, for various reasons, to write complete, equity-like debt contracts that require such policies (for example, because courts could not verify the economic variables to which debt service would be indexed). In such circumstances, a well-informed "crisis insurance fund," which bails out countries if and, only if, they get into trouble *in spite of the fact* that they have pursued good policies, may be able to remove inefficient debt crises altogether. Bad luck defaults could no longer exist because transfers from the fund enable countries to repay their debts. Bad policy defaults could not exist because the conditions of fund lending would deter such defaults (countries with bad policies would not be bailed out, and countries which would not be deterred from bad policies in these circumstances would not receive any lending to begin with). By making its actions conditional on information that for some reason could not be written into contracts, the fund would effectively "complete the contracts," achieving the same outcome as if complete contracts were in place (Jeanne 2001).[5]

A country insurance fund could be imagined as a (very significant) extension of the existing IMF, in two respects. First, unlike the IMF, the fund would provide transfers in addition to loans. Hence, it could bail out countries with unsustainable debts, rather than just lend to countries suffering a liquidity shortage. One could imagine the fund having two "windows": a lending window that provides liquidity as a protection against sudden capital flow reversals unrelated to shocks to the country's repayment capacity; and transfers that restore the debt burden to sustainable levels following such solvency shocks. Like any insurance, these transfers would need to be financed by premium payments ex ante. Second, countries would have to "prequalify" for assistance in the sense that the fund's loans and transfers would be conditioned on good policies before the crisis. This is different from the current IMF practice, in which the country's policies before the crisis are not relevant to the decision whether or not to lend to a country in crisis (except to the extent that a country's track record casts doubt on its willingness or ability to carry out the adjustment measures required by the IMF after the crisis).

Practical objections against such a fund can be leveled at both aspects that would distinguish it from the current IMF. As far as the fund's prequalification policy is concerned, the most obvious objection is that in practice, there may be disagreement on what "good policies" exactly means. In addition, country policies may not, in fact, be fully observable. As a result, any real-life prequalification policy would be imperfect in the sense that it may sometimes result in the bailout of countries that did not deserve it, and turn away countries that did. Depending on exactly how well the policy would work in practice, this might still be an improvement over the status quo (while not fully achieving the first best), or it might make matters worse, by rewarding crisis countries with bad policies (with transfers, not just loans).[6] A second objection is that prequalification policies are generally not "time consistent." If the country insurance fund cares about the welfare of the countries that apply for help (as a public institution presumably would), it will be tempted to extend loans or transfers to all countries hit by a crisis, regardless of what caused it. Hence, prequalification only works if the fund can commit not to bail out countries that went into crisis because of bad policies.

These are serious objections, but they do not, in our view, imply that the idea of prequalification in the international community's response to a crisis should be dropped altogether. In what follows, we will pursue the idea further in the context of pure crisis *lending*. A more devastating problem is that a crisis insurance fund would have to levy premia (presumably large ones) from participating countries in a way that would be actuarially fair. This is a problem for two reasons. First, political economy constraints may prevent countries from wanting to pay such large premia for unlikely "accidents." This phenomenon is well known from the fact that countries tend to underinsure against catastrophes, even when they are caused by purely exogenous events. Second, there have not been enough debt crises to figure out what a fair premium would be. Moreover, the causes and costs of debt crises have been evolving. Even the most recent generation of crises that is studied in this book have been so heterogeneous that they provide very slim information on how to price insurance adequately against future crises.

Sovereign Bankruptcy Mechanisms

Proposals for sovereign bankruptcy mechanisms—rules and procedures for "orderly workouts" in the event of a crisis, anchored either in contracts or statutes—have been part of the policy debate on debt crises since the early 1980s (see Rogoff and Zettelmeyer 2002 for a history of the idea). They gained prominence in the aftermath of the 1995 Mexican crisis (Sachs 1995; Eichengreen and Portes 1995) and again between 2001 and 2003, when the creation of a statutory mechanism of this type, the "Sovereign Debt Restructuring Mechanism" (SDRM)

(Krueger 2001, 2002; IMF 2002b; IMF 2003c; Hagan 2005) was proposed by IMF management and staff (but ultimately dropped after it became clear that the United States, which has veto power over amendments of the IMF's articles, would not support it).[7]

The central premise of such mechanisms is that the cost of sovereign debt crises are to a significant extent related to coordination failures and free riding. Debt crises may occur unnecessarily because uncoordinated creditors fail to roll over. Furthermore, coordination failures may make unavoidable debt restructurings (in cases when debt is unsustainably high) more difficult to resolve. Quick and comprehensive debt restructurings may be obstructed by litigation before or during the restructuring negotiations, or by the prospect of "holdouts" that do not participate in the negotiations and may litigate for full repayment after some agreement has been reached (see chapter 3). To deal with these potential problems, proposals for sovereign bankruptcy procedures have focused on mechanisms that make the outcome of agreements between a majority (or supermajority) of creditors legally binding on "holdouts" and shield creditors from litigation while negotiations are ongoing.

Assuming that coordination failures do, in fact, play a role in making debt crises more likely and more costly, there is no question that a sovereign bankruptcy mechanism would be beneficial for countries that are already *in a crisis*. However, such a mechanism would not necessarily make a potential crisis country better off ex ante. In particular, if the difficulties of restructuring debt in an orderly fashion reflect deliberate contractual choices by market participants in the face of problems such as debtor moral hazard, a mechanism that makes debt restructurings easier could backfire, making sovereign debt more expensive, and perhaps cutting some countries off from international capital markets altogether. This is the line of argument that was used by some SDRM critics (e.g., Shleifer 2003).

One does not have to agree fully with this argument to see that a sovereign restructuring mechanism that improves creditor coordination in a debt crisis can have ambivalent welfare effects. Whether or not they reflect deliberate creditor and debtor choices (such as a preference for short-term debt), coordination failures that precipitate or prolong debt crises will have two incentive effects on countries. First, they deter both repudiations and policies that make debt crises more likely. This is the disciplining effect emphasized by the critics of sovereign bankruptcy mechanisms.[8] But there is an additional, countervailing effect: to the extent that debt crises are triggered by bad luck, the prospect of having a debt crisis *in spite of* good policies will discourage a creditor from implementing those policies in the first place (Jeanne 2001, 2004; Corsetti, Guimarães, and Roubini 2006). Hence, the incentives effect of sovereign bankruptcy mechanisms is ambiguous. If "bad luck" plays a big role in precipitating defaults, a (mandatory) sovereign bankruptcy mechanism would, in fact, improve incentives and improve welfare; if not, it might not.[9]

Aside from this incentives argument, there is a more pragmatic criticism of sovereign bankruptcy proposals: the problem that they promise to solve—creditor coordination failures, particularly in the aftermath of a crisis—may not, in fact, be a very big part of the costs of default. As argued in chapter 3, creditor litigation does not appear to have posed a major risk to successful debt restructurings, even after creditors became more diffuse and uncoordinated in the 1990s. Creditor runs which can trigger rollover crises may be a more important factor, and arguably played a role in several of the debt crises studied in this book, but stopping those runs does not require a bankruptcy mechanism: a unilateral payments moratorium will do. The role of a bankruptcy mechanism in this context could be to legitimize such a moratorium, and hence to reduce its adverse reputational effects. However, this was not the primary objective of the mechanisms that have been proposed in the past decade, and whether it would work is doubtful. Hence, rather than going *too far* and perhaps throwing the baby (the sovereign debt market) out with the bathwater (high crisis costs), the main limitation of sovereign bankruptcy proposals as they have been discussed in the policy community could be that they would not, in fact, go very far at all in mitigating default costs. This would render the previous discussion about the incentives effects of such a mechanism a bit academic.

How would a bankruptcy mechanism have to be designed in order to be both effective—in the sense of substantially reducing crisis costs and preventing some crises altogether—and incentive-friendly? In order to reduce the costs of crises effectively, such a mechanism would have to be very extensive. It would have to deal not just with the holdout problem, but legitimize payments moratoria, and most likely other measures, such as capital controls, that governments may be forced to take to deal with the "secondary runs" that generate the steep output declines that often follow debt crises (chapter 2). It may also have to address the "debt dilution problem": the impossibility of committing countries either to refrain from additional borrowing in the future, or assign current creditors priority. One could imagine a very intrusive international debt restructuring mechanism that addresses this problem by giving earlier creditors priority over later creditors (Bolton and Skeel 2004). Finally, in order to achieve not just a reduction in crisis costs ex post but a welfare improvement ex ante, a bankruptcy mechanism of this kind would have to involve prequalification; that is, it should be open only to countries that follow responsible macroeconomic and debt management policies before the crisis.

A sovereign bankruptcy mechanism that embodies all these characteristics might be nearly as effective as the (hypothetical) comprehensive crisis insurance fund discussed in the previous section. It is not difficult to see why. Behind all the trappings—and ignoring the debt dilution problem and the issue of seniority for the sake of simplicity— a bankruptcy mechanism with prequalification would work almost the same as a crisis insurance fund. In well defined circumstances, namely, if debtors run into debt servicing difficulties in spite of having undertaken responsible policies, countries would receive a transfer that restores their solvency. The difference is that in the case of the crisis insurance fund, the transfer would come from an international institution and would be financed by insurance premia. In contrast, in the case of a bankruptcy mechanism, the transfer would come from the creditors, and be financed by the ex ante risk premium built into sovereign borrowing costs. In a sense, the country would be "insured" by its creditors—against both solvency shocks and self-fulfilling runs—with a neutral institution deciding when the insurance must be paid.[10]

What is the feasibility of such a mechanism? On the upside, it would avoid the main problem of a crisis insurance fund, namely, the need to figure out actuarially fair insurance premia and persuade countries to pay them. Under a bankruptcy mechanism, "insurance premia" would be paid automatically, as part of the interest payment to creditors, and the market would decide the appropriate level. On the downside, the problems of prequalification that were raised in the previous section would remain, and some new problems would arise. In order to have the desired effect, the bankruptcy mechanism would need to be intrusive, require ambitious statutory changes at both the national and international level, and concentrate substantial new powers in the hands of an international institution. In view of the political and legal obstacles that confronted—and ultimately led to the demise of—the

IMF's far more modest SDRM proposal, it is doubtful that a mechanism of this kind will ever see the light of day.

International Crisis Lending with Prequalification

The international financial architecture does presently comprise one important instrument to forestall and mitigate debt crises: IMF-led crisis lending. For the purposes of this discussion, three aspects of how this is organized are important. First, there is no prequalification or "ex ante conditionality." A country's policy track record may have an impact on the decision to lend, but only indirectly, through the credibility of the country's promises to carry out policy actions ex post.[11] Second, the IMF only provides loans, not transfers, and charges an interest rate that is arguably in line with the risk it faces (Jeanne and Zettelmeyer 2001, Zettelmeyer and Joshi 2005).[12] Third, by the standard of the debt flows that are typical for emerging market countries and the magnitude of capital flow reversals that was experienced during the crises of the 1990s, the size of IMF lending is rather limited.

There is a consistency between the first of these aspects (no prequalification) and the last two. If the IMF were to provide transfers rather than loans, then the absence of prequalification would result in a very significant moral hazard problem. Countries would be rewarded with international taxpayer money for going into crisis. The fact that the IMF *lends*, seeks to lend only to countries that are solvent in principle, and does so at an actuarially fair rate, eliminates a significant source of moral hazard. So long as the future repayment record of IMF borrowers remains in line with their past repayment record, moral hazard cannot happen at the expense international community (Jeanne and Zettelmeyer 2005b). However, in situations where debtor country governments do not fully represent the interests of their citizens, moral hazard could still arise at the expense of *domestic* taxpayers. The reason is that the "safety net" provided by IMF lending may make it easier for countries with irresponsible fiscal policies to attract funds internationally. Once a debt crisis happens and the IMF lends, it is the domestic taxpayer that foots the bill, in the form of higher taxes or lower public expenditure after the crisis. Without requiring prequalification, this brand of moral hazard can be kept at bay only if the IMF safety net is not very extensive to begin with, that is, if the amounts that the IMF can lend are limited.

While there is no doubt consistency between these characteristics of IMF lending, it is very unlikely—based on the body of economic thought that has guided our discussion so far—that they are jointly optimal, given the information that the IMF has and the constraints that it faces. From an incentives perspective, ignoring precrisis policies entirely in deciding whether to lend or not (except to the extent that they carry information about the likely postcrisis policies) seems an extreme position to take. Economic logic would justify this position only if the IMF were entirely uninformed about a country's precrisis policies (or the link between these policies and the crisis), or if it were entirely unable to commit, that is, if it could never follow through ex post on the intention to only lend to prequalified countries. Neither is likely to be true. While imperfectly informed, the IMF clearly has some notion both of what defines good policies in emerging markets and what policies countries actually undertake (otherwise the process of "IMF surveillance," in which the IMF observes country policies and recommends changes, would make no sense). It also has some, albeit imperfect, capacity to commit. Most of the IMF's current lending policies assume some degree of commitment, including the central premise of IMF lending, namely, that lending is interrupted to countries that fail to carry out IMF conditionality (ex post).

In principle, it should thus be possible to improve IMF-led crisis lending by linking it to the quality of country policies before the crisis. Doing so would increase welfare by "shifting out" the trade-off between moral hazard and the size of crisis lending. It would either allow the IMF to reduce any currently existing moral hazard for current volumes of crisis lending, or to expand the scale of its crisis lending without creating moral hazard. This welfare gain would occur through two channels: first, through stronger incentives for countries to take measures that prevent crises; and second, by discouraging capital flows to countries that fail to do so. Hence, countries with poor policies or institutions would have less scope to build up financial sector and fiscal imbalances that are effectively liabilities of the average taxpayer. This implies that a prequalification policy could benefit even countries whose governments fail to respond to the strengthened incentives created by the policy.

While the basic case for prequalification is straightforward, it is also clear that the devil is in the details: a flawed prequalification system—for example, one that excludes too many countries from the IMF's safety net—could obviously do more harm than good. How these details should look like is beyond the scope of this chapter, but based on the discussion so far, the following principles are likely to be relevant. First, since the purpose of prequalification is to withhold IMF "insurance" from countries that accumulate large contingent liabilities that could explode in a crisis, prequalification criteria would need to focus on public debt, including debt management, and financial sector practices and institutions.[13] Second, what is "sound" in one area depends on the strength of policies in other areas, on the characteristics of the economy, and on the state of the economic cycle; hence, the thresholds defining sound policy could differ both from country to country and over time. Third, because of this complexity, it seems unlikely that prequalification could be purely rules-based; it would require some element of discretion (e.g., exercised in the context of the IMF's surveillance process). Finally, because the prequalification process could lead to mistakes that are only apparent with hindsight, the policy may have to allow exceptions (see Ostry and Zettelmeyer 2005 for details).

The Achilles heel of prequalification, particularly if the policy is to allow for exceptions, remains the time consistency problem, which was already briefly discussed. Traditionally, the IMF has always had some, albeit imperfect, capacity to commit to rules. Better public scrutiny via enhanced transparency of IMF operations and watchdog bodies, such as the Independent Evaluation Office, has improved this capacity over the last decade. Nevertheless, the IMF will sometimes find it difficult—particularly when political interests are involved—to withhold large scale lending to crisis countries even when they have manifestly violated the prequalification criteria and no exception is warranted. To prevent this from happening, some authors have suggested steps that would increase the operational independence of the Executive Board from the national capitals (De Gregorio et al. 2000; Cottarelli 2005; Ostry and Zettelmeyer 2005).

An Emerging Market Debt Price Stabilization Fund

Almost all debt crises discussed in this book were directly or indirectly related to the "sudden stop" in capital flows to emerging markets that followed the Russian default of August 1998. If this is true—and more generally, if debt crises tend to follow busts in international capital markets (chapter 1)—would it not make sense to mitigate sudden stops directly, rather than at the level of each individual country? As Guillermo Calvo (2002) has observed, IMF-led crisis lending "operates more like a fire department than like a central bank. Liquidity is sprayed where fire is found, not on the system as a whole in the manner of a central bank faced with a liquidity crisis."

To "spray liquidity on the system as a whole," and thereby prevent the fire from spreading, Calvo (2002, 2005) proposes the creation of an "emerging market fund" (EMF) that would stabilize a broad index of emerging market debt, such as J. P. Morgan's Emerging Market Bond Index EMBI+, or the EMBI Global. To the extent that financing conditions in emerging markets deteriorate as a result of movements in the aggregate EMBI, as was the case in 1995 and 1998–1999, this would remove or reduce a key source of contagion, and hence prevent a chain reaction of crises such as witnessed after 1998 (from Russia to Brazil and Ecuador, among others; from Brazil to Argentina; and from Brazil and Argentina to Uruguay). In turn, this might obviate or reduce the need for IMF crisis lending (except perhaps to the country that triggered the chain reaction).

Calvo envisages the EMF as an intervention fund endowed with G-3 debt instruments. Because the level of emerging market debt is small compared with G-3 debt, only about 1 percent of G-3 debt would suffice to capitalize the fund in the amount of about one third of EMBI+ debt. The fund would intervene only in the event of very large fluctuations such as witnessed at the time of the Tequila and Russian crises, and it would only "lean against the wind." For example, the fund could buy emerging market debt if prices fall more than x percent relative to a moving average. This means that the fund would eventually sell emerging market debt again, converging to a situation where it does not hold emerging market debt anymore, regardless of whether prices recover or not. However, whether or not prices recover will obviously determine whether the fund makes profits or losses. Hence, Calvo does not propose a mechanical intervention rule; rather, intervention would be decided on a case-by-case basis depending on whether a downturn seems to be driven by fundamentals or not. Calvo (2005) argues that the fund could outperform the market for two reasons: it is not subject to regulations such as collateral constraints that may prevent it from taking advantage of arbitrage opportunities, and capital market information may be undersupplied due to an externality (it provides a free benefit to agents other than those that supply it).

One objection to Calvo's idea is that the fund might suffer large losses when it guesses wrong; though if his logic is right, these losses would wash out in the long run. A related worry is that the fund could give rise to moral hazard. Note that the source of moral hazard, if any, would be quite different from that of IMF crisis lending discussed previously: because the EMF's intervention would not result in any liabilities at the expense of emerging market country taxpayers, the "victim" of any moral hazard would be the global taxpayer financing the fund. Calvo (2002) argues that "the EMF is less subject to the moral hazard criticism because it supports the asset class, rather than the bonds of an individual country." This would be certainly true if the members of the EMBI+ were small and uncoordinated. But if individual countries make up a large share of the index, as they have in the past, or if the three or four largest members collude, then moral hazard could become an issue.

Perhaps for this reason, Calvo (2002) argues, without going into details, that "countries protected by the EMF should submit to new rules in order to prevent moral hazard." In other words, one could envisage an EMF with a "code of conduct" for countries that benefit from EMF stabilization, somewhat analogous to the prequalification criteria for large scale IMF lending that were discussed in the previous section. This "code" would have to be focused on good economic housekeeping (particularly with regard to the public debt) that ensures the solvency of the country. The debt of countries that violate the code would be excluded from EMF intervention. In these circumstances, it is difficult to imagine that an EMF could do much harm, and for the reasons explained by Calvo, it might do a lot of good.

Financial Innovation

As previously argued, debt crises are closely related to the incompleteness of debt contracts. If debt contracts embodied more risk sharing between debtors and creditors, or were written in ways that made countries less vulnerable to rollover crises or exchange rate movements, debt crises would be both less frequent and less severe. So far, we have taken the position that debt contracts are incomplete for deep reasons that cannot be addressed directly, and have considered changes in international institutions or crisis management policies that in some sense substitute for more complete contracts. We now return to the question of whether there are ways in which the prevailing contract incompleteness could be addressed more directly. In principle, there could be three avenues for doing so. First, the international community could find ways of extending the set of contingencies that can be reflected in private contracts, by creating or improving institutions that disseminate information or allow it to be verified. Second, to the extent that certain types of financial contracts are already feasible but do not occur because of first mover or other coordination problems, international financial institutions could coordinate the parties involved, or give potential first movers (such as large emerging market countries) a nudge. Third, international financial institutions could conceivably become a party to some contracts that private parties are reluctant to undertake on their own. We now consider a variety of potential financial innovations that the international community could encourage through any of these channels.

Indexation to Real Variables

Suppose that self-fulfilling runs are not the issue, or that current institutions such as the IMF offer adequate protection against such runs. Then, the main contingency which one would want to write into debt contracts in order to prevent "bad luck defaults" are solvency shocks: unforeseen developments with an impact on a country's capacity to pay. Bond contracts would specify an upward or downward adjustment to the country's debt service in relation to a variable which influences (or proxies for) the country's ability to pay. In the limit, one could imagine contingencies in which a portion of the debt is written down entirely. Such a situation would look like a default on plain vanilla bonds, but because the debt write down occurs in a contingency that is contractually prespecified—and not the fault of the debtor—reputational and other default costs would not arise.

For some countries, there are indeed observable variables outside the control of policy that are highly correlated with the country's capacity to service its debts. Examples include commodity prices (for energy exporters or highly dependent energy importers), natural disasters, and measures of external demand (e.g., growth in trading partners' GDP). For other countries, however, exogenous factors affecting solvency might be too diffuse for the purposes of indexing debt service to these variables. In such cases, only broad economic variables such as GDP or exports might be reliably correlated with debt service capacity. These broad economic variables may also have the advantage that they are fairly uncorrelated across countries (as can be shown empirically for GDP growth; see Borensztein and Mauro 2004) so that the risk associated with fluctuations in these variables is easily diversifiable. However, because they are partly endogenous to economic policy, indexation to these variables raises a potential moral hazard issue. For this reason, fiscal revenue, for example, is generally not a suitable variable for indexation purposes: although it is partly endogenous, it is too easily controlled by policy actions, even in the short run.

There is a long and distinguished history of proposals arguing for the benefits of indexation to real variables.[14] Yet, there are very few examples of bonds issues indexed to real variables (or, for that matter, insurance arrangements with private parties that condition on similar variables). For the case of indexation to broad economic variables such as GDP, debtor moral hazard could be part of the explanation: although governments may not have an incentive to engineer low growth in order to save on interest payments, GDP indexed bonds may induce them to be a bit less careful about avoiding recessions, and may also provide an incentive to misreport GDP data. But these arguments do not explain the absence of simple insurance against purely exogenous shocks, such as natural disasters, which are easily observable and verifiable. Underinsurance in these cases could be due to three reasons: moral hazard arising from the expectation that international aid will be forthcoming in the event of a large bad shock; the fact that creating liquid markets in indexed instruments requires either large issues or coordination; and political economy problems (voters might not be easily persuaded that insurance against rare contingencies is worth public funds that might also be spent on health, education, or tax reductions).

A recent survey of market participants (Borensztein et al. 2005, appendix) suggested that it is probably a mix of these factors that prevent investors from demanding (and countries from issuing) GDP indexed bonds. The top obstacles to growth-linked bonds identified by the study included, in order of importance: (1) concerns about growth measurement; (2) concerns about lack of liquidity of growth-linked instruments; and (3) difficulty in pricing such instruments. These obstacles do not seem insurmountable. Difficulties in pricing indexed securities are amenable to research (see Ceballos 2005 and Chamon and Mauro 2005 for recent examples) and will decline with use, as markets become more familiar with real indexation. Concerns about lack of liquidity depend on the size of the indexed debt issue relative to nonindexed debt. Finally, concerns about misreporting could be dealt with by delegating growth measurement to an independent agency or a process that is subject to international audits.

In sum, indexation to real variables is an obvious way of reducing the risk of debt crises, and it is at least partly amenable to encouragement by international institutions. The international community could help develop markets for indexed debt in two ways: (1) through surveillance over the process for measuring the variables to which bond contracts are indexed; and (2) by helping to internalize the good externality that countries create when they experiment, and hence familiarize markets, with indexed instruments. In addition, to the extent that policymakers reject such instruments because of moral hazard or domestic political economy problems, international institutions could create offsetting incentives for their adoption, for example, ranging from moral suasion in the course of IMF surveillance to prequalification policies as discussed in the previous section.

The international financial institutions should also explore ways of building real indexation into their own lending terms, particularly in their longer-term lending.[15] In principle, IFIs are well positioned to absorb GDP risk (or risk related to exogenous variables affecting repayment capacity) because they can diversify some of this risk through their broad lending portfolios, and because they should be in a better position to verify GDP measurement than private investors. However, because there is no market that would price such loans, the terms of the indexed IFI lending would have to be carefully designed.

Contingent Reserves and Related Hedging Strategies

Even if they could index debt service payments to relevant real variables, this may not protect countries from liquidity crises—triggered, for example, by a sudden stop in international capital flows. IMF lending is supposed to deal with these types of crises, but IMF intervention did not prevent most crisis countries in the 1990s from suffering large current account reversals and output contractions (Ghosh et al. 2002). This experience may have contributed to the large surge in emerging market reserve holdings that can be observed since the late 1990s, as governments attempted to self-insure. But self-insurance is inefficient, and makes countries vulnerable to exchange rate and interest swings in the international currencies that are being held as reserves. This leads to the question of whether there are ways of protecting emerging market countries from sudden stops—other than new or reformed official institutions, as discussed previously—that do not require massive reserve accumulation. What one would want is a financial instrument that supplies ample international reserves when they are needed, but does not force the country to pay the carry cost of reserves all the time.

During the 1990s, this idea led several emerging market countries, including Argentina and Mexico, to enter contracts with major international banks which allowed them to swap or sell sovereign bonds in return for international reserves on preset terms. Argentina's repo line, which was contracted by the BCRA as a backstop for providing liquidity to the financial system in time of need, was quite significant, amounting to $6.2 billion. Argentina did, in fact, draw $1.3 billion from this credit line in September 2001.

However, credit lines of this type suffer from two potential problems. First, they might be susceptible to moral hazard. For example, suppose the facility is a put option that allows the country to sell government bonds to banks at a prespecified price at a moment of its choosing. This would make the banks vulnerable to country actions that lower the market value of the bonds after the contract has been agreed, which in turn will be reflected in a high-risk premium at the time of signing (or restrictions on when the option can be exercised). This problem can be reduced through the design of the facility. For example, Argentina's facility was a repo line: when drawing, Argentina was required to deposit bonds valued at current market prices rather than a prespecified price; moreover, deterioration of the market price after drawing required Argentina to supply additional bonds. Even so, a moral hazard problem might remain to the extent that at the time of drawing, the country has private information about current or future actions that is not revealed to the market and hence not reflected in the market price of its bonds.[16]

Second, there is a question whether banks or investors that are the counterparties of private contingent credit lines can engage in transactions that might somehow undo the benefit of the facility. Clearly, repo lines cannot be used to force a bank to take on more exposure to the debtor country than it otherwise would, since the bank can reduce its exposure, for example, by holding fewer government bonds. Moreover, when a country draws on the facility, banks are free to sell the government bonds that they have just received. Does this negate the purpose of the facility? Not quite, if its purpose is to obtain liquidity in an emergency rather than extra financing for the budget. Repo lines can be useful in that they provide liquidity at a time when the primary market for government bonds has dried up completely, though perhaps at the price of an additional drop in secondary market bond prices.

While well-designed repo lines may hence have a place in the financial architecture, one can ask whether there are alternative "contingent reserves" contracts that are not susceptible to these problems. The ideal variable for conditioning reserves payments would have three properties: it would be exogenous to country actions; it would be highly correlated with events (such as sudden stops) in which a country needs extra reserves; and it would attract investors who do not ordinarily invest in emerging markets, hence avoiding crowding out of demand for other emerging market assets. Caballero and Panageas (2004, 2005) have recently proposed one variable along these lines: the Volatility Index (VIX) compiled by the Chicago Board Options Exchange, an index of near term U.S. financial market volatility based on the prices of S&P500 stock index options. They show that spikes in the VIX are highly correlated with sudden stops in emerging markets (the probability of observing a statistically significant jump in the VIX conditioning on a sudden stop is about 0.7).

Because jumps in the VIX are independent of country actions, VIX-based contracts are immune to the moral hazard problem that may hamper contingent credit lines (and, to a lesser extent, GDP-indexed bonds). Furthermore, jumps in the VIX in excess of a contractually determined threshold would result in a transfer of reserves, not in a loan; hence, there is no sense in which VIX payments can be "undone" by an offsetting transaction. Whether or not VIX-type instruments could be successful thus boils down to how expensive they would be, assuming that emerging market countries purchase them en masse (as they would have to for the instruments to be useful), and whether flooding the market with instruments whose returns are correlated with those of emerging market securities would crowd out the latter. The answer to the last question depends on whether the class of investors that would be interested in holding VIX risk would extend beyond the class currently holding emerging market assets—as it well might. As for the price, there should be gains from trade between an emerging market country for which a dollar is worth much more than a dollar in times of crisis and an advanced country investor for whom a dollar basically just equals a dollar at all times.

In principle, there should thus be a potential market for insurance mechanisms such as VIX-based transfers. From the perspective of an emerging market country, the main worry may be whether there will continue to be a reliable relationship between the VIX (or similar advanced country financial variables) and emerging market crises going forward (i.e., whether the VIX would indeed supply reserves when needed). It would be more reassuring to purchase a contingent reserves contract that conditions on variables which are directly related to emerging market crises, such as credit default swaps, or aggregate debt price indices such as the EMBI. But the latter are not exogenous to the actions of large emerging market countries, and much less likely to tap investors that currently do not hold emerging market assets. Hence, there is a trade-off.

VIX and related options could also play a useful role in the *official* sector response to sudden stops. For example, one could imagine a VIX-based crisis insurance fund, whose members are both emerging markets that suffer from sudden stops and advanced countries that do not. Emerging markets would pay an insurance premium to the advanced countries in return for a payment triggered by VIX jumps. As long as sudden stops involve a deadweight loss, and assuming the VIX signal is sufficiently good proxy of times of need for the insured, there could be efficiency gains from such an arrangement.

One could also imagine official *lending* based on VIX-type variables. A VIX jump within a certain time window of a lending request would make it more likely that the origins of a crisis are external and systemic, and hence less likely that it is the debtors fault. Hence, it would make sense to use the VIX (along with other information) as an input in the decision on whether or not to extend large scale crisis loans. How official lending policies could be designed to trade off VIX-type signals and other information about precrisis policies and crisis origins optimally might be a subject worth further study.

Bond Covenants

In principle, debt contracts can try to distinguish between "bad luck" and "bad policies" in two ways: by making payments contingent on exogenous variables and hence defining cases in which bad luck can be legitimately passed on to creditors ex post, or by identifying and prohibiting debtor behavior which is harmful to creditor interests. The latter is a bit like trying to untie the Gordian knot of moral hazard by cutting it, that is, by attempting to condition bond contracts directly on debtor actions. For the reasons discussed at the beginning of this chapter, this may be very difficult. For one, the list of debtor actions which could potentially harm creditor interests (or conversely, the code by which debtors would have to live in order to conform to creditor interests) may be too long and unpredictable to write down ex ante. Moreover, observable "policy variables" that reflect debtor actions, such as deficits or money growth, are also partly endogenous to shocks outside the debtor's control.

However, there is a tradition of using "negative covenants" in corporate debt contracts to achieve just that objective, that is, to place ex ante restrictions on debtor actions that might harm creditors (Smith and Warner 1979; Asquith and Wizman 1990; Goyal 2003). These include restrictions on the firm's financing policies, including restrictions on net worth or total debt, in some cases excluding subordinated debt; dividend policies; and investment or divestment policies (such as mergers and the sale of firm assets). The main aim of these restrictions is to protect creditor claims from dilution through payments or new liabilities issues to third parties such as equity holders (in the case of dividends) or future debt holders (in the case of new debt). The question is whether similar restrictions could play a useful role at the sovereign debt level, and, if so, what could potentially be done to promote their use.

It is difficult to imagine a list of restrictions on debtor policies that will comprehensively protect creditor interests. Nevertheless, based both on the cases we have reviewed in previous chapters and the literature surveyed in chapter 2, one can easily imagine a few economic variables, such as total debt, or reserves as a share of short-term debt, that can both be influenced by debtors and are important determinants of solvency and liquidity. There is no question that constraining debtors with respect to these policies would benefit creditors; indeed, some official creditors—notably, the IMF and the World Bank—do impose such restrictions on its debtors over a portion of the lifetime of their loans, in the form of "conditionality."[17] The fact that these variables may reflect economic shocks well as policy actions alone could be dealt with by combining covenants on policy variables with indexation to real variables that are entirely or mostly outside the debtor's control, as suggested previously.[18]

Another reason why "negative covenants" in bond contracts deserve consideration is that several of the most recent debt crises involved dilution of earlier creditors by subsequent creditors in a way that is quite analogous to the dilution of corporate debt (see Borensztein et al. 2005 for a discussion). To take one example, the holder of a Russian GKO issued in December 1997 received the same treatment in Russia's 1999 restructuring as the holder of a June 1998 GKO, even though the 1997 holder paid a much higher price. If Russia had not aggressively issued new GKOs in the first half of 1998, holders of the December GKO would have been much better off, even if Russia had defaulted in 1998 just like it eventually did, because they would have had to share the recovery value of Russian debt with a much smaller number of competing creditors. As argued by Bolton and Jeanne (2005), this fear of dilution could be one reason why creditors seek debt forms that are hard to restructure (but make crises more likely and deeper when they occur).

This leads to the question why "negative covenants" that restrict the debtor's financial policies are not already used in sovereign bond contracts.[19] One candidate answer is that they could not be legally enforced. But this argument is not entirely convincing, since it also applies to other terms in sovereign debt contracts, including the payment terms. Yet such terms are written, and by and large respected. Restrictions on financial policies in sovereign debt could be enforced in the same way payment terms are enforced, namely, by defining the violation of those terms as a default, triggering acceleration and cross-default clauses, and hence reputational and other punishments unless the creditor immediately repays in full. One could also imagine slightly softer options such as making bonds "putable" if the debtor violates the financial restrictions laid out in the contract. Nothing prevents a sovereign debtor from giving the creditor the contractual right to demand early repayment, if, for example, a certain level of external debt has been exceeded.

A more plausible explanation is that bond covenants of this type are not used because of a combination of the general barriers to financial innovation mentioned earlier in this chapter, and the fact that the debt dilution problem in sovereign debt—though recognized for some time, by authors such as Sachs and Cohen (1982) and Kletzer (1984)—may only recently have acquired practical significance. (During the 1970s and 1980s, debt dilution was less of an issue, because creditor banks formed a cartel, and bond finance was of secondary importance.) In addition, there may be measurement problems, in particular, the lack of an international registry that would comprehensively and reliably document the level and composition of public debt for each sovereign.[20]

In sum, the obstacles to greater use of negative covenants in debt contracts (or put options that condition on debtor behavior) could be quite similar to the obstacles that face GDP-linked bonds: measurement issues, pricing difficulties, and a "novelty premium" facing first users. Hence, the international community could potentially promote these contracts in similar ways that have been suggested above for GDP-linked bonds and other forms of real indexation. This said, the idea of using sovereign bond contracts as devices through which countries could commit to good policies has been much less explored than the subject of real indexation of debt payments, and one would want to see more research on the issue before jumping to policy conclusions.

Local Currency Instruments

As documented in the preceding chapters of this book as well as some of the cross-country studies surveyed in chapter 2, currency mismatches in public sector balance sheets contributed significantly to most of the large debt crises in the past decade, by creating a direct link between currency crises and debt service capacity. These mismatches could have been reduced or avoided if countries had issued a far larger share of their public debts—particularly their public *long-term* debts—in local currency (whether in nominal or CPI-indexed terms). The question is why foreign currency debt contracts were adopted instead, and whether there is a role for international institutions in promoting local currency debt, including by attempting to create local debt markets at the international level.

To a first approximation (see Borensztein et al. 2005; Goldstein and Turner 2004 for details), there are two views on why foreign currency debt has been the preferred form of issuing long-term debt in emerging market countries. They roughly coincide with the "two views on financial architecture" described at the beginning of this chapter. The first view argues that the inability of issuing local debt in domestic currency is a *symptom* of the moral hazard problems that have been discussed in the course of this chapter, in particular, the inability to credibly commit to policies that would maintain the currency stable (Calvo and Guidotti 1990; Jeanne 2000, 2003; Caballero, Cowan, and Kearns 2004; Rajan 2004a, among others). In view of this lack of commitment, investors prefer debt instruments that are both inflation and currency crisis-proof. But the downside is that this may leave the public sector with a balance sheet structure that exposes it to self-fulfilling runs and shocks unrelated to country policies, and creates a link between currency crises and debt crises.

The second view emphasizes the lack of liquid *international* markets in local currency instruments as the critical reason for why countries choose to issue debt in U.S. dollars or other international currencies. This view, sometimes referred to as the "original sin hypothesis," is backed by evidence that the ability of countries to issue bonds in international markets is largely related to country size, and not so much to problems with country policies or institutions (Hausmann and Panizza 2003; Eichengreen, Hausmann, and Panizza 2005b). Consequently, these authors argue that financial innovation needs a big push from international institutions, which ought to become directly involved in setting up local debt markets at the international level.

As argued previously, the two views are not necessarily inconsistent. Commitment and moral hazard—"domestic" problems—could well be the deep reason for financial dollarization. At the same time, it is possible that lack of liquidity and other startup problems have in the past prevented even countries with credible policies from issuing local currency debt in international markets. In other words, an "international problem" may exist along with a domestic problem. Which problem deserves more emphasis depends on one's views on where policy efforts are likely to have the greater impact, but also on what one is ultimately trying to achieve. If the primary objective is to break the link from currency crises to sovereign debt crises, the focus should be on reducing public sector currency mismatches. From this perspective, developing international markets in local currency instruments is not necessary—issuing long-term local currency debt *domestically* will do just fine. On the other hand, if the objective is to insure countries as a whole against "sudden stops" in international capital flows, then domestic residents should be net debtors in local currency instruments, so that when the currency depreciates and real incomes decline, there is a countervailing effect on their net worth. In this case, the focus should be on persuading *foreigners* to buy local currency debt. This may or may not require issuing such debt in international markets, but if it does, improved policy credibility may not be enough, and barriers to financial innovation may need to be overcome.

What is the recent experience with local currency debt issues, at both the domestic and international level? A number of emerging market countries, including Colombia, India, Singapore, South Africa, China, and Thailand, have traditionally issued long-term local currency in domestic markets. This reflects long histories of low or moderate inflation, in some cases combined with financial repression. The question is whether countries with histories of financial instability can undertake policy steps towards the same objective, without resorting to financial repression. The experience of the last decade is surprisingly encouraging. A number of emerging market countries with relatively recent inflation or devaluation experiences, including Brazil, Chile, Israel, Mexico, Peru, and Poland, have been able to issue long-term local currency debt, usually within a decade of stabilizing their currencies and undertaking steps to develop credible monetary and fiscal policy institutions. Hence, it appears that countries can take the development of domestic debt markets in local currency in their own hands, without waiting for actions by international institutions (though international institutions could, of course, play a supportive role in helping national authorities achieve greater policy credibility).

What about international debt in local currencies? The World Bank and the InterAmerican Development Bank have in recent years issued debt in a number of emerging market currencies, allowing international investors to gain exposure to these currencies without facing sovereign default risk. Eichengreen and Hausmann (2005) and Levy-Yeyati (2003) have proposed significant expansions of this role; the former to tap more effectively international demand for emerging market currency debt, and the latter to tap domestic savings from the emerging markets itself. These proposals have been controversial (Rajan 2004b; Goldstein and Turner 2004), in part because of doubts that the IFIs could in fact issue emerging market debt in large amounts more cheaply than the emerging market governments themselves. At the same time, however, a number of emerging market issuers including Brazil, Colombia, and Uruguay, as well as a number of banks or corporations in Mexico, Brazil, China, Korea, and South Africa, have for the first time been successful in placing long-term local currency debt in international markets, albeit in relatively small amounts. This has been helped by the low yield environment in emerging market debt in the last few years, but it also shows that lack of liquidity is not an insurmountable problem in issuing local currency debt internationally.

Taking together local and international markets, local currency long-term debt issues are clearly on an upward trend. The origins of this trend precede the latest boom phase in emerging market financing that set in during 2003–2004; hence, one would hope that it is not just a cyclical phenomenon. In August 2005, the EMTA quarterly survey showed that the overall volume of trading in local currency debt instruments had surpassed the volume of Eurobond trading for the first time in history. Moreover, foreigners have increasingly taken positions in long-term local currency instruments issued in local markets (i.e., under domestic law), rendering the distinction between domestic and international markets much less relevant than it has been in the past.

Overall, this makes for a very different picture compared with the possible financial innovations discussed in the previous subsections. In emerging market countries with recent track records of macroeconomic stability, currency mismatches in both public sector and national balance sheets appear to be on a path of gradual self-correction, as these countries increase their shares of local currency debt, and a significant share of these new issues is absorbed by foreigners. The same cannot be said with respect to the dearth of debt contracts that are contingent on real variables, or that would allow the debtor to commit to good policies.

Conclusions

The purpose of this chapter was to discuss both the conceptual motivation and practical obstacles of some ideas for reforming the international financial architecture, not to advocate particular reform proposals. Nevertheless, there are a few general lessons that one can take away from this discussion.

First, it is possible to think of new institutional designs so comprehensive that they would eliminate costly debt crises. Examples include a well-informed crisis insurance fund with the power of making extensive transfers to countries with good policies, or a very comprehensive framework for restructuring sovereign debts and containing the associated secondary runs. However, these institutions appear unfeasible, either because their informational requirements are too demanding, or because of political obstacles, or a mix of the two.

Second, and related to the first point, changes that address the deep informational and contractual incompleteness problems that are at the root of debt crises are more likely to occur at the country level—through improvements in policies, domestic institutions, and eventually credibility—than at the international level. The fact that, improvements in macroeconomic credibility have recently enabled an increasing number of emerging market countries to move away from dangerous debt structures (in particular, short-term and foreign currency-denominated debt) is encouraging in this regard.

Third, one can make a case for a variety of contractual and financial innovations which would help insure countries against shocks that might precipitate crises, and strengthen country commitments to good policies. For many of these innovations, the informational and institutional prerequisites appear to be in place even now; yet they are not being adopted. We need to obtain a better understanding of why this is the case—in particular, whether it is due to barriers to contractual innovations in financial markets, or a reluctance on the side of domestic policymakers—and what the international financial community can do to help.

Finally, as long as emerging market finance remains relatively unstable and boom-bust cycles in international credit flows are the norm—as they have been for the last two centuries—there will be a role for official financial institutions and related facilities that provide liquidity in the event of a sharp reversal in private debt flows. However, ways need to be found to deliver this liquidity in a way that is faster, more effective, and more incentives-friendly. In particular, the prospect of liquidity support must not encourage excessive debt flows to countries that are not well-equipped to absorb them, and should hence be linked to good macroeconomic and financial sector policies in the borrowing countries. There may also be a case for creating a facility that mitigates the instability of emerging market debt flows at the center, by leaning against very sharp swings in emerging market debt prices, rather than just by lending to countries that suffer from the effect of such swings.

Appendix: Tools for the Analysis of Debt Problems

The purpose of this appendix is to review a number of tools that help an observer assess the likelihood and proximate causes of debt crises, evaluate likely restructuring scenarios, and estimate possible financial implications for the government. We divide our exercise in six parts: solvency and liquidity indicators, debt dynamics decompositions, debt sustainability analysis, estimating the probability of default, estimating recovery values, and assessing the financial impact of default from the perspective of the defaulting government.

Solvency and Liquidity Indicators

The most commonly used measures of a country's capacity to service its debt are "debt ratios" that measure debt and debt service obligations in terms of the debtor's economic size or income. The simplest and most famous is of course the *debt-to-GDP ratio*, which we have used extensively in our case studies; another is the *interest-to-GDP ratio* which measures debt service payments due each year as a percentage of GDP. Public debt levels and debt service are also sometimes related to taxes or revenues, and external public debt is often related to export earnings, particularly in the case of countries that have little access to world capital markets and whose main sources of foreign exchange are trade related.

As the empirical literature that we discussed in chapters 2 and 11 shows, debt ratios have some power to predict debt crises: everything else equal, countries with higher indebtedness relative to economic size or income are more likely to default. At the same time, the literature shows that many other variables and indicators also help predict defaults, and that the informativeness of the debt-to-GDP ratio and similar solvency indicators—in particular, whether a specific debt ratio is viewed as "dangerously high" or not—may depend on these other factors. Looking at debt ratios alone does not get one very far in predicting which countries are in danger of experiencing a crisis and which are not.

Table A.1 illustrates the usefulness as well as the limitations of debt ratios. The table considers two groups of emerging economies. The first is a group of countries that defaulted or restructured their debts in recent years. The second is an arbitrarily selected group of emerging market nondefaulters, of about similar size and geographic location. To see whether debt ratios provide a good signal of impending crises, all numbers for the first group refer to the year prior to default. Two messages emerge from this table. First, on average, the defaulters did, in fact, have significantly higher interest and debt burdens than did the nondefaulters. Two countries in the defaulting group, Pakistan and Ecuador, show much higher debt burdens than the others, and two—Russia and, again, Pakistan—exhibit much higher interest burdens as a ratio of revenue. Hence, if one had been forced to pick five crisis countries out of this group of nine, without any extra information, these three would presumably have been among them. However—and that is the second message from the table—the other two countries, Argentina and Ukraine, would have been completely indistinguishable from the nondefaulters shown on the right. The debt ratios simply did not offer clues that these countries were particularly at risk. Apart from the fact that debt ratios do not, of course, carry any information about domestic or external shocks to which these economies might be exposed—nor about the flexibility with which policies and institutions might or might not respond to these shocks—there are fundamentally three reasons why debt ratios may not provide particularly good crisis signals.

First, they may not be very good measures of even the concept that they are supposed to proxy, namely, a country's fundamental ability to pay, or *solvency*. This is because solvency is intrinsically an intertemporal concept: it refers to a country's ability to make payments in the future. Current income and face value outstanding as well as current interest payments might not be good guides to these future flows. Future income depends on future economic growth and real exchange rate movements, while future liability streams depend on the structure of amortizations and coupon payments. The latter are obviously not reflected in the face value of debt, and may or may not be reflected in today's interest payments. A country with a relatively small debt but

Table A.1
Solvency indicators: Crisis countries versus noncrisis countries (in percent)

	Debt crisis countries						Noncrisis countries				
	Argentina (2000)	Ecuador (1998)	Pakistan (1998)	Russia (1997)	Ukraine (1997)	Average	Colombia (2000)	Mexico (2000)	Venezuela (2000)	Poland (2000)	Average
Interest/GDP	3.4	4.2	6.1	5.0	1.8	4.1	4.0	4.3	2.9	2.6	3.5
Interest/Total revenue	17.4	20.8	46.4	38.0	4.8	25.5	15.9	20.5	9.4	6.9	13.2
Public debt/GDP[a]	51.1	81.1	76.8	55.2	34.0	59.6	47.7	49.1	28.1	38.7	40.9

Source: National authorities, IMF.

Note: Uses broadest fiscal concept when several are available; that is, general government or total public sector.
[a] Debt stock in local currency evaluated at end-period exchange rates, divided by local currency GDP.

large future interest payments may be insolvent in spite of a low debt-to-GDP or interest-to-GDP ratio. Conversely, it may have a high debt-to-GDP ratio but with debt at very low rates and therefore be relatively safe. Hence, to fully appraise a country's solvencies, one needs to explicitly consider these future streams, and the risk that future liabilities might exceed capacity to pay. This is the business of debt sustainability analysis, while we return to later.

Second, the public debt levels that are reflected in debt ratios may not be an accurate measure of what a sovereign may actually end up owing in a crisis. One potential reason is simply poor measurement, as some explicit government debt may not be on the official books. These "skeletons" then have a habit of showing up in crisis times, when debtors are forced to make an inventory of their overall liabilities. Beyond this, most governments have "quasifiscal" liabilities, in the form of implicit bailout guarantees that benefit particular constituencies that may get into trouble. In particular, no government can afford to let its financial system, or its pension system, go completely broke. But compensating the financial sector for crisis losses, for example, can easily cost the government 10–20 percent of GDP, as we saw in several of the recent crises.

Hence, solvency analysis requires assessing the extent of implicit liabilities, and the chances that they may become explicit. There may be several dimensions to this. First, looking at private balance sheets—particularly in the financial sector, and the corporate sector on which the financial sector may have claims—that may increase the public debt in a systemic crisis. Second, looking beyond the central government to municipal and local government indebtedness that may prompt intervention from the center. Finally, adjusting for the type of pension system. In countries with pay-as-you-go systems, the public debt may understate actual public liabilities because it does not include the implicit liability of future pensions. In contrast, in countries with privatized social security, this liability is usually explicit, in the form of public debt in the hands of the pension funds. Hence, everything else equal, government solvency in countries with pay-as-you-go systems requires lower explicit public debt levels than in countries with privatized systems.

Third, as emphasized in chapter 2, even if a country is solvent in the sense that its future revenue streams and assets exceed its total liabilities in a present value sense, a debt crisis may still arise if a country lacks the liquidity to pay at any given point in time. And debt ratios say nothing about liquidity. A country may be perfectly capable of repaying its debt if spread out over time, for example, but may not have the cash to make a bullet repayment, triggering a default unless it can coordinate its creditors on rolling over, or obtain temporary financing from official sources.

To both assess a country's vulnerability to liquidity problems and, at the same time, get a better sense of solvency if things go wrong, debt ratios can be supplemented through information about a country's liquidity as well as its debt *structure*. *Liquidity indicators* typically compare government debt coming due in the short-term with its liquid assets and short-term income. A classic measure is the ratio of international reserves to short-term debt on a remaining maturity basis; a low ratio (in particular, below one) has been shown to predict liquidity trouble. To the extent that financial or corporate sector liquidity matters for government liquidity, broader economy-wide measures of dollar liquidity may also be important. One example is the gap between short-term dollar liabilities and dollar reserves in the banking system (Jeanne and Wyplosz 2001).

Beyond specific benchmarks, *financing requirements* are an indicator of potential liquidity problems. Financing requirements measure how much debt is coming due during a given period of time, be it government debt, private sector debt, or both. Computing financing requirements requires knowing the amortization structure of the debt. For example, a T-bill with a three-month maturity of $3 billion will enter in the financing requirement numbers for the following year as $12 billion, as it will have to be rolled over four times during that period. If its maturity is one year, the financing requirement would just be $3 billion over the coming year. As long as the market rolls over existing debt automatically, amortizations are usually not considered an important part of the debt problem. But once rollover is in question, knowing how many resources the market will have to provide becomes essential. In the case of Ukraine in 1998 total debt was relatively low (table A.1), but financing requirements were high, due to a bunching of amortizations. When these requirements met an unreceptive market, a crisis arose.

In addition to the maturity and amortization structure, other aspects of the public (as well as financial and corporate) sector debt structure are also important. Perhaps the most important one, discussed at length in previous chapters, is currency composition and/or indexation of debt to the exchange rate or domestic interest rates. In table A.1, Argentina's low debt ratio masked the fact that it was vulnerable to a currency crisis that could lead this debt ratio to double overnight, as a large share of debt was denominated in foreign currency. Other relevant aspects include the creditor composition (official or private, domestic or external) and governing law. These can have implications for the scope and terms of rolling over or restructuring the debt in a crisis.

Finally, there is a question whether external debt stocks should be measured in gross terms or net of foreign assets held by local residents and governments. Many countries provide "net debt" statistics that subtract liquid foreign assets in the hands of the public sector (usually central banks) from the debt stock. However, this assumes that these assets will be used to repay debt, an assumption that may not come true (e.g., if reserves are used to intervene in the foreign exchange market or to stop a run on banks). In no case should foreign assets held by private local residents be subtracted when analyzing debt sustainability, since these assets are seldom available in times of crises. In other words, when liquidity or solvency problems arise, countries cannot count on these resources to provide a counterweight to the burden of debt. An exception may be the assets of local firms abroad or those held by the foreign headquarters of local firms, as in both cases the firm may be willing (or forced) to commit some resources in order to stay afloat during a debt crisis.

Debt Dynamics Decompositions

For all its limitations, the public sector debt-to-GDP ratio remains the most important summary measure of public indebtedness, and its analysis over time can yield important clues both to why a debt crisis occurred, or, if it has not occurred, to where the debt ratio is heading. In this regard, an often used tool is to decompose changes in the debt-to-GDP ratio into the changes of macroeconomic variables—the primary fiscal balance, interest rates faced by the government, the exchange rate, economic growth, and so on—that might be driving it. Because this exercise relies on an accounting identity, there is nothing particularly analytical about it. A good analogy is growth accounting—decomposing real economic growth over time into changes in the capital stock, labor, and total factor productivity. Just as growth accounting tells us nothing about the fundamental reasons driving high growth, debt dynamics decompositions cannot explain why a debt crisis really occurred; but they can offer important clues on where to start looking.

There are many different ways of doing debt dynamics decompositions, because there are alternative ways of measuring debt to GDP, and because the terms in an accounting identity can be "collected" in different ways. In the following, we concentrate on four decompositions: a "nominal" and "real" decomposition, respectively, starting either from a debt-to-GDP ratio based on converting all debt into foreign currency or a debt-to-GDP ratio based on debt in domestic currency terms. The latter distinction may appear a bit surprising: Aren't these unitless ratios, in which debt is ultimately expressed in GDP terms, regardless of how we go about computing the ratio? Well, yes, but there is a subtlety that comes from the fact that we are dividing an end-period stock, debt, through a flow, GDP. Hence, if exchange rates need to be applied to transform everything into the same currency units (as will be the case if some portion of the debt is denominated in domestic currency), debt stocks in local currency units will be based on a different exchange rate—an end of period rate—than GDP in foreign currency, which uses a period average exchange rate:

$$\frac{D_t^f S_t^{eop} + D_t^d}{Y_t} \neq \frac{D_t^f + D_t^d / S_t^{eop}}{Y_t / S_t^{ave}}, \quad \text{where } S_t \equiv \frac{\text{local currency}}{\$}$$

where the superscripts f and d denote foreign currency denominated debt and domestic currency denominated debt, respectively, and *eop* and *ave* stand for "end of period" and "period average." In situations when the exchange rate is depreciating, $S_t^{eop} > S_t^{ave}$; hence the "local currency debt-to-GDP ratio" will appear larger than the "foreign currency debt-to-GDP ratio."

Which of the two approaches is better? Neither—they simply represent different conventions. Traditionally, expressing all debt in dollars and dividing through dollar GDP has been the approach favored by emerging market countries, perhaps because it made their debt to GDP ratios look smaller in depreciating environments, or because it made the ratio less volatile (as annual average exchange rates are more stable than end-of-period rates). However, some countries, such as Pakistan, have traditionally followed the "everything in local currency" approach, and this approach seems to have become more popular recently. In our case studies, we have used the "everything in foreign currency" approach, both because it has been more widely used and so tends to generate the debt-to-GDP ratios that people are used to, and because it leads to a slightly easier debt dynamics decomposition, as will become clear in what follows.

In the remainder of this section, we use the following notation:

$$D_t \equiv D_t^d + D_t^f S_t^{eop}$$

$$D_t^\$ \equiv D_t / S_t^{eop}$$

$$\alpha \equiv \frac{D_t^d}{D_t}$$

So α is the share of local currency denominated debt in total debt.

Debt Dynamics Based on a Dollar Debt Accumulation Equation

Ignoring nondebt financing of the fiscal deficit (such as privatization receipts and grants) as well as changes in the debt stock that are not driven by the deficit (such as debt restructuring, or issuance of compensation bonds to banks), the basic dollar debt accumulation equation can be written as follows (the superscript "*ave*" has been suppressed to avoid clutter):

$$
\begin{aligned}
D_t^\$ - D_{t-1}^\$ &\equiv -\frac{P_t}{S_t} + \frac{I_t}{S_t} + \frac{D_{t-1}^d}{S_{t-1}^{eop}}\left[\frac{1/S_t^{eop}}{1/S_{t-1}^{eop}} - 1\right] \\
&\equiv -\frac{P_t}{S_t} + \frac{I_t}{S_t} + \alpha D_{t-1}^\$\left[\frac{S_{t-1}^{eop}}{S_t^{eop}} - 1\right]
\end{aligned}
$$

(A.1)

where P_t and I_t are the local currency primary balance and interest bill, respectively, from the fiscal accounts. Now

• Rewrite the term in square brackets in terms of the rate of nominal depreciation, $1 + s_t^e \equiv S_t^{eop}/S_{t-1}^{eop}$. Thus, $S_{t-1}^{eop}/S_t^{eop} - 1 \equiv -s_t^e/(1 + s_t^e)$.
• Divide both sides by $Y_t^\$(\equiv Y_t/S_t)$.
• Subtract $D_{t-1}^\$/Y_{t-1}^\$$ from both sides. Then, equation (A.1) becomes

$$\frac{D_t^\$}{Y_t^\$} - \frac{D_{t-1}^\$}{Y_{t-1}^\$} = -\frac{P_t}{Y_t} + \frac{I_t}{Y_t} - \alpha\frac{s_t^e}{1 + s_t^e}\frac{D_{t-1}^\$}{Y_t^\$} + \frac{D_{t-1}^\$}{Y_t^\$} - \frac{D_{t-1}^\$}{Y_{t-1}^\$}.$$

(A.2)

At this stage, there are two ways to proceed. First, one could rewrite (A.2) in terms of inflation, real growth, and the nominal exchange rate contributing to the debt dynamics. This uses the fact that, by definition,

$$Y_t^\$ \equiv \frac{(1 + \pi_t)(1 + g_t)}{(1 + s_t)}Y_{t-1}^\$,$$

(A.3)

where π_t equals the (local currency) GDP inflation rate, g_t equals the real growth rate, and s_t equals the (period average) rate of exchange rate depreciation.

Substituting into equation (A.2) and rearranging, one obtains

$$d_t^\$ - d_{t-1}^\$ = -\frac{P_t}{Y_t} + \frac{I_t}{Y_t} - \frac{d_{t-1}^\$}{(1+\pi_t)(1+g_t)}$$

$$\times \left\{ \left(\alpha \frac{s_t^e(1+s_t)}{1+s_t^e} - s_t \right) + \pi_t + g_t + \pi_t g_t \right\}. \tag{A.4}$$

We can then call the first term on the right-hand side the "primary balance contribution" to the increase in the debt to GDP ratio, and the second term the "interest contribution." By multiplying the factor outside the curly brackets with each of the terms inside the curly brackets, we obtain the "exchange rate contribution," "inflation contribution," and "real growth contribution," as well as a "theoretical residual" consisting of the cross-terms. In addition, there will be "statistical residual" reflecting debt stock operations, nondebt financing, and measurement error.

The disadvantage of this decomposition is that in flexible exchange rate or adjustable peg environments with high inflation, there will be big terms with opposite signs (a high inflation term with a negative sign and a high nominal exchange rate term with a positive sign). Basically, high inflation pulls the debt-to-GDP ratio down ceteris paribus by pushing up nominal GDP, but ceteris paribus doesn't hold because high inflation leads to nominal depreciation. The relevant question is whether the depreciation effect more than offsets the inflation effect (as will generally be the case in a currency crisis). To bring this out, it is more informative and useful to look at a decomposition in terms of "real" variables only, including real exchange rate depreciation. Starting again from equation (A.2), we use

$$Y_t^\$ \equiv \frac{(1+\pi_t^\$)(1+g_t)}{(1+e_t)} Y_{t-1}^\$, \tag{A.5}$$

where e_t, the rate of real exchange rate appreciation, is *defined* by

$$(1+e_t) \equiv (1+s_t)\frac{1+\pi_t^\$}{1+\pi_t}. \tag{A.6}$$

This yields

$$d_t^\$ - d_{t-1}^\$ = -\frac{P_t}{Y_t} + \frac{I_t}{Y_t} - \frac{d_{t-1}^\$}{(1+\pi_t^\$)(1+g_t)}$$

$$\times \left\{ \left(\alpha \frac{s_t^e(1+e_t)}{1+s_t^e} - e_t \right) + \pi_t^\$ + g_t + \pi_t^\$ g_t \right\}. \qquad (A.7)$$

Now one can call the first term in the curly brackets the "real exchange rate contribution" to the debt accumulation (which isn't completely right because the "attenuation term" reflecting the presence of domestic denominated debt that is added to $-e_t$ in the bracket continues to involve the nominal exchange, but this is a small point). Finally, one can combine the interest effect and the U.S. inflation effect into just one "real interest rate effect," by expanding the interest term as follows:

$$\frac{I_t}{Y_t} \equiv \frac{I_t/S_t}{D_{t-1}^\$} \frac{D_{t-1}^\$}{Y_t/S_t} \equiv i_t^\$ \frac{D_{t-1}^\$(1+e)}{Y_{t-1}^\$(1+\pi_t^\$)(1+g)}, \qquad (A.8)$$

where $i_t^\$$ is the average dollar interest rate on the public debt. Substituting in (A.7) gives

$$d_t^\$ - d_{t-1}^\$ = -\frac{P_t}{Y_t} + \frac{d_{t-1}^\$}{(1+\pi_t^\$)(1+g_t)}$$

$$\times \left\{ (i_t^\$ - \pi_t^\$) - \left(\alpha \frac{s_t^e(1+e_t)}{1+s_t^e} - e_t \right) - g_t + i_t^\$ e - \pi_t^\$ g_t \right\}. \qquad (A.9)$$

So if one multiplies out the square brackets, one now has a decomposition in terms of a "real interest rate contribution," a "real exchange rate contribution," and a "real growth contribution." For emerging market countries with high shares of dollar-denominated debt (i.e., a small α) and a balance-of-payments crisis ahead of the debt crisis—implying large swings in both inflation and nominal exchange rates—this may be the neatest decomposition.

Debt Dynamics Based on a Local Currency Debt Accumulation Equation

The starting point is a local currency debt dynamics equation:

$$D_t - D_{t-1} \equiv -P_t + I_t + D_{t-1}^f S_{t-1}^{eop} \left[\frac{S_t^{eop}}{S_{t-1}^{eop}} - 1 \right]$$

$$\equiv -P_t + I_t + (1-\alpha)D_{t-1}s_t^e \qquad (A.10)$$

(using the same definition of α as before). The analogous equation to (A.2) is thus

$$\frac{D_t}{Y_t} - \frac{D_{t-1}}{Y_{t-1}} = -\frac{P_t}{Y_t} + \frac{I_t}{Y_t} + (1 - \alpha)s_t^e \frac{D_{t-1}}{Y_t} + \frac{D_{t-1}}{Y_t} - \frac{D_{t-1}}{Y_{t-1}}. \tag{A.11}$$

Using the identity

$$Y_t \equiv (1 + \pi_t)(1 + g_t)Y_{t-1} \tag{A.12}$$

to substitute Y_t in the third and fourth term on the right-hand side, this can be rewritten as

$$d_t - d_{t-1} = -\frac{P_t}{Y_t} + \frac{I_t}{Y_t} + \frac{(1 - \alpha)d_{t-1}}{(1 + \pi_t)(1 + g_t)}s_t^e$$

$$+ \frac{d_{t-1}}{(1 + \pi_t)(1 + g_t)}\{-\pi_t - g_t - \pi_t g_t\}. \tag{A.13}$$

So this is now a decomposition in terms of a primary balance effect, an interest effect, a nominal exchange rate effect, an inflation effect, and a real growth effect (plus the cross-term). Note that by using the expansion

$$\frac{I_t}{Y_t} \equiv \frac{I_t}{D_{t-1}}\frac{D_{t-1}}{Y_t} \equiv i_t \frac{D_{t-1}}{Y_{t-1}(1 + \pi_t)(1 + g)}, \tag{A.14}$$

we can also put the interest effect inside the curly bracket; that is,

$$d_t - d_{t-1} = -\frac{P_t}{Y_t} + \frac{(1 - \alpha)d_{t-1}}{(1 + \pi_t)(1 + g_t)}s_t^e$$

$$+ \frac{d_{t-1}}{(1 + \pi_t)(1 + g_t)}\{i_t - \pi_t - g_t - \pi_t g_t\}. \tag{A.15}$$

Then we could talk about a "real interest effect" (some authors call it a "growth adjusted real interest effect").

Finally, we can decompose the second term on the right-hand side into a real exchange rate depreciation and an end-of-period interest differential. This uses

$$s_t^e \equiv \frac{(1 + e_t^e)(1 + \pi_t^e)}{1 + \pi_t^{\$e}} - 1 \equiv \frac{e_t^e + \pi_t^e - \pi_t^{\$e} + e_t^e\pi_t^e}{1 + \pi_t^{\$e}}. \tag{A.16}$$

Substituting into (A.13) and rearranging gives

$$d_t - d_{t-1} = -\frac{P_t}{Y_t} + \frac{d_{t-1}}{(1+\pi_t)(1+\pi_t^{\$})(1+g_t)}$$

$$\times \{i_t - \pi_t + (1-\alpha)e_t^e - g_t + (1-\alpha)(\pi_t^e - \pi_t^{\$e}) + c\}, \quad (A.17)$$

where the cross-terms, c, are

$$c \equiv \pi_t^{\$e}(i_t - \pi_t - g_t) - (1 - \pi_t^{\$e})\pi_t g_t + (1-\alpha)e_t^e \pi_t^e. \quad (A.18)$$

Again, there are various ways of lumping together the terms in the curly brackets. For example, one could combine the inflation terms into one term, $(1-\alpha)(\pi_t^e - \pi_t^{\$e}) - \pi_t$. Note that the cross-term here is potentially much bigger than in the previous three decompositions because of the term $(1-\alpha)e_t^e \pi_t^e$, which can be large for countries with high inflation and depreciation and a lot of dollar denominated debt. Thus, this decomposition is good mainly for countries with large shares of local currency denominated debt and relatively low inflation environments.

Debt Sustainability Analysis

Debt sustainability is one of the most used and abused concepts in the recent discussions on preventing and resolving sovereign debt crises. Because debt sustainability has to do with the feasibility of paying debts over the indefinite future, coming to an agreement on when this is possible is not an easy task. Governments will claim that they can make the payments and generate the needed primary surpluses to do so, even when history or common sense tends to suggest that such primary surpluses are not attainable. The issue is further complicated by the fact that what is attainable depends on growth, interest, and real exchange rate forecasts on which governments, international financial institutions, and the markets often disagree.

Hence, assessing debt sustainability is an art rather than a science, and involves a large number of alternative methodologies. Fortunately, there is an excellent survey by Chalk and Hemming (2000) on the traditional literature and its practical application to developing countries; and several recent papers, including Diáz Alvarado, Izquierdo, and Panizza (2004), Mendoza and Oviedo (2004), and Levy-Yeyati and Sturzenegger (2006) contain overviews of developments since then. The purpose of this section is not to provide a new survey of this by now vast literature, but rather to convey three key ideas on the subject: the basic intertemporal approach, which gives a rule of thumb for evaluating sustainability if one assumes that the economy is in steady state; the link between the exchange rate and sustainability in economies that have some of their public debts denominated in foreign currency; and ways to evaluate sustainability in the face of uncertainty about future economic growth and market conditions.

The Basic Intertemporal Approach

We start again from a basic debt accumulation equation such as (A.1) or (A.10), but ignore the distinction between local currency and foreign currency debt for the time being (i.e., we assume all debt is in local currency):

$$D_{t+1} - D_t = i_{t+1}D_t - P_{t+1}, \tag{A.19}$$

where P_{t+1} is the primary surplus of period $t+1$, D_{t+1} is the total end-of-period $t+1$ public debt stock, and i_{t+1} is the period $t+1$ interest rate.[1] Dividing both sides by GDP and rearranging, as before, we obtain

$$d_{t+1} = \frac{(1+i_{t+1})}{(1+g_{t+1})}d_t - p_{t+1}, \tag{A.20}$$

where lower-case letters denote ratios-to-GDP and g_{t+1} is the GDP growth rate from period t to period $t+1$.

Substituting forward and imposing the "transversality condition" that the present value of endpoint debt as a percentage of GDP value must converge to zero, we obtain the present value budget constraint:

$$d_t = \sum_{v=0}^{\infty} R_{t+1,v} p_{t+1+v}, \tag{A.21}$$

where $R_{t+1,v} \equiv \prod_{s=0}^{v}(1+g_{t+1+s})/(1+i_{t+1+s})$. This just says that the debt stock has to equal the present value of future primary surpluses.

In what sense is (A.21) a "debt sustainability condition"? Other than imposing the transversality condition—which follows from the very basic idea that individuals holding government debt will not allow the government to run a "Ponzi game" in which debt is rolled forever, because this would be dominated by not holding any debt all—we have derived equation (A.21) using only accounting identities. Hence, the present value budget constraint is little more than an accounting identity; it tells us only that there must be consistency between today's debt stock and the projected path of primary surpluses, interest rates, and growth, but not how this consistency is to be achieved. For example, it could be achieved by adjusting the present debt stock through a restructuring, or through inflation (which raises nominal growth relative to interest rates and hence the discount factor R). Therefore, the present value budget constraint is *a condition on future required primary surpluses* only if one assumes that the government wants to avoid these "disorderly" ways of adjusting—that is, if the current debt stock as well as the path of g and i are taken as given, and not something that the government can or should mess with (except through policies that act on real growth).

However, even when this assumption is made, the present value budget constraint imposes little "discipline" in the sense that there are, of course, infinitely many primary surplus paths that will make the equation hold. Whether debt is sustainable or not boils down to the question of whether at least some of these paths are feasible, but how can one decide that? To answer this question, essentially three approaches have been suggested and applied in practice:

First, one can impose "discipline" artificially, by way of a thought experiment, by pretending that the economy is in steady state, and considering only flat primary surplus paths (this is sometimes known as *"static sustainability analysis"*). In other words, we assume that the interest rate and GDP growth rate are constant, so that equation (A.21) becomes

$$d_t = \sum_{v=0}^{\infty} \left(\frac{1+g}{1+i} \right)^{v+1} p_{t+1+v}. \tag{A.22}$$

If, in addition, we assume the primary surplus to be constant over time, we obtain

$$p = d_t \left[\frac{1+i}{1+g} - 1 \right] = d_t \left[\frac{i-g}{1+g} \right], \quad \text{assuming } 0 < \frac{1+g}{1+i} < 1. \tag{A.23}$$

Equation (A.23) gives the level of primary surplus that makes the current debt sustainable under the growth rate and interest assumptions made.[2] It can be computed very easily, and it helps us answer a well defined question: "Suppose that future growth is g and the future interest rate is i. In these circumstances, is the current primary balance sustainable in the sense that the government could run it forever and repay its debt"? The answer is yes or no, depending on whether the current balance is higher or lower than the balance indicated by equation (A.23).

Table A.2
Permanent primary surplus required to make debt sustainable (in percentage points of GDP unless otherwise stated)

Public debt to GDP	GDP growth rate (in percent)					
	1.0	2.0	3.0	4.0	5.0	6.0
35	2.1	1.7	1.4	1.0	0.7	0.3
40	2.4	2.0	1.6	1.2	0.8	0.4
45	2.7	2.2	1.7	1.3	0.9	0.4
50	3.0	2.5	1.9	1.4	1.0	0.5
55	3.3	2.7	2.1	1.6	1.0	0.5
60	3.6	2.9	2.3	1.7	1.1	0.6
65	3.9	3.2	2.5	1.9	1.2	0.6
70	4.2	3.4	2.7	2.0	1.3	0.7
75	4.5	3.7	2.9	2.2	1.4	0.7
80	4.8	3.9	3.1	2.3	1.5	0.8
85	5.0	4.2	3.3	2.5	1.6	0.8
90	5.3	4.4	3.5	2.6	1.7	0.8
95	5.6	4.7	3.7	2.7	1.8	0.9
100	5.9	4.9	3.9	2.9	1.9	0.9
110	6.5	5.4	4.3	3.2	2.1	1.0
120	7.1	5.9	4.7	3.5	2.3	1.1
130	7.7	(6.4)	5.0	3.8	(2.5)	1.2
140	8.3	6.9	5.4	4.0	2.7	1.3
150	8.9	7.4	5.8	4.3	2.9	1.4
160	9.5	7.8	6.2	4.6	3.0	1.5

Source: Calculated from equation (23), assuming $i = 7$ percent.

An example is presented in table A.2. The table assumes an annual interest rate of 7 percent but allows for different GDP growth rates and initial debt stocks. Given the expected rate of growth and the current debt to GDP ratio, the table indicates the permanent primary surplus needed for that debt to be sustainable. For example, if a country has a debt to GDP ratio of 130 percent and its expected growth rate is only 2 percent, it would need to achieve a 6.4 percent primary surplus to make the debt sustainable in this static approach. If expected growth is 5 percent, the required surplus falls to 2.5 percent. Obviously, the higher the growth rate the smaller the required primary surplus as a share of GDP.

While (A.23) is very useful as a rule of thumb, the static sustainability approach that underlies it is obviously incomplete, in a number of ways. It does not deal with possible uncertainty regarding GDP and interest rate paths, and it abstracts away from complications that arise if a portion of the debt is in foreign currency. The next two subsections will briefly deal with these issues. In addition, one implication of static sustainability analysis is that it delivers something stronger than we actually need, namely, not just a primary surplus path that will make the debt sustainable, but a primary surplus that keeps it constant at its current level. But there is no reason to assume that the current debt to GDP ratio is optimal, for many reasons, including that jumping to a higher primary surplus overnight (if the current one is not sustainable) can hardly be optimal. A further problem is that the static framework, by itself, gives us no clues on whether the "required" primary surplus is feasible or not.

In practice, the last set of problems can be dealt with in two ways. One approach is a more flexible version of the static one, in which equation (A.23) is used to calculate the required *long-run* primary surplus, while the short- and medium-run debt dynamics that might lead to that long-run are simulated, typically in a spreadsheet, assuming alternative short and medium-term paths for interest rates, growth rates, and the primary surplus. For example, one can ask the question whether the debt is sustainable under current policies (assuming a constant primary surplus) for a set of assumption of how g and i will evolve in the next few years as well as their assumed long run values. If the answer is no, one can then use the same spreadsheet-based analysis to determine whether there might be "realistic" paths for the primary surplus, based on the authorities' political and economic constraints and the way in which the country has dealt with these constraints in the past, so that it eventually reaches the long run level implied by equation (A.23) that makes the debt sustainable. This is the way in which debt sustainability analysis has traditionally been conducted by country authorities and international institutions such as the IMF (Chalk and Hemming 2000).

An alternative approach, based on Bohn (1998) has recently been applied to developing countries (IMF 2003a; Abiad and Ostry 2005). The idea is to model the primary surplus explicitly as a function of the debt stock, growth, interest rates, and perhaps other variables that can be projected for the future. Past data on these variables is used to regress primary surplus observations for the country on these determinants. The question whether debt is sustainable or not can then be answered by comparing the present value of fitted primary surpluses (conditioning on projected interest and growth paths) with the debt outstanding. The advantage of this approach is that it is much less ad hoc than the alternative previously sketched: it systematizes the historical experience which otherwise enters informally, and perhaps too judgmentally, in deciding whether a particular surplus path is realistic. The disadvantage is that it assumes that the ability of the authorities or the country to generate primary surpluses will be the same in the future as it was in the past. In particular, it assumes that exceptional fiscal performance, which is sometimes observed in the face of crises or after crises, most recently in countries such as Turkey, Brazil, and Argentina, cannot be sustained. This may be unduly pessimistic, if the crisis changes something fundamental (see Abiad and Ostry 2005 for refinements of the endogenous primary surplus approach that attempt to address this objection). Another limitation of the approach is, of course, that it continues to rely on the projected fundamentals, which are uncertain. We return to this issue later.

How Does a Devaluation Affect Debt Sustainability?

Because the currency denomination of debt may differ from that of GDP or government resources, it may be a critical determinant of the impact of devaluations on debt sustainability.[3] Ignoring the distinction between end of period and period average exchange rates, and focusing on the real exchange rate as the relative price of tradables and nontradables, the debt to GDP ratio d can be expressed as

$$d = \frac{D + eD^*}{Y + eY^*}, \tag{A.24}$$

where e is the real exchange rate (defined as the price of nontradable goods relative to tradable goods), D is debt payable in domestic currency, D^* is debt payable in foreign currency, Y is output of nontradables, and Y^* is output of tradables.

Mismatches between debt and output composition can imply a substantial impact of a real exchange rate depreciation on the debt-to-GDP ratio. At one extreme, consider the case in which all output is denominated in nontradables, and all debt is foreign denominated, that is, $d = eD^*/Y$. This is the worst-case scenario, in which a real exchange rate depreciation has the most detrimental impact on sustainability. At the other extreme, suppose $(D/eD^*)/(Y/eY^*) = 1$, so that the composition of debt and output is perfectly matched. In that case, a depreciation has no effect on debt ratios. Table A.3, taken from Calvo, Izquierdo, and Talvi (2003) shows how some Latin American countries

Table A.3
Public-sector debt currency mismatches

	Argentina	Ecuador	Colombia	Brazil	Chile
D/eD^*	0.08	0.02	0.59	1.76	1.30
Y/eY^*	8.63	2.94	6.36	12.34	2.85
$(D/eD^*)/(Y/eY^*)$	0.01	0.00	0.09	0.14	0.45

Source: Calvo et al. (2002), table 6. Values for 1998.

Table A.4
Fiscal sustainability after a 50 percent real exchange rate depreciation (in percent of GDP unless otherwise stated)

	Argentina	Brazil	Chile	Colombia	Ecuador
Real interest rate (percent)	7.1	5.8	5.9	7.3	6.3
Real GDP growth (percent)	3.8	2.0	7.5	3.6	2.6
Actual public debt	36.5	51.0	17.3	28.4	81.0
Required primary surplus	1.2	1.9	...[a]	1.0	2.9
With 50 percent depreciation					
Imputed public debt	50.8	58.1	18.7	34.9	107.2
Required primary surplus	1.6	2.2	n.a.	1.2	3.9

Source: Calvo et al. (2002). Values refer to 1998.
[a] Real interest rate smaller than real GDP growth, so sustainability is not a concern.

ranked in terms of their mismatch at the time of the Russian crisis. A value of 1 in the last line of the table indicates a perfect match between the share of foreign debt in total debt and the share of tradables in GDP. The table shows that the highest mismatches existed for Ecuador and Argentina, the second most closed economy in the group, with a very high proportion of dollar debt. On the other side of the spectrum lies Chile, with a value of 0.45.

Consider now the effects of a depreciation of the real exchange rate of 50 percent. Argentina and Ecuador would be the hardest hit. Focusing only on the relative price adjustment—that is, assuming that interest rates on public debt and GDP growth remain unchanged—Argentina's debt-to-GDP ratio jumps from 36.5 percent of GDP to 50.8 percent. Quite a different scenario plays out for Chile, where the debt revaluation effect is minimal: public sector debt as a share of GDP increases from 17.3 percent to 18.7 percent. The increase in the required primary surplus is shown in table A.4, also taken from Calvo, Izquierdo, and Talvi (2003).

While this analysis suggests that devaluations can be a big problem for debt sustainability—the more so, the more mismatched the debt structure—it is also true, however, that in most of the cases studied in this book, large devaluations did not prevent the debt to GDP ratios from coming down very quickly after the default. Many, or most, of the mismatched countries appear to have reestablished sustainability in the postdefault phase. This occurred in spite of the fact that in most cases—Argentina being the notable exception—the debt restructurings themselves did not, in fact, play a very big role in reducing debt-to-GDP ratios,[4] or indeed in providing much debt relief in present value terms (chapter 11). What made the difference in lowering debt ratios in most cases were impressive improvements in the primary balance, combined with real appreciations, and in some cases high growth.

The fact that most devaluations and defaults were followed by large real appreciations suggests that the exchange rate had overshot, which means that the effect of devaluations on debt sustainability is to some degree self-correcting—of course, only after a possibly very costly crisis. In addition, the striking increases that are often observed in the primary surplus in the aftermath of a crisis points to another factor that has to be taken into account when considering the effect of devaluations on debt sustainability: the fact that the devaluation may have a positive impact on the feasible primary surplus. One reason for this is already internalized in the preceding analysis, namely, that a certain fraction of GDP, and hence tax revenues, are foreign currency linked. But there is an important additional consideration: the fact that the main liability of governments is not explicit debt but spending promises, most of which, particularly wages and pensions, are quoted in domestic currency. Thus, as long as wages and pensions lag behind prices and the exchange rate, there is an automatic improvement in the primary surplus as a result of the devaluation.

Hence, to obtain a complete sense of the effects of devaluation on fiscal sustainability, one needs to compare the effect of the devaluation on debt ratios with the effect of a devaluation on primary surpluses. The elasticity of the primary surplus relative to a devaluation will be higher, the higher the wage bill in government spending and the smaller the wage pass-through (i.e., the change in local wages after a devaluation). The recent experience in Latin America and other crisis countries, where pass through has been quite limited, suggests that there is significant scope for a positive sustainability effect through this channel.

Dealing with Uncertainty

From the preceding discussion, it is clear that projected paths of output, interest rates, real exchange rates, as well as any (additional) determinant of the primary surplus will be critical for debt sustainability. But most of these variables are highly uncertain. How can one sensibly deal with this uncertainty? This is an area in which research has exploded in recent years.

As in the case of deciding what a "reasonable" primary surplus projection means, two broad approaches have been applied in practice. One approach, popular among practitioners, is to submit particular debt sustainability scenarios to "stress tests," which assume different paths of the critical variables in response to domestic and external shocks. Hence, these stress tests answer the question whether the debt is still sustainable if, say, there is a sharp rise in international interest rates, negative terms of trade shock, a slowdown in growth, and so forth. In order to decide what "reasonable" shocks are, and whether they should be assumed to be permanent or transitory, one can calibrate shocks based on the stochastic behavior of the relevant variables in the past (IMF 2005c).

Though this approach is useful in giving a sense of the sensitivity of the debt sustainability analysis to a range of plausible scenarios, it would be, of course, more satisfactory to capture the effects of a whole distribution of shocks that can hit the economy, rather than that of a "typical" shock. Moreover, the stress test approach disregards correlations among shocks, and the *joint* dynamic response of the variables that might be relevant for the debt dynamics. In response, a number of authors (Ferrucci and Penalver 2003; Garcia and Rigobón 2004; Mendoza and Oviedo 2004; Celasun, Debrun, and Ostry 2006; Levy-Yeyati and Sturzenegger 2006) have recently attempted to estimate the variance-covariance structure of the relevant shocks, and used these estimates to generate probabilistic forecasts of the debt dynamics.[5] These forecasts can then be used to generate probabilities that the debt to GDP ratios will fall below its current level, or that it will rise beyond a specified threshold.

The methods applied in these papers differ, in particular, with respect to the way in government behavior is modeled, if at all, with respect to the estimation, and the presentation of the results. However, several papers seem to share a basic approach, namely, to estimate a vector autoregression in the main variables determining the debt dynamics, to treat fiscal policy as endogenous (either by including the primary balance in the vector autoregression, or by separately estimating a policy reaction function), and to use Monte Carlo simulations to generate probability distributions for the debt-to-GDP ratio in the future. The results can be presented in highly intuitive ways; for example, Celasun, Debrun, and Ostry (2006) use "fan-charts" familiar from inflation forecasting to illustrate the likely path of debt-to-GDP, and Garcia and Rigobón (2004) use their framework to generate impulse responses that show the trajectory of the debt-to-GDP ratio in response to a variety of shocks—in the spirit of "stress tests," but much better founded. Hence, in this sense, the new approaches encompass the more traditional approaches, and we would imagine that they will gradually replace them in applied work.

Estimating the Probability of Default Based on a Fixed Recovery Value

Estimation Based on Sovereign Spreads

If one is willing to make an assumption about the share of principal that can be recovered in the event of default (see next section), it is fairly easy to "back out" the probability that the market assigns to a default from observed bond prices. To start with the simplest case, consider a sovereign bond that matures in one period.[6] Assuming risk neutrality, the expected return on the sovereign bond should equal the rate of return of a risk-free asset:

$$(1 - \pi)(1 + i) + \pi R = (1 + r), \tag{A.25}$$

where π refers to the implicit probability of default, i denotes the yield on the sovereign bond, R the recovery value of the bond in the event of default, and r the yield on a U.S. treasury bond (or other risk-free asset) with identical maturity and liquidity as that of the sovereign bond. Hence, the implied probability of default during the life of the bond is

$$\pi = \frac{S(1 + r)}{S(1 + r) + (1 + r - R)}, \tag{A.26}$$

where $S \equiv (1 + i)/(1 + r) - 1 = (i - r)/(1 + r)$ denotes the interest spread of the risky bond over the risk-free one.[7]

Using equation (A.26), the implied default probability can be read off spreads and international interest rates, conditioning on an assumption

about the expected recovery. The higher spread, the higher the probability of default conditioning on R.

The simple formula (A.26) applies only to the special case of a bond
that pays all its interest (if any) at the end of its life. However, with an
extra assumption, it is not hard to derive an analogous formula for a
multiperiod coupon bond. The assumption that keeps things tractable
is that the risk of default is evenly distributed over the life of the bond.
Specifically, assume a multiperiod bond with a constant probability of
default that we will model as a Poisson process with parameter λ (i.e.,
with a constant probability of default in every instant). The probability
of no default from time zero until time t is $e^{-\lambda t}$. The probability of default over one period is hence $(1 - e^{-\lambda})$, which is approximately λ
when λ is not too large.

Under the assumption of recovery value R for one dollar of principal, the market price of a bond paying annual coupon C should be

$$P = \sum_{i=1}^{n} C \frac{1}{(1+r)^i} e^{-i\lambda} + \frac{1}{(1+r)^n} e^{-n\lambda} + R \sum_{i=1}^{n} \frac{1}{(1+r)^i} [e^{-(i-1)\lambda} - e^{i\lambda}]$$

$$= \sum_{i=1}^{n} C \frac{1}{(1+r)^i} \frac{1}{(1+\Lambda)^i} + \frac{1}{(1+r)^n} \frac{1}{(1+\Lambda)^n} + R \sum_{i=1}^{n} \frac{1}{(1+r)^i} \frac{\Lambda}{(1+\Lambda)^i},$$

where $\Lambda = e^\lambda - 1$. $1/(1+\Lambda)^i$ is thus the probability of no default and
$\Lambda/(1+\Lambda)^i$ the probability of default between time 0 and time i.

Now consider a par floater paying an annual coupon of $1+i =
r + S + rS$. Then the price of the par floater is

$$1 = \sum_{i=1}^{n} (r + S + rS) \frac{1}{(1+r)^i} \frac{1}{(1+\Lambda)^i} + \frac{1}{(1+r)^n} \frac{1}{(1+\Lambda)^n}$$

$$+ R \sum_{i=1}^{n} \frac{1}{(1+r)^i} \frac{\Lambda}{(1+\Lambda)^i}$$

$$1 = \frac{\overbrace{\sum_{i=1}^{n} (r + \Lambda + r\Lambda) \frac{1}{(1+r)^i} \frac{1}{(1+\Lambda)^i} + \frac{1}{(1+r)^n} \frac{1}{(1+\Lambda)^n}}^{= 1}}{}$$

$$+ (S + rS - \Lambda + R\Lambda - r\Lambda) \sum_{i=1}^{n} \frac{1}{(1+r)^i} \frac{1}{(1+\Lambda)^i}.$$

Subtracting 1 on both sides, we obtain the coupon spread

$$S(1+r) = \Lambda(1-R+r)$$

which gives, once again, an implicit probability of default:

$$\pi = \frac{\Lambda}{1+\Lambda} = \frac{S(1+r)}{S(1+r) + (1+r-R)}. \qquad (A.27)$$

Table A.5 presents the implicit default probabilities using equation (A.27) for different assumptions regarding recovery values and spreads, given a risk-free interest rate of 7 percent. For example, the table indicates that for a recovery value of 50 percent and a spread of 350 basis points the market is assigning a 6.2 probability of default over the upcoming year.[8] The probabilities of default increase as we move to the right in the table. Higher recovery values for a *given* spread can only be rationalized if there is a higher probability of default. Likewise, the higher are the spreads, the higher the probability of default.

Using Credit Default Swaps to Estimate Default Probabilities

A credit default swap (CDS) is an insurance contract in which the seller (the insurance provider) promises to make the buyer whole in the event of default (or another well-defined "credit event") by covering the *loss to par*.[9] Within thirty days of the default, the buyer delivers a (defaulted) bond and receives the par value (say, $100) in exchange. Hence, the transfer to the buyer at the time of default equals the difference between the par value and the price of the cheapest (foreign currency denominated) bond that the buyer can find to deliver to the seller. If one makes an assumption about the price of that bond—that is, about the recovery value at the time of default—it is thus possible to back out the probability of default from observed CDS spreads (i.e., the "premium" charged to the buyer), much as one can back out default probabilities from observed bond spreads. The advantage of using CDS spreads is that CDS contracts over relatively short horizons (say, one year or six months) may be more liquid than markets with bonds of similar horizons, so that default probabilities can be inferred from CDS spreads without either using relatively illiquid instruments or making assumptions about the distribution of default risk over the life of longer bonds.

The one period risk premium on a CDS must be equal to the expected transfer that the buyer stands to receive in the event of

Table A.5
Implicit probabilities of default as a function of recovery value and spreads (in percent)

Spread (in basis points)	Recovery value (as a percent of principal)[a]								
	10	20	30	40	50	60	70	80	90
50	0.5	0.6	0.7	0.8	0.9	1.1	1.4	1.9	3.1
100	1.1	1.2	1.4	1.6	1.8	2.2	2.8	3.8	5.9
150	1.6	1.8	2.0	2.3	2.7	3.3	4.2	5.6	8.6
200	2.2	2.4	2.7	3.1	3.6	4.4	5.5	7.3	11.2
250	2.7	3.0	3.4	3.8	4.5	5.4	6.7	9.0	13.6
300	3.2	3.6	4.0	4.6	5.3	6.4	8.0	10.6	15.9
350	3.7	4.1	4.6	5.3	6.2	7.4	9.2	12.2	18.1
400	4.2	4.7	5.3	6.0	7.0	8.3	10.4	13.7	20.1
450	4.7	5.2	5.9	6.7	7.8	9.3	11.5	15.1	22.1
500	5.2	5.8	6.5	7.4	8.6	10.2	12.6	16.5	23.9
550	5.7	6.3	7.1	8.1	9.4	11.1	13.7	17.9	25.7
600	6.2	6.9	7.7	8.7	10.1	12.0	14.8	19.2	27.4
650	6.7	7.4	8.3	9.4	10.9	12.9	15.8	20.5	29.0
700	7.2	7.9	8.9	10.1	11.6	13.7	16.8	21.7	30.6
750	7.6	8.4	9.4	10.7	12.3	14.6	17.8	22.9	32.1
800	8.1	9.0	10.0	11.3	13.1	15.4	18.8	24.1	33.5
850	8.6	9.5	10.6	12.0	13.8	16.2	19.7	25.2	34.9
900	9.0	10.0	11.1	12.6	14.5	17.0	20.7	26.3	36.2
950	9.5	10.5	11.7	13.2	15.1	17.8	21.6	27.4	37.4
1000	9.9	11.0	12.2	13.8	15.8	18.5	22.4	28.4	38.6
1050	10.4	11.4	12.7	14.4	16.5	19.3	23.3	29.4	39.8
1100	10.8	11.9	13.3	14.9	17.1	20.0	24.1	30.4	40.9
1150	11.3	12.4	13.8	15.5	17.8	20.7	25.0	31.3	42.0
1200	11.7	12.9	14.3	16.1	18.4	21.5	25.8	32.2	43.0
1250	12.1	13.3	14.8	16.6	19.0	22.2	26.6	33.1	44.0
1300	12.5	13.8	15.3	17.2	19.6	22.8	27.3	34.0	45.0
1350	13.0	14.2	15.8	17.7	20.2	23.5	28.1	34.9	45.9
1400	13.4	14.7	16.3	18.3	20.8	24.2	28.8	35.7	46.8
1450	13.8	15.1	16.8	18.8	21.4	24.8	29.5	36.5	47.7
1500	14.2	15.6	17.2	19.3	22.0	25.5	30.3	37.3	48.6
1550	14.6	16.0	17.7	19.8	22.5	26.1	31.0	38.1	49.4
1600	15.0	16.4	18.2	20.4	23.1	26.7	31.6	38.8	50.2
1650	15.4	16.9	18.7	20.9	23.6	27.3	32.3	39.5	50.9
1700	15.8	17.3	19.1	21.4	24.2	27.9	33.0	40.3	51.7
1750	16.2	17.7	19.6	21.8	24.7	28.5	33.6	41.0	52.4
1800	16.6	18.1	20.0	22.3	25.3	29.1	34.2	41.6	53.1
1850	16.9	18.5	20.5	22.8	25.8	29.6	34.9	42.3	53.8
1900	17.3	18.9	20.9	23.3	26.3	30.2	35.5	43.0	54.5

Table A.5
(continued)

Spread (in basis points)	Recovery value (as a percent of principal)								
	10	20	30	40	50	60	70	80	90
1950	17.7	19.3	21.3	23.7	26.8	30.7	36.1	43.6	55.1
2000	18.1	19.7	21.7	24.2	27.3	31.3	36.6	44.2	55.7
2500	21.6	23.5	25.8	28.5	31.9	36.3	42.0	49.8	61.1
3000	24.9	27.0	29.4	32.4	36.0	40.6	46.5	54.3	65.4
3500	27.9	30.1	32.7	35.9	39.7	44.3	50.3	58.1	68.8
4000	30.6	33.0	35.7	39.0	42.9	47.7	53.6	61.3	71.6
4500	33.2	35.6	38.5	41.8	45.8	50.6	56.5	64.1	73.9
5000	35.5	38.1	41.0	44.4	48.4	53.2	59.1	66.5	75.9
5500	37.8	40.3	43.3	46.8	50.8	55.6	61.4	68.5	77.6
6000	39.8	42.5	45.5	48.9	53.0	57.7	63.4	70.4	79.1

Source: Computations based on equation (4).
[a] Assuming a risk-free interest rate of 7 percent.

default times the probability of that event.[10] Let R stand for the expected price of the cheapest to deliver bond, and π, as before, for the default probability. Then[11]

$$\pi(100 - R) = \text{premium}. \tag{A.28}$$

Consider an example. Since credit default swaps are quoted on an annual basis, a spread of 1600 basis points implies an "insurance premium" of $16 for twelve months per $100 of bond insured. Assume the bond price in the aftermath of default is $20. The implicit probability of default, over the one-year time frame, would then be

$$\pi = \frac{\text{premium}}{(100 - R)} = \frac{16}{100 - 20} = 0.2. \tag{A.29}$$

Finally, a word of warning. We have so far confined the discussion to showing how to "back out" default probabilities from market variables for given assumptions about recovery values. In reality, of course, markets form views on both default probabilities and recovery values, and revise *both* in response to new information. Hence, changes in default probabilities and expected recovery values should be correlated, because they are driven by related fundamentals. For example, overborrowing by a sovereign will both make a crisis more likely, and lower the expected recovery value for each unit of face value issued, because more creditors have to share a limited "pie." Hence, when observing a sharp increase in CDS spreads or bond spreads, it is generally incorrect to evaluate the default probability implied by the higher spreads using the same recovery value assumption as before (see Singh 2003; Singh and Andritzki 2005 for a criticism of market practice along these lines). Rather, recovery value assumptions need to be revisited along with the recomputation of the implicit default probability. Put differently, it makes more sense—though it is, in practice, much more difficult—to estimate default probabilities and expected recovery values *jointly* based on market data, than to assume one in order to derive the other. This is a subject to which we now briefly turn.

Estimating Recovery Values

One possible guide for assumptions about default recovery values are estimates from the U.S. corporate bond market, where large amounts of evidence about past defaults make the task of estimating recovery values much easier. Table A.6 shows historical recovery rates for this market taken from Jarrow, Lando, and Turnbull (1997). As can be seen, recovery rates increase with the seniority of the debt. The weighted average recovery rate for U.S. corporates is 39 percent.

In the context of sovereign bonds, two approaches have been used to estimate actual or expected recovery values. As mentioned earlier, one approach is to estimate recovery values implicit in bond prices, after imposing an identifying condition that allow one to separate default probabilities and recovery values. Merrick (2001) uses the information provided by that fact that bonds sometimes include cross-default clauses (thus having the *same* default probability) to achieve this identification. He finds that for the Russian default, recovery values were substantially lower than those of U.S. corporates, while recovery values implicit in Argentine bonds during the 1998 Russian crisis remained high and similar to a senior unsecured U.S. corporate. Sosa Navarro (2002), using a similar framework, estimates recovery values for Argentina in 2001 using data right up to the crisis. By then, expected recovery values had fallen considerably, to just over 20 percent. Andritzky (2005) disentangles default probabilities and expected recovery values for Argentina over the 2000–2002 period, using the assumption that bonds receive equal compensation after a default, and finds broadly similar results.

An alternative approach is to compute ex post realized recovery values from the treatment that bondholders actually receive in debt

Table A.6
Recovery values in previous restructurings (in percent)

Study	Issuer	Instrument or time period	Estimate (mean)	Standard dev.
Jarrow et al. (1997)	U.S. corporates 74–91	Senior secured	67.1	
		Senior unsecured	46.5	
		Senior subordinated	32.1	
		Subordinated	26.4	
		Junior subordinated	18.0	
Merrick (1999)	Russian Eurobond	Pre-GKO default 07/23/1998–04/12/1998	27.3	
		Post-GKO default 08/17/1998–12/14/1998	10.3	
	Argentina	Pre-GKO default 07/23/1998–08/14/1998	51.2	
		Post-GKO default 08/17/1998–12/14/1998	49.3	
Sosa Navarro (2002)	Argentina	12/10/01–12/20/01	21.7	
		Post-default: 12/21/01	20.8	
Andritzky (2005)	Argentina	Mid-2000–mid-2001	40–50	
		July 2001–October 2001	30–40	
		December 2001–April 2002	20–30	
Sturzenegger and Zettelmeyer (2005)	Russia	GKO/OFZs-residents (3/99)	54.3	4.5
		GKO/OFZs-nonresidents (3/99)	38.5	3.2
		MinFin3 (2/00)	39.0	…
		Prins/IANs (8/00)	30.8	0.7
	Ukraine	OVDPs-residents (8/98)	81.8	12.6
		OVDPs-nonresidents (9/98)	40.8	1.9
		Chase Loan (10/98)	69.3	…
		ING Loan (8/99)	62.0	…
		International bonds (4/00)	59.9	9.2
	Pakistan	Eurobonds (12/99)	69.6	1.9
	Ecuador	International bonds (8/00)	40.0	7.3
	Argentina	Phase 1 (residents) (11/01)	41.9	9.4
		Pesification (2/02)	41.2	12.5
		2005 International (3/05)	33.0	9.1
	Uruguay	External (5/03)	73.8	7.8
		Domestic (5/03)	63.8	8.8
	Dominican Republic	International bonds (5/05)	101.0	4.1

restructurings. This is the approach we have taken in this volume when presenting "haircut" estimates, namely, estimates of investor losses during crises. Conceptually, the difference between these haircut estimates and the "haircut" implicit in recovery values is that the latter refers to the face value of the original bond, while we quote haircuts as a percent of the net present value of the original bond, evaluated at post-restructuring yields. However, recovery values that are analogous to those estimated by the previous literature can, of course, be inferred from the same data, and we present averages and standard deviations of these values in table A.6, where the standard deviations refer to the cross-section of original bonds tendered at the various exchanges (see Sturzenegger and Zettelmeyer 2005 for details).

There are two main insights from table A.6. First, on average, realized recovery values in sovereign bonds restructurings have been higher than those in corporate restructurings, with median recovery rates in the 40–70 percent range. This corresponds to *senior* corporate debt, and is much higher than the benchmark 20 percent recovery rate that is reportedly often assumed in CDS pricing (Singh and Andritzki 2005). Second, there are very large variations across default episodes. The lowest ex post recovery rates for foreign currency debt, in Russia and Argentina, were about 30 percent. The highest recovery rates, among the involuntary exchanges, were obtained in Uruguay, at close to 75 percent, followed by Pakistan (the Dominican Republic, by this measure, should no longer be regarded as an involuntary exchange). Hence, these realized recovery rates do not offer all that much guidance in making recovery rate assumptions, other than that 30 percent appears a conservative assumption, and median recovery rates have in fact been higher.

In view of the large variation in observed realized recovery rates, one would ideally want to forecast recovery rates by modeling realized recovery rates in terms of economic and political fundamentals, and computing fitted recovery rates based on current and projected fundamentals for each risky borrower. However, the sample of realized recovery rates that we have compiled is so far too small for a regression exercise along these lines. Nevertheless, the results in table A.6 seem to support the common sense idea that recovery values were lower, the higher the initial debt burden, namely, the larger the reduction in the debt that was required to regain sustainability.[12] On that basis, maximal recovery values could be forecast by assuming that the debt write down will be at least as large as is required to regain sustainability.

The results of such an exercise, of course, depend on the debt sustainability approach that is applied. For illustrative purposes, consider the simplest static approach, assume a long-term growth rate of 3 percent, an average interest rate of 10 percent, and a long-term primary surplus of 3 percent. Using (23), the maximum sustainable level as a share of GDP is

$$d_t = p \left[\frac{1+g}{i-g} \right] = 3 \left[\frac{1.03}{0.07} \right] = 44 \text{ percent.}$$

Inspired by the example of Argentina, assume that the postdefault debt-to-GDP ratio is 130 percent. Hence, if the debt restructuring lowers the debt to the maximum sustainable level, the recovery value in this example would have been 44/130 = 34 percent. This happens to coincide roughly with the average realized recovery value in the case of Argentina's external debt.

Estimating the Interest Cost Impact of Debt Restructurings

A debt restructuring has obvious implications on the interest costs of the government, through at least three channels. First, it leads to a lower net debt burden, and hence lower debt servicing cost on the outstanding debt. Second, it improves solvency, lowering risk premia through that effect. Third, there may be a reputation effect that increases future interest costs. The last two effects, which run in opposite directions, will, of course, impact the government only after it starts refinancing its existing debt. What is the likely combined impact of these effects on financing costs? Could the net effect be to increase the government's interest bill going forward? If so, the restructuring would have been counterproductive from a solvency perspective (though it might still have been justified from a liquidity perspective).[13]

One way to approach this question is through a model of equilibrium spreads, for example, as estimated by Ades et al. (2000). In that model, spreads are estimated to relate to both debt levels as well as default history. According to that model each percentage point reduction in the debt-to-GDP level implies a reduction of 7 basis points in spreads. On the other hand, the same model estimates a reputation cost to be equal to 165 basis points, as identified by a restructuring dummy in the model, though our discussion of chapter 1 indicates that this may be a relatively high estimate.[14] As a restructuring also reduces the total amount of debt, the net effect is ambiguous.

Table A.7
Change in debt service costs after a restructuring (in percent of GDP unless otherwise stated)

Debt reduction assumption (in percent of the original debt stock)

Original debt stock	0 Debt rollovers (in percent per year)			10 Debt rollovers (in percent per year)			20 Debt rollovers (in percent per year)			30 Debt rollovers (in percent per year)			40 Debt rollovers (in percent per year)		
	50	25	12.5	50	25	12.5	50	25	12.5	50	25	12.5	50	25	12.5
30	4.7	4.3	3.6	0.7	0.4	-0.1	-3.2	-3.4	-3.8	-7.0	-7.1	-7.4	-10.6	-10.7	-10.9
40	6.3	5.8	4.8	0.7	0.3	-0.4	-4.6	-5.0	-5.4	-9.8	-10.0	-10.3	-14.8	-14.9	-15.1
50	7.9	7.2	6.1	0.6	0.1	-0.7	-6.3	-6.7	-7.2	-13.0	-13.2	-13.5	-19.3	-19.3	-19.4
60	9.4	8.6	7.3	0.3	-0.2	-1.1	-8.2	-8.6	-9.1	-16.4	-16.6	-16.8	-24.1	-24.1	-24.1
70	11.0	10.1	8.5	0.0	-0.6	-1.6	-10.3	-10.7	-11.2	-20.2	-20.2	-20.4	-29.2	-29.1	-29.0
80	12.6	11.5	9.7	-0.5	-1.2	-2.2	-12.7	-13.0	-13.5	-24.2	-24.1	-24.1	-34.7	-34.5	-34.1
90	14.2	12.9	10.9	-1.1	-1.8	-2.9	-15.3	-15.6	-15.9	-28.4	-28.3	-28.1	-40.5	-40.1	-39.4
100	15.8	14.4	12.1	-1.8	-2.5	-3.7	-18.1	-18.3	-18.5	-33.0	-32.7	-32.3	-46.6	-46.0	-45.1
110	17.3	15.8	13.3	-2.7	-3.4	-4.6	-21.1	-21.2	-21.3	-37.9	-37.4	-36.7	-53.0	-52.2	-50.9
120	18.9	17.3	14.5	-3.6	-4.4	-5.6	-24.4	-24.3	-24.2	-43.0	-42.4	-41.4	-59.8	-58.7	-57.0
130	20.5	18.7	15.7	-4.7	-5.5	-6.6	-27.9	-27.5	-27.3	-48.4	-47.6	-46.2	-66.8	-65.5	-63.4
140	22.1	20.1	16.9	-5.9	-6.6	-7.8	-31.7	-31.0	-30.5	-54.1	-53.0	-51.3	-74.2	-72.6	-70.0
150	23.6	21.6	18.2	-7.3	-7.9	-9.1	-35.7	-34.7	-34.0	-60.0	-58.7	-56.6	-81.9	-80.0	-76.8

Note: Changes in NPV of debt service costs, using a 10 percent discount rate, and based on the interest rate changes described in the text.

Summarizing the three effects, the financial impact of a restructuring is the NPV of the change in debt payments:

Change in debt payments (% of GDP)

$$= -\sum_{t=0}^{\infty}\left(\frac{1}{1+r^*}\right)^t (r_t^{before} d_t^{before} - r_t^{after} d_t^{after}).$$

The interpretation of the formula is very simple: it just compares the stream of payments before and after default. The Ades et al. (2000) specification allows comparing the *before* and *after* borrowing cost using the following formula (in basis points):

$$r^{after} = r^{before} + 165 - 7 * (\text{debt reduction in percent of GDP}).$$

Table A.7 shows our estimates for the change in debt service costs using this formula. All values are computed as present discounted values at the arbitrary rate of 10 percent and expressed as percentages of GDP. The table is computed for several restructuring scenarios and several maturity assumptions for the debt. If 50 percent of the debt has to be refinanced each year, debt structure is shorter and the change in costs kicks in quickly. In the case that only 12.5 percent has to be refinanced each year, the costs change more slowly. The table shows that for the assumed parameters, and in spite of the relatively large assumed reputation cost, the three effects combine to reduce debt service costs, except in cases when the debt reduction is very small (less than 20 percent).

Notes

1 Sovereign Defaults and Debt Restructurings: Historical Overview

1. Because we are interested in these episodes as antecedents of the most recent set of sovereign debt crises studied in chapters 4–10 of this book, we focus on crises and restructurings involving sovereign, privately held debt. See Rieffel (2003) and Marichal (1989) for accounts involving broader definitions of debt crises and defaults (including defaults involving official lenders, and subnational defaults).

2. This is true even if repeated debt rescheduling agreements with the same country in the 1980s are excluded (including such rescheduling results in over two hundred commercial debt restructuring deals since the 1970s alone; see World Bank 2002, appendix II; Rieffel 2003, 104).

3. As is standard, we reserve the expression "repudiation" for defaults that clearly reflect unwillingness to pay, even though the means to service debt were available.

4. To these, one might add an ongoing boom that began in 2003; see IMF (2005d).

5. Eichengreen and Portes (1989) report that by the 1930s, the miscellaneous members also included representatives of the Association of Investment Trusts, the British Insurance Association, the Bank of England, and the stock exchange.

6. Until about 1950, the concept of sovereign immunity was interpreted much more broadly than it is today (see chapter 3). This said, there were cases in which individual bondholders challenged a deal reached by the CFB in U.K. courts, usually on the grounds of different treatment compared to other bondholders (Mauro, Sussman, and Yafeh 2006). These suits were directed against the CFB rather than the debtor.

7. As explained by Rieffel (2003), the origin of the term could be that the first BACs in the late 1970s met in London; however, Paris and, especially, New York were also venues for negotiations in the 1980s.

8. For example, Beim and Calomiris (2001) report that the "fair market value" of Mexico's discount bond was about 51 cents on each dollar of face value of the new debt, while the corresponding value of the par bond was about 37 cents. Hence, the value offered to investors for each dollar of old debt was about 33 cents (0.65 times 0.51) and 37 cents, respectively. Assuming that the present value of the old claim was $1 on the dollar (this loan had already come due), this means that the present value loss suffered

by the banks was about 65 percent—much higher than the 35 percent discount in face value.

9. This was also the case in Argentina's 2001 Phase I restructuring of international bonds aimed mostly at domestic bondholders.

2   The Economics of Sovereign Debt and Debt Crises: A Primer

1. Several excellent surveys exist, including Eaton and Fernandez (1995), Kletzer (1994), and Obstfeld and Rogoff (1996, chap. 6).

2. Eaton and Gersovitz allow for retaliation through direct punishment in addition to exclusion from future credit. However, direct punishments are not necessary to sustain sovereign debt in their model.

3. In Eaton and Gersovitz's model, the insurance motive comes through concavity in the utility function, that is, risk aversion: the country prefers smooth consumption to choppy consumption. This is the way in which international borrowing has usually been motivated in the literature, but it is not the only way; for example, one could assume linear utilities and concavity in *production*, together with the assumption that production requires capital (Cole and Kehoe 1998; Wright 2004). What these stories have in common is that they generate potential gains from trade between borrowers and lenders *that go on forever*. While there may be other motives for borrowing that do not have this property— for example, impatience to consume, or acceleration of capital accumulation—these can generally not be exploited to enforce repayment (Eaton, Gersovitz, and Stiglitz 1986, 491). The reason is that they imply a point in time after which the motive for borrowing disappears (e.g., because the capital stock has been built up to the point where the marginal return to capital equals the international interest rate). At that point—call it T—the country does not care about capital market access any more, and will default. Anticipating that point, lenders will refuse new lending at $T - 1$. This takes away the incentive to repay at $T - 1$, which in turn leads lenders to refuse new lending at $T - 2$, and so forth.

4. In addition, there is little empirical justification for this assumption.

5. These three approaches do not encompass all avenues that have been suggested to overcome the Bulow-Rogoff objection. One additional approach involves "bubbles" in supporting debt (see Hellwig and Lorenzoni 2003, among others). The basic idea is that defaulting and depositing the repayment does not make sense if the interest rate on debt is low enough—namely, less than the (debtor country) growth rate. Creditors may be willing to hold debt at such a low rate of return if it provides the holder with liquidity. While there are examples where this is the case—for example, sight deposits, or highly liquid T-bills issued by industrial countries such as the United States—we find it difficult to relate this idea to emerging market debt, which generally involves a higher interest than the growth rate.

6. Alternatively, the presence of multiple *borrowers* might create an incentive for bank collusion, as banks can gain by cooperating in punishing each others' defaulting borrowers, and punish banks that defect from this cooperative arrangement by offering the defector's debtor a deposit contract that induces it to default.

7. See Gul and Pesendorfer (2004) for a result that relies on the same intuition—namely, that saving cannot replace borrowing for consumption smoothing purposes if the debtor has a self-control problem—but involves a different characterization of the self-control problem.

8. Since this is a finite horizon game, default and exclusion from credit markets constitute the unique subgame perfect equilibrium after a borrower has been identified as belonging to the "bad" type, so renegotiation is not an issue.

9. If cash-in-advance contracts are possible, then "bad" governments will be tempted to occasionally default and save. If this goes on for sufficiently long time periods, lenders will eventually become convinced that the government is indeed "bad." In the limit for $T \to \infty$, no borrowing can be sustained.

10. There is also a question as to why external creditors would want to lend to countries that overborrow, but that is easier to answer: for the reasons later explained, governments may borrow amounts that could be socially too high from a debtor country perspective, but still below their credit ceiling. In competitive credit markets, creditors will be compensated for the additional risk through higher borrowing spreads.

11. The problem is mostly lack of good data on liability dollarization for the economy as a whole. Recently, however, some studies have started using the foreign liabilities of the domestic financial sector as a proxy, which is available for many countries. Using this measure, Calvo, Izquierdo, and Mejía (2004), find that liability dollarization is a strong predictor of "sudden stops" (sudden net capital outflows). These could, in turn, trigger a debt crisis, but this link is not made explicit in the paper.

12. For example, high volatility of macroeconomic variables could mean that "solvency shocks" triggering default become more likely, but also that countries have a greater incentive to repay, as a volatile country is more dependent on foreign borrowing to smooth its consumption (Eaton and Gersovitz 1981). A recent paper by Catão and Sutton (2002) shows that the "solvency effect" outweighs any "willingness-to-pay" effect.

13. This has led the IMF and IDA (2004) to propose that "sustainable thresholds" of debt-to-GDP (or debt-to-export ratios) in low-income countries be defined in relation to their institutional quality: countries with good institutions can "afford" more debt.

14. They also find a much higher interest penalty (about 500 basis points) for countries that manage to reaccess international capital markets while still in default. Hence, it is fair to summarize the evidence as suggesting that prior to reaching a settlement with their creditors, defaulting debtors either cannot access capital markets at all or only at very high costs.

15. A useful comparison in this regard is between the crises in Argentina (2002) (currency crisis and default) and Brazil (1999) (currency crisis but no default). The capital account reversal was much worse in Argentina. In Brazil, debt flows collapsed, but FDI held steady and even increased. In Argentina, both debt flows and FDI collapsed, in spite of the fact FDI was not directly affected by the default.

16. The link between *currency* and banking crises has received much more attention; see Kaminsky and Reinhart (1999), Barro (2001), and Burnside, Eichenbaum, and Rebelo (2001, 2004).

17. Because most restructurings covered in this book are too recent to enter the sample, the results are mostly driven by the defaults in the 1980s.

18. As in most models that emphasize exclusion from capital markets as the reason why countries repay, the purpose of sovereign borrowing in their model is consumption smoothing. It is conceivable that stronger results could be obtained if foreign borrowing were used to finance production (as in Cole and Kehoe 1998 or Wright 2004). It is also possible that exclusion from capital markets might have more punch if output shocks

can lead to changes in growth trends rather than just fluctuations around a growth trend (see Aguiar and Gopinath 2004).

3 Legal Issues in Sovereign Debt Restructuring

1. The law on this matter is not entirely uniform, particularly across European countries. As a result, sovereigns have been concerned about attachment of central bank reserve assets in some European jurisdictions (see Singh 2003).

2. The development of the Eurobond market was influenced by tax considerations. In 1963, the United States imposed an Interest Equalization Tax (IET) on foreign securities held by U.S. investors. This forced non-U.S. corporations to pay a higher interest rate to attract U.S. investors, encouraging the development of the Eurobond market, which was not subject to the IET. The IET was repealed in 1974, but by then the market was firmly established.

3. What this means precisely, and in particular whether or not it implies that payments to creditors in the event of default must be made pro rata, has been the subject of recent controversy.

4. New York law governed emerging market bonds registered with the U.S. Securities and Exchange Commission ("Schedule B" issues), have traditionally provided each bond-holder the right to accelerate and litigate his or her own bond following certain events of default such as a missed payment of principal or interest, or in some bond issues, the declaration of a debt moratorium. Starting in 2003, however, Schedule B bonds have routinely required collective action for acceleration, in line with the trend toward inclusion of collective action clauses in New York law bonds.

5. The Trust Indenture Act was motivated by actions of several American companies whose equity holders began buying the companies' bonds at heavily discounted prices after the stock market crash of 1929. Once they had achieved the necessary creditor majority, they could use this power to defer payments of the bonds, effectively inverting the priority of bondholders over equity holders. Unilateral consensus for changing the payments terms was introduced to prevent such abuse.

6. On this subject, see also Roubini and Setser (2004).

7. In addition, a large number of suits has been filed in Argentine courts. By May 2005, nine of the fifteen class action suits filed in the United States had been certified.

8. In May 2002, in *Applestein v. Republic of Argentina and Province of Buenos Aires*, plaintiffs sought to attach the representation office of the province in New York. Investors have also requested the attachment of diplomatic facilities, as well U.S. accounts of Correo Argentino S.A. (the renationalized postal service). All these requests have been denied. The only successful attachments so far appear to be attachments of small cash balances related to commercial transactions of Argentina in Germany.

II Introduction

1. In addition, because it shared many features with the Uruguay restructuring we briefly cover a recent debt restructuring in the Dominican Republic, although this was not an outgrowth of the bust cycle of 1998–2003 but had idiosyncratic origins.

2. Of the remaining seven cases listed in table 1.1, three—Indonesia in 1999, Seychelles in 2002, and Gabon in 1999 and 2002—involved reschedulings or payments arrears on debt held by foreign commercial banks. Côte d'Ivoire defaulted on Brady bond payments in 2000 in the context of a political and fiscal crisis that led to large arrears to domestic and both official and private external creditors; these bonds remain in default following the continued civil war in that country. In February 2003, Paraguay defaulted on domestically issued dollar denominated debt which was partly held by foreign banks; later in the year, this debt was restructured, with maturities extended by three years. After accumulating external arrears, Dominica and Grenada undertook comprehensive debt restructurings in 2004 and 2005 involving both private and official creditors; in both cases, exchange offers were used (see IMF 2005a, 2005b for details).

3. The data reproduced in this book reflects information that was available to us in November 2005, except for end-2005 data for Argentina and Uruguay reported in the tables in chapters 8 and 10. This data was updated in July 2006.

4. Alternatively, one can start with a debt accumulation equation with all debt converted to local currency units, and subsequently divide through local currency GDP. Because this only uses end-period exchange rates—whereas period average exchange rates are used when converting local currency GDP into U.S. dollars—the two approaches differ somewhat (see the appendix). We stick to the first approach because this is the one that has traditionally been used in emerging market countries with large shares of dollar debt, and because it yields a particularly simple debt dynamics decomposition in term of "real variables," with a small cross-term. Its main disadvantage is that because devaluations are reflected in period average rather that end-of-period exchange rates, there is a "carry-over effect" in the sense that a devaluation will generally be reflected in a rise in the end-year public debt ratio both in the year in which it occurs and in the following year.

4   Russia

This chapter draws on Kharas, Pinto, and Ulatov (2001), Central Bank of the Russian Federation (1998), Owen and Robinson (2003), Odling-Smee (2004), JP Morgan (2000), published or publicly accessible IMF country reports, and material gathered through the Russian Studies Database of the Norwegian Institute for International Affairs (NUPI).

1. The measurement and interpretation of the output decline is controversial; in particular, official statistics may overstate the true output decline to the extent that they miss economic activity in the informal sector, as well as product improvements. See Gavrilenkov and Koen (1994) and Johnson, Kaufman, and Shleifer (1997).

2. In hindsight, the GKO-Eurobond swap has been called a failure on the grounds that of the $41 billion GKOs eligible for the exchange, only $4.4 billion were actually exchanged (IMF 2003b, Box 4; Santos 2003). However, this ignores the fact that only $2–10 billion GKOs were targeted in the first place, as the terms of the exchange were structured in a way that would be attractive only for holders of GKOs maturing in August and September.

3. Prior to default, the Russian government had proposed to exchange stocks of GKO owned by nonresidents against five-year dollar bonds with interest rated slightly above LIBOR. Residents, instead, would have received three-year ruble bonds earning a 30 percent interest rate. This dual treatment, though possibly more favorable to international investors than the one they eventually received, was rejected by foreign creditors.

4. The first week after August 17 was marked by a short boom in the sales of cars and durable goods, as households anticipated an acceleration of inflation. The first queues in front of banks began appearing around August 20, before extending to the larger part of the banking sector in the following week. Access to cash from abroad with credit cards issued by Russian banks also became almost impossible at that time.

5. This section draws on Robinson (2003) and publicly available IMF staff reports.

6. Nonresidents could also elect to convert and repatriate restricted rubles earlier, but only at a more depreciated exchange rate.

7. Interestingly, these figures are still nowhere near estimates of nonresident GKO investor losses cited in market commentary at the time of the exchange, which were as high as 95 percent (Santos 2003). The likely explanation for the discrepancy is that these very high loss estimates reflected not only the effect of the debt restructuring but also the effect of the preceding currency crisis and devaluation.

5 Ukraine

The sources used for this chapter include news reports, newsletters, and chronologies published by the Ukrainian-European Policy and Legal Advice Centre (UEPLAC), IMF Country Reports (in particular, No. 97/109, No. 99/42, and No. 02/146, all available online at http://www.imf.org), as well as unpublished but publicly available IMF reports. For related literature, see Eichengreen and Rühl (2001), Lipworth and Nystedt (2001), IMF (2001), and Huang, Marin, and Xu (2004).

1. Like other countries on the territory of the former Soviet Union, Ukraine signed an agreement with Russia, in December 1994, under which Ukraine would not be responsible for Soviet external debt in exchange for renouncing its claims on Soviet external assets.

2. Actual "usable" reserves were much lower, because it turned out that the National Bank of Ukraine had engaged in a number of transactions that effectively rendered a portion of its reserves illiquid (e.g., indirect onlending to commercial banks); see IMF News Brief No. 00/15 and IMF News Brief No. 00/26. In early September, IMF staff estimated "usable" reserves at end-August to be as low as $320 million; see IMF European II department, "Ukraine—Request for Extended Arrangement—Supplementary Information," EBS/98/144 (unpublished report to the Executive Board available under the IMF archives policy, International Monetary Fund, Washington, DC, August 14, 1998).

3. The program's floor on net international reserves of the NBU was set in a way that left the government with no option but to restructure the debt falling due in the fall 1998, given the available official financing. Debt restructuring was also declared an explicit objective of the program (see IMF Press Release No. 98/38, http://www.imf.org/external/np/sec/pr/1998/pr9838.htm). At the same time, the program contained a performance criterion prohibiting accumulation of external arrears, which implied that the government had to seek negotiations with creditors. In its September 4, 1998, Letter of Intent to the IMF, the government stated that it was involved in such negotiations and that it expected payments that were falling due to external creditors that year to be rolled over (see http://www.imf.org/external/np/loi/090498.htm).

4. Only a week earlier, the IMF's managing director had condemned the Russian default as "highly regrettable and extremely unfortunate," and stated that "we do not regard that

(unilateral) approach as a constructive one for any other country to follow" (transcript of a press conference held on August 28, 1998, at IMF headquarters, http://www.imf.org/external/np/tr/1998/tr980828.htm).

5. For illustrative purposes, the values of the old and new instrument are computed and compared at a rate of 60 percent (the end-August one-year T-bill rate). However, because of the special structure of the new instrument—a floating rate bond after the first year—the discount and coupon rates approximately cancel after the first year, and the haircut is very insensitive to the discount rate assumed (in particular, for restructured T-bills with maturity close to one year). See Sturzenegger and Zettelmeyer (2005) for details.

6. The upfront cash portion of the exchange amounted to about US$76 million, which was repaid out of reserves, in contravention of the initial understanding with the IMF. In the event, the IMF accepted this relative small payment as an inevitable sweetener for the deal to go forward. See IMF European II department, "Ukraine—Request for Extended Arrangement—Financing Assurances Review, and Request for Waivers and Modification of Performance Criteria," EBS/98/176 (unpublished report to the Executive Board available under the IMF archives policy, International Monetary Fund, Washington, DC, October 22, 1998), p. 5.

7. Ukraine offered to value their existing holdings either at 55 cents to the dollar or at 75 cents to the dollar if investors put in new money equal to at least 15 percent of their holdings. According to news reports, investor interest was mainly in the second option.

8. Coupon payments for the new bonds were set on a quarterly basis, with no grace period for interest payments. Amortization was to occur twice a year, with 3 percent at each amortization date in 2001, 5 percent in 2002, and 9.33 percent at each date between 2003 and 2007.

6   Pakistan

This chapter relies on Helbling (2001), Burki (2000), IMF Country Reports (No. 97/120, No. 01/11, No. 01/24, No. 01/222, No. 02/246, No. 02/247, No. 03/338, and No. 04/411), the IMF Staff Report for the 1998 Article IV consultation, EBS/98/231 (unpublished report to the Executive Board available under the IMF archives policy, International Monetary Fund, Washington, DC, December 29, 1998), financial sector newsletters, and news reports.

1. Through this book, we use the best data available to us as of November 2005. In the case of Pakistan, this data implies a substantially lower debt-to-GDP ratio—by over 10 points—than was perceived at the time, on account of a large revision of nominal GDP in the interim. Moreover, as explained in the introduction to Part II, our debt-to-GDP ratios are based on converting all debt in U.S. dollars and dividing by dollar GDP, which gives slightly lower ratios, in depreciating exchange rate environments, than if debt is converted into local currency at end-period rates. As a result of the combination of these two effects, the debt ratios that were publicly perceived in the mid-1990s were closer to 90 percent of GDP.

2. This refers to net consolidated public debt, defined as the sum of government (federal and provincial) debt minus government deposits, excluding central bank assets and liabilities (in particular, debt owed to the IMF) (see Helbling 2001, 46).

3. In part for that reason, Pakistan's balance of payments and debt crisis did not lead to a banking crisis—an exception among the cases discussed in this book—in spite of fragilities in the banking system resulting from a history of direct state involvement and weak supervisory and regulatory capacity (see IMF Staff Report for the 1998 Article IV consultation, EBS/98/231 (unpublished report to the Executive Board available under the IMF archives policy, International Monetary Fund, Washington, DC, December 29, 1998), Box 1; IMF Country Report No. 02/247, Section IV). Moreover, banks were not directly exposed to currency risk, since they were forced to purchase forward exchange cover from the State Bank of Pakistan to close their open foreign exchange positions (IMF Staff Report for the 1998 Article IV consultation, Box 3).

7 Ecuador

This chapter is based on Jácome (2004), Fischer (2001), Beckerman and Solimano (2002), Peterson (1999), Buchheit (2000), selected IMF Country Reports, and news reports.

1. See IMF Country Report No. 00/125, Chapter III.

2. A Paris Club agreement of January 1992 restructured $339 million of bilateral debts falling due between January 1, 1992, and January 1, 1993, on "Houston terms." A further Paris Club agreement in June 1994 granted Houston terms to $292 million additional loans. On February 28, 1995, Ecuador's Brady deal restructured $7.8 billion of debt owed to commercial banks. Ecuador's debt was reduced by $1.8 billion in nominal terms. The menu offered to banks included discount bonds (which carried a 45 percent discount), par bonds with reduced fixed interest rate, PDI bonds, and interest equalization bonds. As in most Brady deals discount and par bonds had a thirty-year maturity and thirty-year zero coupon bonds as collateral for the principal. However, Ecuador's Brady deal was tougher than previous deals that had typically carried only a 35 percent discount.

3. The reasons for this included lack of expertise and the regional distributional consequences of applying purchase and assumption operations, which would have implied the takeover of Guayaquil-based banks by Quito-based banks (Jácome 2004).

4. Ecuador's external commercial debt consisted of two types of Eurobonds issued in April 1997—a US$350 million fixed rate bond due in 2002, and a $150 million floating rate bond due in 2004—and four types of Brady bonds with total face value of US$6.115 billion—discount and par bonds due in 2025 ($1.479 billion and $1.655 billion, respectively), PDI bonds due in 2015 ($2.838 billion), and interest equalization bonds due in 2004 ($143 million).

5. In addition to a fully collateralized principal, Brady discount and par bonds carried interest collateral covering any first two missed coupon payments. Upon default, this could be released from a New York Federal escrow account at the request of 25 percent of the bondholders. Once released, the debtor had twelve months to resume debt service.

6. There are parallels with the case of Argentina here, where domestic residents were restructured ahead of the main external debt restructuring (Phase 1 exchange, see chapter 8) and it is difficult to ascertain the size of the haircut at the time because the bonds that were still trading were bonds that were expected to be restructured.

7. These haircuts represent an upper bound with respect to the haircuts suffered by domestic bonds maturing between October 28, 1999, and end-2000, since the high yields would have depressed the present values of the longer instruments compared with instruments maturing on October 28.

8. Paragraph 47, Memorandum of Economic Policies dated April 4, 2000, available online at http://www.imf.org.

9. The 2025 principal repayments scheduled for the par and discount bonds are discounted using the U.S. long treasury bill rate, since these repayments were collateralized and not subject to country risk. Ceteris paribus, collateralization thus increases both the present value of the old instruments and the value received in the exchange (since the latter involved the release of the collateral).

8 Argentina

For alternative views on the Argentine crisis, see Perry and Serven (2002); Hausman and Velasco (2002); Powell (2002); de la Torre, Levy-Yeyati, and Schmukler (2003); and Calvo, Izquierdo, and Talvi (2003). On the background of the crisis and the relationship between Argentina and the IMF, see Mussa (2002), the Independent Evaluation Office of the IMF (2004), and Daseking et al. (2004). On the recovery from the crisis and the 2005 debt restructuring, see Sturzenegger (2003), IMF Country Report No. 05/236, Gelpern (2005), and Porczekanski (2005). Datz (2005) analyzes the crisis from the perspective of the pension funds.

1. In some cases, such as with the sale of the energy company YPF, these liabilities were cancelled with privatization proceeds.

2. $13.7 billion from the IMF, $1 billion from Spain, $2.5 billion from BID, and $2.5 billion from the World Bank. The package included some degree of "private sector involvement" (private financing commitments), through participation of local financial institutions, though in a non-binding way.

3. The syndicate received an exchange commission of 0.55 percent of nominal value, except for bonds exchanged by the central bank, which did not pay the fee, and those presented by three government-owned institutions, which paid a lower commission. Local pension funds were treated like any other investor (thus paying the full commission), to avoid the risk of the exchange being declared a technical default or involuntary by rating agencies.

4. During the 1990s, the BCRA had signed a series of contracts with major foreign banks in which it obtained the right to put government bonds at a preset price in time of systemic distress. In exchange, the government paid an insurance or option premium.

5. In an August 17, 2001, interview with CNN, Treasury Secretary Paul O'Neill famously questioned the wisdom of pouring more IMF money into Argentina, stating that "Argentina is now, after the $41 billion intervention, in a very slippery position. We are working to find a way to create a sustainable Argentina, not just one that continues to consume the money of the plumbers and carpenters in the U.S." (quoted from a Dow Jones newswire report).

6. The "guarantee" that was supposed to back the new loans was given comparatively little importance as all government debt is guaranteed by tax collection.

7. There was no secondary market for the new domestic instruments after the exchange, and hence no "exit yield" with which we could discount old and new payment streams. As a result, we use two alternative discount rates. First, yields of the old instruments, which continued to be held by nonresident and some resident bondholders, and were

traded after the exchange. Because the government had announced that the new instruments would in effect be treated as senior—the declared intention was to restructure the old instruments in a second phase while attempting to service the new ones—these yields can be regarded as an upper bound for the unobservable yield of the new instruments. Second, the government eventually issued postdefault debt in U.S. dollars, Bodens, which began trading in September 2002; the yields of these instruments can be used to compute an alternative, lower discount factor with which to discount the instruments swapped in the Phase 1 exchange (see Sturzenegger and Zettelmeyer 2005 for details). However, by September 2002 much legal and political uncertainty had been resolved, and the economy was recovering. Thus, the observed yields at that time will almost certainly understate what the "exit yield" would have been in November 2001.

8. These risks turned out more benign than initially expected. The strong recovery of asset prices after the exchange strongly improved financial institutions' solvency. Moreover, the Supreme Court upheld the constitutionality of pesification for a subset of deposits in July 2004.

9. In the March letter of intent, the government also committed to "an appropriate minimum participation threshold necessary for a broadly supported restructuring." In the event, no such threshold was set.

10. However, the first detailed description of payment terms ("18-K" filing to the SEC, June 10, 2004) envisaged slightly higher coupons than were revealed in November, in the event that participation were to exceed 70 percent.

11. Also missing are a handful of U.S. dollar and Arg dollar issues for which we could not verify the payment terms.

12. For the IMF staff's views on the debt restructuring approach and a government rebuttal, see IMF Country Report No. 05/236 and the attached statement of the IMF executive director for Argentina. The quotes are from an April 1, 2004, speech by the IMF managing director, and an IMFC communiqué of April 16, 2004.

13. Post-exchange debt stocks are evaluated under the assumption that participation was 100 percent. In actual fact, of course, participation was only 76.3 percent, leading to a federal government debt of $126.5 billion, or 73 percent of GDP excluding the claims of holdouts (face value about $20 billion, plus PDI of around $5 billion). The total debt burden depends on how holdout debt is valued. A standard approach is to value holdout debt under the terms of the exchange, that is, as if holdouts had taken the exchange offer. Given the contractual and domestic legal barriers that Argentina has created to commit itself not to give holdouts better terms, this may be a reasonable assumption.

9 Moldova

This chapter is based mostly on published IMF documents and press reports, in particular, IMF Country Report No. 02/190 and IMF Country Report No. 04/39, and IMF (2003b).

1. The main difference with respect to a HIPC country was that prior to 1997, Moldova borrowed from its official creditors mainly on nonconcessional terms. Moldova became IDA eligible only in 1997 and ESAF/PRGF eligible in March 1999.

10   Uruguay

This chapter draws on IMF reports, particularly IMF Country Report No. 03/247, which contains a detailed description of the exchange in appendix II, and IMF Country Report No. 05/202, Salmon (2004), Gelpern (2003), and news reports.

1. Holders of the Samurai bond, the Global 2027, two Brady bonds, and one domestic bond were not given a choice.

2. The Uruguayan authorities retained the law firm Cleary, Gottlieb, Steen & Hamilton, which had also advised Ecuador in 2000 and had pioneered the use of "exit consents" in sovereign debt at that time (Buchheit and Gulati 2000).

Afterword: The Dominican Republic

This draws on Hausmann, Rodrik, and Velasco (2004), IMF (2005b), and news reports.

11   Debt Crises from the Perspective of an Emerging Market Economy Policymaker

1. Depending on the currency denomination of exports, the currency composition of foreign currency debt may also be important to stabilize shocks to export earnings and exchange rate swings between the major industrial currencies; see Levy-Yeyati and Sturzenegger (2000).

2. Another strand (Hausmann and Panizza 2003; Eichengreen, Hausmann, and Panizza 2005b) examines the determinants of currency composition in *international* markets. Policy proposals in this area are discussed in chapter 12.

3. If this is not the case, privatizing the pension system could make the public debt structure more vulnerable. For example, after Argentina privatized its pension system in 1994, wage earner contributions were funneled to private pension funds that invested heavily in government bonds denominated in dollars. The pension reform thus transformed implicit liabilities of the pay-as-you-go system which were naturally GDP-indexed—because public sector pension benefits were indexed to future tax income—into explicit dollar debt, thus increasing the balance sheet mismatch of the public sector and the economy as a whole.

4. There is also a new literature in this area (García and Soto 2004; Jeanne and Rancière 2006) that estimates welfare maximizing reserve levels based on calibrated intertemporal macromodels. The results vary according to parameter assumptions, but seem to support the relevance of the Greenspan-Guidotti rule.

5. For this reason, some countries, including Argentina and Mexico, contracted "contingent credit lines" with major international banks during the 1990s, giving them the right to swap bonds with international reserves on preset terms. The experience with these credit lines has been mixed (see chapter 12 for a discussion).

6. Mexico has issued bonds indexed to oil prices, as have other countries in the context of the Brady deal. The State of Alaska buys and sell options in the oil market to stabilize its oil receipts. Bulgaria issued GDP-indexed bonds and so has Argentina in the latest debt

exchange. But Bulgaria has been trying to swap these bonds with more liquid "plain vanilla" instruments, and market reception to the Argentine proposal initially was not very favorable.

7. Legal considerations may play an important role in this context. A foreign financial sector can develop either through "subsidiaries" or through "branches." The latter are accountable to depositors in the country of origin, while subsidiaries are not. However, U.S. courts have ruled that depositor claims against U.S. banks are curtailed if the balance sheets of banks are modified by the government of the country where the branch was established. Thus, when Argentina pesified at different rate assets and liabilities, it took away the depositors' rights to sue the branches of foreign banks in their country of origin.

8. Galindo, Micco, and Powell (2004) point out a particular tradeoff that international banks may impose on emerging economies. They show that while it is true that international banks with a diversified asset base are less default prone, they may also react more quickly to reductions in lending opportunities within the country.

9. In reality, the policymaker will, of course, have to decide not just on whether to fight the default per se, but on the intensity with which to fight it, that is, on the adjustment or reform effort. To capture this more general case, p and c could be written as functions of the reform effort, and inequality (1) would have to be evaluated at the level of reform effort which maximizes utility conditional on attempting to fight the default.

10. To these, one might be tempted to add a third, namely, increases in debt (e.g., to international financial institutions) that is not restructured in either default scenario. However, these increases in debt involve an offsetting increase in country assets (e.g., in the case of debts to the IMF, gross international reserves). Hence, they imply a loss only to the extent that these assets are run down between the time of early and late defaults. This is already captured by the loss in reserves mentioned in the preceding paragraph.

11. In September 2005, Argentina's sovereign spread fell below Brazil's sovereign spread. However, the price of Argentine bonds included nondetachable GDP warrants. Once one accounts for the value of these warrants, Argentine postrestructuring bonds traded at a slightly higher spread than Brazilian bonds, on the order of 90 basis points.

12. Emerging market countries with default histories and a limited capacity to commit to prudent fiscal policies may, in fact, benefit from a constraint that limits new external borrowing.

13. Why could a debt exchange conceivably be successful in such circumstances, namely, when it is clear to all that the country will be insolvent as a result? The answer is that the new bondholders acquire a claim on the recovery value of the debt, at the expense of incumbent creditors. Hence, if the discount is large enough, it might make sense to participate in such an exchange.

14. For local currency rates, we took some version of the interbank rate at the time of the exchange as the local currency risk-free rate. Because inflation expectations change dramatically at the time of debt restructurings we cannot, in this case, ignore the specifics of each case in choosing the discount rate.

15. Principal reinstatement also provides a strong incentive to keep current in the future, thus reducing significantly future default risk. In cases where the stream of interest is reduced, one could think of analogous *interest reinstatement*.

16. Investment banks charge a fee for such exchanges, which depends on the size of the restructuring. In the case of pure liquidity operations, such as Argentina's June 2001 Megaswap, outsourcing the exchange entirely may have the advantage that rating agencies may be less likely to classify the exchange as "distressed" if it is handled by an investment bank (since it makes it easier to confirm that creditors were not coerced). This argument does not apply to debt restructurings leading to a present-value loss, which are always classified as "distressed."

12   International Financial Architecture

1. In particular, Cline (1995), Eichengreen and Portes (1995), Eichengreen (1999, 2002), Rogoff (1999), Council on Foreign Relations Taskforce (1999), Kenen (2001), Roubini and Setser (2004), and Isard (2005).

2. This point was made, from different angles, in two classic papers by Sachs and Cohen (1982), and Atkeson (1991). More recent references include Jeanne (2004), Bolton and Jeanne (2005), and Tomz and Wright (2005).

3. Note that for this reason, risk sharing by creditors is efficient even if creditors do not diversify this risk across countries. If they were able to diversify this risk, this would create an additional rationale for equity-like contracts.

4. Importantly, in this view, the fundamental cause of costly debt crises is *not* that sovereign debtors can repudiate their debts—the classic "willingness to pay problem"—but rather the presence of unobservable actions on the side of the debtor that impact his capacity to repay, and which contracts cannot directly condition on. Provided there are ways—whether reputational or direct—of "punishing" defaulting debtors, the pure repudiation problem could be resolved efficiently by punishing debtors selectively, depending on whether defaults are "excusable" by economic conditions or not (Grossman and Van Huyck 1988). The problem is that these punishments are applied indiscriminately, regardless of the cause of the default, because a moral hazard problem exists *in addition* to the "willingness to pay" problem. This point appears to have been first clearly recognized by Atkeson (1991).

5. A variant of the crisis insurance fund idea was proposed by George Soros (1997, 1998) following the Asian crisis. Soros envisaged an insurance, financed by a country fee at the time of issuing a new loan, for debt issues below a total debt ceiling set by the IMF (or a similar institution) based on the country's macroeconomic and structural fundamentals. Debt issues in excess of the ceiling would not be insured. Hence, the Soros proposal can be viewed as a special case of the crisis insurance fund described above, in which the decision to guarantee debts depends only on whether the preset debt threshold at the time when the debt was issued had been exceeded or not. All countries—not just those with good policies—would benefit from the insurance, but the insurance would cover higher levels of debt in countries with better policies relative to countries with poor policies.

6. In that case—namely, when the fund has a weak capacity to define and observe good policies—one could also imagine an adverse selection problem, in the sense that countries that intend to pursue suboptimal policies are drawn to the fund, deterring participation from countries that intend to pursue good policies, both due to the effect on premia and due to the negative signal associated with fund membership.

7. Amendments to the IMF's Articles of Agreement require the backing of three-fifths of members holding 85 percent of the total voting power. The United States presently holds 17.4 percent of the votes.

8. The implicit assumption here is that this disciplining effect is a good thing. This need not always be the case. In particular, in situations when politicians have incentives to undertake "gambles for redemption"—attempts to avoid the crisis that are not in the national interest, as discussed in chapter 11—a bankruptcy mechanism that tempts countries into defaulting earlier would be unambiguously welfare-improving (Powell and Arozamena 2003).

9. All arguments made in this paragraph apply both to statutory and contractual mechanisms (collective action clauses) if the latter are mandatory, namely, if they are forced on market participants through international pressure. *Optional* collective action clauses can never be welfare-reducing. Whether or not promoting such optional clauses in soft ways, through information and moral suasion is better than a mandatory system is an open issue: if one believes that a mandatory system would in fact improve welfare, it might be better than simply offering collective action clauses because it would deal with coordination problems more comprehensively.

10. The reason why such a mechanism might not quite achieve the relief of a comprehensive insurance fund is that it might not eliminate all default costs. A country would still have to restructure its debts, and the debt restructuring would still take some time and effort, and might lead to an interruption in capital inflows. In contrast, a perfectly designed crisis insurance fund would eliminate the need for a debt restructuring.

11. This is a consequence of the fact that under its Articles, IMF members are *entitled* to access IMF's general resources (subject to the conditions of the Articles and IMF policy, which include requiring assurances that the country will repay). An access policy based on prequalification may hence require an amendment to the Articles.

12. Technically, IMF financial support works like a repo line: a country swaps its own currency against a reserve currency when it accesses IMF resources, and swaps it back at maturity. For this reason, borrowing from the IMF's general resources is called a "purchase" (of another member's currency) in IMF-speak, while repayment is called a "repurchase" (of the borrower's own currency).

13. Prequalification criteria were also discussed by a Council on Foreign Relations Task Force (1999), the International Financial Institutions Advisory Commission (2000), Jeanne and Zettelmeyer (2001, 2005b), Cordella and Levy-Yeyati (2005), and indeed the IMF itself in the context of its "Contingent Credit Line," a lending facility that existed between 1999 and 2004 to provide faster and less onerous access to crisis lending to prequalified countries, but did not replace standard large-scale lending, and was never used (probably for that reason). See Ostry and Zettelmeyer (2005) and Truman (2006a,b).

14. See Privolos and Duncan (1991) and Claessens and Duncan (1993) for two edited volumes that contain many of the classic papers on commodity indexation. Borensztein et al. (2005, Box 6) provide a concise survey that discusses indexation to real variables other than commodity prices.

15. When there is a short-run trade-off between either reforms and output or stabilization and output, indexing IFI debt service to GDP might distort the incentives *of the IFI* (in the form of an expansionary bias) if the latter has some influence over a country's economic policies. This would argue against GDP indexation in short-term IFI lending.

16. For example, the country could know that it intends to default, draw just before defaulting, and not repurchase its defaulted bonds. Note that this did not occur in Argentina, where the bonds that collateralized the September 2001 drawing were repurchased

by the central bank in line with the repo agreement. Hence, even though the Argentine government defaulted on its bonds, the central bank did not default on the repo line.

17. The analogy is not perfect, of course, since a breach of covenant typically would trigger acceleration, while missing a performance criterion merely triggers suspension of further lending by the IMF or World Bank.

18. This would be analogous to the IMF's practice of granting "waivers" if performance criteria are missed for excusable reasons.

19. There are exceptions, notably the negative pledge clause, which prohibits sovereign debtors from issuing collateralized debt unless incumbent creditors are given an equal claim on the collateral (see chapter 2). But restrictions on total debt or fiscal policy are virtually absent.

20. The World Bank's Global Development Finance database is currently the closest thing to such a registry, but it relies on debtor reporting and it does not encompass domestically issued debt.

Appendix   Tools for the Analysis of Debt Problems

1. This section draws on Blanchard (1990) and Chalk and Hemming (2000).

2. If this condition is not satisfied, then the government can sustain any level of debt as it grows faster than the interest cost of the debt, meaning that at each point and for any level of debt growth is sufficient to reduce debt ratios over time. In practice, this cannot be, as interest rates would eventually climb above growth rates if debt levels are sufficiently high.

3. This section closely follows Calvo, Izquierdo, and Talvi (2003).

4. This is clear from fact that, with the notable exception of Argentina, the residual in the debt dynamics decompositions that we presented in each country chapter is not very large in debt restructuring years. In percentage points of GDP, we have −27 for Argentina (2005), −13 for Ecuador (2000), −6.9 for Ukraine (2000), −6.5 for Russia (1999), and −5.5 for Russia (2000). In all other cases (of which some—namely, Uruguay, Argentina in 2001, Pakistan, and Moldova—did not involve face value reductions at all) the residual was close to zero or even positive.

5. A related approach applies Value at Risk techniques common in assessing risks faced by banks and portfolios to the central bank (Blejer and Schumacher 1998) or the public sector (Barnhill and Kopits 2003).

6. What matters here is not how long that period is, but that there are no interest or coupon payments other than at the end of the period. Hence, this case covers a six-month instrument with all interest paid at the end, but also a five-year zero-coupon bond.

7. The spread defined here is the geometric spread, that is, the ratio of the rates of return on two assets. This definition of S is preferred to the usual approximation $i - r$, which may be poor when either i or r are large. In addition, the implied probability of default will always be between 0 and 1, as it should.

8. This assumes an annual coupon payment. In the more standard case of semiannual coupon payments, the risk-free rate would need to be expressed on a semiannual basis and the implicit default probability would apply to that period.

9. This section follows Merrill Lynch (2002).

10. The risk neutrality assumption that is made here may seem surprising at first, since the fact that the buyer wants to buy insurance implies that at least he must be risk averse. However it is a standard assumption. It can be justified by assuming that sellers can diversify risk, and that there is free entry in offering such contracts. In that case, it is appropriate to assume risk neutrality for the purposes of pricing the contract.

11. Condition (A.28) abstracts from complications arising from accrued premia or accrued interest on the deliverable bond (see Singh and Anritzki 2005, appendix, for a fuller discussion that does not make these simplifying assumptions).

12. The outlier here is Pakistan, but it must be borne in mind that Pakistan's sovereign bond debt was small relative to its remaining public debt (in particular, official external debt), and that it received debt relief from official sources at the same time.

13. The implicit assumption here is that the default or restructuring was not motivated by an unsustainable debt situation. If it were, debt service could not go up (in net present value) as a result of the restructuring, because this would imply that the debt is still unsustainable after the default. In such a situation, the government would be forced to curtail any rollovers of the restructured debt (and hence to adjust through other means such as increasing the fiscal surplus) so that the debt service is reduced to a sustainable level, which must be lower than the prerestructuring level.

14. Ades et al. (2000) try a default dummy and a dummy that captures whether the instrument originates in a restructuring. Only the latter is significant, and is the estimate we use here. Other authors, such as Dell'Ariccia, Schnabel, and Zettelmeyer (2006) found a default dummy to be statistically significant, but somewhat lower than the 165 basis point estimate of Ades et al.

References

Abiad, Abdul, and Jonathan D. Ostry. 2005. "Primary Surpluses and Sustainable Debt Levels in Emerging Market Countries." IMF Policy Discussion Paper 05/6. Washington, DC: International Monetary Fund.

Ades, Alberto, Federico Kaune, Paulo Leme, Rumi Masih, and Daniel Tenengauzer. 2000. "Introducing GS-ESS: A New Framework for Assessing Fair Value in Emerging Markets Hard Currency Debt." Global Economics Paper No. 45. June. New York and London: Goldman Sachs.

Agénor, Pierre-Richard. 2004. "Macroeconomic Adjustment and The Poor: Analytical Issues and Cross Country Evidence." *Journal of Economic Surveys* 18, no. 3: 351–408.

Aghion, Philippe, Philippe Bacchetta, and Abhajit Banerjee. 2001. "Currency Crises and Monetary Policy in an Economy with Credit Constraints." *European Economic Review* 45 (June): 1121–1150.

Aghion, Philippe, Philippe Bacchetta, and Abhijit Banerjee. 2004. "A Corporate Balance Sheet Approach to Currency Crises." *Journal of Economic Theory* 119, no. 1 (November): 6–30.

Aguiar, Mark, and Gita Gopinath. 2004. "Emerging Market Business Cycles: The Cycle is the Trend." NBER Working Paper No. 10734. Cambridge, MA: National Bureau of Economic Research.

Alesina, Alberto, Alessandro Prati, and Guido Tabellini. 1990. "Public Confidence and Debt Management: A Model and a Case Study of Italy." In *Public Debt Management: Theory and History*, ed. Rudiger Dornbusch and Mario Draghi, 94–118. Cambridge: Cambridge University Press.

Allen, Frankin, and Douglas Gale. 1994. *Financial Innovation and Risk Sharing*. Cambridge, MA: MIT Press.

Amador, Manuel. 2003. "A Political Economy Model of Sovereign Debt Repayment." Unpublished paper, Stanford University, Stanford, CA.

Andritzky, Jochen R. 2005. "Default and Recovery Rates of Sovereign Bonds: A Case Study of the Argentine Crisis." *Journal of Fixed Income* 7: 97–107.

Arellano, Cristina, and Jonathan Heathcote. 2003. "Dollarization and Financial Integration." Unpublished paper, University of Minnesota, Minneapolis, and Georgetown University, Washington, DC.

Arellano, Cristina, and Enrique G. Mendoza. 2002. "Credit Frictions and 'Sudden Stops' in Small Open Economies: An Equilibrium Business Cycle Framework for Emerging Markets Crises." NBER Working Paper No. 8880. Cambridge, MA: National Bureau of Economic Research.

Asquith, Paul, and Thierry Wizman. 1990. "Event Risk, Covenants, and Bondholder Return in Leveraged Buyouts." *Journal of Financial Economics* 27: 195–213.

Atkeson, Andrew. 1991. "International Lending with Moral Hazard and Risk of Repudiation." *Econometrica* 59, no. 4: 1069–1089.

Barnett, Barry C., Sergio J. Galvis, and Ghislain Gouraige, Jr. 1984. "On Third World Debt." *Harvard International Law Journal* 25 (Winter): 83–151.

Barnhill, Theodore, and George Kopits. 2003. "Assessing Fiscal Sustainability under Uncertainty." IMF Working Paper 03/79. Washington, DC: International Monetary Fund.

Barro, Robert J. 2001. "Economic Growth in East Asia before and after the Financial Crisis." NBER Working Paper No. 8330. Cambridge, MA: National Bureau of Economic Research.

Becker, Törbjörn I., Anthony J. Richards, and Yunyong Thaicharoen. 2003. "Bond Restructuring and Moral Hazard: Are Collective Action Clauses Costly?" *Journal of International Economics* 61: 127–161.

Beckerman, Paul, and Andres Solimano. 2002. *Crisis and Dollarization in Ecuador.* Washington, DC: World Bank.

Beim, David O., and Charles W. Calomiris. 2001. "Emerging Financial Markets." *Finance, Insurance, and Real Estate.* Boston: McGraw-Hill Irwin.

Berg, Andrew, and Jeffrey Sachs. 1988. "Debt Crisis: Structural Explanations of Country Performance." *Journal of Development Economics* 29, no. 3: 271–306.

Blanchard, Olivier J. 1990. "Suggestions for a New Set of Fiscal Indicators." OECD Working Paper No. 79. Paris: Organisation for Economic Cooperation and Development.

Blejer, Mario I., and Liliana Schumacher. 1998. "Central Bank Vulnerability and the Credibility of Commitments: A Value-at-risk Approach to Currency Crises." IMF Working Paper 98/65. Washington, DC: International Monetary Fund.

Bohn, Henning. 1990. "A Positive Theory of Foreign Currency Debt." *Journal of International Economics* 29 (November): 273–292.

Bohn, Henning. 1998. "The Behavior of U.S. Public Debt and Deficits." *Quarterly Journal of Economics* 113 (August): 949–963.

Bolton, Patrick. 2003. "Towards a Statutory Approach to Sovereign Debt Restructuring: Lessons from Corporate Bankruptcy Practice around the World." *Staff Papers* (International Monetary Fund) 50, Special Issue: 41–71.

Bolton, Patrick, and Olivier Jeanne. 2005. "Structuring and Restructuring Sovereign Debt: The Role of Seniority." NBER Working Paper No. 11071. Washington, DC: National Bureau of Economic Research.

Bolton, Patrick, and Davis A. Skeel. 2004. "Inside the Black Box: How Should a Sovereign Bankruptcy Framework Be Structured?" *Emory Law Journal* 53: 763–822.

Bordo, Michael D., and Anna J. Schwartz. 1999. "Under What Circumstances, Past and Present, Have International Rescues of Countries in Financial Distress Been Successful?" *Journal of International Money and Finance* 18: 683–708.

Borensztein, Eduardo, Marcos Chamon, Olivier Jeanne, Paolo Mauro, and Jeromin Zettelmeyer. 2005. "Sovereign Debt Structure for Crisis Prevention." IMF Occasional Paper 237. Washington, DC: International Monetary Fund.

Borensztein, Eduardo, and Paolo Mauro. 2004. "The Case for GDP-indexed Bonds." *Economic Policy* 39 (April): 165–206.

Boughton, James M. 2001. *Silent Revolution: The International Monetary Fund 1979–1989.* Washington, DC: International Monetary Fund.

Broner, Fernando A., Guido Lorenzoni, and Sergion L. Schmukler. 2004. "Why Do Emerging Economies Borrow Short-term?" Unpublished paper, Universitat Pompeu Fabra, Barcelona.

Broner, Fernando, and Jaume Ventura. 2005. "Sovereign Risk, Anonymous Markets, and the Effects of Globalization." Working Paper No. 837. Barcelona: Universitat Pompeu Fabra.

Brownlie, Ian. 2003. *Principles of Public International Law*, 6th ed. New York: Oxford University Press.

Buchheit, Lee C. 1986. "Sovereign Immunity." *Business Law Review* (February): 63–64.

Buchheit, Lee. 1990. "Sovereign Debt: Change of Hat." *International Financial Law Review* 9 (June): 12.

Buchheit, Lee. 1991. "Advisory Committees: What's in a Name?" *International Financial Law Review* 10, no. 1: 9–10.

Buchheit, Lee. 1995. "The Sovereign Client." *Journal of International Affairs* 48 (Winter): 527–540.

Buchheit, Lee. 1998a. "The Collective Representation Clause." *International Financial Law Review* 17: 9–11.

Buchheit, Lee. 1998b. "Changing Bond Documentation: The Sharing Clause." *International Financial Law Review* 17: 17.

Buchheit, Lee. 1998c. "Majority Action Clauses May Help Resolve Debt Crises." *International Financial Law Review* (August): 17–18.

Buchheit, Lee. 2000. "How Ecuador Escaped the Brady Bond Trap." *International Financial Law Review* 19, no. 12: 17–20.

Buchheit, Lee. 2002. "The Search for Intercreditor Parity." *Law and Business Review of the Americas* 8: 73–80.

Buchheit, Lee, and Mitu Gulati. 2000. "Exit Consents in Sovereign Bond Exchanges." *UCLA Law Review* 48 (October): 59–84.

Buchheit, Lee, and Mitu Gulati. 2002. "Sovereign Bonds and the Collective Will." *Emory Law Journal* 51, no. 4: 1317–1364.

Buchheit, Lee C., and Jeremiah S. Pam. 2004. "The Pari Passu Clause in Sovereign Debt Instruments." *Emory Law Journal* 53 (Special Edition): 869–922.

Bulow, Jeremy, and Kenneth Rogoff. 1988. "Multilateral Negotiations for Rescheduling Developing Country Debt: A Bargaining-theoretic Framework." *Staff Papers* (International Monetary Fund) 35 (December): 644–657.

Bulow, Jeremy, and Kenneth Rogoff. 1989a. "Sovereign Debt: Is to Forgive to Forget?" *American Economic Review* 79 (March): 43–50.

Bulow, Jeremy, and Kenneth Rogoff. 1989b. "A Constant Recontracting Model of Sovereign Debt." *Journal of Political Economy* 97 (February): 155–178.

Burki, Abid A. 2000. "Governance of Foreign Aid and Its Impact on Poverty in Pakistan: A Critical Review." LEAD-Pakistan Occasional Paper No. 8. Lamabad: LEAD-Pakistan.

Burnside, Craig, Martin Eichenbaum, and Sergio Rebelo. 2001. "Prospective Deficits and the Asian Currency Crisis." *Journal of Political Economy* 109: 1155–1197.

Burnside, Craig, Martin Eichenbaum, and Sergio Rebelo. 2004. "Government Guarantees and Self-fulfilling Speculative Attacks." *Journal of Economic Theory* 119, no. 1 (November): 31–63.

Bussière, Matthieu, and Christian Mulder. 1999. "External Vulnerability in Emerging Market Economies: How High Liquidity Can Offset Weak Fundamentals and the Effects of Contagion." IMF Working Paper 99/88. Washington, DC: International Monetary Fund.

Caballero, Ricardo J., Kevin Cowan, and Jonathan Kearns. 2004. "Fear-of-sudden-stop: Lessons from Australia and Chile." NBER Working Paper No. 10519. Washington, DC: National Bureau of Economic Research.

Caballero, Ricardo J., and Stavros Panageas. 2004. "Contingent Reserves Management: An Applied Framework." NBER Working Paper No. 10786. Washington, DC: National Bureau of Economic Research.

Caballero, Ricardo J., and Stavros Panageas. 2005. "A Quantitative Model of Sudden Stops and External Liquidity Management." NBER Working Paper No. 11293. Washington, DC: National Bureau of Economic Research.

Calvo, Guillermo. 2002. "Globalization Hazard and Delayed Reform in Emerging Markets." *Economia* 2, no. 2: 1–29.

Calvo, Guillermo. 2005. "Crises in Emerging Market Economics: A Global Perspective." NBER Working Paper No. 11305. Washington, DC: National Bureau of Economic Research.

Calvo, Guillermo, and Pablo E. Guidotti. 1990. "Management of the Nominal Public Debt Theory and Applications." IMF Working Paper 90/115. Washington, DC: International Monetary Fund.

Calvo, Guillermo, Alejandro Izquierdo, and Ernesto Talvi. 2003. "Sudden Stops, the Real Exchange Rate, and Fiscal Sustainability: Argentina's Lessons." NBER Working Paper No. 9829. Washington, DC: National Bureau of Economic Research.

Calvo, Guillermo, Alejandro Izquierdo, and Luis-Fernando Mejía. 2004. "On the Empirics of Sudden Stops: The Relevance of Balance-sheet Effects." IADB Working Paper No. 509. Washington, DC: Inter-American Development Bank.

Catão, Luis, and Sandeep Kapur. 2004. "Missing Link: Volatility and the Debt Intolerance Paradox." IMF Working Paper 04/51. Washington, DC: International Monetary Fund.

Catão, Luis, and Bennett Sutton. 2002. "Sovereign Defaults: The Role of Volatility." IMF Working Paper 02/149. Washington, DC: International Monetary Fund.

Ceballos, Francisco. 2005. "Valuación Mediante Simulaciones de Monte Carlo de las Unidades Ligadas al Crecimiento Emitidas por la República Argentina." Unpublished manuscript, Universidad Torcuato Di Tella, Buenos Aires.

Celasun, Oya, Xavier Debrun, and Jonathan D. Ostry. 2006. "Primary Surplus Behavior and Risks to Fiscal Sustainability in Emerging Market Countries: A "Fan-chart" Approach." IMF Working Paper 06/67. International Monetary Fund, Washington, DC.

Central Bank of the Russian Federation. 1998. *Annual Report.* Moscow: Central Bank of the Russian Federation.

Chalk, Nigel Andrew, and Richard Hemming. 2000. "Assessing Fiscal Sustainability in Theory and Practice." IMF Working Paper 00/81. Washington, DC: International Monetary Fund.

Chamon, Marcos. 2002. "Why Can't Developing Countries Borrow from Abroad in Their Currency?" SSRN Working Paper Series. New York: Social Science Research Network. Available online at http://papers.ssrn.com/sol3/papers.cfm?abstract_id=320001.

Chamon, Marcos. 2004. "Can Debt Crises Be Self-fulfilling?" IMF Working Paper 04/99. Washington, DC: International Monetary Fund.

Chamon, Marcos, and Paolo Mauro. 2005. "Pricing Growth-Indexed Bonds." IMF Working Paper 05/216. Washington, DC: International Monetary Fund.

Chuhan, Punam, and Federico Sturzenegger. 2005. "Default Episodes in the 1980s and 1990s: What Have We Learned?" In *Managing Economic Volatility and Crises,* ed. Joshua Aizenman and Brian Pinto, 471–519. Cambridge: Cambridge University Press.

Claessens, Stijn, and Ronald C. Duncan. 1993. *Managing Commodity Price Risk in Developing Countries.* Baltimore, MD: Johns Hopkins University Press.

Cline, William R. 1984. *International Debt: Systemic Risk and Policy Response.* Washington, DC: Institute of International Economics.

Cline, William R. 1995. *International Debt Reexamined.* Washington, DC: Institute for International Economics.

Cline, William R. 2001. "The Role of the Private Sector in Resolving Financial Crises in Emerging Markets." In *Economic and Financial Crises in Emerging Market Economies,* ed. Martin Feldstein, 459–496. Chicago and London: The University of Chicago Press.

Cohen, Daniel, and Richard Portes. 2004. "Towards a Lender of *First* Resort." CEPR Discussion Paper No. 4615. London: Centre for Economic Policy Research.

Cole, Harold L., and Patrick J. Kehoe. 1995. "The Role of Institutions in Reputation Models of Sovereign Debt." *Journal of Monetary Economics* 35 (February): 46–64.

Cole, Harold L., and Patrick J. Kehoe. 1996. "A Self-fulfilling Model of Mexico's 1994–1995 Debt Crisis." *Journal of International Economics* 41, no. 3–4: 309–330.

Cole, Harold L., and Patrick J. Kehoe. 1998. "Models of Sovereign Debt: Partial versus General Reputations." *International Economic Review* 39 (February): 55–70.

Cole, Harold L., and Patrick J. Kehoe. 2000. "Self-fulfilling Debt Crises." *Review of Economic Studies* 67, no. 1: 91–116.

Cordella, Tito, and Eduardo Levy-Yeyati. 2005. "A (New) Country Insurance Facility." IMF Working Paper 05/23. Washington, DC: International Monetary Fund.

Corsetti, Giancarlo, Bernardo Guimarães, and Nouriel Roubini. 2006. "The Trade-off between an International Lender of Last Resort to Deal with Liquidity Crisis and Moral Hazard Distortions: A Model of the IMF's Catalytic Finance Approach." *Journal of Monetary Economics* 53, no. 3: 441–471.

Cottarelli, Carlo. 2005. "Efficiency and Legitimacy: Trade-offs in IMF Governance." IMF Working Paper 05/07. Washington, DC: International Monetary Fund.

Council on Foreign Relations Task Force. 1999. *Safeguarding Prosperity in a Global Financial System: The Future International Financial Architecture*. Washington, DC: Institute for International Economics.

Daseking, Christina, Atish R. Ghosh, Alun H. Thomas, and Timothy D. Lane. 2004. "Lessons from the Crisis in Argentina." IMF Occasional Paper 236. Washington, DC: International Monetary Fund.

Datz, Giselle. 2005. "Pension Privatization and the Politics of Sovereign Default in Latin America." Unpublished paper, Rutgers University, Newark.

De Gregorio, José, Barry Eichengreen, Takatoshi Ito, and Charles Wyplosz. 2000. "An Independent and Accountable IMF." Geneva Reports on the World Economy 1. Geneva and London: International Center for Monetary and Bank Studies and Centre for Economic Policy Research.

De la Torre, Augusto, Eduardo Levy-Yeyati, and Sergio Schmukler. 2003. "Living and Dying with Hard Pegs: The Rise and Fall of Argentina's Currency Board." *Economía* 5, no. 2: 43–99.

Dell'Ariccia, Giovanni, Isabel Schnabel, and Jeromin Zettelmeyer. 2006. "How Do Official Bailouts Affect the Risk of Investing in Emerging Markets?" Forthcoming in *Journal of Money, Credit and Banking*.

Detragiache, Enrica. 1994. "Sensible Buybacks of Sovereign Debt." *Journal of Development Economics* 43: 317–333.

Detragiache, Enrica, and Antonio Spilimbergo. 2001. "Crises and Liquidity: Evidence and Interpretation." IMF Working Paper 01/2. Washington, DC: International Monetary Fund.

Detragiache, Enrica, and Antonio Spilimbergo. 2004. "Empirical Models of Short-term Debt and Crises: Do They Test the Creditor-run Hypothesis?" *European Economic Review* 48, no. 2: 379–389.

Díaz Alvarado, Carlos, Alejandro Izquierdo, and Ugo Panizza. 2004. "Fiscal Sustainability in Emerging Market Countries with an Application to Ecuador." IADB Working Paper No. 511. Washington, DC: Inter-American Development Bank.

Dooley, Michael P. 2000. "Can Output Losses Following International Financial Crises Be Avoided?" NBER Working Paper No. 7531. Washington, DC: National Bureau of Economic Research.

Drazen, Allan. 2000. *Political Economy in Macroeconomics*. Princeton, NJ: Princeton University Press.

Duffie, Darrell, Lasse Heje Pedersen, and Kenneth Singleton. 2003. "Modeling Sovereign Yield Spreads: A Case Study of Russian Debt." *Journal of Finance* 58, no. 1: 119–160.

Dujovne, Nicolás, and Pablo Guidotti. 2001. "El Sistema Financiero Argentino y su Regulación Prudencial." In *Crecimiento y Equidad en la Argentina. Bases de una Politica Económica para la Década*, 131–211. Buenos Aires: FIEL.

Easterly, William. 2001. "Growth Implosions and Debt Explosions: Do Growth Slowdowns Explain Public Debt Crises?" *Contributions to Macroeconomics* 1, no. 1: 1–24.

Eaton, Jonathan. 1996. "Sovereign Debt, Reputation and Credit Terms." *International Journal of Finance & Economics* 1 (January): 25–35.

Eaton, Jonathan. 2004. "Standstills and an International Bankruptcy Court." In *Fixing Financial Crises in the Twenty-first Century*, ed. Andy Haldane, 261–276. London: Routledge.

Eaton, Jonathan, and Raquel Fernandez. 1995. "Sovereign Debt." In *Handbook of International Economics, Vol. 3*, ed. Gene M. Grossman and Kenneth Rogoff, 2031–2077. Amsterdam: North-Holland.

Eaton, Jonathan, and Mark Gersovitz. 1981. "Debt with Potential Repudiation: Theoretical and Empirical Analysis." *Review of Economic Studies* 48 (April): 289–309.

Eaton, Jonathan, and Mark Gersovitz, and Joseph E. Stiglitz. 1986. "The Pure Theory of Country Risk." *European Economic Review* 30 (June): 481–513.

Eichengreen, Barry. 1999. *Toward a New International Financial Architecture: A Practical Post-Asia Agenda*. Washington, DC: Institute for International Economics.

Eichengreen, Barry. 2000. "Can the Moral Hazard Caused by IMF Bailouts Be Reduced?" Geneva Reports on the World Economy Special Report 1. London: Centre for Economic Policy Research.

Eichengreen, Barry. 2002. "*Financial Crises and What to Do about Them.*" Oxford: Oxford University Press.

Eichengreen, Barry, and Ricardo Hausmann. 1999. "Exchange Rates and Financial Fragility." NBER Working Paper No. 7418. Cambridge, MA: National Bureau of Economic Research.

Eichengreen, Barry, and Ricardo Hausmann. 2005. "Original Sin: The Road to Redemption." In *Other People's Money: Debt Denomination and Financial Instability in Emerging Market Economies*, ed. Barry Eichengreen and Ricardo Hausman, 26–288. Chicago: University of Chicago Press.

Eichengreen, Barry, Ricardo Hausmann, and Ugo Panizza. 2005a. "The Pain of Original Sin." In *Other People's Money: Debt Denomination and Financial Instability in Emerging Market Economies*, ed. Barry Eichengreen and Ricardo Hausman, 13–47. Chicago: University of Chicago Press.

Eichengreen, Barry, Ricardo Hausmann, and Ugo Panizza. 2005b. "The Mystery of Original Sin." In *Other People's Money: Debt Denomination and Financial Instability in Emerging Market Economies*, ed. Barry Eichengreen and Ricardo Hausman, 233–265. Chicago: University of Chicago Press.

Eichengreen, Barry, and Ashoka Mody. 2004. "Do Collective Action Clauses Raise Borrowing Costs?" *Economic Journal* 114, no. 495: 247–264.

Eichengreen, Barry, and Richard Portes. 1986. "Debt and Default in the 1930s: Causes and Consequences." *European Economic Review* 30: 599–640.

Eichengreen, Barry, and Richard Portes. 1989. "After the Deluge: Default, Negotiation, and Readjustment during the Interwar Years." In *The International Debt Crises in Historical Perspective*, 12–47. Cambridge, MA: MIT Press.

Eichengreen, Barry, and Richard Portes. 1995. *"Crisis? What Crisis? Orderly Workouts for Sovereign Debtors."* London: Centre for Economic Policy Research.

Eichengreen, Barry, and Christof Rühl. 2001. "The Bail-in Problem: Systematic Goals, Ad Hoc Means." *Economic Systems* 25: 3–32.

Emerging Market Trader's Association. 1999. "Is Burden-sharing Being Pushed Too Far?" *EMTA Bulletin* (4th Quarter).

English, William B. 1996. "Understanding the Costs of Sovereign Default: American State Debts in the 1840s." *The American Economic Review* 86, no. 1: 259–275.

Esteves, Rui Pedro. 2004. "Sovereign Debt and Bondholders' Protection the European Capital Markets before 1914." Unpublished paper, University of California, Berkeley.

Fallon, Peter R., and Robert E. B. Lucas. 2002. "The Impact of Financial Crisis on Labor Market Household Incomes and Poverty. A Review of Evidence." *World Bank Research Observer* 17, no. 1: 21–45.

Fernandez, Raquel, and Robert W. Rosenthal. 1990. *Review of Economic Studies* 57 (July): 331–349.

Ferrucci, Gianluigi, and Adrian Penalver. 2003. "Assessing Sovereign Debt Under Uncertainty." *Bank of England Financial Stability Report* 15 (December), 151–159. London: Bank of England.

Fischer, Stanley. 2001. "Ecuador and the International Monetary Fund." In *Currency Unions*, ed. Alberto Alesina and Robert Barro, 1–11. Stanford, CA: Hoover Institution Press.

Fishlow, Albert. 1985. "Lessons from the Past: Capital Markets During the 19th Century and the Interwar Period." *International Organization* 39, no. 3: 383–439.

Fishlow, Albert. 1989. "Lessons of the 1890s for the 1980s." In *Debt, Stabilization and Development*, ed. Guillermo Calvo, Ronald Findlay, Pentti Kouri, and Jorge de Macedo, 19–47. Oxford: Basil Blackwell.

Flandreau, Marc. 2003. "Crises and Punishment: Moral Hazard and the Pre-1914 International Financial Architecture." CEPR Discussion Paper No. 3742. London: Centre for Economic Policy Research.

Flandreau, Marc, and Frédéric Zumer. 2004. *The Making of Global Finance, 1880–1913*. Paris and Washington: Organisation for Economic Cooperation and Development.

Galindo, Arturo, Alejandro Micco, and Andrew Powell. 2004. "Loyal Lenders or Fickle Financiers: Foreign Banks in Latin America." Business School Working Papers Series 08/04. Buenos Aires: Universidad Torcuato di Tella.

Garcia, Marcio, and Roberto Rigobon. 2004. "A Risk Management Approach to Emerging Market's Sovereign Debt Sustainability with an Application to Brazilian Data." NBER Working Paper No. 10336. Cambridge, MA: National Bureau of Economic Research.

García, Pablo, and Claudio Soto. 2004. "Large Hoardings of International Reserves: Are They Worth It?" Working Papers Central Bank of Chile No. 299. Santiago: Central Bank of Chile.

Gavrilenkov, Evgeny, and Vincent R. Koen. 1994. "How Large Was the Output Collapse in Russia? Alternative Estimates and Welfare Implications." IMF Working Paper 94/154. Washington, DC: International Monetary Fund.

Gelos, Gaston, Ratna Sahay, and Guido Sandleris. 2004. "Sovereign Borrowing by Developing Countries: What Determines Market Access?" IMF Working Paper 04/221. Washington, DC: International Monetary Fund.

Gelpern, Anna. 2003. "How Collective Action Is Changing Sovereign Debt." *International Financial Law Review* (May): 19–23.

Gelpern, Anna. 2004. "Building a Better Seating Chart for Sovereign Restructurings." *Emory Law Journal* 53, Special Edition: 1115–1161.

Gelpern, Anna. 2005. "After Argentina." Policy Brief in International Economics No. PB05-2. September. Washington, DC: Institute for International Economics.

Ghosh, Atish R., Timothy D. Lane, Marianne Schulze-Gattas, Aleš Bulir, Javier A. Hamann, and Alex Mourmouras. 2002. "IMF-Supported Programs in Capital Account Crises: Design and Experience." IMF Occasional Paper No. 210. Washington, DC: International Monetary Fund.

Goldstein, Morris, and Philip Turner. 2004. *Controlling Currency Mismatches in Emerging Markets.* Washington, DC: Institute for International Economics.

Goyal, Vidhan, K. 2003. "Market Discipline of Bank Risk: Evidence from Subordinated Debt Contracts." Unpublished paper, University of Science and Technology, Hong Kong.

Gramlich, Ludwig. 1981. "Staatliche Immunität für Zentralbanken?" In *Rabels Zeitschrift für Ausländisches und Internationales Privatrecht* 45: 545–603.

Greenwood, Christopher, and Hugh Mercer. 1995. "Considerations of International Law." In *Crisis? What Crisis? Orderly Workouts for Sovereign Debtors,* ed. Barry Eichengreen and Richard Portes, 103–117. London: Centre for Economic Policy Research.

Grossman, Herschel I., and John B. Van Huyck. 1988. "Sovereign Debt as a Contingent Claim: Excusable Default, Repudiation, and Reputation." *American Economic Review* 78, no. 5: 1088–1097.

Guidotti, Pablo, Federico Sturzenegger, and Agustín Villar. 2004. "On the Consequences of Sudden Stops." *Economía* 4, no. 2: 171–214.

Gul, Faruk, and Wolfgang Pesendorfer. 2004. "Self-control and the Theory of Consumption." *Econometrica* 72, no. 1: 119–158.

Gulati, Mitu G., and Kenneth N. Klee. 2001. "Sovereign Piracy." *The Business Lawyer* 56: 635–651.

Hagan, Sean. 2005. "Designing a Legal Framework to Restructure Sovereign Debt." *Georgetown Journal of International Law* 36, no. 2: 299–403.

Haldane, Andy. 1999. "Private Sector Involvement in Financial Crisis: Analytics and Public Policy Approaches." In *Bank of England Financial Stability Report* 7 (November), 184–202. London: Bank of England.

Hausmann, Ricardo, and Ugo Panizza. 2003. "The Determinants of Original Sin: An Empirical Investigation." *Journal of International Money and Finance* 22, no. 7: 957–990.

Hausmann, Ricardo, Dani Rodrik, and Andrés Velasco. 2004. "Growth Diagnostics." Unpublished paper, Kennedy School of Government, Harvard University, Cambridge, MA.

Hausmann, Ricardo, and Andrés Velasco. 2002. "Hard Money's Soft Underbelly: Understanding the Argentine Crisis." In *Brookings Trade Forum: 2002*, ed. Susan M. Collins and Dani Rodrik, 59–119. Washington, DC: Brookings Institution Press.

Helbling, Thomas. 2001. "Debt and Debt Sustainability Issues in Pakistan." In *Pakistan: Selected Issues and Statistical Appendix*. IMF Country Report No. 01/11, chapter II, 23–70. Washington, DC: International Monetary Fund.

Hellwig, Christian, and Guido Lorenzoni. 2003. "Bubbles and Private Liquidity." Unpublished paper, University of California, Los Angeles.

Higginbotham, Brian, and Kurt Schuler. 2002. "The Subsidy in IMF Lending." Washington, DC: Joint Economic Committee, United States Congress. Available online at http://www.house.gov/jec/imf/imfpage.htm.

Huang, Haizhou, Dalia Marin, and Chenggang Xu. 2004. "Financial Crisis, Economic Recovery, and Banking Development in Russia, Ukraine and Other FSU Countries." IMF Working Paper 04/105. Washington, DC: International Monetary Fund.

IMF Country Report No. 97/109. 1997. *Ukraine: Recent Economic Development*. Washington, DC: International Monetary Fund.

IMF Country Report No. 97/120. 1997. *Pakistan: Recent Economic Developments*. Washington, DC: International Monetary Fund.

IMF Country Report No. 99/42. 1999. *Ukraine: Recent Economic Developments*. Washington, DC: International Monetary Fund.

IMF Country Report No. 00/125. 2000. *Ecuador: Selected Issues and Statistical Annex*. Washington, DC: International Monetary Fund.

IMF Country Report No. 01/11. 2001. *Pakistan: Selected Issues and Statistical Appendix*. Washington, DC: International Monetary Fund.

IMF Country Report No. 01/24. 2001. *Pakistan: 2000 Article IV Consultation and Request for Stand-by Arrangement—Staff Report; Staff Supplement; Public Information Notice and Press Release on the Executive Board Discussion*. Washington, DC: International Monetary Fund.

IMF Country Report No. 01/222. 2001. *Pakistan: Request for a Three-year Arrangement under the Poverty Reduction Growth Facility (PRGF)—Staff Report; Staff Statement; Press Release on the Executive Board Discussion; and Statement by the Executive Director*. Washington, DC: International Monetary Fund.

IMF Country Report No. 02/146. 2002. *Ukraine: 2002 Article IV Consultation—Staff Report; Staff Supplement; Public Information Notice on the Executive Board Discussion; and Statement by the Executive Director for Ukraine*. Washington, DC: International Monetary Fund.

IMF Country Report No. 02/190. 2002. *Republic of Moldova: 2002 Article IV Consultation, First Review Under the Three-year Arrangement Under the Poverty Reduction and Growth Facility and Request for Waiver of Performance Criteria—Staff Report*. Washington, DC: International Monetary Fund.

IMF Country Report No. 02/190. 2002. *Republic of Moldova: 2002 Article IV Consultation, First Review under the Three-year Arrangement under the Poverty Reduction and Growth Facility and Request for Waiver of Performance Criteria—Staff Report; Public Information Notice and News Brief on the Executive Board Discussion*. Washington, DC: International Monetary Fund.

IMF Country Report No. 02/246. 2002. *Pakistan: Article IV Consultation, Poverty Reduction and Growth Facility Arrangement, and Request for Waivers of Performance Criteria—Staff Report; Staff Statement; Public Information Notice on the Executive Board Discussion; and Statement by the Executive Director for Pakistan*. Washington, DC: International Monetary Fund.

IMF Country Report No. 02/247. 2002. *Pakistan: Selected Issues and Statistical Appendix*. Washington, DC: International Monetary Fund.

IMF Country Report No. 03/247. 2003. *Uruguay: 2003 Article IV Consultation and Third Review under the Stand-by Arrangement and Request for Modification and Waiver of Applicability of Performance Criteria—Staff Report; Staff Supplement; Staff Statement; Public Information Notice and Press Release on the Executive Board Discussion; and Statement by the Executive Director for Uruguay*. Washington, DC: International Monetary Fund.

IMF Country Report No. 03/338. 2003. *Pakistan: Sixth and Seventh Reviews under the Three-year Arrangement under the Poverty Reduction and Growth Facility and Request for Waiver of Performance Criteria—Staff Report; Staff Statement; Press Release; and Statement by the Executive Director for Pakistan*. Washington, DC: International Monetary Fund.

IMF Country Report No. 04/39. 2004. *Republic of Moldova: 2003 Article IV Consultation—Staff Report; and Public Information Notice on the Executive Board Discussion*. Washington, DC: International Monetary Fund.

IMF Country Report No. 04/411. 2004. *Pakistan: 2004 Article IV Consultation, Ninth Review under the Three-year Arrangement under the Poverty Reduction and Growth Facility, and Request for Waiver of Performance Criteria—Staff Report; Staff Statement; Public Information Notice and Press Release on the Executive Board Discussion; and Statement by the Executive Director for Pakistan*. Washington, DC: International Monetary Fund.

IMF Country Report No. 05/202. 2005. *Uruguay: Ex Post Assessment of Longer-term Program Engagement—Staff Report; Public Information Notice on the Executive Board Discussion; and Statement by the Executive Director for Uruguay*. Washington, DC: International Monetary Fund.

IMF Country Report No. 05/236. 2005. *Argentina: 2005 Article IV Consultation—Staff Report; Staff Supplement; Public Information Notice on the Executive Board Discussion; and Statement by the Executive Director for Argentina*. Washington, DC: International Monetary Fund.

IMF News Brief No. 00/15. 2000. "Allegations about the Use of Ukraine's International Reserves." March 14. Washington, DC: International Monetary Fund.

IMF News Brief No. 00/26. 2000. "Release of Pricewaterhouse Coopers Report on the National Bank of Ukraine." May 4. Washington, DC: International Monetary Fund.

IMF Press Release No. 98/38. 1998. "IMF Approves Three-year Extended Fund Facility for Ukraine." September 4. Washington, DC: International Monetary Fund.

Independent Evaluation Office of the IMF. 2004. *Report on the Evaluation of the Role of the IMF in Argentina, 1991–2001*. Washington, DC: International Monetary Fund.

International Financial Institutions Advisory Commission. 2000. *Report*. Washington, DC: U.S. Congress. Available online at http://www.house.gov/jec/imf/meltzer.htm.

International Monetary Fund (IMF). 1998. "Russian Federation—Use of Fund Resources—Request for Augmentation of Extended Arrangement and Request for Purchase under the Compensatory and Contingency Financing Facility," EBS/98/120, Supplement 1. Unpublished report to the Executive Board available under the IMF's archives policy, International Monetary Fund, Washington, DC, July 17, 1998.

International Monetary Fund (IMF). 2000. "Private Sector Involvement in Crisis Prevention and Resolution: Market Views and Recent Experience." In *International Capital Markets: Developments, Prospects, and Key Policy Issues*, 115–151. Washington, DC: International Monetary Fund.

International Monetary Fund (IMF). 2001. *Involving the Private Sector in the Resolution of Financial Crises—Restructuring International Sovereign Bonds*. International Monetary Fund, Washington, DC. Available online at http://www.imf.org/external/pubs/ft/series/03/IPS.pdf.

International Monetary Fund (IMF). 2002a. *Sovereign Debt Restructurings and the Domestic Economy: Experience in Four Recent Cases*. International Monetary Fund, Washington, DC. Available online at http://www.imf.org/external/np/pdr/sdrm/2002/022102.pdf.

International Monetary Fund (IMF). 2002b. *The Design of the Sovereign Debt Restructuring Mechanism—Further Considerations*. International Monetary Fund, Washington, DC. Available online at http://www.imf.org/external/np/pdr/sdrm/2002/112702.htm.

International Monetary Fund (IMF). 2002c. *Crisis Resolution in the Context of Sovereign Debt Restructuring: A Summary of Considerations*. International Monetary Fund, Washington, DC. Available online at http://www.imf.org/external/np/pdr/sdrm/2003/012803.pdf.

International Monetary Fund (IMF). 2003a. "Public Debt in Emerging Markets: Is It Too High?" *World Economic Outlook* (September): 113–150.

International Monetary Fund (IMF). 2003b. *Reviewing the Process for Sovereign Debt Restructuring within the Existing Legal Framework*. International Monetary Fund, Washington, DC. Available online at http://www.imf.org/external/np/pdr/sdrm/2003/080103.htm.

International Monetary Fund (IMF). 2003c. *Proposed Features of a Sovereign Debt Restructuring Mechanism*. International Monetary Fund, Washington, DC. Available online at http://www.imf.org/external/np/pdr/sdrm/2003/021203.pdf.

International Monetary Fund (IMF). 2003d. *Collective Action Clauses: Recent Developments and Issues*. International Monetary Fund, Washington, DC. Available online at http://www.imf.org/external/np/psi/2003/032503.pdf.

International Monetary Fund (IMF). 2003e. *The Restructuring of Sovereign Debt—Assessing the Benefits, Risks, and Feasibility of Aggregating Claims*. International Monetary Fund, Washington, DC. Available online at http://www.imf.org/external/np/pdr/sdrm/2003/090303.pdf.

International Monetary Fund (IMF). 2004. *Progress Report to the International Monetary and Financial Committee on Crisis Resolution*. September. International Monetary Fund, Washington, DC. Available online at http://www.imf.org/external/np/pdr/cr/2004/eng/092804.htm.

International Monetary Fund (IMF). 2005a. *Progress Report to the International Monetary and Financial Committee on Crisis Resolution.* April. International Monetary Fund, Washington, DC. Available online at http://www.imf.org/external/np/pp/eng/2005/041205.htm.

International Monetary Fund (IMF). 2005b. *Progress Report on Crisis Resolution.* September. International Monetary Fund, Washington, DC. Available online at http://www.imf.org/external/np/pp/eng/2005/092105.htm.

International Monetary Fund (IMF). 2005c. *Information Note on Modifications to the Fund's Debt Sustainability Assessment Framework for Market Access Countries.* International Monetary Fund, Washington, DC. Available online at http://www.imf.org/external/np/pp/eng/2005/070105.htm.

International Monetary Fund (IMF). 2005d. *Global Financial Stability Report: Market Developments and Issues.* September. International Monetary Fund, Washington, DC.

International Monetary Fund (IMF), and International Development Association (IDA). 2004. *Debt Sustainability in Low-income Countries—Further Considerations on an Operational Framework and Policy Implications.* Washington, DC. Available online at http://www.imf.org/external/np/pdr/sustain/2004/091004.pdf.

Isard, Peter. 2005. *Globalization and the International Financial System: What's Wrong and What Can Be Done.* Cambridge: Cambridge University Press.

Ize, Alain, and Eduardo Levy-Yeyati. 2003. "Financial Dollarization." *Journal of International Economics* 59: 323–347.

Ize, Alain, and A. Powell. 2004. "Prudential Responses to De Facto Dollarization." IMF Working Paper 04/66. Washington, DC: International Monetary Fund.

Jácome, Luis Ignacio. 2004. "The Late 1990s Financial Crisis in Ecuador: Institutional Weaknesses, Fiscal Rigidities, and Financial Dollarization at Work." IMF Working Paper 04/12. Washington, DC: International Monetary Fund.

Jarrow, Robert A., David Lando, and Stuart M. Turnbull. 1997. "A Markov Model for the Term Structure of Credit Risk Spreads." *Review of Financial Studies* 10: 481–523.

Jeanne, Olivier. 2000. "Foreign Currency Debt and the Global Financial Architecture." *European Economic Review* 44: 719–727.

Jeanne, Olivier. 2001. "Sovereign Debt Crises and the International Financial Architecture." Unpublished paper, International Monetary Fund, Washington, DC.

Jeanne, Olivier. 2003. "Why Do Emerging Economies Borrow in Foreign Currency?" IMF Working Paper 03/177. Washington, DC: International Monetary Fund.

Jeanne, Olivier. 2004. "Debt Maturity and the International Financial Architecture." IMF Working Paper 04/137. Washington, DC: International Monetary Fund.

Jeanne, Olivier, and Pierre-Olivier Gourinchas. 2004. "The Elusive Gains from International Financial Integration." IMF Working Paper 04/74. Washington, DC: International Monetary Fund.

Jeanne, Olivier, and Romain Rancière. 2006. "The Optimal Level of International Reserves for Emerging Market Countries: Formulas and Applications." Unpublished paper, International Monetary Fund, Washington, DC.

Jeanne, Olivier, and Charles Wyplosz. 2001. "The International Lender of Last Resort: How Large Is Large Enough?" NBER Working Paper No. 8381. Washington, DC: National Bureau of Economic Research.

Jeanne, Olivier, and Jeromin Zettelmeyer. 2001. "International Bailouts, Moral Hazard and Conditionality." *Economic Policy* 33: 407–424.

Jeanne, Olivier, and Jeromin Zettelmeyer. 2005a. "Original Sin, Balance Sheet Crises and the Roles of International Lending." In *Other People's Money: Debt Denomination and Financial Instability in Emerging Market Economies*, ed. Barry Eichengreen and Ricardo Hausman, 95–121. Chicago: University of Chicago Press.

Jeanne, Olivier, and Jeromin Zettelmeyer. 2005b. "The Mussa Theorem: And Other Results on IMF Induced Moral Hazard." *Staff Papers* (International Monetary Fund) 52, Special Issue (September): 64–84.

Johnson, Simon, Daniel Kaufman, and Andrei Shleifer. 1997. "The Unofficial Economy in Transition." *Brookings Papers on Economic Activities* 2, no. 1: 159–221.

Jorgensen, Erika, and Jeffrey Sachs. 1989. "Default and Renegotiation of Latin American Foreign Bonds in the Interwar Period." In *International Debt Crisis in Historical Perspective*, ed. Barry Eichengreen and Peter H. Lindert, 48–83. Cambridge, MA: MIT Press.

JP Morgan. 2000. *Russia: A Rough Guide to the Prin/IAN Exchange for 2010 and 2030 Eurobonds*. London: JP Morgan.

Kaletsky, Anatole. 1985. *The Costs of Default*. New York: Priority Press.

Kaminsky, Graciela L., and Carmen M. Reinhart. 1999. "The Twin Crises: The Causes of Banking and Balance-of-payments Problems." *American Economic Review* 89, no. 3: 473–500.

Kharas, Homi, Brian Pinto, and Sergei Ulatov. 2001. "An Analysis of Russia's 1998 Meltdown." *Brookings Papers on Economic Activity*, no. 1: 1–50.

Kelly, Trish. 1998. "Ability to Pay in the Age of Pax Britannica, 1890–1914." *Explorations in Economic History* 35: 31–58.

Kenen, Peter B. 2001. *The International Financial Architecture: What's New? What's Missing?* Washington, DC: Institute for International Economics.

Kindleberger, Charles P. 1973. *The World in Depression, 1929–1939*. Berkeley: University of California Press.

Kletzer, Kenneth M. 1984. "Asymmetries of Information and LDC Borrowing with Sovereign Risk." *Economic Journal* 94 (June): 287–307.

Kletzer, Kenneth M. 1994. "Sovereign Immunity and International Lending." In *The Handbook of International Macroeconomics*, ed. F. van der Ploeg, 439–479. Oxford: Blackwell.

Kletzer, Kenneth M., and Brian D. Wright. 2000. "Sovereign Debt as Intertemporal Barter." *American Economic Review* 90 (June): 621–639.

Klingen, Christoph, Beatrice Weder, and Jeromin Zettelmeyer. 2004. "How Private Creditors Fared in Emerging Debt Markets, 1970–2000." IMF Working Paper 04/13. Washington, DC: International Monetary Fund.

Kohlscheen, Emanuel. 2005a. "Sovereign Risk: Constitutions Rule." Unpublished paper, University of Warwick, Coventry.

Kohlscheen, Emanuel. 2005b. "Why Are There Serial Defaulters? Quasi-experimental Evidence from Constitutions." Unpublished paper, University of Warwick, Coventry.

Kraay, Aart, and Vikram Nehru. 2004. "When Is External Debt Sustainable?" World Bank Policy Research Working Paper 3200. Washington, DC: The World Bank.

Krajnyak, Kornelia, and Jeromin Zettelmeyer. 1998. "Competitiveness in Transition Economies: What Scope for Real Appreciation?" *Staff Papers* (International Monetary Fund) 45, no. 2: 309–362.

Kremer, Michael, and Seema Jayachandran. 2003. "Odious Debt." NBER Working Paper No. 8953. Cambridge, MA: National Bureau of Economic Research.

Krueger, Anne O. 2001. "International Financial Architecture for 2002: A New Approach to Sovereign Debt Restructuring." Address given at the National Economists' Club Annual Members' Dinner, November. American Enterprise Institute, Washington, November.

Krueger, Anne O. 2002. *A New Approach to Sovereign Debt Restructuring*. Washington, DC: International Monetary Fund.

Kruger, Mark, and Miguel Messmacher. 2004. "Sovereign Debt Defaults and Financing Needs." IMF Working Paper 04/53. Washington, DC: International Monetary Fund.

Krugman, Paul. 1999. "Balance Sheets, The Transfer Problem, and Financial Crises." In *International Finance and Financial Crises: Essays in Honor of Robert P. Flood, Jr.*, ed. Peter Isard, Assaf Razin, and Andrew K. Rose. Boston and Washington, DC: Kluwer Academic and International Monetary Fund.

Kumhof, Michael. 2004. "Fiscal Crisis Resolution: Taxation versus Inflation." Unpublished draft, International Monetary Fund, Washington, DC.

Kumhof, Michael, and Evan Tanner. 2005. "Government Debt: A Key Role in Financial Intermediation." IMF Working Paper Working Paper No. 05/57. Washington, DC: International Monetary Fund.

Lane, Philip R. 2004. "Empirical Perspectives on Long-Term External Debt." *Topics in Macroeconomics* 4, no. 1: 1–21.

Lee, Paul. 2003. "Central Banks and Sovereign Immunity." *Columbia Journal of Transnational Law* 41: 327–396.

Levy-Yeyati, Eduardo. 2003. "Financial Dedollarization: A Carrot and Stick Approach." CIF Working Paper 8/2003. Buenos Aires: Universidad Torcuato di Tella.

Levy-Yeyati, Eduardo, and Federico Sturzenegger. 2000. "Implications of the Euro for Latin American Banking and Financial Sectors." *Emerging Markets Review* 1, no. 1: 53–81.

Levy-Yeyati, Eduardo, and Federico Sturzenegger. 2006. "The Balance Sheet Approach to Debt Sustainability." Unpublished paper, IADB.

Lindert, Peter H., and Peter J. Morton. 1989. "How Sovereign Debt Has Worked." In *Developing Country Debt and Economic Performance*, ed. Jeffrey Sachs, 39–106. Chicago: University of Chicago Press.

Lipson, Charles. 1985. *Standing Guard: Protecting Foreign Capital in the Nineteenth and Twentieth Centurites*. Berkeley: University of California Press.

Lipson, Charles. 1989. "International Debt and National Security: Comparing Victorian Britain and Postwar America." In *The International Debt Crisis in Historical Perspective*, ed. Barry Eichengreen and Peter H. Lindert, 189–226. Cambridge, MA: The MIT Press.

Lipworth, Gabrielle, and Jens Nysted. 2001. "Crisis Resolution and Private Sector Adaptation." *Staff Papers* (International Monetary Fund) 47, Special Issue: 188–214.

Lorie, Henri, and Zafar Iqbal. 2005. "Pakistan's Macroeconomic Adjustment and Resumption of Growth, 1999–2004." IMF Working Paper No. 05/139. Washington, DC: International Monetary Fund.

Manasse, Paolo, and Nouriel Roubini. 2005. "'Rules of Thumb' for Sovereign Debt Crises." IMF Working Paper 05/42. Washington, DC: International Monetary Fund.

Manasse, Paolo, Nouriel Roubini, and Axel Schimmelpfennig. 2003. "Predicting Sovereign Debt Crises." IMF Working Paper 03/221. Washington, DC: International Monetary Fund.

Marichal, Carlos. 1989. *A Century of Debt Crises in Latin America: From Independence to the Great Depression, 1820–1930*. Princeton, NJ: Princeton University Press.

Mauro, Paolo, Nathan Sussman, and Yishay Yafeh. 2006. *Emerging Markets and Financial Globalization. Sovereign Bond Spreads in 1870–1913 and Today*. Oxford: Oxford University Press.

Mauro, Paolo, and Yishay Yafeh. 2003. "The Corporation of Foreign Bondholders." IMF Working Paper 03/107. Washington, DC: International Monetary Fund.

McBrady, Matthew R., and Mark S. Seasholes. 2000. "Bailing-in." Unpublished paper, Harvard University, Cambridge, MA.

McFadden, Daniel, Richard Eckaus, Gershon Feder, Vassilis Hajivassiliou, and Stephen O'Connell. 1985. "Is There Life after Debt? An Econometric Analysis of the Creditworthiness of Developing Countries." In *International Debt and the Developing Countries*, ed. Gordon Smith and John Cuddington. Washington, DC: The World Bank.

Mendoza, Enrique G. 2002. "Credit, Prices, and Crashes: Business Cycles with a Sudden Stop." In *Preventing Currency Crises in Emerging Markets*, ed. Sebastian Edwards and Jeffrey A. Frankel. Chicago: University of Chicago Press.

Mendoza, Enrique G., and P. Marcelo Oviedo. 2004. "Public Debt, Fiscal Solvency and Macroeconomic Uncertainty in Latin America: The Cases of Brazil, Colombia, Costa Rica, and Mexico." NBER Working Paper No. 10637. Cambridge, MA: National Bureau of Economic Research.

Merrick, Jr. John. 2001. "Crisis Dynamics of Implied Default Recovery Ratios: Evidence from Russia and Argentina." *Journal of Banking & Finance* 25, no. 10: 1921–1939.

Merrill Lynch. 2002. *Emerging Markets Debt Monthly*. August.

Mitchener, Kris James, and Marc D. Weidenmier. 2005. "Supersanctions and Sovereign Debt Repayment." NBER Working Paper No. 11472. Cambridge, MA: National Bureau of Economic Research.

Mussa, Michael. 2002. *Argentina and the Fund: From Triumph to Tragedy*. Washington, DC: Institute of International Economics.

Nolan, John. 2001. "Emerging Market Debt and Vulture Hedge Funds: Free-Ridership, Legal and Market Remedies." *Special Policy Report 3, Financial Policy Forum*. Washington, DC: Derivatives Study Center.

Obstfeld, Maurice, and Kenneth Rogoff. 1996. *Foundations of International Macroeconomics.* Cambridge, MA: MIT Press.

Odling-Smee, John. 2004. "The IMF and Russia in the 1990s." IMF Working Paper No. 04/155. Washington, DC: International Monetary Fund.

Ostry, Jonathan D., and Jeromin Zettelmeyer. 2005. "Strengthening IMF Crisis Prevention." IMF Working Paper No. 05/206. Washington, DC: International Monetary Fund.

Owen, David, and David O. Robinson. 2003. *Russia Rebounds.* Washington, DC: International Monetary Fund.

Özler, Sule. 1993. "Have Commercial Banks Ignored History?" *American Economic Review* 83 (June): 608–620.

Pernice, Sergio A., and Federico López Fagúndez. 2005. "Valuation of Debt Indexed to Real Values I, The Case of the Argentinean Growth Coupon: A Simple Model." Unpublished paper, Universidad del Cema, Buenos Aires.

Perotti, Roberto. 1996. "Redistribution and Non-consumption Smoothing in an Open Economy." *Review of Economic Studies* 63, no. 3: 411–433.

Perry, Guillermo, and Luis Servén. 2002. "The Anatomy of a Multiple Crisis: Why Was Argentina Special and What Can We Learn from It?" Policy Research Working Paper No. 3081. Washington, DC: The World Bank.

Pescatori, Andrea, and Amadou N. R. Sy. 2004. "Debt Crises and the Development of International Capital Markets." IMF Working Paper 04/44. Washington, DC: International Monetary Fund.

Peterson, Michael. 1999. "A Crash Course in Default." *Euromoney*, no. 366 (October): 47.

Porzecanski, Arturo C. 2005. "From Rogue Creditors to Rogue Debtors: Implications of Argentina's Default." *Chicago Journal of International Law* 6 (Summer): 311–332.

Powell, Andrew. 2002. "*Argentina's Avoidable Crisis: Bad Luck, Bad Economics, Bad Politics, Bad Advice?*" In *Brookings Trade Forum: 2002*, ed. Susan M. Collins and Dani Rodrik. Washington, DC: Brookings Institution Press.

Powell, Andrew, and Leandro Arozamena. 2003. "Liquidity Protection versus Moral Hazard: The Role of the IMF." *Journal of International Money and Finance* 22, no. 7: 1041–1063.

Power, Philip J. 1996. "Sovereign Debt: The Rise of the Secondary Market and Its Implications for Future Restructurings." *Fordham Law Review* 64, no. 6: 2701–2772.

Prasad, Eswar S., Kenneth Rogoff, Shang-Jin Wei, and Ayhan Kose. 2003. "Effects on Financial Globalization on Developing Countries: Some Empirical Evidence." IMF Occasional Paper 220. Washington, DC: International Monetary Fund.

Privolos, T., and R. Duncan. 1991. *Commodity Risk Management and Finance.* Washington, DC: The World Bank.

Rajan, Raghuram G. 2004a. "Dollar Shortages and Crises." NBER Working Paper No. 10845. Cambridge, MA: National Bureau of Economic Research.

Rajan, Raghuram G. 2004b. "How Useful Are Clever Solutions?" *Finance and Development* (March): 56–57.

Reinhart, Carmen M. 2002. "Default, Currency Crises, and Sovereign Credit Ratings." *World Bank Economic Review* 16 (August): 151–170.

Reinhart, Carmen M., Kenneth S. Rogoff, and Miguel A. Savastano. 2003. "Debt Intolerance." *Brookings Papers on Economic Activity*, no. 1: 1–74.

Rieffel, Lex. 2003. *Restructuring Sovereign Debt: The Case for Ad Hoc Machinery.* Washington, DC: Brookings Institution Press.

Robinson, David O. 2003a. "Banking Crisis and Recovery." In *Russia Rebounds*, ed. David Owen and David O. Robinson, 121–153. Washington, DC: International Monetary Fund.

Robinson, David O. 2003b. "Macroeconomic Policymaking." In *Russia Rebounds*, ed. David Owen and David O. Robinson, 25–56. Washington, DC: International Monetary Fund.

Rodrik, Dani, and Andrés Velasco. 2000. "Short-term Capital Flows." In *Proceedings of the 1999 Annual Bank Conference on Development Economics*, ed. B. Pleskovic and J. E. Stiglitz, 59–90. Washington, DC: The World Bank.

Rogoff, Kenneth. 1999. "International Financial Institutions for Reducing Global Financial Instability." *Journal of Economic Perspectives* 13, no. 4: 21–42.

Rogoff, Kenneth, and Jeromin Zettelmeyer. 2002. "Bankruptcy Procedures for Sovereigns: A History of Ideas, 1976–2001." *Staff Papers* (International Monetary Fund) 49, no. 3: 470–507.

Rose, Andrew K. 2005. "One Reason Countries Pay Their Debts: Renegotiation and International Trade." *Journal of Development Economics* 77, no. 1: 189–206.

Rose, Andrew K., and Mark M. Spiegel. 2004. "A Gravity Model of Sovereign Lending: Trade, Default, and Credit." *Staff Papers* (International Monetary Fund) 51, Special Issue: 50–63.

Roubini, Nouriel, and Brad Setser. 2004. *Bailouts or Bail-ins? Responding to Financial Crises in Emerging Economies.* Washington, DC: Institute for International Economics.

Sachs, Jeffrey D. 1984. "Theoretical Issues in International Borrowing." *Princeton Studies in International Finance*, no. 54 (July).

Sachs, Jeffrey D. 1989. "Introduction." In *Developing Country Debt and Economic Performance*, vol. 2, ed. Jeffrey D. Sachs, 1–35. Chicago: University of Chicago Press.

Sachs, Jeffrey D. 1995. "Do We Need an International Lender of Last Resort?" Frank D. Graham Lecture, Princeton, NJ, April. Unpublished paper. Available online at http://www.earthinstitute.columbia.edu.

Sachs, Jeffrey D., and Daniel Cohen. 1982. NBER Working Paper No. 1925. Cambridge, MA: National Bureau of Economic Research.

Salmon, Felix. 2004. "Uruguay's Elegant Transformation." *Euromoney* 35, no. 418 (February): 86–91.

Sandleris, Guido. 2005. "Sovereign Defaults: Information, Investment and Credit." Unpublished paper, School of Advanced International Studies, Johns Hopkins University, Baltimore, MD.

Santos, Alejandro. 2003. "Debt Crisis in Russia: The Road from Default to Sustainability." In *Russia Rebounds*, ed. David Owen and David O. Robinson, 154–183. Washington, DC: International Monetary Fund.

Schneider, Martin, and Aaron Tornell. 2004. "Balance Sheet Effects, Bailout Guarantees and Financial Crises." *Review of Economic Studies* 71, no. 3: 883–913.

Shleifer, Andrei. 2003. "Will the Sovereign Debt Market Survive?" *American Economic Review* (Papers and Proceedings) 93, no. 2: 85–90.

Schwarcz, Steven L. 2000. "Sovereign Debt Restructuring: A Bankruptcy Reorganization Approach." *Cornell Law Review* 85: 101–187.

Singh, Manmohan. 2003. "Recovery Rates from Distressed Debt—Empirical Evidence from Chapter 11 Filings, International Litigation, and Recent Sovereign Debt Restructurings." IMF Working Paper 03/161. Washington, DC: International Monetary Fund.

Singh, Manmohan, and Jochen R. Andritzky. 2005. "Overpricing in Emerging Market Credit-default-swap Contracts: Some Evidence from Recent Distress Cases." IMF Working Paper 05/125. Washington, DC: International Monetary Fund.

Smith, Cliff, and Jerald Warner. 1979. "On Financial Contracting: An Analysis of Bond Covenants." *Journal of Financial Economics* 7, no. 2: 117–161.

Soros, George. 1997. "Avoiding a Breakdown: Asia's Crisis Demands a Rethink of International Regulation." *Financial Times* (December).

Soros, George. 1998. *The Crisis of Global Capitalism.* New York: Public Affairs Press.

Sosa Navarro, Ramiro. 2002. "Estimación de Tasa de Recupero y Probabilidades de Cesación de Pagos para Bonos Argentinos: Crisis Financiera Diciembre 2001." Unpublished paper, Universidad Torcuato Di Tella, Buenos Aires.

Sturzenegger, Federico. 2003. *La Economía de los Argentinos.* Buenos Aires: Editorial Planeta.

Sturzenegger, Federico. 2004. "Toolkit for the Analysis of Debt Problems." *Journal of Restructuring Finance* 1, no. 1: 201–230.

Sturzenegger, Federico, and Jeromin Zettelmeyer. 2005. "Haircuts: Estimating Investor Losses in Sovereign Debt Restructurings, 1998–2005." Working Paper 05/137. Washington, DC: International Monetary Fund.

Summers, Lawrence. 2001. "An Analysis of Russia's 1998 Meltdown: Comments and Discussion." *Brookings Papers on Economic Activity*, no. 1: 51–57.

Suter, Christian. 1989. "Long Waves in the International Financial System: Debt-default Cycles of Sovereign Borrowers." *Review of the Fernand Braudel Center for the Study of Economies, Historical Systems and Civilizations* 12 (Winter): 1–49.

Suter, Christian. 1992. *Debt Cycles in the World Economy: Foreign Loans, Financial Crises, and Debt Settlements, 1820–1990.* San Francisco: Westview Press.

Suter, Christian, and Hanspeter Stamm. 1992. "Coping with Global Debt Crises: Debt Settlements 1820–1986." *Comparative Studies in Society and History* 34, no. 4: 645–678.

Taylor, John. 2002. "Sovereign Debt Restructuring: A U.S. Perspective." Remarks at the conference "Sovereign Debt Workouts: Hopes and Hazards?," Institute for International Economics, Washington, DC. Available online at http://www.treas.gov/press/releases/po2056.htm.

Tirole, Jean. 2002. *Financial Crises, Liquidity, and the International Monetary System.* Princeton, NJ: Princeton University Press.

Tomz, Michael. 1999. "Do Creditors Ignore History?" Unpublished paper, Harvard University, Cambridge, MA.

Tomz, Michael. 2006. *Sovereign Debt and International Cooperation*. Forthcoming. Princeton: Princeton University Press.

Tomz, Michael, and Mark L. J. Wright. 2005. "Sovereign Debt, Defaults and Bailouts." Unpublished paper, Stanford University, Palo Alto, CA.

Truman, Edwin M. 2006a. "Overview on IMF Reform." In *Reforming the IMF for the 21st Century*, ed. Edwin M. Truman, 31–126. Washington, DC: Institute for International Economics.

Truman, Edwin M. 2006b. *A Strategy for IMF Reform*. Washington, DC: Institute for International Economics.

United States Court of Appeals for the Second Circuit. 1984. *Allied Bank International v. Banco Credito Agricola de Cartago*, 733 F. 2d 23 (2d Cir. 1984).

United States Court of Appeals for the Second Circuit. 1985. *Allied Bank International v. Banco Credito Agricola de Cartago*, 757 F. 2d 516 (2d Cir. 1985).

United States Court of Appeals for the Second Circuit. 2005. *EM Ltd. et al. v. The Republic of Argentina*, Summary Order, May 13.

Van Rijckeghem, Caroline, and Beatrice Weder. 2004. "The Politics of Debt Crises." CEPR Discussion Paper No. 4683. London: Centre for Economic Policy Research.

Waibel, Michael W. 2003. "Sovereign Debt Restructuring." Unpublished paper, University of Vienna, Vienna.

Wijnholds, J. Onno de Beaufort, and Arend Kapteyn. 2001. "Reserve Adequacy in Emerging Market Economies." IMF Working Paper 01/143. Washington, DC: International Monetary Fund.

Williamson, John. 2001. "An Analysis of Russia's 1998 Meltdown: Comments and Discussion." *Brookings Papers on Economic Activity*, no. 1: 57–62.

Winkler, Max. 1933. *Foreign Bonds, An Autopsy: A Study of Defaults and Repudiations of Government Obligations*. Philadelphia: Swain.

Wood, Philip. 2003. "Pari Passu Clauses—What Do They Mean?" *Butterworths Journal of International Banking and Financial Law* 18: 371–374.

World Bank. 2002. "Financing the Poorest Countries." *Global Development Finance*. Appendix II. Washington, DC: World Bank.

Wright, Mark L. J. 2002a. "Creditor Coordination and Sovereign Risk." Unpublished paper, Stanford University, Palo Alto, CA.

Wright, Mark L. J. 2002b. "Reputations and Sovereign Debt." Unpublished paper, Stanford University, Palo Alto, CA.

Wright, Mark L. J. 2004. "Coordinating Creditors." Unpublished paper, Stanford University, Palo Alto, CA.

Zettelmeyer, Jeromin, and Priyadarshani Joshi. 2005. "Implicit Transfers in IMF Lending, 1973–2003." IMF Working Paper 05/8. Washington, DC: International Monetary Fund.

Index